WEEDS LIKE US

by

GUNTER NITSCH

Bloomington, IN Milton Keynes, UK

authorHOUSE®

AuthorHouse™
1663 Liberty Drive, Suite 200
Bloomington, IN 47403
www.authorhouse.com
Phone: 1-800-839-8640

AuthorHouse™ UK Ltd.
500 Avebury Boulevard
Central Milton Keynes, MK9 2BE
www.authorhouse.co.uk
Phone: 08001974150

This book is a work of non-fiction. Unless otherwise noted, the author and the publisher make no explicit guarantees as to the accuracy of the information contained in this book and in some cases, names of people and places have been altered to protect their privacy.

First published by AuthorHouse 10/18/2006

ISBN: 1-4259-6755-8 (sc)

Library of Congress Control Number: 2006908729

Printed in the United States of America
Bloomington, Indiana

This book is printed on acid-free paper.

DEDICATION

With heartfelt gratitude to the late Daniel J. and Naomi Peachey whose CARE packages sustained my mother and me in a West German refugee camp and who, years later, made my wife and me unofficial members of their family in Pennsylvania.

ACKNOWLEDGMENTS

My thanks go to the many people who helped me to fill in the gaps in my story: my cousins Ilse in Izmir, Turkey, and Gerda in Berlin, Germany, and my fellow East Prussians Günther Allenberg, Elsbeth Dardat, Hilde Gehrmann, the late Erna Krause, Dr. Klaus-Eberhard Murawski and Dora Opfermann who kindly offered thoughts and details about their own experiences in East Prussia both during and after World War II.

My appreciation goes also to everyone in the United States who gave my manuscript a critical reading: Annie Desbois, Robert Dumont, Helen-Jean Arthur Dunn, Michael Dunn, Agnès Gallet, Liz Gordon, Lane Gutstein, and Harriet Langsam-Sobol.

Last but not least, special thanks to my wife Mary for the editing and re-editing of my numerous drafts and to my sons Michael and Frederick for their invaluable contributions.

PROLOGUE

You won't find East Prussia, where most of this book takes place, on any map. At the end of World War II, this easternmost province of Germany, with a population of nearly two and one-half million people, an area slightly larger than the state of Maryland, ceased to exist. In 1945, the Potsdam Conference awarded the southern two-thirds of the province to Poland and the northern one-third to the Soviet Union. Today the northern one-third forms the Russian region called Kaliningradskaja Oblast. Hugging the Baltic Sea, the Russian portion of former East Prussia is walled off from the Russian motherland by Lithuania on the east and Poland on the south and west.

Although East Prussia was a part of Germany, its people took pride in their separate history, boasting how Frederick I crowned himself "King in Prussia" in Königsberg, the capital, in 1701, and honoring their native son, the philosopher Emmanuel Kant. To an East Prussian, the rest of Germany to the west was called the "Reich" (Empire). To other Germans, East Prussia was a world apart. East Prussians had the reputation for being stubborn and hard-working. Their broad East Prussian accent, distinguished by a rolling "r" and the peculiar habit of tacking diminishing syllables onto many nouns and first names often made East Prussians the butt of jokes.

At the end of World War I, the Treaty of Versailles gave Poland access to the Baltic Sea by creating the Polish Corridor. This land barrier virtually cut off East Prussia from the Reich from 1920 to 1939. Adolf Hitler's promise to reclaim the land in the Polish Corridor won him widespread support in East Prussia.

On September 1, 1939, Hitler's war machine started World War II by invading Poland. In the aftermath of that brutal war, a mass westward exodus from the region began as East Prussians, in horse-drawn wagons and by ship, tried to escape the advancing Russian front. Between 400,000 and 600,000 East Prussians, together with thousands of French and Belgian prisoners of war (whose exact number is unknown), perished in the attempt. As many as 800,000 others, trapped behind Russian lines, remained in the region when it fell under Russian and Polish control. My mother, brother and I were among those left behind.

I was born in Königsberg, East Prussia, on December 3, 1937. My paternal grandfather made his fortune before World War I as the owner of a chain of upscale women's clothing stores specializing in expensive suits and furs. When he sold his business, he invested the proceeds in a two hundred sixty-two acre farm in Altenberg, just outside of Königsberg, and became a "gentleman farmer."

The Nitsch family photograph album bulged with pictures dating back to the turn of the century; a family tree proudly traced our ancestors all the way back to a "musketeer" born in 1755. In Altenberg, culture and education were highly prized. A grand piano dominated the living room in my grandparents' substantial farmhouse. When my Aunt Käte played, her younger brothers and sisters were required to sing along. A sharp rap to the side of the head was my grandfather's way of enforcing this rule. Most of the men in my father's family were members of the Nazi party. Nominally Lutheran, my Altenberg grandparents were churchgoers only on Easter and Christmas, and at baptisms, confirmations, weddings, and funerals.

My father, Willi Nitsch, was the black sheep of his family. Expelled from middle school for brawling, he was the only one of the five children who did not complete a formal education. Instead, following a lengthy apprenticeship, he became a master pastry chef, a profession considered unmanly by his relatives. When he married my mother, Margarete Recklies, in 1935, several members of his family expressed their disgust with my father's low social status by choosing not to attend the wedding.

The newlyweds opened a small café and pastry shop in Königsberg and worked hard to make a go of it before the war forced them to close the place down. After my father was drafted into the German army in 1939, my mother and I went to live with her parents, Gottfried and Berta Recklies, whose small farm in Langendorf near Schippenbeil, sixty kilometers southeast of Königsberg, was less than one-fourth the size of the Altenberg property. Opa and Oma, my Langendorf grandparents, were a simple, hardworking couple, devout Lutherans who went to church every Sunday, rain or shine. Aside from the Farm Journal, Opa never read anything other than his Bible, a heavy volume with covers made of thin wooden boards wrapped in shiny brown leather, the first letter in each Book decorated with red and gold spiraled illuminated letters. Over one hundred years old, the Bible had been handed down to Opa from his grandfather, and from his grandfather's grandfather before him.

Oma and Opa considered Hitler's politics to be pernicious and ungodly from the very beginning. Still, against their advice, all five of their children, including my mother, supported the regime. Only after Germany invaded Russia, directly threatening the safety of East Prussia, did the entire family agree that Hitler was a dangerous madman.

A succession of prisoners of war worked alongside Opa in the fields. A war disabled World War I veteran who lived on a nearby farm brought Opa's prisoners to him and, after a while, took them away and brought us new ones. Some were Poles; others were Frenchmen, Belgians, and

Russians. Arriving prisoners wore faded uniforms with KG (Prisoner of War) painted on the back of their shirts, but after a few months they replaced their threadbare uniforms with work clothes provided by the farmers. Since my father and my uncles rarely came home on leave, Opa and our prisoners were the men in my life.

The little bit of formal learning I received was in a one room elementary school just down the road. But what a strange education it was! On cold, rainy days we stayed indoors, writing arithmetic problems and spelling words on our slates and singing catchy German folk songs, but our lessons were often interrupted by our teacher's somber warnings about terrifying potato-eating bugs released from American and British high-flying airplanes, and toy cars dropped by the Russians to blow small children like us to bits. At dismissal time, she reminded us to draw the shutters tight at night to maintain a total blackout.

On nice days, when we had gymnastics class on the sports ground, my teacher, Fräulein Durbach, changed into black shorts. A small swastika emblem of the League of German Maidens was stitched into her snow-white athletic top. We spent entire school days out in the fields, wearing special aprons and collecting wild flowers and herbs to dry in our attics so they could be used to produce medicines for the troops. My friends, Sigrid and Horst, and I threw ourselves into the war effort, competing to see who could bring in the most iron, rags, paper, and even old bones, all of which, Fräulein Durbach assured us, would help secure the "final victory" for the Fatherland.

The highlight of the school year came on the 20th of April 1944, when we celebrated the Führer's birthday. Our principal, Herr Tellmann, spoke enthusiastically about Adolf Hitler's life, how he came from a humble background, and how bravely he had fought in the First World War. His voice quivering with emotion, he assured us that the Führer was the "savior of Germany." When he had finished speaking, Fräulein Durbach poured each of us a tiny cup of hot chocolate, measuring carefully to be sure everyone would have enough. After the festivities, as Horst and I walked home from school clutching our little paper swastika flags on thin wooden sticks, I puzzled over our principal's words. How could Herr Tellmann claim the Führer as our savior when Opa always taught me that our Savior was the Lord Jesus Christ?

During the fall school vacation, I spent every day in the fields with Opa and the prisoners, bringing in the potato crop. In the late afternoon, potatoes skewered on willow branches and roasted over a burning pile of dried plants warmed us up.

A fifteen minute walk along the tree-lined road from Opa's farm brought us to the Alle River Bridge at the edge of Schippenbeil. I often walked there with Mutti to bring fresh eggs from our farm to the Buchmanns, Oma's sister and brother-in-law, who owned an immaculate bakery in town, or to visit Uncle Schulz, the Schippenbeil station master. Uncle Schulz lived over the train station on Bahnhofstrasse near Adolf-Hitler Platz in an apartment filled with fierce, colorful masks, ornate lances, and bows and arrows, souvenirs of the three years he spent in Africa working for the German railroad before World War I. When Mutti was growing up, Jewish families had owned some of the shops in Schippenbeil, but they were long gone. In fact, until I was nearly seven years old, I cannot remember ever hearing the word "Jew." Then, late in 1944, the SS opened a sub-camp of the Stutthof Concentration Camp at the Schippenbeil military airport, where nearly one thousand Jewish women, yellow stars sewn on their loose-fitting clothing, toiled day and night. At Sunday services, I heard whispers that the emaciated bodies of dead camp inmates lay buried in unmarked graves in our church cemetery.

There were other ominous signs even a six-year-old could understand: the red glow in the sky from the bombing of Königsberg, only a one-hour train ride away; the sudden decision of my friend Sigrid's mother to return with her children to the Reich; the arrival of refugee families in Langendorf, the odor of diarrhea clinging to their clothes. Nazi officials placed two families with my Aunt Liesbeth and her five children at their large farm further down the road. Soon it was our turn. Suitcases and bundles were stacked up against our farmhouse walls; comforters were spread on the floor. For the ten days the strangers stayed with us, I resented being forced from my own room, resented the break in our family's routine.

Still, most frightening was the possibility that we might lose the war. Every evening when the war news, interspersed with peppy march music, blared from the radio in the living room, the announcers still claimed we were winning on all fronts. Fräulein Durbach repeated the same upbeat reports every day in school. Yet when we visited my father's family in Altenberg or when Vati or Mutti's brothers, Uncle Ernst and Uncle Herbert, came home on leave, the conversation always turned to the approaching Russian front, and to considerations of our own escape. On those occasions I was gripped by the feeling that something dreadful was about to happen.

In reality, the Russians were closing in on East Prussia from three sides. Only the coast along the Baltic Sea remained securely in German hands and time was running out.

CHAPTER 1

*O*pa's white stucco farmhouse had a red tiled roof with a steep gable and two windows over the double entrance doors. A strange blend of scents from salted herring and raw onions; pungent, stomach-turning tripe; and the sweet aroma of warm milk dumpling soup wafted from Oma's kitchen. Dark yellow fly catcher strips hung in big curls from the dining room ceiling, drifting slowly back and forth. Attracted by the smell of Tilsiter cheese and fried bacon, a small army of flies invaded the farmhouse.

Every afternoon in late summer 1944 Oma packed a basket with crusty rye bread, sweet wheat bread the color of egg yolk sprinkled with poppy seeds, butter, homemade cooked cheese with caraway seeds, gooseberry or rhubarb jam, and thick buttermilk to carry out to Opa, the prisoners and me as we worked in the fields.

Opa had squinty blue eyes surrounded by crinkly laugh lines. He wasn't especially tall, but he was lean and bony, and very strong. He was the first one up in the morning and, in the evening, the last one to go to bed. His large hands were rough and weathered and his palms were calloused from hard work. Most evenings, just after supper, Opa would take the heavy Bible from its stand in the living room and I would curl up next to him on the big wooden bench. When the weather

1

turned colder at the end of October, I snuggled against the pillows in the glow of the wood burning in the tile stove, never tiring of listening to stories about Jonah, and Moses, and Jesus, until Opa dozed off and began to snore.

By late November 1944, when deep snow covered the farm, Opa decided to slaughter a hog in defiance of Nazi Party prohibitions, even if doing so put our family at risk. Under a pitch black early morning sky in the faint light of the electric lamp hung from the eaves of the pig sty, our warm breaths formed little puffs of fog in the frosty air. By the time I had slipped out of bed and sneaked outside to watch, Armand and Gustave, the French prisoners now working on our farm, had already tied one hind leg of the huge squealing hog to an iron hook in the wall. Four metal buckets and a few razor-sharp knives lay ready on a low table. Each Frenchman held a piece of rope and, as the hog tried desperately to escape, Opa whacked it on the head with a giant sledge hammer. Throwing down the hammer, Opa tied the hind legs of the hog together and our prisoners hoisted the bloodied creature up off the ground, using the pulley block attached to the strong beam jutting out from under the roof.

Starting right after breakfast, Mutti and Oma set to work, grinding meat into sausage and preparing meat for canning, while Opa salted the hams and the sides of pork and hung them up in the smoke house. Later, he added fresh blood sausage, liver sausage, and smoked meat sausage. Around lunchtime, everyone, even the prisoners, sat together around the kitchen table, feasting on freshly cooked blood sausage spiced with marjoram, liverwurst, and small crusty breaded cutlets fried in butter, with applesauce and sweet pickled pumpkin cubes on the side. During our feast, my two-year-old brother Hubert enjoyed a place of honor on Oma's lap.

School closed for vacation in early December 1944, two weeks ahead of schedule. We heard rumors that our area was unsafe. Some people in Schippenbeil claimed that escaped Russian and Polish prisoners of war were working as partisans for the encircling Russian Army. Twice before Christmas, German military police searched our farm for escaped prisoners.

Until the last minute, I hoped that, by some miracle, Vati, or Uncle Ernst, or Uncle Herbert would come for the holidays, but none of them came. Oma and Mutti once again prepared a wonderful meal featuring roast goose stuffed with apples and then we sat around the big table near the tiled stove while Opa read the Christmas story from the Bible. Later, we sang Christmas carols. Despite the festivities, the Christmas spirit of past years was somehow missing. Opa tried to find some carols on the radio, but all we got were reports from the front.

On January 21, 1945, the radio announced alarming news. The Russians had captured Gumbinnen, a small town in the eastern part of East Prussia, only eighty kilometers from Langendorf. First thing the next morning, once again disobeying the orders of the high command, Opa worked with Armand to cover our best wagon. Gustave, our other French prisoner, had slipped away during the night.

* * *

By the 25th of January, demolition charges had been packed around the concrete columns of the Alle River Bridge, less than a kilometer from Opa's farm. Yet our local Nazi party leaders were adamant. Word once again spread from farm to farm: "They still won't let us leave."

That same evening, about two hours after supper, while the war news blared on the radio, the telephone rang.

Mutti answered. "Hallo?" She covered the receiver to whisper, "It's Liesbeth." As Mutti listened, the color drained from her face.

"Well, what is it?" Oma asked as soon as Mutti hung up. "Are the Reimanns all right?"

"Just before Liesbeth called, a lieutenant from the infantry and two soldiers barged into her house. 'What? You're still here?' he asked her. And then they left without another word. She's at a loss what to do."

Opa cleared his throat. "Well, it looks as though the Party and the Army have different opinions. One says we'll be shot if we leave; the other says we'll be shot if we stay. I hope things will be clearer in the morning. What else did Liesbeth say?"

"Nothing, she's totally dissolved."

"The poor girl. She and the children are much too isolated in that house with Alfred away. I wish they lived a bit closer to us."

Opa called Aunt Liesbeth back and tried to calm her down. Then we all went to bed. Under my comforter, my heart beat faster than usual.

Before I fell asleep, I said a short prayer. Dear God, please help the grownups decide what to do. And please protect us and our farm. Amen.

* * *

The very next day, January 26, 1945, electrifying news spread through Langendorf. Mayor Tetzlaff, a loyal Nazi Party member, had stowed a bulging briefcase in the trunk of his car and driven away with his family during the night. Although there was still no official blessing, it was suddenly "Every man for himself." Everyone began to make hasty preparations.

The mood in our house was gloomy as Mutti, Oma and Opa hurriedly packed clothes, towels, and linens. Our living room was soon filled with boxes, suitcases, and bundles of blankets and coats. The grownups were still hard at work long after sunset.

"Günter, it's time for you to go to bed," Mutti announced.

"It's not fair," I protested. "Why don't you let me pack? I'm not a baby."

"Of course not. You're a big boy of seven, but tomorrow's going to be a long day. You'll be much more help to us after a good night's sleep."

"All right, all right, I'm going."

4

Just as I started to drag my feet towards my room, I heard Senta, our big German Shepherd, barking outside. She must have heard someone along the road. I turned back to Mutti.

"Can Senta sleep next to me in the wagon?" I asked, full of hope.

Mutti, who had been smiling, looked suddenly serious. "No, I don't think so. Let's talk about Senta in the morning. Sleep tight!"

Before crawling under the covers, I studied Vati's framed photograph on my small night table. He looked serious in his pressed Luftwaffe uniform, no curve of a smile around his mouth; his service cap was tipped slightly to one side leaving his right eye partially in shadow. His nose leaned in the same direction as his hat, its crooked shape a souvenir of a brawl between his Storm Troopers and the Communists. He was staring straight ahead. I could not meet his gaze.

I compared his picture to the one next to it, showing me as a delighted little boy, proudly wearing my father's hobnailed military boots and his Luftwaffe garrison cap, tilted to the left. The eagle decorating the cap carried a swastika in its claws, just like the ones on my father's uniform. The straps holding up my shorts were crossed over my chest. I wore a long-sleeved checkered shirt. Hidden underneath it were the hated rubber suspenders, sewn to my short undershirt to hold up my leggings. My spindly legs, in their scratchy thigh-high woolen stockings, showed between the tops of my father's shiny leather boots and the bottom of my short knitted pants. Mutti always joked that I would have lots of growing to do before I filled boots like those.

* * *

Mutti and Oma stayed up working most of the night. Now, at dawn, they were busy packing food in the kitchen. Gradually our supplies filled up the barn. There were dark rye breads packed into wooden boxes. Earthenware jugs filled with lard. Smoked sausages and hard sausages. Sides of bacon marbled with fat. Dried apple slices, flour, and sugar in linen bags. Jam, liver sausage, and blood sausage in jars.

5

Piles of pots and pans stacked to one side. Along one wall of the living room, still waiting to be loaded, were boxes and suitcases crammed full of clothes, linens, dishes, two large oriental rugs, and half a dozen runners.

Since everyone was busy, I kept my questions bottled up inside. There were many of them. Where would we sleep during the nights? Wouldn't we be too cold on the wagon? Where would we cook?

Hubert nudged me. "Can we go to the barn again?"

"Sure," I said, helping him with his coat, his woolen cap, and his boots.

In the barn, Opa was filling burlap sacks with oats for our horses. Then he and Armand loaded everything onto our wagon. For a late breakfast the grownups ate scrambled eggs and bacon. As a special treat, Hubert and I had scrambled eggs with homemade cherry marmalade.

"If Senta isn't sleeping with me, where will she sleep?" I asked Mutti, as I stirred the marmalade into my eggs.

"Senta's not coming with us," Mutti said, looking down at her plate.

"Not coming? But she's our watch dog! Who's going to protect us along the way?"

"I'm sorry," Opa said sadly. "I know how much you love Senta. We all do, but we have to leave her behind."

I didn't give up easily. "I'll take care of her. Whatever she needs. She won't be any trouble."

Mutti shook her head. "Senta's a smart dog. She'll manage somehow on her own. If she came along, she'd just be another mouth to feed."

After breakfast, I rushed outside to look for Senta. She bounded out of her dog house at my approach. As I bent down to pet her, she licked my hand. I buried my face in her fur and sobbed.

* * *

Around noon, twelve more people arrived in two covered wagons. The first wagon was driven by a Russian prisoner of war. My Aunt Liesbeth and her five children: Ilse, eleven, Dora, ten, Gerda, eight, Helga, three, and Dieter, who was one, were inside. Their maid, Emma, a young woman with dirty blond hair, accompanied them. Aunt Liesbeth's in-laws and the sharecropper couple who worked their farm were in the second wagon. They joined us for a lunch of sandwiches and pound cake. While Oma, Emma and Mutti cleared the dishes, Opa and Aunt Liesbeth listened to the radio.

The color drained from Opa's face. Aunt Liesbeth started to cry.

"Berta! Gretel! Come in here!" Opa called. Oma and Mutti rushed out of the kitchen, drying their hands on their aprons.

"What is it? What's wrong?"

"We're encircled," Opa said. "Two hundred thousand Russian soldiers have overrun nearly all of East Prussia. Worse than that, we're cut off from the Reich. They've captured Tolkemit near the Baltic Sea. We have to reach Pillau at all costs."

Mutti broke the silence following this announcement.

"Why all the long faces? We all knew something like this might happen. If it has to be Pillau, then Pillau it is."

7

CHAPTER 2

*O*n Saturday, January 27, 1945, late in the afternoon, all of us left in the three covered wagons, each pulled by two horses. In our wagon were Mutti, Hubert, Armand, Oma and Opa, and me. The weather was cold and frosty. We could faintly hear the far away boom of cannons. Mutti and Oma were crying. I couldn't believe how fast our situation had changed. I tried to pretend I was going off on a great adventure, like one of Uncle Schulz's safaris, but I was too overwhelmed and frightened. How could we leave everything behind? Our farm, our house, our furniture, most of our food, our cows, our chickens, my toys, even my electric train. However, the worst for me was leaving Senta. She raced after our wagon, her tail wagging furiously.

"Stay!" Opa had commanded and she had sat down obediently in front of the cow stable. As the wagons lurched down the driveway, I could still see her through my tears, running back and forth with excitement.

Wagons clogged the road to Schippenbeil. We moved so slowly, Opa and Armand were able to walk alongside, Opa holding the reins of the horses. Mutti moved to the front opening of the wagon and I joined her to get a better view. Bypassing Schippenbeil on the left, we took the road to Landskron. Someone yelled, "The factory's on fire!"

Black smoke hung on the horizon, but Opa kept his eyes on the road straight ahead.

We heard several distant rumblings, followed by loud explosions.

"Sounds like the soldiers are blowing up the military airport," Opa commented bitterly to Mutti. "I wonder what happened to all the prisoners there."

"The Russians must be even closer than we thought," Mutti replied. Her eyes scanned the horizon as she spoke. The sun was an odd shade of crimson.

"We're in God's hands," Opa said quietly.

I slipped down from the front seat and crawled way back inside the wagon. Curled up under a cozy down comforter and three blankets, I dozed off. My sleep was often interrupted by our sudden stops and starts, the sounds of people yelling, the neighing of the horses outside.

Senta must be worried by now. Was she standing at her post on the sand pile next to the barn, watching the top of the driveway for our return? Or had she gone to look for us because the cows had not been milked, because the chickens were unfed? I heard Senta's whimpering, and then the warmth of her body nestled against mine, but woke to find Hubert snuggling closer to me for extra warmth. I worried that Mutti had forgotten to lock the house before we left. Would the Russians find the door open, or would they be forced to break it down? I dreamed a Russian boy was in my room, shaking out the contents of my cigar boxes, knocking over my pictures, playing with my leather soccer ball. Leaving behind the cozy safety of Opa's farm, I was being jostled and bumped toward an uncertain future.

* * *

The sun finally rose after a seemingly endless night. According to Opa, we had only traveled a few kilometers. Everyone looked miserable and tired. All around us, the grown ups were talking about how fast the Russian front was closing in. Since our wagon wasn't moving yet,

I climbed out to take a look around. Suddenly I felt very shivery and hungry.

"May I have a cup of milk?" I asked Mutti through chattering teeth.

She shook her head. "I'm afraid not. Our milk froze solid in the metal drum."

Without warning, the line of refugee wagons began to move again and we were swept along with them. Three civilian automobiles zoomed past.

"There go more party bosses. A few days ago they ordered us 'to hold out to the end.' Now look at them skedaddle," Opa observed.

"We couldn't move any faster if we tried," Mutti said. The line of wagons stretched far ahead of us to the horizon. We could not see the first wagon in the column, but still it set the pace for the rest of us. On every country lane, to the right and to the left, more wagons waited to merge onto the paved road.

By mid-afternoon, Mutti and Aunt Liesbeth decided we could not go on without a rest. We looked for shelter in the houses along the road, only to find them already filled with refugees. There wasn't a room to spare. Finally, we turned to the left down a country road where we discovered a large farm. The owners were packing their wagon, getting ready to leave the next day. Three or four refugee families were already staying the night and we were invited to join them. Aunt Liesbeth and Mutti were grateful for the fresh milk which the farmer's wife gave us. The farmer and his wife even let us keep our horses in their stable where they were provided with hay and oats. The knotholes on the weathered boards reminded me of the marks my toy potato shooter had left on the wall of Opa's barn. I wondered what had happened to my friend Horst. Together we could have worked up some cheerful mischief. Thinking he might be among the refugees crammed in the farm house, I went to look for him.

"Did you happen to see Horst?" I asked Mutti.

"There's no one here I recognize," she said. "Funny, it's the first time I wouldn't mind seeing that little troublemaker."

"I feel bad we haven't played together since school closed. I don't even know when they left Langendorf."

"Wherever we end up tomorrow night, we can look for him there," Mutti said, but without much conviction.

* * *

The large kitchen was the busiest place in the house. All of the mothers, including Mutti, were cooking soup, frying bacon, and toasting frozen bread. After we ate, Mutti, Oma, Opa, Hubert, Armand, and I bedded down in the nursery. We curled up on the floor under blankets and comforters retrieved from our wagon. My bed back home was more comfortable, but at least I wasn't being jostled about on a rutted road. Feeling warm and cozy, I stared up at the ceiling and tried to imagine my little Stuka plane hanging there. I soon dozed off.

It was still dark the next morning when I was awakened by Aunt Liesbeth's voice. I pretended to be asleep so that I would not interrupt the conversation.

"He just thanked me for everything and said 'Au revoir'," Opa was explaining

Now I was nosy. I opened my eyes and asked, "Who're you talking about?"

"Armand. He's gone," Opa said. "He decided to join some of his countrymen in another wagon."

* * *

No sooner had our wagon caravan started to move again, when three army motorcycles with sidecars caught up with us. Military policemen wearing metal shields on their chests forced us off the paved road. All of the refugees were directed to use a frozen track beaten by farm wagons across the nearby fields. As we jolted along, pails, wash basins, shovels,

11

saws and axes which had been hung on the outside of the wagons were bumped off into the snow. Nobody stopped to pick anything up. No one seemed to care.

The detour infuriated Mutti. Opa tried his best to soothe her.

"The Lord will lead us to safety," he said with his usual calm.

After crisscrossing country paths, we returned to a paved road whenever we could but, most of the time, we were forced to travel through the fields and forests. As time went on, the grownups began to worry that we were hopelessly lost. No one had a map. There were no road signs. We could not ask directions because all of the local farmers had already left. We could not even guide ourselves by the sun. Even when it wasn't snowing, the sky was often the color of slate. Hoping for the best, we sat in our wagons, plodding aimlessly ahead.

"We're going in circles," Oma complained. "That's the same barn we passed two hours ago."

"Is this the road to Pillau?" I called out to Opa anxiously.

"No doubt about it," he comforted me. Opa could always be relied on to see us through.

* * *

From where I was sitting under the canvas in the back, I could barely catch a glimpse of the outside, but I was aware of how often we were forced to stop. Our wagons slipped on the frozen tracks. We covered only a few kilometers each day. More than once I wished I could wave a magic wand and be back in Langendorf.

Since we were forced to rely on melted snow for our drinking water, it wasn't long before the smallest children got upset stomachs. Dieter, who was the youngest, cried constantly. The smell of sickness filled the wagon. I worried that we would never find a place to stop and rest.

* * *

One evening, just at sunset, after seven days on the road, we reached the town of Preussisch Eylau. Soldiers and refugees crammed the tree-lined streets. We had no hope of finding a warm place to sleep. In desperation, Opa approached a German soldier, sitting astride a motorcycle.

"Excuse me, sir; do you have any idea where we could stay the night?"

The soldier was forced to raise his voice so that he could be heard over the noise of his idling engine.

"Try that place over there. They'll tell you they're full, but stand your ground!" he yelled.

Crowds of refugees were already inside the large building the soldier had pointed out. The floor was covered with huge burlap sacks filled with straw. To our great relief, we were soon squeezed into assigned spaces in the hall on the main floor. The Reimanns were given straw mattresses next to ours. Despite the cramped conditions, the room was warm and dry, a welcome change after the cold nights we had spent huddled in our drafty wagons.

"Thank you, Lord, for sending us this miracle!" Opa proclaimed.

We shared a kitchen with many other families and a few German soldiers. When Mutti got her turn to use the stove, she hung up her coat on a peg and began to cook a huge pot of potato soup with sausage. Before peeling the potatoes, she slipped her everyday wristwatch into her coat pocket. Later she discovered that her watch had been stolen. Angrily, Mutti searched through our bags until she found the fancy dress watch Vati had given to her for special occasions. She wore that watch from then on.

After supper we waited patiently on line for a chance to take our first baths since we left Langendorf. It was wonderful to be clean again.

When I woke up at dawn, I felt as though my belly was going to explode. Tiptoeing past my family, I looked forward to using the toilet, but by the time I reached the bathroom, more than a dozen people, including mothers clutching babies and clean diapers, were ahead of me on line.

My tummy told me loud and clear that I could not wait. Stepping outside, the icy wind hit my face. We were no longer in the countryside; although plenty of bare trees lined the street, there were no bushes to provide protective cover. Frantically, I rushed along the slushy sidewalk, searching for a place where I could have some privacy. The street was lined with refugee wagons and from a number of wagons I could hear low voices. Suddenly a group of broken-down wagons, one of them without wheels, caught my eye. Approaching as close as I dared, I called out, "Is anyone there?" but there was no answer.

I crept inside and stood with my dirty shoes on a pile of soft, striped blankets. Picking my way over open suitcases and boxes full of clothes, my urge became greater. In the back of the wagon, I climbed onto a tall wooden packing crate and relieved myself on the down comforters piled up behind it. To clean myself, I went through an entire stack of white linen napkins. Leaving the wagon, I grabbed a big yellow towel. After using the snow outside to wash my hands until they turned blue, I dried myself with the towel and then I threw it away.

Even though I felt guilty about what I had done, I comforted myself with the thought that the owners had fled and all of their possessions would soon fall into Russian hands. At the same time that my conscience was pricking me, I was also curious about what else might have been left behind. In search of a dry towel to wrap around my frozen fingers, I climbed into another abandoned wagon. Rummaging through the contents of a suitcase, I discovered two flat, round cans of military chocolate. It didn't take me long to decide to put the chocolate into my pocket.

When I got back to the hall, Mutti was upset. "Where were you all this time? I was worried sick about you."

"Sorry, but I had diarrhea and the line for the toilets was too long."

"Did you walk all the way back to Langendorf?"

"Once I finished, I snooped around some abandoned wagons. Look what I found!"

"It's the same kind of chocolate your father brought us when he came home on leave," Mutti said, slowly turning over a tin in her hand.

"Yes, I know. Isn't it wonderful?"

"None of that chocolate for you, young man," Oma piped up. "Not with a sick stomach."

I looked to Mutti for support, but she shook her head. "Oma's right. The army packs that stuff with caffeine. The soldiers break off only a little bit at a time to keep themselves awake." Instead Oma made me eat two pieces of charcoal which she took from the little pill box in her handbag where she kept her medications. Ilse, Dora and Gerda also needed charcoal from Oma's "pharmacy."

"That should help you until we leave here tomorrow," she said, "but be sure to come back and see me if you need another dose."

* * *

Trusting in Oma's remedy, I set out to explore the town. In a square not far from where we were staying, a German army truck had towed in an enormous soup cauldron on wheels. A young soldier was ladling out pea soup to a long line of refugees. Pieces of red sausage were floating in the soup. The smell was irresistible. Full of hope, I joined the line. When my turn finally came, I realized I was the only one there who had not brought along a container.

"Well, what are we going to do about you?" the soldier asked. "No bowl, eh?"

"No, sir," I replied timidly.

"Step aside, please. We'll think of something. Just don't run away though."

"Thank you. I won't budge."

15

While continuing to ladle soup into bowls, he called back over his shoulder to some other soldiers:

"I need an army canteen kit, on the double!"

The people in line plodded slowly forward. After five more were served, the soldier was handed a kit. He filled the canteen with steaming hot soup and snapped on the cover. Smiling, he handed me the canteen.

"Enjoy it, young man. You can keep the kit. Compliments of the German Army."

"Thank you very much!" I stammered. "But are you sure it's all right?"

With a glance at his comrades, the friendly soldier shrugged. "If I had given you an army canteen a week ago, it would have meant a court martial, but now, with the Russians so close, it really doesn't matter."

Clutching the warm container, I rushed back to the hall. A flat knife was attached to the canteen kit. Next to it hung a funny utensil, a combination spoon and fork. The monogrammed silver soup spoon I had carried in my pocket since leaving Langendorf had been a baptism gift from Oma, but I proudly used my new Army gadget instead. As Dorchen, Gerda and I shared the soup, Opa hurried over to the soup kitchen with a small pail to get some more for the rest of the family. By the time he arrived, it was all gone.

That same evening Mutti and Aunt Liesbeth heard more rumors about the fast approaching Russian Army. Some people had even left during the night. For the sake of the children, Mutti and Aunt Liesbeth decided to wait until daybreak.

The next morning German Army units rushed through the streets; refugees tried desperately to get away. In the confusion, we were afraid we would get separated from Aunt Liesbeth. Somehow we were all still together when we reached the outskirts of town.

* * *

When we left Preussisch Eylau, there was no oncoming traffic. Everyone was moving in the same direction, away from the Russian front somewhere behind us. As far ahead as we could see, evenly spaced trees with white-painted trunks lined the road.

"Who painted them to look like birch trees?" I asked Opa.

"I guess soldiers, because the drivers of trucks and cars aren't allowed to turn on their headlights at night," he began.

"Just like blacking out our windows at Langendorf during the night, right?"

"That's right," Opa replied. "The white paint on the trees acts like a guidepost in the dark."

One of the refugee wagons passing by us had no roof. Bundled in several layers of clothing, the people inside looked like dark, misshapen dolls. Every so often, their driver's hand flicked the reins, but the rest of them sat so still, I thought they might have already frozen to death. Crowded among the military vehicles and covered wagons were refugees traveling on foot. Some people had hand carts or baby carriages; others pushed bicycles loaded with bags and little packages tied together in pairs.

We had been underway for hours. Numb with cold, I climbed down from the wagon and walked alongside with Opa. The ditch on the right side of the road was cluttered with boxes, suitcases, carpets, toy trains, baby strollers, and abandoned wagons. Pink-faced dolls lay like tiny frozen bodies on the ice.

"Why do you suppose some people prop some stuff up next to the trees instead of dumping it in the ditch?" I asked Opa.

"The things you notice!" Opa said. "Maybe they think someone else will see it and put it to good use."

A large dog, flattened by a tank, lay like a bloody carpet in the middle of the road just ahead of us, reminding me of frogs crushed by harvest wagons back in Langendorf. My thoughts drifted back to Senta. Was she still alive? If she had tried to follow us into Schippenbeil,

Gunter Nitsch

she might also have been squashed like that. The thought made me shudder.

Farther along the road, four horses lay dead.

"They must have broken their legs," Opa explained. "It's the kindest thing to shoot them so they don't suffer too long."

Blood, spilt from the bullet holes in the horses, had melted the snow and then refrozen.

"It looks as though their heads are resting in red ice," I commented to Opa, a shiver running down my spine.

"It's been like this for days," he told me. "Maybe you'd be better off tucked inside the wagon with your Mutti and Hubert. The view out here is a bit hard to stomach."

"If it's all the same to you, I'd rather stay out here. Walking warms me up."

Without warning, the wagon in front of us slowed down. Then everybody ahead of us, including the military vehicles next to us, came to an abrupt stop. No one budged for more than an hour. A few refugees ventured out of their wagons to start little fires on the right side of the road so that they could heat up some coffee or soup. Thick black smoke rose up as the frozen wood started to burn. Mutti was also tempted to cook, but Oma took the pot out of her hand and suggested that we stretch our legs instead.

Clinging to the right side of the road, Mutti and I walked up ahead a little way. The odor from piles of human waste disgusted me; yellow colored snow spoke of many "relief stops." As we went on, we saw soldiers pacing up and down next to their truck. Mutti and I overheard one of them grumbling about "the awful refugees who were responsible for the terrible traffic jam."

Jerking his thumb towards the cluster of wagons, another young soldier nodded in agreement. "If it were up to me, we'd use our tanks to push all that refugee scum right off the road."

I grabbed Mutti's hand as she and I rushed back to our wagon.

18

All along the side of the road, refugees, encouraged by the long stopover, were busy with their cooking. Suddenly, the line of traffic began to move. The frustrated cooks grabbed their red-hot pots off of the fires and held them in the snow. Lugging the heavy containers by their handles, they walked along next to their wagons, waiting for the liquid inside to cool down.

With howling motors, army trucks, track laying vehicles, sometimes even a tank with its tracks squealing and clattering, passed us recklessly. Any semblance of discipline was gone. Our horses, although underfed and very tired, became skittish. Opa and the other wagon drivers had a rough time.

A huge vehicle pulled alongside us. It had wheels in front like a truck, but from the middle to the back it had treads like a tank.

"What d'you call that thing?" I asked Opa.

"A soldier told me it's a half-track towing vehicle. Just look how many other vehicles it's pulling! They must have run out of gas or broken down along the way."

I watched in amazement. The half-track moved only a little faster than our wagon. I counted nine military vehicles in tow. The steel ropes between the vehicles were so taut I thought they might snap any second. Opa and I choked on the dark-blue exhaust fumes.

When the last vehicle finally passed us, Opa stared up ahead. With concern in his voice, he turned to me and exclaimed, "This is too much! Look!"

Following Opa's gaze, I saw that, far ahead of us, the road curved to the right. The half-track had carefully rounded the curve and disappeared, but the vehicles in the middle of the convoy, with no one to steer them, did not go properly into the curve. Instead, as they began to straighten out, they edged close to the right side of the road forcing three horse-drawn wagons to veer sharply off to the right and roll down the slope. We could hear the cracking of splintered wood as a few small trees on the slope broke off like match sticks.

Two of the drivers managed to ride down the slight slope onto a snowed-in field. One wagon took the slope too fast and flipped upside down at the bottom of the ditch. The cries of the people trapped inside were heartbreaking, but the military convoy kept on going as if nothing had happened.

The refugee wagons in front of ours came to an abrupt halt. An old farmer from one of the other wagons clambered down the slope to help. Carrying a baby in his arms, he brought the whole family up to ride with him on his wagon. All of the family's belongings had to be left behind.

Another man tried to help by unhitching the horses from the broken wagon, but the animals were so badly injured, they could not walk. Meanwhile, the drivers of the other wagons at the bottom of the slope tried without success to get back onto the road. The convoy was gone by now, but individual military vehicles continued to pass us on the left side. People behind us started to yell, "Let's go!"

"I wish I could help," Opa told Mutti, "but our horses are too weak to pull them out of the ditch." We just moved on like everyone else.

CHAPTER 3

We traveled slowly. Sometimes we were stuck for half a day; sometimes for an entire day. I worried that we would get stuck so long, the Russian tanks would roll right over us. We could hear artillery rumbling constantly like distant thunder. When we were able to make some progress, we pushed forward as late into the evening as possible. The lonely houses we passed were empty until noon, but then they filled up fast. So we were usually forced to spend the night in our wagons. Hubert, Helga, and Dieter cried most of the time. Wiping their tears and runny noses was a never-ending task for Mutti and Aunt Liesbeth. Many times I also broke down in tears. All of us were sick. Oma's charcoal no longer helped.

One morning, my cousin, Ilse, came over to tell Mutti that Aunt Liesbeth's eighty-three year old mother-in-law had died during the night. Opa and Ilse tried to dig a grave for her, but the ground was frozen solid. Old Mrs. Reimann was covered with a blanket and laid into the snow. A mound of snow piled on top was her only marker and more snow was already falling as her husband stood slumped over at the side of the road.

"Come ride in our wagon," Aunt Liesbeth said, gently tugging her father-in-law's arm.

By the time we moved on, the whole landscape looked as if it had been covered with a giant white bed sheet. My teeth chattered and my breath was visible in the air. Crossing my arms across my chest to try to stop my shivering, I worried that my feet would turn into blocks of ice.

As we continued on our way, the right side of the road became even more cluttered with furniture, pots and pans, boxes, suitcases, and dead horses. How many people lay just beneath the surface of the snow? Who among us would be next to die? Perhaps all of us were doomed. Would our wagons end up one day along the side of the road, piled with our dead bodies?

* * *

One day as we stopped around lunchtime, Oma discovered that all of our glass jars of canned sausage and fruits had burst from the frost. Five wooden boxes of broken glass landed in the clutter on the right side of the road. Trying not to look discouraged, Mutti struggled to make a fire so she could cook some barley soup with sausage. It was rough going because frozen wood burned slowly. Just as Mutti had called out that the soup was almost ready, we heard a terrifying noise. Soldiers jumped from their vehicles. One of them yelled, "Low flying airplanes! Everybody down!"

Bursts of automatic gunfire rapidly ripped up the ground nearby. By the time I had fallen to the ground the Russian airplanes were gone, their drone replaced by the dreadful shrieks of the wounded mixed with the agonizing screams of injured horses. Right behind our wagon, people and horses lay where they had been hit by volleys of machine gun fire, some already dead, others writhing in pain. Terrified I was going to die, I looked up and saw, to my astonishment, that Mutti was still stirring the barley soup. For a second I did not know whether to laugh or to cry.

Set back from the tree-lined road, a farm building was ablaze. Thick black smoke belched toward the lead-colored sky.

"Do you think those were incendiary bombs?" I asked Opa as I watched the flames consume the farm house roof. "Like the ones the radio announcer said were dropped on Berlin and Hamburg?"

"They wouldn't waste stuff like that on us," Opa answered, shaking his head. "Maybe they hit a fuel tank. That's probably what caused the fire."

"I hope our farm is still safe."

"No need to worry," Opa replied, but his eyes, like mine, were focused on the burning building.

I tugged at his sleeve. "Opa, who's milking our cows and feeding the chickens? Did you remember to ask someone to do it?"

"There was no one to ask. They all left, just like us," he replied.

"Well, one thing's for sure. Senta's too smart to go hungry. Do you think, if she were starving, she'd kill one of the chickens for food?"

Opa had no time to answer me. Without warning, the planes returned, raining down more deadly machine gun fire and bombs. The earth trembled beneath our feet and we were deafened by the piercing sounds from above. I was sure the end of the world had come. The attack was followed by more cries, more bleeding, more wounded, more dead. Some military vehicles, also hit, burst into flames. To my relief Mutti, who had been crouching motionless next to the kettle, looked up at us and smiled weakly.

All of us began to cry at the sight of such incredible misery. The pungent smell of scorched people and horses and of gasoline and burning rubber hung over us. No one could help the victims. Dead people, some with their eyes and mouths still open, lay crumpled in the snow or sprawled across demolished vehicles.

In their terror, our mares tried to bolt. As our wagon skidded behind the horses, Opa used all of his strength to regain control. Other refugees were less fortunate. Some lost all of their possessions on the icy road. Some wagons broke apart.

"The Lord is my shepherd...," I heard Opa praying softly.

23

How much longer would we live? How many more minutes did we have left?

Mutti cooled off the pot by dipping it several times into the snow at the side of the road. She put on the lid and carried the soup to our wagon. "Let's get out of here," she pleaded, "before they come back."

Opa, checking over our gear, nodded grimly. "May God forgive us for leaving the dead and wounded behind."

We rejoined the endless caravan of refugees. All bundled up, I was sitting in the front of our wagon. Military vehicles continued to pass us on the left, transporting soldiers with grime-caked faces and shredded uniforms. Many wore blood-soaked bandages. Some had a crazed look in their eyes; others just looked frightened and miserable. Most awful of all, some of the wounded soldiers didn't look much older than Ilse, who was nearly twelve.

I hopped down to walk with Opa. The closer I was to him, the safer I felt. All of a sudden, the pace of the wagons up ahead slackened, then ground to a halt. Climbing onto our wagon, we could see far enough ahead to find out what was going on. At a roadblock up ahead, a tank was clearing away the debris.

We finally reached the spot where the tank had been. Demolished wagons and Army trucks, dead people and horses, suitcases and rucksacks, destroyed rifles and burning tires lay, still smoldering, in a jumbled heap on the slope leading down from the road. I heard footsteps and looked over my shoulder, fully expecting to see the Devil with his clubbed foot close behind, but it was only Mutti, who had joined us to view the grim scene.

"Wouldn't we be better off taking the next country road?" she asked Opa. "The planes are targeting the military, not us."

"I think the main road's best for now," Opa replied. He patted one of the mares on her haunches. "The pavement's icy, but the horses would have to struggle even harder in deep snow. They barely have any strength left as it is."

* * *

That night was horribly cold. We huddled together in the back of the wagon, trying without success to ignore the wails of grief from nearby wagons. At dawn, we set out again. I joined Opa on the front seat. Sitting up there, I was much colder than I had been in the back of the wagon, but at least the air was fresh and I could see what was going on. As the military vehicles moving along to our left picked up speed, a motorcycle approached us from the opposite direction and screeched to a halt one wagon further ahead.

"Trouble," Opa whispered.

A giant of a young SS officer, in an immaculate uniform complete with cuffed leather gloves, jumped off the back of the motorcycle. Raising his right hand, he commanded the driver of the wagon ahead of ours to go down the slope to the right of the road. At the bottom of the slope was a small meadow and, beyond the meadow, only forest. As ordered, the driver carefully maneuvered his wagon off the road.

Opa climbed down from our wagon and approached the SS officer. Bowing slightly, Opa quietly spoke his mind.

"Officer, how can you do this to us? You know we can't get ahead there. You're sending us to our death."

The SS officer's face flushed. His gray eyes narrowed into angry slits. He rushed forward, shoved his pistol into Opa's chest and snarled, "This is a strategic retreat! Civilian swine like you have no business being on a paved road. Get off, or I'll shoot you!"

I stared at the menacing face of the SS officer. For the first time in my life, I hated someone so much I wished with all my heart that he would die. How could this monster say such a thing to Opa?

It seemed forever before Opa moved. He climbed slowly back onto our wagon. Shaking his head in disgust, he turned our horses off the road. The incline was so steep, I was sure we would flip over and be

25

crushed. When we reached the bottom and were still all in one piece, I thanked God for having saved us once again.

Followed by the other refugee wagons, we continued on the snow-covered meadow between the road and the forest. Sometimes a grove of trees blocked our way and we had to struggle to get close to the road again. High snow drifts severely handicapped the horses. They strained forward, the muscles bulging in their necks. As we inched along, retreating army vehicles of all kinds rushed by on the pavement up above us. In all of the confusion, the wagon driven by the Reimanns' sharecroppers had become separated from the other two wagons in our group. We never saw them again.

* * *

We eventually brought our wagons back up onto the pavement. Still, as a precaution, whenever a convoy towed by a half-track was about to pass us on a curve, Opa and the other drivers drove onto the shoulder of the road if it were at all possible.

One morning, in light snow, we were passed by a half-track pulling a long line of broken down vehicles loaded with wounded soldiers. The road ahead made a wide curve. As the half-track vehicle disappeared to the left, the towed vehicles came dangerously close to the edge of the road. Those soldiers who could react quickly enough jumped out to the right side onto the pavement. Just at that moment the trucks and trailers at the end of the convoy slid off the icy pavement and tumbled down the slope. Like a heavy chain whipped to the left by a giant, nearly all of the towed vehicles dropped off the edge. I covered my ears to shut out the screams of the men who were trapped in the vehicles and stared out at the incredible line of overturned trucks. Their wheels, some still spinning, pointed to the iron gray sky. Wherever I looked, soldiers lay bleeding. Many were begging for help; others were silent forever, but the refugee wagons on the right side of the road just kept rolling.

"War is a terrible thing," Opa said, gently putting his arm around my shoulders. "I knew that long ago. The Kaiser sent me to trenches in France in the last war, and that was more than enough for me."

"I was thinking about Vati, and Uncle Ernst, and Uncle Herbert," I said, my voice husky. "One of them could be lying down there."

"Try not to worry," Opa said, "and always pray whenever you feel the need. With God's mercy, we'll all get through this in one piece."

* * *

As we approached the coast, the road became more crowded.

"How can they call this a strategic retreat?" Opa asked Mutti. "Any fool can see this is the end."

"We should be pretty far ahead of the Russians by now. Don't you think so, Opa?" I asked.

Opa shook his head. "In all this time, we've hardly traveled any distance at all," he explained. "The Russian front is encircling us like a net. Each day the net is tightening around us."

"Like my butterfly net in Langendorf?"

"No, not like that. More like the noose we used to hoist up the hog."

I visualized that poor animal, struggling on the rope just before Opa slit its throat. "I hope we don't end up like that," I said with a shiver.

* * *

As we neared the town of Heiligenbeil, we found ourselves in the middle of a war zone. Our wagon caravan was strafed by low flying Russian military planes three more times. Each time the planes came over, I began to sob uncontrollably. Even holding on to Mutti did not help to calm me down. Sometimes when I cowered in the back of our wagon during an air raid, I silently asked God to spare our lives one more time, but sometimes I felt such terror, I wished we would be killed by the machine gun fire and bombs from the Russian planes. At least then, we would all be safe in heaven.

When the shooting stopped I joined Opa. He had lit a fire between two bricks so that he could heat up a big pot of "coffee" made from roasted barley. I held my hands over the fire and let the warmth crawl up my arms. Slurping down the hot coffee made me feel better. It tasted good even without milk.

As Opa bridled the horses and prepared to set out on foot, I began to worry. "Don't you get tired, walking all day long?" I asked.

"It's funny you ask," Opa replied. "When I worked on our farm, I could keep going from sunrise to sunset. Not bad considering I'm going to have my 67th birthday in May. I always considered myself a tough old bird. But ever since we left home, I've felt tired nearly all of the time. It's not from the walking, though. It's from the lack of sleep."

When we moved on a short time later, I draped myself in a blanket from head to foot. Under it I wore all the sweaters I owned, a coat, and two woolen caps, yet I still felt cold. I was so bundled up I could barely walk.

Opa put his hand on my shoulder. "A skinny tadpole like you is better off inside under the covers."

"All the same, Opa, I prefer to walk with you."

We were following a paved road, leading through a small village. Far ahead, in the early morning fog, I saw what looked like stiff scarecrows hanging from two tall trees. A glance at Opa's face told me something was wrong.

Opa pulled on the reins and the horses stopped.

"Gretel, can you come out here for a moment?" he called. Mutti poked out her head, her breath turning into little clouds in front of her face.

"Is something the matter?"

"Those may be the bodies of German soldiers. Do you think we've crossed into a Russian area?"

28

Mutti climbed down. She, Opa, and I cautiously approached the corpses dangling from the trees, hands tied behind their backs, their features frozen in death. Hastily scribbled posters were pinned to their chests.

"What do they say?" I asked Mutti.

"This one says, 'I'm a German deserter.' That one over there says, 'I was too much of a coward to fight.' Do you want to hear the rest?"

I shook my head.

"The poor soldiers," Opa said. We stood in silence for a moment, shocked by the grisly scene. Finally Mutti spoke.

"It looks like we're still in a German-controlled area," she said quietly.

As we walked slowly back to the wagon, I tugged Opa's hand. "Opa, who hung them up like that?"

"Probably one of their commanding officers. Someone who still believes in the final victory," Opa said.

I tried to digest this stunning news. "Opa," I finally asked, "if a German could do that to our own soldiers, what would the Russians do to us if we're caught?"

"No need to worry," he said, putting a strong arm around me. "It's German soldiers they're after, not us. They have no bones to pick with women and children and old men like me."

* * *

Nearly three weeks after leaving Langendorf, we reached Heiligenbeil. We had traveled only one hundred kilometers. Oma decided we should stay in Heiligenbeil for two nights to rest before attempting to cross to the other side of Frisches Haff Bay where we could board the ferry to Pillau.

Opa drove through town twice before finding quarters for us in a farm house. The owners of the farm had left and other refugees had already been there for a day. When we had settled in, Aunt Liesbeth and

29

Mutti cooked noodle soup with sausage pieces floating in it. I slurped down three bowls. Mutti looked worried.

"I know you're hungry, but if you don't stop, you might burst."

"Don't you worry about me," I assured her, helping myself to more.

"Look what I got!" Opa said, setting down a pail half full of fresh milk.

"Where'd that come from?" Aunt Liesbeth asked.

"I found some refugees milking cows in the cow stable. So another man and I joined them. We just helped ourselves," he replied.

Mutti and Aunt Liesbeth spent many hours in the kitchen baking bread. It smelled good and tasted even better after all of the cold stale bread we had been eating.

Later in the afternoon, a truck pulled up carrying five military policemen. Everyone gathered around the sergeant in charge who was wrapped in a warm woolen coat.

"Please listen carefully. I don't have time to tell you twice," he began gruffly. As he spoke, he ticked off each point on his fingers. "As you probably already know, the Frisches Haff Bay separates the East Prussian mainland from the Baltic Sea. Once you go out onto the ice, it's about 12 kilometers to the narrow spit of land called Frische Nehrung. If you get there safely, be sure to turn right when you get to the road or else you'll end up in Danzig instead of at the ferry slip to Pillau. I've saved the most important advice for last. If you cross the frozen Haff at night, you'll be less likely to be targeted by Russian planes. Maintain a distance of at least forty to fifty meters between wagons to avoid breaking through the ice."

"How much weight can the ice carry?" an old farmer standing near me asked.

"That's hard to say. We can't keep track of everyone who's fallen through and drowned. For your own safety, try to lighten your loads as much as possible."

"Thanks for the advice, sergeant," said Opa. "We'll do our best."

Just then we heard a commotion near the barn. The other soldiers approached us, guns drawn. Three prisoners of war, their hands held above their heads, marched in front of them. Aunt Liesbeth's Russian prisoner was among them.

She rushed after the sergeant. "Please, sir, I have five children, my old father-in-law and a young servant with me in my wagon. Our Russian driver is indispensable to us. I wouldn't know what to do without him."

The sergeant's eyes turned the color of cold steel. "Sorry, ma'am. We have to take all of them into custody. I have my orders."

I watched in horror as they dragged the man away.

* * *

"No more ships are leaving Pillau," Mutti reported early the next morning.

"I heard the same thing," Oma added. "That's all everyone's talking about in the kitchen."

"Apparently some people have decided to stay in Heiligenbeil, rather than risk crossing the Haff," Aunt Liesbeth said.

"But there really isn't much choice, is there?" Mutti asked. "The coast is in front of us and all of the traffic is moving in this direction. We're trapped if we stay here."

"We've come this far, the least we can do is give it a try," Opa resolved. "I'm not ready to give up yet."

* * *

After Russian planes bombed the military airport in Heiligenbeil during the afternoon, Opa decided we should leave right away. It took us quite a while to cover the short distance to the Haff. I huddled next to Opa in the front of the wagon to get a better view. Having listened to Opa and Mutti, I expected a narrow strip of ice, something like a frozen river, so my first glimpse of the bay took my breath away. It looked cold, endless, frightening, and as vast as the sea.

It was twilight and should have been nearly dark, but the ice served as a mirror. Glistening stars appeared and the moon hung like a yellow giant lamp in the sky. In the far distance, the faint glimmer of lights jutted out on a spit of land. Abandoned luggage cluttered the shoreline. Lacquered with transparent ice and layers of frozen snow, barrels, wooden boxes, pails, shovels, saws, small pieces of furniture, slabs of spoiled pork and beef, pots, infants' bathtubs, and clothing lay strewn about.

Opa and Mutti unloaded Oma's Singer sewing machine, a box full of cooking pots and frying pans, several runners and the two large oriental rugs, one from our living room and the other from our dining room.

"We may as well dump these, too," Opa said, tossing three heavy sacks of rock-solid potatoes out of the wagon. "Once they're frozen, they're no good anyhow."

After weeks of being crowded together with other refugees, it was eerie to be nearly alone. Only two other refugee wagons were visible ahead of us. Our horses shied when their hooves touched the ice. I was afraid they would bolt, but Opa quickly calmed them.

"Liesbeth, are you all right back there?" Opa called over his shoulder.

A moment later Aunt Liesbeth's wagon pulled alongside. Ilse was driving the horses.

"Aren't you the brave one!" Opa exclaimed. "Hold tight on the reins. They have to know who's boss!"

"I'm glad they switched places," Mutti said with obvious relief as our wagon pulled to what we hoped was a safe distance ahead. "Liesbeth has always had such poor night vision."

"That granddaughter of mine sure knows horses," Opa added proudly. "She handles them like a Cossack!"

* * *

The moonlight shone on a row of tall thin poles which poked out of the ice at regular intervals. Like guideposts, they led us slowly forward. Sometimes the ice creaked, threatening to give way. Sometimes a layer of water floated on the surface, coloring it black. Partly submerged wagons and the carcasses of horses jutted out, the broken crust of the ice refrozen around them. A thin layer of snow lay on top. The scene was unearthly.

Far to our right, we heard occasional faint hissing sounds. The glow of flares illuminating the sky spooked our horses. Each time, Opa and Ilse struggled to regain control.

"Now what?" Oma grumbled. "First they warn us to travel under cover of darkness and then they turn night into day."

"Perhaps it's the Russians," Mutti whispered.

After that, no one said a word as we moved on; we listened instead for the drone of approaching Russian airplanes. The wagon wheels ground against the ice. The horses snorted as their hooves rhythmically tapped the hard surface. Once in a while one of the animals slipped and my heart skipped a beat. I had seen what happened to horses with broken legs. It was agonizing to watch their slow progress; how much worse it would be if we were forced to abandon our wagons and travel on foot.

As my eyes scanned the starry sky for the moving lights of Russian fighter planes, a hand tapped me on the shoulder from inside the wagon. Oma slipped me five cubes of gingerbread. I stashed four pieces into my coat pocket and popped the fifth one into my mouth. The gingerbread was frozen solid and I sucked on it until it was soft enough to chew.

Opa hopped down to walk alongside the wagon on the ice. I decided to join him. Glancing back at the Reimanns' wagon, I saw a bulky silhouette. Under multiple layers of warm clothing, Ilse was guiding the horses. I waved at her, but she did not see me. She was only a few years older than I was. I admired her tremendously.

Hours passed. Suddenly the silence was broken. Somewhere far off to our right we heard the sharp cracking of the ice followed by shrill human screams and the piercing sounds of terrified horses.

Mutti and Oma peered out of the wagon.

"What's going on?"

I could hear the fear in Mutti's voice.

"Calm down, everyone. We're not in any danger," Opa said. "Sound travels very far on the ice. When my brothers and I used to go skating, we could practically talk from one side of Lake Spirding to the other." Opa always found the right words in a crisis.

"It's a good thing we have these posts to follow," Mutti said. "Those poor souls must have tried to find their own path."

In what appeared to be a burst of caution by the drivers, the two wagons in front of us slowed down considerably. We also slackened our pace. Renewed screams from off to our right made everyone anxious. It seemed forever until the cries subsided. All of us were jittery. In our wagon, only little Hubert slept. Suddenly the two wagons in front of us veered off to the left, away from the guiding poles. We soon saw why. Up ahead the ice had cracked. Abandoned wagons and dead horses lay on the ice in dark pools of brackish water. Others drifted on large loose-floating frozen chunks.

Dear God, I whispered under my breath. We've come so far. Please don't abandon us now. Amen.

Driving through ankle-deep water, I felt time standing still as we went around that huge open area. It might have taken us half an hour or several hours; there was no way to tell. When we finally returned to the markers, everyone felt relieved.

It was nearly dawn when the weather turned a bit foggy. We got close enough to see the trees. "It won't be long now," Opa assured me. All our hopes were directed toward reaching that spit of land safely.

At sunrise, our exhausted horses used their last bit of strength to pull the wagons up the slope onto the shore. I had looked forward to seeing the Baltic Sea again. When I was three or four years old, Mutti and I had vacationed at the coast in Rauschen in the summertime. I had run in and out of the waves, collecting wet sand in my pail, building sand castles, then retreating to the huge wicker beach chairs when the sun had gotten too strong. But instead of the Baltic Sea, I saw nothing but trees, bushes, and abandoned refugee wagons in the fog.

"Where's the water?" I asked Opa.

"It's somewhere there," he replied, pointing away from the icy Bay we had just crossed. "Once we move on, you'll probably catch a glimpse of it off to the left."

Together with the occupants of the other two wagons, we stopped for breakfast in a little forest. Opa and Aunt Liesbeth had just walked over to chat with one of the other two drivers when an Army vehicle screeched to a halt alongside our wagon. A soldier rolled down the window.

"That's what I call dumb luck!" he called out to us. "We've been watching you for a while, hoping you'd make it."

"Thanks for your interest," one of the other drivers said. "We had our doubts back there for a while ourselves."

"You've missed my point. The place where you crossed has been off limits for days."

Opa spoke up. "Is that why there weren't any other wagons? Come to think of it, it was a bit odd."

"The route you took was heavily traveled until the Russians bombed it a while back. We put up the wooden poles as a warning. The ice is still much too thin."

"Imagine that," Aunt Liesbeth said. "And yet we still got across."

The young soldier lit a cigarette before continuing. "You were doubly lucky. Last night the ice broke on the official route. Nearly a dozen wagons fell through. Some of our men are searching for survivors, but I doubt they'll find any."

No one spoke for a moment. I was convinced Opa was saying a prayer. He knew it wasn't just luck which had brought us to safety.

"How do we get to the ferry slip from here?" an old woman finally asked.

"I gather you're heading towards Pillau and not in the direction of Danzig?" the soldier replied.

"Yes, to Pillau."

"Just keep bearing to the right, another twelve kilometers or so, and you'll come to Neutief. You can't miss it. The ferry will take you from there to Pillau."

We set out again as soon as the soldiers had driven away.

"It must be a pretty big ferry, to hold the wagons and the horses," I commented to Opa.

"I imagine so," he replied with a warm smile.

After quite a while Opa pointed to the left, "Over there, if you look through the trees. That should be the Baltic Sea."

I had never seen the sea in winter. In the bitter cold morning air, the immense expanse of water looked like a majestic gray carpet, as though it were really only dense fog and not water at all. I dozed off. Opa shook me awake and suggested that I lie down in the back of the wagon.

"Yes, Opa." I crawled back and fell asleep right away, dreaming we were back in Langendorf and the war was over. When I woke up, the ferry had already docked in Pillau and our wagons were rolling over a ferry slip onto the pier.

* * *

Pillau looked like a flattened anthill with a light tower on the edge. Civilians, soldiers and sailors scurried in all directions. There was no apparent system, no order, everyone going this way and that.

To our surprise, a soldier from the Military Police shouted up at Opa.

"Hey you! I suppose you're looking for quarters?"

Opa yelled back, "Yes sir, we are."

"It's pretty bad. The Teachers' College, schools, everything's filled up, but there are some barracks at the edge of town," the soldier yelled, pointing straight ahead.

I fell asleep again and when I woke up, our wagon had stopped. In a state of exhaustion, I was barely aware of the makeshift refugee camp that sat back from a road pockmarked with gaping bomb craters.

Together with the others, I stumbled behind Opa and Mutti into a large room. Since there weren't enough straw mattresses to go around, I lay down directly on the floor in a small patch of sunlight and slept right through to the following morning.

A few ships were still leaving Pillau, some of them headed to Kiel and to Lübeck, German ports near Denmark. Mutti, Aunt Liesbeth, and Opa went to the harbor to try to get steamer tickets. Aunt Liesbeth's father-in-law leaned like a heap of misery against the wall. Oma and Aunt Liesbeth's maid, Emma, took charge of the children.

All of the refugee children were cranky and restless. Many were sick. Some whimpered; others threw tantrums. Diapers were scarce; food and water were in short supply. Suddenly the room seemed to spin around. I felt Oma's hand on my forehead.

"You have a fever, young man," she said. I heard her voice as though from far away, and then I drifted back to sleep.

I woke up when Mutti, Opa, and Aunt Liesbeth returned. It was already dark.

"What did you find out?" Oma asked impatiently. "Did you get the tickets?"

"We stood on line all day and have nothing to show for it," Opa replied, "but we did pick up some information."

"Out with it!" Oma snapped.

"Really, Mother," Mutti said. "We're just as frustrated as you are. It seems they're still running ships, but less frequently. Two ships, the Wilhelm Gustloff and the General Steuben, were torpedoed by the Russians. The Steuben just two weeks ago. Thousands of refugees were lost."

"We've been debating for hours what we should do," added Opa. "From what I've heard, our troops are pushing back the Russians. Maybe we'd be better off just to stay here until we can go home to Langendorf."

"Nonsense!" Oma said. "We've seen with our own eyes that our army is doing no such thing. You'll try again tomorrow for tickets."

After two days on line, Mutti and Aunt Liesbeth finally acquired our steamer tickets, but by then even Oma was no longer inclined to use them. The grim fate often awaiting the crowded steamers was endlessly discussed. The odds of making the two or three day crossing safely looked increasingly slim.

"It mightn't be so bad, staying here," Opa said. "Remember 1914? We'd been warned for years about atrocities but the Russian soldiers who came to my father's farm only took a cow, two hogs, and some grain. No one was hurt and that was the end of it."

"It might be different this time," Mutti pointed out.

"Well, anything's better than drowning at sea," Oma said with a shudder.

"The big question is, where should we go? I've heard during the last few days a lot of people are heading further north, to wait out the war," Mutti said.

"Then that's the answer," Aunt Liesbeth chimed in. "Remember our neighbors in Langendorf? The Brenners? They have relatives in Bieskobnicken. It's less than thirty kilometers north of here. Let's try to stay with them."

"Of course I know the Brenners," Oma said, "but what makes you think their family will still be there?"

38

"At least it's worth a try," Opa decided. "What have we got to lose?"

CHAPTER 4

On March 1, 1945, long before daylight, we boarded our wagons and headed north, together with half a dozen other refugee wagons. Gripped with fever, I drifted in and out of sleep, catching only snatches of conversation along the way.

"It looks like we weren't the only ones who decided against going by boat," I heard Opa say.

"Yes, but did you notice the military vehicles? They're all heading the other way," Mutti replied.

I fell back to sleep, dreaming of my cozy bed in Langendorf. When I awoke, our wagon had stopped. I crawled up to the front although I felt cold and shivery. Mutti was holding the reins.

"How much farther?" I asked, trying to rub the sleep out of my eyes.

"Hello, sleepy-head," Mutti said, with a laugh. "We've been traveling all day. It's nearly suppertime. We're already there!"

Opa's eyes were closed, his hands clasped in prayer. Secure in the belief that Opa had worked things out with God, I looked forward to the comfort of a real bed on the Brenner's farm.

* * *

Relying on directions from passers-by, Mutti stopped our wagon at the third farm along the road. A young girl watched us from the driveway.

"Is this the Brenner farm?" Opa called out to her.

The girl shrugged her shoulders.

"The Brenners who have family in Langendorf," Opa persisted. "Is this their farm?"

"I guess," the girl mumbled.

As the girl sprinted towards a large two-story house with double chimneys, we climbed out of our wagons. In our excitement, we had not heard Mr. Brenner come up behind us. Mr. Brenner had thick white hair. Even his eyebrows were bushy white. He gaped at the thirteen of us as though we were a plague of locusts.

"Gottfried Recklies," Opa said with a little bow. "We're neighbors of your brother in Langendorf. I believe we met there some time ago."

Mr. Brenner's face brightened. "Of course! Now I know who you are. We met in Schippenbeil at my nephew's confirmation, and again at my niece's wedding. My brother told me you're a pillar of that congregation, but that was a long time ago, in peacetime."

"It's hard to believe how much things have changed. Can you imagine? Pillau is only about a hundred kilometers from Schippenbeil, and we needed four weeks to get there."

"Everyone's been telling me the same story. That's why we decided to stay put and wait things out."

"I've been wondering whether we shouldn't have stayed home, too," Opa said.

"How long did it take you from Pillau to here?"

"We left in the wee hours of the morning and did the whole trip today, so I really can't complain."

"You can say that again," Mr. Brenner said.

41

"I know we're a large group," Opa said, glancing over his shoulder at his assembled family, "but is there any chance you could put us up here until things blow over a bit?"

"I'm sorry, Mr. Recklies. I just wish you'd come sooner. Our house is already full of refugee families. The army keeps sending them up here from Pillau. We can squeeze eight or nine of you at most into the two small rooms in our attic."

"In that case, the Reimanns should stay here," Opa said. "That'll leave just five of us to find accommodations somewhere nearby."

"I'd suggest the Wittkes across the road," Mr. Brenner said, as the Reimanns began to unload their wagon. "Come, I'll walk over with you to make the introductions."

"We're much obliged to you," Opa said.

* * *

Mr. Wittke and his wife must have seen us coming. They greeted us warmly at their farmhouse door.

"Mr. Recklies and his family are neighbors of my brother's," Mr. Brenner said, by way of introduction.

"Welcome to Bieskobnicken," Mr. Wittke said, shaking Opa's hand.

"With the latest arrivals, we've got guests practically hanging from the rafters at our place," Mr. Brenner added. "Any chance you could take on five more?"

"If you think you could squeeze into a tiny upstairs guest room. That's all we have left."

"No need to apologize," Mutti hastened to say. "That will do just fine."

Mr. Wittke turned to Opa. "I'd suggest you unload only what you really need. Otherwise you won't have room to turn around. Your things will be safe on your wagon in the barn, and I can put up your horses in the stable."

"You're too kind, sir. We haven't seen much of the Christian spirit in the past four and half weeks. It does a person good!"

Mr. Brenner easily picked up two of our heaviest suitcases and carried them into the house. Opa and Mutti lugged in two more pieces each; Oma and I carried our comforters; Hubert clutched Mutti's sleeve and did his best to keep up.

Mr. Wittke called after us. "After your wagon is in the barn, take care of your family first. I'll bed down your horses."

* * *

Our room was sparsely furnished, with only a large wardrobe and two beds, but it was cozy. Mrs. Wittke came in a few minutes later, staggering under an armful of sheets, four fluffy pillows and two blankets. The dampness which had clung to our possessions during the long weeks on the road quickly evaporated in the warmth of the room.

As we got settled, the delicious aroma of home fries mixed with onions and bacon wafted up from the kitchen. After the discomfort of sleeping in our cold wagon, followed by the terror of crossing the frozen Haff, I thought our tiny quarters overlooking the farmyard were heavenly.

"We can unpack later," Mutti said with a grin. "It would be rude not to join everyone for supper!"

Five other refugees were already sitting around the kitchen table with Mr. and Mrs. Wittke when we came down. The table was only large enough to seat eight people.

"We're just finishing up," a young mother with three small children said. "Please take our places."

"We don't want to disturb you," Oma said. "We can come back later."

"Don't worry," Mrs. Wittke chirped. "We've been eating in shifts around here for weeks."

43

The middle of the table was crowded with platters heaped with food, and white crockery pitchers filled with creamy milk. I helped myself to three glasses, hardly taking a breath between each gulp.

"If this were the finest restaurant in Königsberg, the food couldn't look any better!" Mutti exclaimed. "Are you sure you can spare it?"

"I've stopped worrying about it," Mrs. Wittke replied. "I'm thinking of posting a sign in my kitchen: 'Eat, drink and be merry for tomorrow...'" Mr. Wittke cut her off in mid sentence.

"There are children here," he reminded her.

"Well, all the same," concluded his wife, "there doesn't seem much point in hoarding it, does there?"

"At least let us help in some way," Oma said.

"Give yourselves a day or two to get settled," Mrs. Wittke replied. "Then you and your daughter are welcome to join us in the kitchen. Feel free to help yourselves to anything you need from the pantry and the smokehouse."

"What's the latest from the front?" Opa asked. "Are we holding the line?"

"The Russians already paid us a visit at the beginning of February," Mr. Wittke said bitterly.

"Here? In Bieskobnicken?"

"They were right here on the farm, but our troops beat them back. At this very moment we're being protected by twenty-five soldiers, a mobile antiaircraft gun, three ambulances, and a field kitchen. They're parked on our meadow, out back of the barn."

That was good enough for me. Feeling safe and secure, I went upstairs to bed right after supper. Before lying down on my comforter, I knelt to say my prayers. Dear God, thank you for bringing us safely to this wonderful place. Amen.

* * *

Hubert and I were suffering from terrible colds and bad coughs when we arrived in Bieskobnicken. Except for meals, he and I snuggled under our comforters and slept for the better part of a week. Free of worries and strengthened by rich, warm food, we gradually recovered.

From the window of our room, I could see a frozen pond surrounded by willow trees just beyond the farmyard. An older boy skated there every afternoon. One day I ventured outside to get a closer look.

"Are you staying here too?" I asked the boy as he effortlessly glided over to the edge of the pond on shiny skates clipped to the soles of his shoes.

"I live down the road," he answered. "Mr. and Mrs. Wittke don't mind my skating. My name's Martin."

"Mine's Günter," I said, reaching out over the ice to shake his hand. "Sure wish I could do that."

"Get yourself a pair of skates and come join me."

"That's easier said than done," I sighed.

Opa, who had been helping Mr. Wittke in the farmyard, watched us from a distance. A few minutes later he came up alongside me.

"No use moping about," he said cheerfully. "Come, let me surprise you."

We walked together to a small tool shed. Opa sawed a wooden board into two pieces, each about a foot long. He placed two thick sections of heavy wire on the ground and laid one of the boards on top. Pulling the wire around to the top edge of the board, he secured the ends with metal clamps. He repeated the process with the other board. Across the top of each board he nailed a wide leather thong which he carefully measured to fit my foot.

"There you go!" he said. "Your very own ice skates."

I slid my foot under the leather strap as though it were a bedroom slipper. "I'll lose them," I said to Opa.

"Not if you know how to use them," Opa assured me. "My friends and I all had skates like that when we were your age. There's just one more thing I need to do and you'll be in business."

Opa cut a broom stick to about my height. He hammered a nail into the sawn off end. Using a pair of pliers, he pinched the head off the nail.

Beaming at me, he said, "That's it. You're all set. Let's go over to the pond and give them a test run."

Martin skated over to the edge of the pond and eyed me suspiciously as I slipped my feet under the leather straps.

"What on earth?" he snickered. "You'll never get anywhere with those clodhoppers."

"Watch and see," Opa said, but Martin continued to smirk.

Opa turned back to me with a reassuring wink. "Here's all you need to do," he instructed. "Bend your knees and spread your feet a little. Now press the pointy end of the stick into the ice and give yourself a push."

I shoved off and slowly glided forward.

"Push and lift; push and lift," Opa called out from the edge of the pond. As I got the hang of it, I began to gain speed.

"Just one more thing," Opa warned. "Don't try to take any sharp turns, or you'll fall down."

After a while, Martin was forced to swallow his pride.

"Mind if I give 'em a try?" he asked. We took turns after that, practicing skate-poling for the rest of the afternoon. Martin's shiny metal skates lay unused at the side of the pond.

* * *

As the days passed, the memory of soldiers forcing us off the road during our escape remained fresh in my mind, and I had not forgotten the SS officer who threatened to shoot Opa. At first, I decided to keep a safe distance from the military camp, but curiosity got the better of me. I wanted a glimpse of the antiaircraft gun, which Mr. Wittke always referred to as FLAK.

I cautiously extended my walks in the direction of the ambulance trucks. One day around lunchtime, I approached close enough to smell the goulash soup cooking in the field kitchen. About fifteen soldiers were lounging around, waiting for lunch. Some wore Luftwaffe uniforms, others had on the uniforms of the infantry. Most men from each group wore white arm bands with a red cross.

A tall man with a winning smile was shouting orders. He wore the epaulets of a Master Sergeant, just like Uncle Ernst; an Iron Cross and an array of other medals decorated the jacket of his uniform. Laugh lines spread like spider webs alongside hazel eyes. Tufts of light brown hair protruded from under his garrison cap.

To my astonishment, he called over to me.

"Hey, young man! Are you hungry?"

"Yes, please!" I started to run toward him when I realized I did not have a container. "I'll be back in a minute," I shouted. Racing to the house, I grabbed my military canteen and went to look for Opa.

"Opa, come quick!" I said, practically dragging him back with me. "There's goulash soup."

The soldier looked at my canteen with admiration. "That's a fine piece of equipment you have there," he said solemnly. "You wouldn't be a military man by any chance?"

"No, sir," I stammered, feeling the color rise in my cheeks. "It was a gift from a soldier in Preussisch Eylau."

"I'm grateful for your kindness to my grandson," Opa said. He extended his hand to the soldier. "Gottfried Recklies."

"Sergeant Hansen at your service," the man replied, as one of the other soldiers ladled soup right up to the brim of my canteen. "This motley bunch of stragglers is under my command. We're supposed to hold the line in case the Russians decide to pay Bieskobnicken another visit."

47

"So I heard from Mr. Wittke," replied Opa. "It's hard to believe they were here. This place is so peaceful."

"You can't have been to the pigsty yet or the barn," Sergeant Hansen said with disgust. "Just take a look around over there and you'll see what kind of vandals we're up against."

Sergeant Hansen's remarks had whetted my curiosity. What could the pigsty tell me about the behavior of the Russians? I decided to find out for myself.

Three soldiers knelt down in the hog pen, thick cloths wrapped around their knees. They gently poked matted piles of straw and dung with short sticks. Every few minutes, the sticks clinked softly against glass and a tiny bottle was extracted from the straw. Sergeant Hansen came up behind me.

"Hello again," he greeted me cordially.

"What're they looking for?" I asked, pointing to the soldiers.

"Ampoules of medicine." My mouth fell open with astonishment.

"You store them in a pig pen?" I gasped.

"Not us, the Russians. When they paid Mr. Wittke a visit, they tossed our supplies all around. Some of the ampoules broke on impact, but many more landed in the straw and managed to slip down inside to safety."

"I nearly forgot to thank you again for the soup. It tasted even better than the pea soup in Preussisch Eylau."

"Don't mention it," Sergeant Hansen chuckled. "There's plenty more where that came from."

"Do you suppose," I asked somewhat timidly, "I might help search for ampoules?"

"Have you any experience working for the war effort?" he replied, trying not to smile.

"Well, we collected all sorts of things for the final victory when I was in first grade," I said proudly. I thought of the swastika on Fräulein Durbach's gym shirt and wondered where she was now. "Our teacher told us the army needed the weeds to make medicine for our soldiers. Maybe these very medicines!"

"In that case, let's see what you can do!"

Sergeant Hansen showed me three ampoules.

"Here are some samples."

One contained clear liquid; in the others, the liquid was the pale yellow color of straw or the color of apple juice. The ampoules ranged in size from the length of my pinky to the length of my index finger.

"So that's what I'm supposed to look for?"

"There are probably twenty or thirty different kinds. We desperately need whatever is unbroken."

"I understand."

"The soldiers are kneeling down, but I don't want you to do that. There's too much broken glass on the floor." He thought for a moment. "How old did you say you were?"

"I don't think I told you. I'm seven, why?"

"At your age, you should be able to squat down while you work."

"That's easy. I used to squat for hours when I floated my toy boats in the village pond back home."

A curious odor of medicine mixed with pig dung filled my lungs as I crouched down to work. Following the example of the others, each time I found an unbroken ampoule, I placed it carefully on a huge woolen blanket spread across a wooden table. As the ampoules were retrieved, a short blond soldier washed them, first with water and then with alcohol. He sorted the tiny bottles by color into neat rows.

"Be sure to bring your canteen when you come tomorrow," Sergeant Hansen told me when I was ready to leave. "A hardworking soldier like you deserves a military lunch."

I spent three days working alongside the soldiers in the pigsty and, afterwards, a few more days in the barn, poking through the muck for vials of medicine.

"Well done," the blond soldier complimented me each time I brought him another bottle. "You're saving the lives of many German soldiers."

"Thank you, sir," I replied. Strange, I thought, how much more inspiring those words had been when Fräulein Durbach had spoken them.

* * *

Lunch was the highlight of the day. Joining the soldiers at the field kitchen, we sat down on tree trunks, ammunition boxes, and crates. I imagined myself in a jungle clearing, on an expedition with Uncle Schulz. Life in Langendorf had never been so exciting.

Once Dorchen and Gerda had stopped by to watch us. They stood at the door to the pigsty, crinkling up their noses at the smell.

"The three of you remind me of my own children," Sergeant Hansen confided to us. "I left two boys and a girl back home in Hamburg."

"Hamburg is pretty far from the Russian front, isn't it?" Dorchen asked. "That must be a comfort to you."

"Far from the Russians, yes." There was a tightness in his voice I hadn't heard before. "Hamburg's been under heavy air attack. My wife and children were evacuated to the countryside quite a while ago. I haven't heard a word from them for months."

"You'll find them after the final victory," I commented, watching to see what his reaction would be. To my surprise, tears welled up in Sergeant Hansen's eyes.

"Time for you to get back to work," he said to me softly. Without another word, he turned and walked away.

* * *

During the weeks since our arrival in Bieskobnicken, the weather turned milder. Spring was approaching and the war scarcely intruded on our lives. Occasionally a few small Russian planes, mostly two-seaters, circled like hawks high overhead. Since they did not bother us, the soldiers at the FLAK station observed them, but did not shoot.

The snow started to melt, and the ice on the pond thinned out. When I threw down small stones, some of them broke through and plopped into the water beneath. My ice skates lay unused in the hallway outside of our room.

After breakfast one morning, I crouched on a big boulder alongside the pond. Water flowed in strange patterns just below the surface. Using a sharp stick, I tried to poke holes in the ice. Mutti caught a glimpse of me from the window and hurried outside.

"Günter, get away from there this instant!" she yelled from the doorway. "The ice is much too thin."

"I'll be done in a moment. I just want to try something."

Just as soon as Mutti turned her back, I rammed my stick into the ice. Greenish water gushed out with a gurgling sound. Bending down to feel the coldness of the water, I lost my balance and tumbled in, head first.

Numbed by the icy water, I desperately tried to figure out which way was up. As I struggled and kicked I only became more confused. The water was so deep I could not touch the bottom with my feet. Just as I was certain I would drown, someone else joined me in the water. Strong arms grabbed me and pulled me out of the pond. When I was safely back on land, I looked up to see Sergeant Hansen, his uniform drenched, wet hair clinging to his forehead.

We raced into the house and up to our room. Mutti and Oma were shocked to see us.

"This young man tried to swim in the pond, but the water was a bit too cold," the Sergeant said through chattering teeth. "I'm sure you'll find a way to warm him up."

"Thank you, Sergeant!" Mutti exclaimed. "I'll take over from here."

As soon as he left the room, Oma began to bark out orders. "Take off those wet clothes! Dry yourself with a towel!"

"Let me deal with this," Mutti said, her eyes blazing with anger. She went to the wardrobe and took out a wooden hanger. Without giving me a chance to change, she put me over her left leg and gave me the thrashing of a lifetime.

"Please stop," I gasped. "I promise not to play any more at the pond." Mutti continued to whack me until she was totally out of breath. In a voice choked with sobs, she finally spoke.

"Will you listen to me from now on? Do you know what would have happened if Sergeant Hansen hadn't pulled you out?"

"Yes, Mutti. I'm sorry."

"Now change out of those wet things. I'll give you a warm bath."

The paddling had made my skin tingle. Instead of feeling cold, I started to sweat. After soaking in a hot tub and eating lunch, Oma made me go to bed for a few hours "to avoid pneumonia" as she put it. She brought me up a steaming cup of chamomile tea with honey.

"Mrs. Wittke thought this would warm you up," she said, as she sat on the edge of the bed and watched me drink.

"I'm all black and blue," I complained, patting my tender bottom.

"You'll survive," Oma said. "That paddling was for your own good."

Oma was right. Unlike Sergeant Hansen, I never caught cold. Mutti's method may have been severe, but it worked.

Everyone teased me over the next few days, the soldiers, the Wittkes, even the other refugees in the house. The young blond soldier from the pigsty called me "polar bear" and, when I came down for meals, Mr. Wittke announced, "Here comes the ice fisherman."

Sergeant Hansen sneezed and coughed for more than a week.

"He needs something more nourishing than soup to build up his strength," Oma explained, as she wrapped up an extra batch of potato pancakes and six thick slabs of fried bacon for me to bring to him.

Some days, Opa walked over with me to the camp. When they had first met, he and the Sergeant had barely spoken to one another, just a polite "Good morning" or "Good afternoon." After my disastrous plunge, the two of them grew closer.

"You know," Opa reflected as we headed back to the farmhouse one day, "I wasn't sure those few soldiers would be much good to us if the Russians ever showed up. If the rest of them are as tough as Sergeant Hansen, we should do just fine."

* * *

A large calendar hung in Mrs. Wittke's kitchen. As she crossed off each day after dinner, she remarked, "Another peaceful day, thank the Lord," and we all answered, "Amen."

Near the end of the first week in April, most of the soldiers packed their medical supplies, gear, rifles and machine guns, and boarded trucks.

I ran to find Opa with the news. "They even have some bazookas with them," I breathlessly explained as we walked back together to find Sergeant Hansen. "Have they been expecting tanks?"

"Is anything in the wind?" Opa asked the Sergeant, as engines revved up in the farmyard.

"Just a redeployment," the Sergeant replied, trying to sound cheerful. "Those men are just going a few kilometers away, to Palmnicken along the Baltic Sea."

"Where the amber comes from? We passed through it on our way here."

"That's the place. That leaves four of us to man the FLAK, and four medics to look after the ambulances. Since we're a little shorthanded, maybe Günter'd like to come by and help us out?"

"I'll be there right after lunch," I replied with enthusiasm.

I gobbled up Oma's potato pancakes and apple sauce and rushed to the FLAK unit. "Reporting for duty," I exclaimed, giving my best salute.

"We're listening for sewing machines," one of the soldiers explained. "Not real sewing machines," he hastened to add.

"I know," I said, eager to show off my military expertise. "That's what you call the Russian reconnaissance planes because of the funny noise their engines make."

Within minutes the faint noise of an approaching sewing machine reached our ears. Soon the biplane was slowly circling above our heads high in the sky.

"He's a bit too close for comfort," a lanky FLAK soldier said under his breath. "Let's show him we're still here."

Sprinting back towards the safety of the house, I saw Opa standing among a group of refugees. I placed myself in front of him and he rested his hands on my shoulders. Everyone's eyes were turned upward. Silhouetted against the blue sky, the biplane drifted slowly downward until the red stars painted on the fuselage were clearly visible. The pilot was alone, the seat behind him empty.

Amidst the noise from the FLAK, little puff clouds in rapid succession exploded closer and closer to the target. The pilot tried to escape by yanking his aircraft higher into the sky. Suddenly a trail of black smoke burst from the tail of the plane. The civilians watched in stunned silence, but there was jubilation at the FLAK.

"We got him! We got him!" a soldier kept screaming at the top of his lungs. "Look! He's coming down."

To my utter amazement, the pilot shot out of the cockpit. His parachute opened instantly. As he drifted slowly down, the airplane went into a tailspin. Within seconds it had crashed into an empty field near a small forest some distance away. There was a tremendous impact followed by a huge cloud of smoke. Three soldiers hopped into a truck and drove over to investigate the wreckage.

In the meantime the Russian pilot, dangling from his parachute, swooped down onto a muddy field about three hundred meters away from the farm. Everybody hurried over to see what would happen next. Remembering the hideous Russian soldiers in the newspaper cartoons back in Langendorf, I felt a mixed sense of dread and curiosity to see one up close.

By the time the pilot had disentangled himself from the parachute, Sergeant Hansen and five of his men, all armed with submachine guns, were at his side. The young pilot slowly removed his goggles and his cap, which had built-in earphones. His blond hair was drenched in sweat, his face a light shade of crimson. If it weren't for the five-pointed Russian star on his square metal belt buckle and his Russian uniform, I would have taken him for the older brother of one of my schoolmates in Langendorf.

Raising his hands into the air, he calmly let one of the soldiers disarm him. There was fear in his eyes, yet around his mouth I noticed the slight hint of a grin. Sergeant Hansen handed the pilot a cigarette. The young man put it between his lips. The Sergeant struck a match and held it towards the prisoner. The two men locked eyes as, with a shaky left hand, the Russian guided the lighted match to his mouth. Taking a deep drag on the cigarette, he relaxed. With a faint smile, he gave Sergeant Hansen a nod and said something in Russian which I presumed meant "Thank you." Since the German soldiers spoke no Russian, and the captured pilot did not speak German, it proved hopeless to interrogate him.

Together with the prisoner, we all walked slowly back to the farm. Two soldiers put the pilot into a truck and drove off in the direction of Palmnicken.

"Where are they bringing him?" I enquired of one of the FLAK soldiers. He ignored me at first, but I persisted. "What will happen to the Russian pilot?"

"He'll be brought to a prisoner of war camp," he said grumpily. "That's where you go when you get captured."

"Well, I guess it's all right then," I said after some reflection. "Pilots like him shot at the refugee wagons during our escape. So it's probably best to lock him up for a while, just to be on the safe side."

Just before supper, Opa and I took a walk in the farmyard.

"It won't be long before everything bursts into bloom," he said. "I've promised to help Mr. Wittke with his spring planting."

The night was clear. I thought about the violent drama we had witnessed that afternoon. "Opa!" I burst out. "What will happen to the Russian pilot in a prisoner of war camp?"

"Who told you about a prisoner of war camp?"

"One of the FLAK soldiers."

Opa sighed. "They're supposed to hold him until the end of the war, and then send him home to Russia in exchange for one of our prisoners."

"Is that what's really going to happen?"

"Lord willing," Opa replied. "Let's keep him in our prayers."

* * *

Towards nightfall in dense fog a few days after the Russian plane got shot down, Sergeant Hansen and what was left of his unit prepared to pull out. Their engines already running, the trucks were stocked with gear. The headlights gave off only a faint glow. I walked around to investigate. Thick canvas, painted with tar, covered the headlights of each truck. Tiny slits cut in the canvas let only a narrow glimmer of light shine through.

"It's camouflage," a FLAK soldier explained. "If we drive slowly enough and keep the lights dim, we'll slip right under the Russians' noses."

Sergeant Hansen glared at the soldier. "No need to scare the boy," he said. He turned to Opa. "We're leaving a supply of canned goods behind. They're stacked near the barn. Feel free to help yourselves to whatever you like."

"Thanks, Sergeant," Opa replied. "We appreciate everything you've done for us."

"Good luck!" the soldiers shouted. "Auf Wiedersehen!"

Just before the trucks pulled out, Sergeant Hansen reached down from the cab of the truck as Opa lifted me up to him. We shook hands solemnly.

"Take good care of your family, soldier," he said, giving me a salute. It was the second time I saw him cry.

* * *

I walked into the kitchen. Mutti and Oma were helping Mrs. Wittke prepare supper. There was none of the usual light conversation. Oma was pouring an enormous pot filled with flour dumpling soup, prunes, and dried apples into a metal milk can. Mutti was wrapping a dozen slices of fried bacon.

"Why have you cooked so much?" I wanted to know.

"We're going over to the Reimanns for a chat," Oma replied.

"A strategy meeting," Mutti corrected her grimly. "Not a chat."

We crossed the road to the Brenner farmhouse. Opa lugged the heavy container of soup and Oma brought the package of bacon. Mutti carried Hubert on her arm while holding my hand tightly.

"I've felt at home here," Oma said. "The Wittkes were total strangers, but they treated us like family."

"Are we leaving?" I asked, suddenly anxious.

"That's what we need to discuss with the Reimanns," Opa replied. "Now that the soldiers have left, we have to decide what to do."

* * *

The Reimanns' two tiny attic rooms were connected by a wide door. The six adults squeezed together on beds and chairs. Hubert and I sat elbow to elbow with our five cousins on the floor. The date was April 13, 1945. Nearly six weeks had passed since the thirteen of us had shared a meal together.

"There's nothing like your dumpling soup," Aunt Liesbeth said to Oma.

"We really have the Wittkes' generosity to thank for it," Oma replied, blushing at the compliment.

Aunt Liesbeth turned to the children. "Now I have a surprise for your Oma," she said with a wink. "Would you like to know what it is?"

We crowded closer to her, hoping for a sweet treat.

"Look what one of the soldiers gave me this morning!" Aunt Liesbeth said as she pulled out a jar of pickled herring from her apron pocket. Twisting off the cap, Aunt Liesbeth offered a little piece to anyone who wanted to try it.

"Well, I'll certainly have some," Oma said quickly. Pickled herring was one of her favorite foods.

"Anyone else?"

"No thanks!" We wrinkled up our noses.

My baby cousin Dieter, who had just learned how to walk, had been darting around the room on his little bow legs. He rushed over to Aunt Liesbeth, his mouth open wide. She put a tiny piece of dripping herring inside and we all waited for him to spit it out in disgust. To everybody's surprise, he swallowed it and gestured for more. As the rest of us giggled, Oma reached out to Dieter.

"That's my boy," she beamed. "Come sit on my lap!"

* * *

After supper, the conversation turned serious.

"The Russians must be nipping at our heels," Aunt Liesbeth said.

"Otherwise the soldiers wouldn't have abandoned us like that," Oma agreed. "The question is, do we wait for them here or do we move closer to the coast?"

"I can't see how it would make much difference either way," Opa said. "We're practically at the coast as it is."

"So what do you suggest?" Mutti asked.

"I think we should give it one more day. At least that way the children will have a place to sleep and food on the table. Agreed?"

Before anyone could reply, we heard heavy footsteps on the stairs, followed by a loud knocking.

"Maybe the decision has already been made for us," Mutti whispered.

"Come in!" Opa called out in a loud voice. He stood and faced the door.

It burst open and there stood Mr. Brenner.

"I hate to interrupt," he said, "but I just heard from our neighbors that the Russians are less than a kilometer away." Before we had a chance to react to this news, Mr. Brenner had already rushed back downstairs.

"That's worse than I thought," said Opa, shaking his head. "I think we'd better put the children to bed and gather up some of our things just to be on the safe side."

It was nearly midnight when we said goodnight to the Reimanns and headed back to our room across the road. Opa carried Hubert, who was sound asleep. I dropped off to sleep as soon as my head hit the pillow.

* * *

The calendar in Mrs. Wittke's kitchen read Saturday, April 14, 1945. Gloom hung over the breakfast table. No one talked. No one smiled. It hardly seemed possible that we had shared so much laughter with the Reimanns the previous evening.

As soon as I finished eating, I rushed outside into the fresh air. Walking along the muddy road until I reached a wooden fence, I leaned against a post and tried to make sense of things. The only Russian soldier I had seen so far did not look so threatening. He was not much older than Ilse, barely a man. If the Russians were like him, why had Sergeant Hansen deserted us? What was everyone so afraid of?

A small, low-flying Russian plane buzzed overhead. I glanced over to where the mobile FLAK unit had been. There was nothing there but an empty field. The plane turned in a wide circle and swooped back in my direction, lower than before. Just as I started to race back to the farmhouse, machine gun bullets pelted the ground a short distance away, ripping a wooden fence to shreds. My heart pounding in my throat, my lungs bursting, I dropped to the ground to catch my breath. The plane, moving even more slowly, passed over me a third time. I looked up and saw the pilot waving at me, a big smile on his face. He was toying with me, like a cat with a mouse.

Shaking my fist at the pilot, I screamed, "Are you crazy?" but, of course, he could not hear me.

The pilot flew one last loop and gave me a friendly salute before heading east. It was only after he was gone that I realized how easily he could have killed me if he had really wanted to. Sobbing, I ran back to Opa's waiting arms.

Trembling more violently than I had when I fell into the icy pond, I let Opa hold me tight.

* * *

Everyone gathered around the radio in the kitchen. I usually avoided listening to the war news, but now I felt safer being inside with the grownups.

"...Russian front...static...strategic withdrawal...static," the announcer gargled. Mr. Wittke fiddled with the dial.

The Russians must be very close," Mrs. Wittke commented, "to jam the transmission like that."

"It looks like we're in for it this time," Mr. Wittke said. "Perhaps before nightfall."

"Things might not be so bad," Opa replied. "During the last war we heard terrible things about the Russians, but when they finally arrived at my father's farm, all they did was confiscate some food."

"The party leaders say the Russians are barbarians. They'll slaughter us all in our beds," commented Mrs. Wittke.

"The Nazi propaganda machine has also been promising us a Final Victory. We don't have to believe everything they tell us," Opa reminded her.

"Thanks for trying to cheer us up," Mutti said, "but I have the feeling we're sinking fast and there's nothing we can do about it."

"I suppose you're right," Opa said glumly, "but as long as there's a glimmer of hope, I'm not ready to throw in the towel."

* * *

Still shaken from my experience in the afternoon, I didn't let Mutti out of my sight. Later that evening, she came up to our room and started to pack a small suitcase. Hubert was already curled up, sound asleep.

"What're you doing?" I asked anxiously.

"Oh, these are just photos, papers, and some jewelry. So it's all together in one place."

"Are we going somewhere?"

"Well, we might have to."

"When?"

"We'll find out tomorrow. Don't worry about it."

"Are the Russians really coming?"

"Just try and sleep. I don't know. No one does."

I crawled under my comforter on the floor, but sleep would not come. I tried to pray, but couldn't think what to ask.

"What will they do to us?" I heard Oma ask Mutti. "What if we get separated?"

"I'm sure we'll be all right. We're unarmed. They're not going to kill us."

"Good night, Gretel," Oma said. "I hope you're right."

"Good night, Mother." A few minutes later I heard Oma snoring. Opa had not yet come upstairs.

"Mutti," I whispered. "Are you sure we're going to make it?"

"You know what I always say," she replied softly. "Weeds like us don't perish."

CHAPTER 5

"What's going on?" I rubbed my eyes, trying to wake up. Mutti peeked out of the window. In a hoarse voice she whispered, "The Ivans are here."

The sky was tinged with the first pink glow of the sunrise. Everyone was awake, even little Hubert. Men were shouting and rushing about in the farm yard down below.

We heard them crashing into the house downstairs. A minute later our door was forced open and a grim Russian soldier with a submachine gun burst in, followed by two other men in earth brown uniforms. While we hurried into our clothes, all three soldiers yelled, "Uhrri, uhrri, uhrri."

Their German was primitive but we understood they wanted "Uhren" (watches). With trembling hands Mutti gave them her wristwatch and Opa gave them his pocket watch. Another soldier grabbed Mutti's hand, spat on her ring finger, and slid off her wedding band. Mutti pulled her hand away and stared at her bare finger. We were all shaking with fear. Hubert and I began to cry.

As soon as the three Russian men had left, three female soldiers came in, roaring with laughter. One of them opened the wardrobe and discovered Mutti's clothes. As we cowered in fright, they tried on her blouses, sweaters, and dresses, one by one, before taking nearly all of them. Whatever they did not want they threw on the floor and trampled.

Barely had the women left with most of Mutti's clothes when another soldier stormed into our room. He was wearing at least five watches on each wrist. The young soldier yelled "uhrri" and waved a pistol. Mutti pulled up the sleeves of her sweater. "No more watches," she said. "We don't have any watches left."

But he did not understand her. He pressed his weapon against Opa's chest, just as the SS officer had done only a few weeks before. Although we did not know any Russian, he was clearly counting. In desperation, Mutti grabbed my little toy watch from the table. The watch had once been filled with tiny candies and I had always treasured it. Satisfied for the moment, the soldier stuffed my toy watch into his pocket and started to search through Mutti's big suitcase. He found a small bottle of cologne and put it to his lips, probably believing it was schnapps.

Mutti yelled "Nein!" but she was too late. He took a swig of the cologne, realized his mistake and spat it out. Cursing us in an angry voice, he stormed back downstairs.

He must be an idiot, I thought, but I was too numb to find anything funny in the situation.

Mutti was putting some of Hubert's clothes into her rucksack when another soldier came in. As he tried to grab Mutti, she started to cry. Snatching up Hubert, she rushed down the staircase followed by the enraged soldier. We all grabbed what we could. I took my little suitcase and we followed Mutti outside.

In the farmyard, dozens of Russian soldiers, waving arms covered in watches nearly up to their elbows, were dancing in celebration. Lured by the festivities, Mutti's pursuer gave up the chase and disappeared among his comrades.

I saw Mutti running with Hubert across a field and Opa, Oma, and I followed her. We were out of breath when we finally caught up. In her excitement Mutti had lost her left shoe. We found ourselves in the middle of a muddy field, not knowing where to turn. We walked for a while when Opa grabbed Mutti's arm.

"I just remembered. I have your shiny brown boots in my big bag."

Mutti put her muddy left foot into one boot and the clean foot into the other.

"What about the Reimanns and Emma?" Mutti asked, out of breath. "Did anyone see them?"

"We passed right by their house, but we didn't dare stop," Oma admitted. "Perhaps we should turn back?"

"No, it's too dangerous. The Russians must be right behind us," Opa decided.

As we continued on without them, Opa said a quiet prayer. "We have to trust in the Lord to reunite us one day."

Plodding aimlessly across the fields, we finally came upon a house on a country lane. At first glance, the place looked abandoned. All of the furniture had been smashed and thrown out of the windows. No one was in the farmyard or in the nearby fields. There were no cows, no horses, and no chickens.

However, inside the farmhouse, dozens of German refugees huddled tightly together on the floor. Quickly we scanned their faces, but Aunt Liesbeth and the others were not among them. Feeling safe in that isolated place, we sat down, took off our shoes, and stretched out to rest.

Moments later, without warning, strange looking soldiers with slanted eyes and big cheek bones barged in. One of the soldiers stole Mutti's boots and snatched my little suitcase right out of my hand. I was furious. What use were our family photographs to the thief?

Mutti put her hand on my arm to calm me. "Let it go," she said softly. "Our lives are more important."

Other soldiers rampaged through the room, stealing whatever tempted them. Suddenly, the soldiers turned their attention to the women on the other side of the room, screaming, "Frau komm!"

We rushed outside, joined by several other families, and wandered until we found a paved road. Refugees and Russians were all moving in the same direction, but we had no idea whether they were going East or West, North or South. As soon as I caught my breath, I asked Opa, "Are the almond-eyed soldiers Russians?"

"They're Mongolians," he explained, "from far away in Asia."

Mutti only had socks on her feet so she put on her high brown skating shoes, her last pair of shoes. All of us clung to the hope that somewhere there was a safe place for us.

The two-way road became a one-way road, trucks and tanks on the left and foot soldiers, in formation, on the right. Most of the foot soldiers had slanted eyes, but the officers looked like us.

Barely tolerated on the very right edge of the road, we walked half in the ditch. Several times foot soldiers bumped into refugees on purpose to push them out of their way, as if we were just so much garbage.

"Where are we going anyhow?" I asked when we stopped to rest.

Mutti sat rubbing her feet. Her skating shoes were much too tight. "I don't even know where we are, much less where we're going." She began to cry.

Opa put his arm around her shoulders. "Well," he said, "I've been thinking. Sometimes it's better not to have a plan. Here we are, right in the middle of the Russian army, and no harm done. Who'd have believed it? I say we just keep on wandering and trust the Lord to lead us to safety."

A steady rumble of tanks rolled by. Russian soldiers clung to them in any way they could. The foul-smelling diesel exhaust fumes and the constant dust clouds nauseated me. My head throbbed and my throat felt tight. Wherever we walked, we heard wild shrieks of laughter. To our right, hordes of Russian soldiers ran in and out of abandoned farm houses. They ransacked the buildings and took away whatever they could carry: clothing, linens, leather boots, and clocks. Heavier items such as tables, chairs, wardrobes, and mirrors came crashing out of the windows.

By late afternoon, we were totally exhausted. We needed to stop and rest. We walked into a forest next to the road and lay down on the ground which was covered with a thick blanket of dried pine needles. We did not expect to sleep. The road, crowded with military vehicles, tanks, soldiers, and refugees, was only a short distance away. Diesel fumes hung heavy in the air. Other refugee families had also settled down for the night. Everyone was miserable, upset, and frightened.

A short time later, when several Russian soldiers left the column on the road and approached the edge of the forest, Mutti jumped up from the ground, cradled Hubert in her right arm, and grabbed me by the hand. We ran towards the road. Opa and Oma and most of the other refugees followed us in a hurry.

We left the road and crossed a vast, hilly pasture. Bushes, planted in neat rows, acted as windbreakers, protecting us from the chilly air.

Towards sundown we found an abandoned covered wagon, blankets piled up inside. I dozed off, although I was sure the grown-ups would not sleep. Sometime during the night, we heard loud voices and there they were, three or four Russian soldiers looking into our wagon with a flashlight.

"Frau komm," one of them commanded Mutti. We all started to holler. At that moment a horse approached at a gallop. A Russian officer barked orders at the soldiers and chased them off. The officer knew a little German.

"No fear, no fear. Soldiers drunk. Too much schnapps," he reassured Opa.

"Danke, Herr Offizier," Opa said as the officer disappeared as suddenly as he had come. After that, no one closed an eye all night.

* * *

At dawn, fortified with bacon and stale bread from the wagon, we set out again. Our arms and legs stiff with cold, we found our way back onto a road, joining scores of other refugee families, women, children, and grandparents, all moving in the same direction, no one sure where the road would lead. Every few minutes, we were forced to make wide detours around demolished army vehicles and field guns which blocked the way. Abandoned possessions lay heaped on both sides of the road: open suitcases, machine guns, laundry, pillows, dented gas mask containers, single shoes, military cable reels, books, letters, cartridge cases, moldy loaves of bread, empty machine gun belts, sides of bacon, used bazookas, rifles, wooden toys, German army rucksacks, and broken down baby carriages. Mutti tried out at least five or six of the carriages, but none was usable.

To our horror we also saw the dead bodies of two women and three small children. A dreadful stench rose from the many spots where people had relieved themselves.

A village appeared up ahead. A young woman, her face covered in bruises, gasped when she saw it.

"Oh, no! We've been going in circles. That's Gross Hubnicken, where the Russians caught us yesterday. There's no way I'm going back to that place."

Her family veered off the road towards the left and a large group of us followed them into the fields.

* * *

Mutti wore a rucksack on her back and held Hubert in her arms. She had covered her high brown skating shoes with mud so that they would not look worth stealing. The skating shoes gave her blisters.

Later in the evening, when it was already almost dark, we reached a nearly deserted village. Most of the houses had been ransacked. We had no idea where we were. After some searching we found a big house with broken windows, the large rooms inside already packed with German women of all ages, at least a dozen children and a few old men, all refugees. On the second floor, we found a spot in one of the big rooms where we could lie down on the floor together with the others.

"There's safety in numbers," Opa said, forcing a smile.

"Mutti," I whispered. "I'll be right back."

Finding a toilet was not easy. The bathrooms in the house were in shambles, the fixtures smashed beyond repair. Seeking privacy, I left the house, pushed my way past the people milling around outside, and found an abandoned house nearby. There in the middle of a ransacked kitchen, I relieved myself. When I returned to our spot in the room on the second floor, I had to climb over the newcomers who had arrived in the meantime.

"Thank goodness you're back. I was worried about you," Mutti said.

"I'm going to sleep. I've never felt so tired." I lay down next to her on the floor and quickly dozed off.

* * *

Loud noises woke me up. My eyes took a minute to get accustomed to the darkness. A gang of Russian soldiers carrying giant flashlights had entered our room. Two soldiers went up to the third floor and chased the men and children down the stairs. The Russian soldiers who remained in our room shined their flashlights in our faces as they picked out women and girls aged twelve and older and motioned to them to come upstairs to the third floor. If a woman did not follow right away, a burly soldier just grabbed her by the arms, yelled, "Davai! Davai!" (Move it! Move it!) and shoved her upstairs. Opa's eyes were closed in prayer. Oma was crying, and Mutti clutched Hubert and wept.

"Don't worry, my darling," she kept repeating. "There's nothing to be afraid of."

I wanted to say something comforting to Mutti, but was unable to find the right words.

A soldier loomed over us, his ugly pockmarked face briefly illuminated by a flashlight. Shining his light on Mutti, he snarled, "Davai! Davai!" Without a sound, Mutti handed Hubert to Oma, got up and followed the other women upstairs. I was so scared, I was sure my heart would stop. Piercing cries cut right through the ceiling. Large groups of soldiers stomped upstairs in their heavy boots. As soon as they came back down, they were replaced by others who had been waiting their turn outside.

I felt helpless, useless. I would have given anything to have been bigger than the burly Russian soldier who had taken Mutti away. I imagined myself, armed with a submachine gun, storming up to the third floor, chasing out all the Russians, shooting them as they tried to escape down the stairs.

Thumps and screams from upstairs ended my fantasy. In the end, all I could do was lean against Oma and cry. Oma held Hubert on her lap and stroked his hair as if to calm herself. No one was lying down anymore; we all sat and wept, waiting for the women and girls to come back. I waited only for Mutti.

She was gone for what seemed to me like an eternity. After several hours, when it was light outside, she and the other women, all weeping, staggered down the wide staircase. Mutti's face was flushed with pain. Under her torn blouse, her neck and her upper chest were covered with bloody scratch marks. Her hair drooped wet and disheveled. She was crying, but there was no sound. She sat down on our spot on the floor and took Hubert in her arms. Oma embraced them both.

All around us, exhausted young women clung to their mothers, their silence even more terrifying to me than the earlier screams had been. Drunk and loud, more than a dozen soldiers thundered down the wide staircase from the third floor. I edged closer to Mutti. Frozen in place, the refugees silently watched them leave.

With the Russians gone, people began to stir. Five or six women collected their crying children and hand baggage and went downstairs. They moved slowly and their eyes were glazed.

"Where are we anyway?" an old man asked no one in particular.

"Kraxtepellen, just outside of Palmnicken," a sad old woman replied.

"Can you imagine that?" Oma said, almost to herself. "As the crow flies, we're probably only four kilometers from the Wittkes' farm in Bieskobnicken and it's taken us two whole days to get here."

"Come look!" Opa was standing next to a wide window frame in which only splinters of glass remained around the edges.

Opa pointed at the Baltic Sea. Rolling dark green waves, churning with whitecaps, reminded me of the waves of Russians during the long night. Cold sea air slapped at our faces. I thought we had reached the end of the world. We had no idea where to go or what to do next.

Mutti started to cry again. "How can we continue in all of this misery?"

"Let's walk into the sea," I said, looking up at her, because at that moment I wanted to die, but Mutti shook her head.

Lifting Hubert up into her arms and trying to look as brave as she could, she straightened her shoulders. "Let's get out of here. I can't spend another minute in this place."

Exhausted and frightened, we walked to Palmnicken, picking our way around furniture, bedding, and mattresses flung from the windows onto the sidewalks; pots and pans, broken bottles, and dishes littered the street. Other dazed refugees, women and children and old people, also walked aimlessly, just like us. Almost all of the women and girls we passed had tear-stained faces. Three or four of them had crazed looks, as though they had gone insane during the night. One elderly woman, her long snow white hair flowing in the wind, called out endlessly, "Irene! Irene!" No one answered. We all ignored her.

Although the sun was shining, white stuff began to swirl down from the sky. For a moment I thought it was snowing. We looked up and saw a Russian soldier leaning out of a second floor window, vigorously shaking out a down comforter. As we walked, the "snow" began to seem more like a blizzard. On both sides of the street Russian soldiers were leaning out of windows, slitting open comforters and shaking them out.

We soon discovered the reason for this bizarre behavior. The Russians were stripping apart the bright red inlets from the comforters and using them to cover wooden boards. Soon big red banners written in Cyrillic letters were stretched across the main street of Palmnicken.

A massive brick Lutheran church loomed over us on the left side of the street. As we passed by, we could see Russians hard at work, gutting the interior.

"How can they destroy a house of worship like that?" Oma asked. "What a bunch of heathens!"

A little farther on Opa found a baby carriage on the sidewalk. It was still in working order and Mutti was relieved not to have to carry Hubert any longer. Eventually we came upon an abandoned house in relatively good condition, despite the piles of broken furniture and other junk strewn about outside. Cautiously Opa peeked through a broken window and then he called us over.

"Here, have a look."

Whatever we could see inside had also been smashed. Everything was covered in filth.

"What do you say we clean up this place and stay here?" Opa asked and we all agreed.

It took us the rest of the day to discard the broken furniture and dishes and to clean up the kitchen and three of the rooms. We left some rooms as we found them.

As Opa put it, "After all, who knows how long we can stay?"

Following the example of the Russians, Opa opened the windows and tossed the collected junk out onto the piles of garbage already in the front yard. During this first rough cleanup, Oma checked the plumbing.

"The toilet doesn't work and there's no running water," she reported with disappointment.

"Well, it'll have to do for now," Mutti said grimly.

After we made the place halfway livable, Opa boarded up the few broken windows and nailed the front door shut.

"Maybe the Ivans won't notice we're in here," he said. "The place sure doesn't look lived in from the outside."

We only used the back door, away from the street. Opa made frequent excursions to find water, collecting it in buckets from rain barrels. Oma boiled it for drinking. She also tried pouring some down the toilet, but it was hopelessly clogged. So we had no other choice but to use the bushes behind the house.

I heard distant thunder and asked Opa, "Is it going to rain?"

"No. From what I hear, there's still fighting going on south of here."

"You mean the war's not over?"

"Well, maybe not for the folks down there. But it certainly is for us, my boy."

* * *

Over the next few days, Mutti and Oma searched through wardrobes and three grime-covered trunks, discovering comforters, linens, underwear, and clothing for all of us.

"They must have taken off in a real hurry, to leave all these nice things behind," Oma remarked.

"I'll bet the man of the house was away at war," Mutti added. "The men's clothing looks brand new."

The children's clothes were too big for Hubert and me, but Oma found a sewing kit and quickly took them in for us. She was a genius with a pair of scissors and a needle and thread. In the pantry Oma even found some flour, salt, and lard which ended up as pancakes on our dinner table for a number of our meals.

"Without eggs and sugar they won't taste anywhere as good as they did in Langendorf," Oma warned us.

"Are you fishing for compliments?" Opa asked.

"No, not at all," Oma replied, the color rising in her cheeks.

I thought they were delicious.

To everyone's delight, Oma also found seven war-issue "Hindenburg lights," small wax candles shaped like flat discs that came in very handy at night, since there was no electricity.

* * *

During the day, whenever Mutti left the house with Opa, she dressed in dark clothes like an old woman. With a black shawl around her head, walking with a slight stoop, she looked older than Oma, who was sixty-three. While they were out, Mutti and Opa scrounged for food in abandoned houses. Sometimes they found flour or dried peas which Oma used to make a wonderful soup.

The distant rumble of artillery went on for days until it suddenly stopped. It was April 25, 1945.

"Word is, the Russians have wiped out the remaining German bridgehead in Pillau," Opa reported. "A few wise guys even claim the Americans are on their way to Palmnicken to liberate us. I'll believe that when I see it."

"Did you ever hear such nonsense?" Mutti said. "No one's coming to rescue us. We're stuck here and we may as well make the best of it."

* * *

Opa went out every day in search of food. One day he brought home eight tiny paper bags of Dr. Oetker's vanilla pudding mix. Since there was no milk available, Oma prepared it with water. The pudding tasted horrible and made me gag. Hungry as I was, I just could not force that pudding down.

Another time Opa brought home a coffee mill. "Look what I found. Sure we have no coffee, but one never knows."

During the day, Palmnicken swarmed with Russians, many of them drunk. I watched in disgust as a tipsy young soldier vomited in the middle of the sidewalk. With a vacant look in his eyes, he mumbled to himself, collapsing into his own mess. Russians and Germans alike simply walked around him.

No one in charge seemed to care what happened to us. Even so, the days were less frightening than the nights. Every night we could hear loud soldiers roaming the street. Sometimes we heard women screaming. Occasionally we heard shooting in the distance. Four or five times soldiers banged on our front door and shouted in Russian as we cowered inside, but each time they left after getting the impression the house was unoccupied.

Another German woman gave Mutti advice on how to protect herself.

"Don't be alarmed," Mutti told me that evening. "Before we go to sleep, I'm going to prepare my face so I look very ugly, sick, and old. You understand why, don't you?"

"Yes, but I still hope nobody comes during the night," I said.

"Better safe than sorry." Mutti smeared some jam on her face and then dabbed on a little bit of flour. The result was horrifying, her smooth skin suddenly covered with festering scabs. Hubert began to shriek and sob and Mutti placed him on her lap to soothe him.

Turning to Oma, she tipped her head to one side. "How do I look?"

"Absolutely dreadful. Remember how angry I was when you and Liesbeth used a little makeup to look prettier? I never imagined I'd see the day when an attractive young woman like you would try to look her worst."

"Well," Mutti said, "times have changed."

Before she lay down on the floor between Hubert and me, Mutti placed a tiny glass of elderberry juice against the wall near her head.

For several more nights the Russians banged on our door, and then went away, but finally our luck ran out. One night they splintered the wooden door with a rifle butt and burst into the house. I thought our end was near. As soon as Mutti heard them come in, she took a sip of elderberry juice, but did not swallow. The moment the flashlights shone into her face she let the juice run slowly down the corners of her mouth. At the same time Opa called out, "Typhus! Typhus!"

The soldiers backed away from Mutti, stumbling over one another to reach the door. When the soldiers had left, Opa closed the door and lit a Hindenburg light. Mutti reached over to stroke Hubert's hair. Her hands were trembling.

"That was quite a performance," Oma said after a while. "I didn't know you two were such fine actors."

Mutti tried to smile. "When we get out of this mess, I may take it up as a career." She turned to Hubert and me. "But now it's time to sleep, you two. The show's over for tonight."

I dozed off watching Opa try to secure the door. In the morning, he was sleeping by the front entrance in case the Russians returned.

During the following weeks Mutti never went to bed without her "makeup." She, Oma, and Opa always lay down fully clothed, ready to run away with us at a moment's notice. Now that the Russians knew our house was lived in, soldiers came often during the night, but each time the makeup trick worked.

In the meantime our living quarters had improved, thanks to Opa's ingenuity. He had repaired five chairs and a table which he had found in abandoned buildings, so the place felt more like home.

* * *

One day Mutti and Opa were ordered to report to the Kommandantura (Russian military headquarters) early each morning to be assigned work.

"The more they get organized, the harder it is on us," Mutti commented with a sigh.

"Well, if we don't do the work around here, who will?" Opa replied.

"I guess it's better than sitting around worrying," Mutti agreed.

"There are no men in Palmnicken between the ages of sixteen and fifty-nine," Opa reported that evening when he came home from work. "The ones who reported for work were a few young teenagers and a lot of old timers like me."

"Most of the women were my age, but I saw a few young girls and some grandmotherly types," Mutti said.

Mutti had to clean houses and cook for Russian officers. Sometimes she was sent to clean big storage rooms or to sort used clothes and bundle them to be shipped. Together with other German men, Opa had to remove debris from dilapidated houses or help with construction work. Usually, but not always, they were paid with a piece of bread once the job was finished.

One day Opa wasn't picked for a job so he was home with us. Late in the afternoon we heard loud banging at the door. Opa opened it a crack and a Russian officer and two soldiers barged in, brushing Opa aside. Scowling, they walked from room to room, making a careful inspection. At last the officer appeared to be satisfied. I was sure Opa would receive a compliment for all our hard clean-up work, but instead the officer merely nodded to one of the soldiers who spoke to Opa in broken German:

"You move now. Tomorrow Red Army live here."

"Where to?" Opa asked, but the soldier just shrugged his shoulders.

After the Russians left we stood there for a while, stunned. Oma, Hubert, and I began to cry, but Opa just started packing a little handcart he had found some time before.

"Hopefully Gretel will get home in time to give us a hand," he said.

Fortunately, Mutti came home earlier than usual that day. Although she was as upset as we were, minutes later she and Opa set out to look for another abandoned house. They came back some time later to announce that they had found one nearby. It was even a little bigger than ours, but full of junk, broken furniture, and filth, just like the one we were using had been before we moved in. Once again, there was neither running water nor a working toilet.

Opa, Mutti, and I were able to make seven trips with the little handcart before darkness fell. We brought over pillows, bed covers, clothes, underwear, pots and pans, and the coffee mill, together with what little food we had left. Opa cleaned out the large vestibule so that we could store everything. We went back one more time to get Oma and Hubert and then we moved in. The next morning Mutti and Opa had to report for work, although we had more than enough work in our "new house."

Not all of the nearby buildings were empty. German refugees lived in five or six of the buildings close to ours. Oma, Hubert, and I went from door to door.

"Excuse me, sir," Oma said to an elderly man two houses down, "but where do you get your water?"

"Not from the faucet, that's for sure," he replied bitterly. "We use rainwater like everyone else. There's a rain barrel under the gutter in back of our house. You can use it 'til you get settled, but only for drinking and cooking, mind you."

"Thank you! We'll take you up on that," said Oma. After a moment's hesitation, she asked, "And what about water for washing?"

"That's another story. Some people use the Kraxte Creek or seawater. It's a long walk either way. The Creek's brackish and the sea's salty. Take your pick."

"Which do you recommend, if I may ask?"

"The best would be to find yourself a rain barrel. I hear there are still some for the taking in Kraxtepellen."

Opa soon found a rain barrel and rolled it back to our house. While we waited for it to fill, we carried water home from the Kraxte Creek for washing. Oma was careful not to waste a drop of the brownish stuff. After washing dishes or clothing, she saved the water in four large pails.

"What's it good for?" I asked Oma as I peered down into the murky liquid.

"Waste not, want not," she reminded me.

With grim determination, for two days, Oma attacked the chunks of plaster clogging our toilet. After each onslaught, she poured in a bucket of water but, to her disappointment, the toilet would not flush.

"We'd need a master plumber to clean out that mess," Mutti said, but Oma was not to be discouraged. On the third day she poked around with a long piece of thick wire, bent into a little hook at one end.

"I'm beginning to worry about Mother," Mutti said to Opa that evening after supper.

"Let her be," he replied. "She's like a bull dog, never quits."

Just then, Oma yelled from the bathroom, "I did it! It works! Come and look!"

We all crowded into the tiny room. Oma, out of breath from bending down for so long, her face flushed, quickly poured a pail of dirty wash water into the toilet bowl. The water disappeared with a loud gurgle.

"What do you say now?" she asked proudly.

"I have to hand it to you," Mutti said, "I was beginning to have my doubts."

"One sorrow less," Opa added. "Sometimes East Prussian stubbornness really pays off."

We were fortunate. Most people were forced to use a spot in the backyard to relieve themselves. The familiar stench of diarrhea was everywhere. Keeping ourselves clean was a never-ending battle. The few cakes of soap we had found in the house were soon used up. Mutti would have filched a piece of soap from the Russian officers she worked for, but they did not have any either. Before long, we all had head lice. Oma and Mutti went to work on us with a fine comb and their fingernails. They washed our hair and scalps with hot water filtered through ashes from the stove, all to no avail.

* * *

At the Kommandantura where the German adults had to line up every morning for work, Mutti and Opa picked up scraps of information.

"We weren't the only ones kicked out of our houses," Mutti reported one evening. "Everyone's complaining about it."

"The way I see it," Opa said, "the Russians do everything backwards."

"How's that?" Oma asked.

"First they smash everything to bits, just for the fun of it. Then it dawns on them that they need the houses for their own people, so they just wait around until we've fixed them back up."

* * *

80

As time went on, finding food in abandoned buildings became nearly hopeless. Three or four times Oma and I went through garbage containers outside Russian-occupied houses to find potato peels. Boiled with a little salt, they didn't taste too bad.

During dry spells, when our rain barrel was nearly empty, Opa brought back water he found trickling from a broken pipe near the amber factory. On Sundays he and I filled our buckets at the water tower pipe near the Palmnicken railroad station. Oma boiled all our drinking water.

Firewood also became scarce. We had to walk eight hundred meters to Kraxtepellen to find unoccupied houses. One morning Hubert and I had gone into a house to look for firewood. I had already stacked a few wooden boards on our little handcart when Oma called to me from the gaping doorframe of another dilapidated house. I pulled the cart over the rubbish. Leaving Hubert outside and clambering over fallen bricks and pieces of plaster, I found Oma in the next room. Under half a dozen wooden boards and a heap of plaster she had found a dust-covered trunk, which we pried open. A ten-kilo bag full of rye lay inside. Oma and I chewed a few of the grains to be sure they had not spoiled. Leaving behind for the time being the wood that we had found, we hoisted the heavy bag onto our handcart, placed Hubert on top of the bag and headed back home. We both had to pull the heavy cart.

As we walked, Oma made plans. "Now that we have the rye, I'm going to bake us some bread."

I was skeptical. "How can you bake bread without flour?" I asked.

Oma paused to consider my question. "Remember the coffee mill your Opa found? It's going into service."

"Can I help?"

"You can crank the handle. My old hands are too stiff."

When Opa ran his fingers through the grain, tears filled his eyes. "The Lord has provided us with bread. Thanks be to God. Amen."

CHAPTER 6

Palmnicken, once a seaside resort town, was swarming with Russian soldiers. Abandoned military vehicles cluttered Linden Boulevard. Gutted villas, stripped of window glass and trimmings, stood forlornly behind the trees lining the road. Towards the side of the village farthest from the Baltic Sea, garbage was strewn among piles of discarded furniture. The foul-smelling carcasses of decaying animals, crawling with maggots and covered with flies, mixed with the repulsive smell of human waste. I desperately missed the peace and quiet of Langendorf and spent many hours searching for places where I could spend some time alone.

One sunny afternoon in May I decided to show Hubert the long bluff along the Baltic Sea I had discovered a few days earlier, where fast-flying swifts lived in holes burrowed into the hardened sand wall of the cliff. I had climbed around there twice before to watch in amazement how the swifts darted high up in the air, swooping back down like dive bombers close to the waves or to the bluff. When they returned to their little sandstone homes, they slowed down for only a second before safely disappearing inside to feed their young.

Hubert was two and one-half years old. I had to walk slowly so he could keep up with me. Once we passed through a sweet-smelling park filled with big leafy trees the path suddenly turned sandy before running downhill to the beach. Standing at the top, my view no longer blocked by trees and bushes, I gasped in astonishment. The beach was not empty as it usually was, nor did I see many swifts. Instead, a vast array of Russian soldiers was engaged in a boisterous celebration.

The soldiers sat on arm chairs, straight-backed chairs, boxes, barrels, mattresses, blankets, and directly on the sand. Four of them had even dragged complete beds to the beach to sit on. Many were shirtless and all of them were drinking tea or vodka. In the middle of each group of soldiers was a campfire from which wafted the delicious aroma of roasting potatoes and fried fish.

Nearly a dozen other German children were also hanging around. The appetizing smells tickled our noses. Still holding Hubert tightly by the hand, I edged a little closer to one group of Russians. In their midst was a soldier with an accordion, playing beautiful music. Some of the other soldiers were singing along. I had never heard the songs before, but I liked the melodies and wished I could join in. Since three or four of the songs had many verses, after a little while I was able to hum along. I felt a tugging at my hand. Hubert was bouncing up and down with the music.

All of a sudden a middle-aged Russian soldier approached us. With a big laugh he grabbed Hubert and lifted him up. I was startled, but did not dare to object. Holding Hubert against his bare chest, the soldier whirled round and round. At the same time, he kept roaring "Chitler kaputt, voyna kaputt" over and over again. He threw Hubert high up in the air three or four times and caught him again. My tiny brother, his light blond hair flying in the wind, shrieked with delight.

I began to feel anxious; Hubert was my responsibility. Finally the soldier put Hubert down and gestured to me to come closer to the campfire. He gave me a slice of bread and a piece of fried fish dripping with fat, more than enough for both of us.

From what the soldier was shouting, I knew that Hitler was dead, but I was puzzled about the word "voyna." So after I thanked the soldier I asked, "What is 'voyna' please?"

He called over one of his comrades who explained, "Voyna means war. War is over. Big party."

The soldier who had held Hubert started dancing again, still screaming, "Chitler kaputt, voyna kaputt" over and over again. Eight soldiers danced in a circle. They locked arms and squatted down, kicking their feet out in front of them. Sand flew in all directions with each step. Other soldiers galloped bareback with incredible skill along the beach. Some raced along the tide line, the water splashing like flying silver drops in the gleaming sunlight, the horses whinnying with delight. I watched with envy. The only horse I had been on was the one that pulled the wagon on Opa's farm.

The sun began to set. Empty vodka bottles littered the beach. The crowd became louder and more rowdy. A few of the men began to shoot their pistols into the air. Along the shore, a man stood ankle deep in the water and emptied the magazine of his submachine gun out over the Baltic Sea. Many of the soldiers in Palmnicken carried similar weapons, with thick barrels punched full of holes and drum magazines shaped like cans of fish. I had first seen them in Bieskobnicken when the Russians caught up with us.

Some lunatic may empty his fish can gun at us next, I thought in sudden panic. I grabbed Hubert and raced for home.

* * *

"You shouldn't have stayed so long," Mutti scolded after I described our adventure that evening. "Russians and schnapps are a dangerous mixture."

"Yes, Mutti, I realize that now."

"Do you think the war is really over?" Mutti asked Opa and Oma.

"It would seem so, thank the Lord," Opa replied. "Perhaps we'll have an easier time of it from now on."

"Maybe in the long run," Oma said, "but with all that schnapps in them, I'd say we're in for a long night."

For safety reasons we all lay down in one room. Opa and Oma stationed themselves next to the door. Hubert and I curled up next to Mutti on blankets on the floor towards the back of the room, where we felt more protected. Our farm animals in Langendorf had also huddled together that way every night.

The later it got, the louder the screaming outside in the street. At least three times we heard rapid bursts of submachine gun fire. Only Hubert fell asleep. It must have been after midnight when we heard the familiar hammering on the door.

Opa whispered, "Don't talk. Don't move. Maybe they'll leave."

But they did not leave; several young, drunk Russian soldiers broke down the door. One of them shined a flashlight into our faces, terrifying us. In their now well-practiced routine Opa called out, "Typhus!" in a booming voice and Mutti began to cough while a trickle of elderberry juice "blood" ran down her lower lip. Cursing at us in Russian, the soldiers staggered back out to the street.

Opa nailed the door shut as best he could and we tried to get back to sleep, but it was impossible. It was a wild, endless night, filled with the screams of women and the rat-a-tat of gunfire. When morning finally came, I was totally exhausted.

A notice was posted on the Kommandantura bulletin board the following afternoon. The war had ended on May 9, 1945. A few days later, another poster announced that the violation of German women by Russian soldiers would no longer be tolerated.

"Just as it says in the good book," Opa remarked. "Swords into plow shares."

"All the same," Mutti said, "I'm still going to put on my 'makeup,' just to be on the safe side."

* * *

In the middle of May Opa took me to the beach along the Baltic Sea for a long walk. It was nearly deserted in the early morning. The sky was cloudless and the sun was shining, but the water was icy cold. Golden pieces of amber shimmered in the sand. I collected five smooth pieces and held them up to Opa.

"Look what I found!"

"You're lucky. Normally there's not that much amber on the beach, but after that storm yesterday, the waves turned up quite a bit. People have been finding amber along this beach for thousands of years. Palmnicken's famous for it."

"Is this where the amber came from for Mutti's pendant?"

"I'm sure it did. Nearly all of the world's amber comes from Palmnicken. Your mother's was an especially nice piece, with a tiny mosquito trapped in the resin. I gave an amber brooch to your Oma, too, when we became engaged. You should give one to your sweetheart some day. It's an East Prussian tradition."

"Mutti and Oma must have felt really bad when that little suitcase was stolen."

"I'm sure they were upset about it at the time," Opa said. "But that's the way it is."

"How do people know that amber is really made of pine resin?"

"Let me have one of the pieces you've collected so far and I'll show you."

I pulled them out of my pocket and he chose a long narrow piece from my hand. Opa lit a match and held the flame against the thin end, taking care not to burn his fingers. The yellow, transparent amber darkened, started to melt, and finally burned away as pitch-black soot, releasing the familiar odor of burning pine resin into the air. Before the amber piece had completely burned up, Opa dipped it into the water. There was a short hissing sound. When he took it out of the water, the little piece of amber no longer looked pretty. Big black bubbles ran along the burned edge, but the pungent smell remained. We continued our walk. Before long, my pocket was crammed full of little amber pieces.

As we turned back, Opa stopped and stared out at the sea. "Everything washes up on the shore in time," he said quietly. "Sometimes things which look bad on the outside really aren't inside. Like when the water chisels and polishes ordinary looking rocks until they become translucent and you can see whether a little leaf or an insect is hidden inside. And sometimes it's the other way around, a thing which sparkles on the outside turns out to be ugly or worthless."

"How can you tell the difference?" I asked.

"If you wait long enough, you'll always find out."

* * *

The Monday after Pentecost (Sunday May 20, 1945) Opa came home and slumped forlornly into a chair. When Mutti got back a short time later, she also looked troubled. Both of them ignored me.

"Did you read the poster at the Kommandantura?" Mutti asked Opa.

"Of course I did. Everyone did."

"What kind of poster?" Oma demanded.

"The Kommandant claims thousands of Soviet women were shot by the SS at a beach near Palmnicken at the end of January. He's asking the Germans for information about mass graves."

"Thousands?"

"Apparently so," Mutti said. "It seems hard to believe something like that went on right around here."

"What do the locals have to say?"

"The ones I saw milling around the Kommandantura were tight lipped," Opa answered.

"If no one's willing to talk about it, there might be some truth to the accusations."

"In that case, God help us all," Oma said.

We ate our thin bread soup in silence. Finally Opa brought up a different subject.

"There was another poster. 'All German men in Palmnicken have to report to the Kommandantura tomorrow morning at 6 A.M.' and then, in capital letters, 'NO EXCEPTIONS!' I wondered about the last part. Normally the Russians aren't so strict with us old-timers."

"I reacted the same way when I saw it," Mutti agreed.

* * *

The next evening Opa looked even more distressed.

"What kind of work did you have to do?" Mutti asked.

"I'd rather not talk about it, if you don't mind," Opa said, "at least not in front of the children."

Nothing more was said during supper. Aside from Hubert, who was slurping his soup, the only noise was the sound of our spoons clinking against the soup bowls. As soon as we finished, Mutti gave me a hard look. I didn't need to be told that I wasn't wanted.

"Please take Hubert along," Mutti said as I headed for the door. "I don't mind if you play for a while outside."

* * *

On Wednesday evening, I asked Opa, "How was your day?" but he looked upset and turned away. He was crying. What's wrong with Opa? I wondered. What are the Russians doing to him? I had never seen him cry before and I was scared.

"Opa worked at the beach today so he's pretty tired. Why don't you go out and play while he rests. You needn't take Hubert along," Mutti told me.

"All right, see you later," I said, slamming the door on the way out. Whenever the grown-ups wanted to talk about things I was not supposed to hear, I got a funny feeling in the pit of my stomach.

I wandered over to the collection of broken mobile searchlights, wrecked trucks, tanks blackened by fire, and anti-aircraft guns rusting away in a small shady park near the dilapidated railroad station. Opa had nicknamed the place "the military junkyard." Three children were playing hide-and-seek among the chestnut trees. Two boys straddled the anti-aircraft guns. With some difficulty, I hoisted myself onto the little seat of one of the five search lights. Perched high above the ground, I was reminded of the metal saddle atop Opa's mowing machine. The crank rotated, but it no longer worked the gears. I imagined turning the huge search light around until I had locked onto a Russian plane just like the anti-aircraft gunners had done in Bieskobnicken.

Three gold-toothed Russian officers approached. One of them, whose map case was hanging from his shoulder strap, said a few friendly words to me in Russian and the others smiled. I supposed he was warning me not to fall down. Lucky for me he could not read my thoughts.

* * *

"Would someone please tell me what's going on?" I begged when I got home.

"Maybe some other time," Mutti said. "Opa doesn't feel like discussing it right now."

Opa left early the next morning and every morning for days. When he returned in the late afternoons, he barely said a word; he had no appetite. He sat hunched over the Bible, reading until the last glimmer of sunlight disappeared. On the rare occasions when he wanted to talk to Oma and Mutti, I was sent out to play. I was afraid we would have to escape again and that was why Opa was upset.

One day when I was sent outside I was determined to find out what was going on. I left whistling in the direction of the little park, then doubled back. Tiptoeing over to an open window, I caught snatches of their conversation. My heart was pounding so loud I was sure they would hear me.

"...and the Russians have been finding bodies ever since they got here," I heard Opa say. "Corpses keep turning up everywhere."

"Not just along the beach?" Mutti asked.

"In Germau. In Kraxtepellen. Three hundred bodies here, two hundred there, and it goes on and on. It makes me sick. They're buried four deep, stacked together like so many sardines. I had more respect for my dead farm animals."

"...you know how many?"Oma asked.

"More than four thousand souls, mostly women, gunned down this past January 31st."

I strained so hard to listen that I nearly forgot to breathe. What could it all mean? Each time a noisy Russian truck rolled by, I was afraid I'd miss something important.

"Who were they?" Oma asked. "Do you have any idea?"

"The Russians call them Soviet heroes. But they were Jewish prisoners. I'm sure of it....six-pointed stars sewn onto one sleeve and on the back. But when we lift them out, the bodies just fall apart."

"What must the Russians think of us?" Oma said sadly. A column of army vehicles rumbled by on the street, muffling the voices inside. Using the noise as cover, I sneaked away from our house. I walked slowly to the park, sat down on an ammunition crate, and tried to understand what I had heard.

All those bodies. Had they been just under our feet at the victory party? Why would anyone shoot them? Something might happen to Opa! I had to find out. Gathering up all my courage, I headed back home, determined to get to the bottom of things.

Storming into the house, I directed my anger at Mutti. "What are you hiding from me? I need to know." Then I turned to Opa. "Please tell me what's going on."

Opa was too choked up to talk so Mutti was the first to speak.

"Well I guess you're going to find out anyhow. Ever since Pentecost, the men have been digging corpses out of the sand with their bare hands. The bodies are in shallow graves along the beach and the Russians want to give them a proper burial."

"Won't Opa get sick? Touching dead bodies like that?"

Opa fought to compose himself. "Don't you worry about me, sonny boy. Your Opa's a tough old farmer."

Opa's eyes did not meet mine. He had just lied to me for the very first time.

"Some of them worked at the Schippenbeil airport," Opa said, his voice barely above a whisper. "They were Jewish prisoners from the Stutthof Concentration Camp."

"Oh, no!" Oma gasped. "Why, Ilse saw one of them trying to escape!"

"Opa," I interrupted, "are Jews soldiers?"

An awkward moment of silence followed my question. Finally Opa cleared his throat.

"No, they're not soldiers. They're people like you and me, but with a different religion. You remember all the Old Testament stories about the people of Israel? Those stories are about the Jews."

"But then why...." Mutti shot me a glance to let me know the subject was closed, but I persisted. "If they weren't soldiers, why did the SS shoot them?"

"I wish I knew," Opa replied.

"What do you think, Mutti?" I asked. "Opa says that Jews have a different religion. Did the SS shoot them because of that?"

Mutti studied her shoes. Without looking up, she answered me in a soft voice, "They shouldn't have, but I think they did."

"That doesn't make any sense," I said, looking to Opa for a better explanation.

"You're right about that," Opa agreed. "I don't understand it either and I never will, so long as I live."

* * *

Day after day Opa dug out corpses from the mass graves. He did this terrible work and he suffered. Although his stomach was empty, he threw up all the time. His gnarled hands were covered in scabs. The awful odor of decomposed bodies clung to his clothes.

Every day he had another heart-wrenching story to tell.

"Yesterday some women were ordered to go to the Anna Pit near the Palmnicken Amber Factory to dig out corpses."

"There too?" Mutti exclaimed.

"Right across from the factory. Hundreds of corpses under a shallow layer of sand and earth. The SS was nothing if not thorough."

Bang! Bang! You're dead. The SS doesn't take any prisoners! the older boys in Schippenbeil used to yell. I remembered the SS officer who had threatened to shoot Opa during our escape. How brave Opa had been to question his orders.

"When is all this going to end?" Oma asked.

"It just gets worse and worse. Did I tell you many of the corpses are wearing belts made from telephone wire? Today I found a body with a German army canteen attached to the wire. There were seventeen bullet holes in the canteen. Can you imagine what those poor people went through before they died?" Opa broke down in sobs.

Poor Opa, I thought with a shudder. I hope he doesn't have to do this much longer.

* * *

As the work continued, more German women were sent to work alongside the men. Mutti was grateful she still was assigned to clean houses and storage rooms.

At long last, after three or four weeks of digging, the horrible task came to an end. Opa, who had been skinny before Pentecost, now looked so emaciated I was afraid he would collapse and die.

Terrifying rumors circulated that the Russians were going to shoot the German men in Palmnicken as revenge for the crimes of the SS, but nothing of the kind happened.

Opa was assigned to the local amber factory as a watchman. When he came home at the end of his shift, he rarely spoke. I tried to talk with him, but he seemed distracted, as though his mind were elsewhere. The strange sadness that had settled over Opa never went away.

CHAPTER 7

*O*ne day in June, when the weather had become quite warm, Oma developed a rash accompanied by a headache, chills, and a high fever. A day or two later I came down with the same symptoms. Mutti rushed us to the nearby hospital in Palmnicken North. Dozens of feverish Germans and a few Russians squeezed together in the waiting room. Hours went by, but no one called us in.

Finally, just as we expected to be told to return the next day, Oma and I were given cursory examinations, first by a German nurse and then by a sharply-dressed Russian military doctor, who spoke excellent German. The doctor nodded at the nurse and then, with a look of concern, he spoke to Mutti.

"I'm sorry to give you the bad news. Both your mother and your son have typhus. They'll need to be under quarantine in the hospital for a few weeks."

Typhus! The word alone was enough to frighten away the Russian soldiers at night, but at that point I was beyond caring. All I wanted to do was lie down and rest. I was startled when Mutti began to cry.

"If I don't come visit you in the hospital," she said, her voice strained, "it's not because I don't care. The doctors won't let anyone in to keep the sickness from spreading. You'll be a brave boy, now won't you?"

Stunned by the frightening news I reached out for Mutti, but she left without giving me a hug. My heart sank as I watched her walk quickly away. At the exit door, she turned to wave at us and then she was gone. I broke down in tears and did not even notice Oma being taken away from me.

Adult patients, asleep or perhaps already dead, lay in wooden bunk beds lining the hallways and in the rooms on either side. My assigned cot was in a large isolation ward with many other children. Three times a day we were each given tiny portions of watery "flour" soup, dry bread, and a glass of water or herb tea. Nurses were seldom around. Even if one of them showed up, it was useless to ask for something to drink. They were too busy. I was thirsty most of the time. The worst torture was to listen to the other children as they called out for water. Some spoke up with loud voices, others were barely audible.

Getting a bed pan was just as difficult. Many of the children lay in soiled bed sheets. Although the windows were open, the stench was horrible.

The endless nights in the ward terrified me. I would sometimes be awakened by the groans of the other children and of the adults in the hallway outside our door. It took me at least a week to accept the idea that neither Mutti nor Opa would come to visit me. A nurse provided some comfort by reporting, "Your Oma is still sick, but it looks as though she'll pull through."

After a few days, I was convinced no one cared about me, not even Mutti. As my fever rose, my thoughts became desperate. I began to worry whether Mutti, Hubert, and Opa had also become patients in the hospital or whether they might have already died.

Delirious though I was, I was keenly aware of the nurses wheeling out several corpses every day. The stretchers they used made a strange squeaking noise because the rubber wheels were out of air and flat. Two children in my ward died in a single night. Many others died during the next few weeks. I fully expected to be next. I felt so sick I was actually waiting for it.

By some miracle, I began to stay awake more often during the day and I started to feel better. My legs above my knees were thinner than my legs below my knees but, with the help of a nurse, I was even able to wobble to the bathroom.

The German nurse tried to cheer me up. "You must come from tough stock," she said. "Your Grandmother is also doing better. You'll both be sent home soon."

With great difficulty I stood up straight. "Well, as Mutti always says," I replied proudly, my voice scarcely above a whisper, "East Prussian blood isn't made of buttermilk."

* * *

Opa and Mutti came to the hospital to pick us up, their eyes glistening with tears when they saw us. I took a few wobbly steps towards them.

"You're a sight for sore eyes," Mutti said to me. "Opa's brought the handcart to bring you home, first Oma and then you."

"I never thought we'd leave this place alive," Oma said.

Oma and I had spent nearly four weeks in the hospital. She was incredibly skinny, her face strangely twisted by sorrow and suffering. When I glanced into a mirror in the lobby, a skeleton covered with skin stared back. I grimaced and the strange boy in the mirror did the same.

"What on earth are you doing?" Mutti asked.

"Just making sure it's really me."

Oma got up from a wheelchair and walked unsteadily towards Opa. If he had not grabbed her at the last moment she would have fallen down. Without saying a word, they hugged one another. I had never seen them embrace before. It was totally unexpected. I felt compelled to look away.

Mutti and I sat on a brick wall near the hospital, waiting for Opa to return. Mutti looked worried.

Always fearful of what the Russian soldiers might do, I asked her, "Did the Russians break in our door while Oma and I were stuck in the hospital?"

"Yes," Mutti sighed. "They came four times but, thank God, the typhus trick worked each time. Whenever they come I think it might be our last hour."

"Four times? I'm sorry I wasn't there to protect you, but I'm glad Opa and Hubert were there. At least the worst didn't happen."

Mutti gave me a strange look. At first I thought she was going to cry, but then she smiled and stroked my hair. "Don't you worry about me," she said, her voice scarcely more than a whisper. "I can take care of myself."

"But, Mutti, you still look worried. What's the matter? Aren't you glad to see us?" I asked.

"Don't be silly. Of course I am. I was just thinking about what the doctor said. That the only way you'll get better is by gaining some weight."

We both knew this was easier said than done. Our diet consisted of thin cabbage and potato peel soup with bread, occasionally supplemented by food scraps scrounged from the garbage.

Our neighbors were quick to pitch in. One friendly lady, who had taken care of Hubert while Oma and I had been in the hospital, gave Mutti a huge bottle of cod liver oil. An elderly German fisherman bartered away six cod livers and half a bucket of smelts in exchange for two pairs of dusty trousers from our attic. Mutti boiled the tiny fish in saltwater and we ate them, head, tail, and all; nothing was thrown away.

* * *

Germans and Russians continued to die of typhus in great numbers, but somehow Oma and I recovered, thanks mainly to the old fisherman. Over the next few weeks he always managed to save a few extra fish from his pail for us. When I was strong enough, he invited Mutti and me out in his tiny rowboat. As we headed out to sea, I studied the man who had saved my life. His face, lower arms, and hands were weathered by wind and sun, his hair snow white. His eyes were as blue as the water on a sunny day. Although he looked older than Opa, he rowed with enormous strength.

When I gazed down at the water, trying to see the fish, he laughed. "We'll be over my favorite spot in a few minutes," he explained, "and then I'll show you how to catch some dinner."

Shielding my eyes from the glare of the sun with my left hand, I saw how he adjusted the oars to cut across the small waves. "The water looks all the same," I said. "How can you tell where to stop?"

"If you'd been fishing these waters as long as I have," he replied, "you'd know, too." After a pause, he added, "When we get there, we'll have to be very quiet or we'll scare away the fish."

When we were quite a distance from the shore, he stopped rowing and the boat rocked gently to and fro. The fisherman worked in silence, using a fishing rod and a large, fine-meshed net that he pulled behind the boat. As we drifted, we heard nothing but the wind and the waves.

I loved having Mutti all to myself. I leaned against her and she put her arm around me. War, fear, even hunger seemed to be so far away. I wished our boat ride would go on forever.

The fisherman caught eight large fish and also three or four buckets full of tiny ones. He gave Mutti and me a small bucket full of the tiny fish to bring home. That night we feasted on fish and boiled potatoes cooked in their jackets.

* * *

One day, out of the blue, the Russians took over the fishing boats and our supply of fresh fish came to an abrupt halt. Mutti was angry when she heard the news.

"What on earth are we going to do now?" she asked. "It wasn't much, but we needed every bit of it."

Opa replied, as I knew he would, "The Lord will provide."

From then on, four or five times a week, three motorized fishing boats, each with a crew of three German fishermen, went out onto the Baltic Sea. On board each boat was a Russian soldier armed with a fish can submachine gun. The fish they brought back were loaded onto a horse drawn wagon driven by a Russian soldier who carted away the catch to the Russian garrison.

"Why is there a soldier on each boat?" I asked Oma one Sunday morning as she, Hubert and I stood watching the return of the small fishing fleet.

"I guess they need all the fish for the soldiers," Oma replied. "And they want to be sure none of the German fishermen try to escape."

"Where would they go?" I asked, looking out at the great expanse of the sea.

"They're not going anywhere," she said, "so it really doesn't matter."

Half a dozen older German boys were helping the fishermen pluck the fish from the nets as they were hauled in. I watched one boy let several fish slip out of his hand, one by one. Without looking down he pressed the silvery creatures into the sand, burying them with his foot. Oma glanced over at me.

"Did you see what that rascal did? He'd better watch out. The Russians deal harshly with anyone who steals."

"I'd do the same thing, given the chance," I said. "Wouldn't you?"

* * *

Mutti continued to report every morning to the Kommandantura where, before dawn, Russian soldiers placed German workers in various jobs. Mutti had cleaned houses, washed, ironed, and cooked for Russian officers for many weeks. A number of times she had also been sent with a group of other German women to help pick weeds and to bring in the rye crop at some big farm. The other women were mostly city dwellers from Königsberg who did not know how to tie a sheaf of rye with straw. Mutti enjoyed teaching them.

One morning at the end of August a Russian officer at the Kommandantura ordered Mutti and a woman named Mrs. Koch to take care of the recently established "Soviet" cemetery in Germau.

"We have to report there first thing in the morning," Mutti told Oma over supper.

"Just the two of you? That's all? How can two women manage there all alone?"

"We'll see what happens. You never know with the Russians. Perhaps they'll send dozens of women," Mutti replied.

Opa sat listless in his chair, his eyes sunken and dull. I had not thought he was paying attention when he suddenly spoke up. "Did he really call it a Soviet cemetery? The men who brought the bodies there from the beach always call it the 'Jewish' cemetery. Why can't they just call it what it really is?"

* * *

That evening when Mutti came back she sank down on the couch next to Opa. Hubert climbed up onto her lap.

"You'd think, after so much effort was put into digging up those poor murdered souls, that they'd finally get a proper resting place. But they're hardly better off than when they were lying under the sand."

Opa sighed deeply. "And I suppose there was nobody else there but the two of you?" Mutti just nodded and clung tighter to Hubert.

As she was tucking me in for bed a few days later, Mutti asked, "Why don't you join us tomorrow at the cemetery? It's a bit of a walk, but you can manage."

"Okay," I replied, curious to find out what the place was really like.

* * *

The weather the next morning was beautiful and we got an early start. Mutti wore a black scarf over her hair.

"Isn't it a bit warm for that thing?" I asked. "You look like Oma."

"I try to look old and ugly until I reach the cemetery. I don't want to attract any attention."

"How far did you say it was?"

"About six kilometers. It's a tree-lined road for the most part, so it's not too hot in the sun. Can you walk that far?"

"Sure. I'll be fine."

We passed through the tiny village of Sorgenau. Near the railroad crossing two small, hungry-eyed children clung to the hands of a ragged woman. They silently watched us go by. Farther on, where a forest edged close to the road, three burned out army trucks stood near the ditch to our left. The trucks were so rusty, I could not tell whether at one time they had been decorated with the black and white German cross or the Russian red star. Long after we passed the trucks, Mutti issued a warning.

"In just a minute you'll need to cover your nose and mouth with your handkerchief."

"Why? What is it?"

By then I had already gotten my first whiff of a terrible stench. A few meters farther on, the nearly decomposed body of a horse lay in some bushes at the side of the road. The sickening, pungent smell was almost unbearable and we quickened our steps to escape from it.

"There's at least one good thing about that horse," Mutti said when we were at a safe distance. "It means we're nearly there."

Gunter Nitsch

A short while later we arrived at the cemetery. I was not prepared for what I saw. The cemetery was at the end of a dirt road in the middle of nowhere.

"This is it? Where's Germau?"

"We've never dared go into the village. What if the Russians checked up on us and we weren't here?"

I had imagined it would be like the huge German soldiers' cemetries in the illustrated magazines back home in Langendorf, the ones with identical crosses lined up like rows of dominoes, but the Germau cemetery was small, surrounded by a big wooden fence with high fence posts. On top of each post and marking each of the mass graves were five-pointed stars, each cut out of weather-beaten boards like the ones on Opa's barn. Mutti called them "Soviet stars." They had been painted red at one time, but the paint had mostly faded away.

Wooden markers tipped to the left and to the right. No one had tried to line them up. Weeds choked the clusters of asters planted at the head of each grave. Only the light blue forget-me-nots brightened the scene. Mutti and Mrs. Koch took rakes, hoes, and watering cans out of a small shed and set to work, pulling out the weeds and watering the flowers.

For a while I poked around among the graves before settling down on a wooden crate to watch them work, but Mutti had other ideas.

"I don't want you to get bored. Why don't you help us with a little weeding?"

"Sure, why not?"

"You can start with that grave over there. Pull out all the weeds and heap them up next to the grave. We'll pick up the piles later."

I set right to work. Soon sweat rolled down my forehead onto my neck.

"Which one should I start on next?" I asked Mutti after a while. I waited for her to admire my efforts.

"You need to pull out the forget-me-nots, too," she said, "but otherwise you did a great job."

102

"But Mutti, I left them on purpose. They're too pretty to be weeds."

"Sorry, but only the asters stay. Why don't you look at the other graves to see what Mrs. Koch and I did?"

Forget-me-nots are just as pretty as asters, I muttered to myself, reluctantly yanking them out by the roots. How do grown-ups decide which are weeds and which are flowers?

* * *

Every so often, I stopped working to admire Mutti. She was slim and not especially tall. Her blue eyes sparkled; her mouth was quick to smile. Even though she pulled her light brown hair into an old-fashioned bun, she was still pretty.

Mrs. Koch was taller than Mutti. She had blond hair. Her husband had been one of the directors in a company in Königsberg which made railroad cars. She had confided to Mutti that she had always had servants and was not accustomed to working with her hands. Most of the work was done in silence, but occasionally Mrs. Koch would talk to Mutti about me. She always referred to me as "our young man" which I found strange since I was only seven.

Around noon the heat became nearly unbearable. There were no shade trees. For lunch Mutti brought some bread and water and Mrs. Koch brought along two or three boiled potatoes, an apple, and water. Mrs. Koch and Mutti chatted during lunch.

"A friend of mine works as a nurse in the Palmnicken North hospital. A few weeks ago almost a dozen patients were dying every day," Mrs. Koch remarked. "She's terrified she'll catch typhus from a patient."

"I can understand how she feels. Günter and my mother spent several weeks in the hospital earlier this summer. They were among the lucky ones. I've heard that nearly half the Germans in Palmnicken have already died of it."

A chill ran down my spine as I looked around at the graves and realized how close I'd come to becoming one of the dead.

Still hungry after lunch, when Mutti and Mrs. Koch returned to work, I went looking for something else to eat. I wandered off quite a distance before discovering a clump of blackberry bushes. After eating my fill of the sweet, juicy berries, I found a giant green leaf. Using the leaf as a pouch, I brought back four handfuls of berries for Mutti and Mrs. Koch.

"Look what I found for you," I said to them.

"Why, thank you," Mrs. Koch teased me. "That's a fine dessert to top off our delicious meal."

Time moved slowly in the afternoon. I helped with the weeding, but after a while I got bored with the work. Squatting down, I observed how hard ants had to struggle to get ahead in the weeds and the flowers. Life wasn't easy, even for them. In the evening, when we walked back to the house in Palmnicken, the walk seemed much longer than it had in the morning.

* * *

One afternoon, after we had been going to the cemetery every day for about a week, a truck arrived. A grouchy Russian sergeant and a private unloaded paint brushes and dozens of containers of red paint. The sergeant explained to Mutti and to Mrs. Koch in pidgin German that they should repaint the red wooden stars. He showed them how to do it.

Mutti pointed to the weeds and made a pulling gesture, but the sergeant replied, half in Russian and half in German, "Ne nado, ne nado, nicht nötig" (not necessary) and then gestured again to the paint containers, to the brush in his hand, and to the wooden stars.

Mutti and Mrs. Koch started to paint. I watched for a while, then took up a brush and picked my own star to paint red. The sergeant smiled at me. He placed himself directly behind me and, while speaking softly in Russian, guided the paintbrush in my right hand in such a way that the bristles were nearly flat against the wood. This prevented the paint soaked bristles from springing back and flinging the paint in my face. Now that he had shown me how to paint, I threw myself into the work. I enjoyed painting the star and made sure I did not miss a spot.

As I painted, the sergeant pulled a neatly folded page from a Russian newspaper out of the right chest pocket of his army tunic. Skillfully he tore off a square piece and, stuffing the remainder of the newspaper back in his right pocket, he took crumbled bits of rotting straw out of his left chest pocket.

"Is he really going to smoke straw? It looks like chaff to me," I whispered to Mutti.

"Careful! I don't know how much German he understands. That stuff's called machorka. It's made from the leftover stems of the tobacco plant," she explained.

Using the paper and the machorka, he rolled himself a cigarette, sealing it with a lot of spit. He crimped the end of the cigarette to keep the straw from falling out, put it in his mouth and lit it at the bent end. The paper burned quickly. He sucked in the smoke as if it were honey coming through a straw.

By now the private had also started to roll himself a cigarette. Since it was a hot day without any noticeable wind, the foul-smelling smoke hovered over the graves. When the sergeant had leaned over me, his breath had smelled worse than onions. Now I understood why.

After the sergeant inspected the work done by Mutti and Mrs. Koch, he checked my star too and paid me a compliment. "Kharosho! Gutt, gutt!" Then he turned to Mutti and Mrs. Koch and said, "Palmnicken!" while making a steering gesture with his hands. We were going back on the truck! I had never ridden one before.

Mutti and Mrs. Koch quickly put the tools, the brushes, and the paint pots away in the little shed. Minutes later the sergeant and the private got into the driver's cabin. I climbed up with Mutti and Mrs.

Koch onto the back of the truck and off we went, all of us holding on for dear life. We flew down the road, faster than the fastest horse in Langendorf. Mutti grabbed her scarf with her left hand to keep it from blowing away. I wished we would never stop!

"Isn't this great?" I yelled at Mutti, but she only nodded in reply.

Soldiers in another open army truck coming from the direction of Palmnicken waved at us as they passed by. I waved back, but Mutti and Mrs. Koch did not. Moments after leaving the cemetery we passed the burned out trucks on our right. I never noticed the smell of the dead horse. When we zoomed through Sorgenau, our truck whirled up so much dust I could barely see the houses.

I was disappointed to reach Palmnicken so soon. The evenly spaced trees on Linden Boulevard whizzed by as we came into town. We pulled up in front of the Kommandantura, a two story red brick building set back from the street, a big red star painted on the wooden archway. Whenever I had walked past there, the star had loomed over me, but now, as I stood on the big truck, it looked a lot less threatening. A huge red hammer and sickle flag hung limp from the flagpole attached to the second floor wall. The truck stopped and as we all jumped down, I suddenly felt the sticky heat of the evening.

"I wish we could travel like that every day. Wasn't it fantastic?" I said to Mutti as we walked home.

"Don't count on it," Mutti replied cheerfully.

The next morning as we walked to Germau, I realized, for the first time, that my feet hurt.

* * *

The routine became boring. Day after day we set out at dawn, walking through Sorgenau, past the burned out trucks and the decomposing horse and then on to the cemetery. After lunch I wandered off in search of blackberries to help fill my empty stomach. There were fewer and fewer to be found; the blackberry season was over.

In the evening we walked back, past the horse, the burned out trucks, through Sorgenau, and then back to Palmnicken. Sometimes when we were at the cemetery, I wished I were back in town where I could have played with the other children on one of the German army search lights. I did not dare complain to Mutti.

It was lonely at the cemetery. In all that time, the only noises were the sounds of the rakes, the flapping wings of birds, and the chirping of insects. Except for the two soldiers at the end of the first week, no Russian official ever visited the cemetery, nor did any person ever come to check our work or even to see whether we did any work at all. No other Germans came either, not even just to say "hello." It was a truly spooky place. I never asked, but I sensed that Mutti and Mrs. Koch felt I could protect them in case Russian soldiers had come. If they only knew how scared I was, just being alone there with them.

Sometimes, during the long walk home to Palmnicken, I thought how terrible it must be to be at the cemetery during the night. My old school friend Horst in Langendorf had once been told by his grandmother that, after midnight, especially during a full moon, the earth opens up and the dead float around in long flowing gauze robes, screaming in pain and howling for a few hours before returning to their graves.

I thought about the hundreds of corpses from the beach who would spook around the cemetery during the full moon after midnight, especially the one Opa had described whose canteen had been riddled with seventeen bullet holes. Imagining her leading all the others in a giant parade in the moonlight, I broke out in a cold sweat. I was glad we always left the cemetery while there was still daylight.

At the end of September, two months before my eighth birthday, two other German women went to work at the cemetery. Mutti was assigned odd jobs by the Kommandantura and I once again was left to roam Palmnicken on my own.

CHAPTER 8

News about lost relatives spread among the refugees by word of mouth. For several months Mutti and Opa asked everyone at work about Aunt Liesbeth Reimann and her five children, but to no avail. One day Opa met an amber stonecutter, a Palmnicken native, who had relatives near Rauschen along the Baltic Sea.

"I think I know whom you mean," he told Opa. "A family by that name recently moved into Karlsberg."

The following Sunday the man took a three-hour walk to Rauschen to visit his relatives. He brought back a message for Opa. "It's them, all right," he confirmed early Monday morning. "I told them you'd find a way to bring them down here somehow."

Opa reported the news to Oma and Mutti as soon as he got home that evening.

"That's wonderful!" Mutti exclaimed. "At least we know they all survived." Opa nodded. A tear rolled down his cheek.

"What a strange way to act!" Oma scolded. "Your daughter and grandchildren are alive and you look like you'd seen a ghost."

"The amber cutter told me something else," Opa said.

"Are the Reimanns all right?" Mutti asked.

"Don't worry. It's not about them," Opa replied. "He told me that at the end of the last century the man who owned the amber factory put up the money to build the Lutheran Church in Palmnicken. The man's name was Moritz Becker."

"Was he related to Mr. Becker, the blacksmith in Langendorf?" I asked.

Opa shook his head. "No, I don't think so, Günter."

"He must have been a very religious man," Oma said.

Opa sighed. "Yes, indeed, I'm sure of that. May his soul rest in peace. But Moritz Becker wasn't a Lutheran. He was Jewish."

Oma's mouth opened wide in amazement. "Jewish?"

"Can you imagine Mr. Becker looking down on Palmnicken from heaven? What must he think about the slaughter of thousands of his fellow Jews by people who considered themselves Christians?" Opa took his Bible and a stool from the kitchen and walked toward the back door of the house. Without another word, Opa stepped outside and gently shut the door.

When I went out back a short while later, I saw Opa slumped over his Bible. He barely looked up as I went past him to play on my favorite searchlight in the military junkyard in the park.

* * *

Opa had a good rapport with the Russian administration at the amber factory and was somehow able to arrange for a truck to pick up Aunt Liesbeth and her five children. In late September of 1945, they arrived in Palmnicken. As Aunt Liesbeth and Mutti shared a long hug and cried tears of joy, I noticed how much the Reimanns had changed since we were last together.

Little Dieter, who was nearly two years old, and Helga, who was four, had always been pudgy. Now they were both as skinny as the rest of us. Dorchen, with her dimples, still looked as pretty as I remembered her, even though she had also lost a lot of weight. My twelve-year-old cousin, Ilse, had recently recovered from a five-week bout with typhus during which she had lost all of her hair. Despite the still mild weather, she wore a woolen cap to hide her baldness.

Only nine-year-old Gerda looked fairly strong. She had grown tall and lanky and still had beautiful dark brown hair. Perhaps because she was a bit of a tomboy, Gerda and I always got along. As soon as I saw her, I realized how lonely I had been for a friend my age. Most of the children I met in Palmnicken had other family members to go out with them when they looked for something to eat. With food so scarce, none of the children had much time for anything else. The only thought we all had was how to fill our bellies. It would be nice to have Gerda as a companion when I scrounged for food and firewood.

* * *

"Sorry I don't have any pickled herring for you this time," Aunt Liesbeth said to Oma as we all sat down together for supper.

The grown-ups and Ilse crowded around our wooden table and Aunt Liesbeth took baby Dieter on her lap. We children sat on wooden crates or on the floor.

"If you're hungry, my turnip soup tastes just as good," Oma replied as she ladled small portions into each bowl while Mutti passed around tiny pieces of bread.

Opa bowed his head. "Dear God. Thank you for your mercy in bringing us all back together. Amen."

"May I say grace?" Dorchen asked. She bowed her head and folded her hands in her lap. "Come, Lord Jesus, and be our guest and bless what Thou hast given us."

"Amen," we all said in unison.

After supper we sat for hours exchanging stories about what we had gone through during the last few months. Mutti brought the Reimanns up to date. Then it was their turn.

"We left Bieskobnicken the same morning you did, April 15, 1945, together with our maid, Emma," Aunt Liesbeth began. "We didn't dare look for you, but we did see Mr. Brenner, lying dead next to his barn, blood still oozing from a bullet hole in his head."

"The poor man. God rest his soul. What about his wife?" Oma asked.

"I have no idea what happened to her. We headed in the opposite direction to the one you took, towards Rauschen, trying to keep off the main roads as much as possible. It was tough going, through fields and forests, too much for my father-in-law. He died along the way."

"We left his body in a narrow wardrobe I found in an abandoned building," Ilse added with a shudder. "At least it kept the birds and rats off him for a while."

"Anyway," Aunt Liesbeth continued, "we finally found ourselves a room on the second floor of a big farmhouse near Karlsberg. Not long after we moved in, Ilse and I came down with typhus."

"Just like Oma and me!" I said.

Dorchen picked up the story at that point. "Without mother and Ilse, we were pretty much left to fend for ourselves. Gerda and I discovered a Russian military mess hall near our house. After the Russian soldiers finished eating, we sneaked inside to devour the leftovers and lick the plates. No matter how many times we were chased away, we kept on going back."

"Like pesky flies," Gerda added.

"Once I began to feel better, I went along with them," Ilse said. "At first I was so weak I had to bump slowly down the staircase on my bottom and crawl to the mess hall."

"I'm convinced those leftovers saved Ilse's life," Aunt Liesbeth added. "After a few weeks, when she and I were strong enough to move, we found a better place to live right in Karlsberg where we had a lot of German neighbors."

"That must have been a great comfort to you," said Opa.

111

"It should have been, but it wasn't. Karlsberg's a long, narrow village, difficult to police. Even though crime was forbidden, incidents happened now and then. Several times our own Emma had to defend herself against the Russian soldiers, but she insisted on staying with us until I was well enough to care for the children. Then one day she up and left. We haven't heard from her since."

"I'm sure she'll be all right," Oma said. "She always had a good head on her shoulders."

"Well now that there are eleven of us under one roof, there should be safety in numbers," Mutti said.

"Thanks be to God for bringing us back together," Opa added. "Where would we be without His protection?"

* * *

Soon after our reunion, Mutti took Aunt Liesbeth along to the Kommandantura in Palmnicken. Aunt Liesbeth was also assigned work by Russian officers and soldiers. A few times she and Mutti even worked on the same job. Since Ilse was still too weak to work for the Russians, she helped Oma take care of the younger children. Often, when Mutti and Aunt Liesbeth came home, they told us stories about their employers. Whenever the Russian officers for whom Mutti did housekeeping spoke German, she made a point of apologizing for the German invasion of Russia. The officers, in turn, would describe with sorrow the hardships suffered by the Russian people during the war.

"How come so many of the officers know German?" Oma asked. "I'm sure our German officers couldn't speak any Russian."

"I asked about that. It's because many of them are Jewish," Mutti explained. "Apparently a lot of Jewish people in Russia speak some German."

"It's not German like we speak," Aunt Liesbeth added. "More like a dialect."

"But some Jewish people speak German just like us," Mutti protested. "Remember my girlfriend in middle school, Rosa Safran? Her parents used to own a clothing store in Schippenbeil. They didn't sound any different."

"It's probably Yiddish," Oma said. "When I was a young woman, Jewish horse traders and cattle dealers from Russia used to come to visit my father's farm. They spoke Yiddish, but we all managed to understand one another."

* * *

Sometimes Mutti would come home from work giggling, ready to share a funny story about her employer. We were puzzled, for example, about a Russian "Kapitan" who occasionally gave Mutti leftovers to take home. Mutti noticed strange imprints across the top of the butter on a plate in his pantry.

"I've solved the mystery," Mutti declared one evening. "I watched him eat his breakfast. First he ripped thick chunks of bread from a big loaf. After each mouthful of dry bread, he ate the butter with his fork." With a twinkle in her eye, Mutti gave us a stern warning. "Should we ever have butter in the house again, I will not permit any 'Russian table manners.' " Times were hard, but we still had a good laugh at the Kapitan's expense.

Aunt Liesbeth also shared a few stories with us. "I've heard about Russian soldiers who fell from their bicycles when they tried to ride them for the first time. Another woman knew a Russian who washed potatoes in the toilet bowl. He became enraged when he pulled at the chain and they flushed away..."

Mutti laughed and cut her off, "Oh come on, Liesbeth. Stop it. I've heard similar tales, but I don't believe them for one minute."

"What Opa used to call propaganda?" I asked.

"I'm sure it is," said Mutti.

Gunter Nitsch

* * *

When Mutti and Aunt Liesbeth cleaned the houses of Russian officers or did their cooking, they were usually paid with potatoes or turnips and a piece of bread. Once in a while, they were paid with leftovers. It all depended on the Russian officers they worked for. Opa had been working in the Palmnicken amber factory since late summer. He was also paid with bread or potatoes. The food they received was barely enough for the three of them, but it also had to be shared with Oma and seven children.

There were still two sacks of potatoes in our basement, but with eleven mouths to feed, they would not last long. There was never enough food to go around.

* * *

In November the weather became cold, although there was still no snow. In growing numbers Russian civilians were moving into Palmnicken and nearby villages. We were concerned that we would have to move again, but no one came from the Kommandantura to order us to leave. As I foraged for food around Palmnicken and nearby Kraxtepellen, I saw Russian women and children wearing gray or brown felt boots, and "ushankas," those wonderful head-warming Russian fur caps with ear flaps. I envied them for their ushankas. Despite wearing two old ragged woolen caps, one on top of the other, my head felt cold most of the time, especially when the wind blew in from the Baltic Sea.

* * *

Nearly a year had passed since we left Opa's farm in Langendorf and a harsh new winter was upon us. On many days the temperature slipped well below zero. Snow began to fall on December 4, 1945, the day after my eighth birthday. I was hungry most of the time. Even so, I

114

somehow managed to stay healthy. Perhaps because they were so much smaller than I was, Hubert and my younger cousins suffered more from the lack of food. Often all of them got sick at the same time. First they would develop bad colds, and then the glands would swell up in their necks. The only doctors in Palmnicken were at the typhus hospital, so whenever the younger children took sick, Oma treated them with her "old home recipe."

First she selected three, four, or five potatoes, depending on their size. Next, she boiled the potatoes in their skins. Taking the potatoes out of the boiling water, she put them into a little cloth bag. If Hubert were to be treated first, Oma held him tightly on her lap as she pressed the cloth bag filled with the boiling hot potatoes against his swollen glands for as long as possible. Especially during the first few minutes of this procedure, Hubert would howl with pain while trying his utmost to escape, but Oma was merciless as she clutched the squirming Hubert tightly in her lap. Watching how skillfully she managed this maneuver, I was reminded of the times back home in Langendorf when she had held a big fat goose and forced food down its gullet.

Eventually the potatoes cooled a bit and Hubert stopped struggling. His screams died down and he began to moan quietly. While all this was going on, Oma's other young patients watched the process with dread, knowing their turns were still to come just as soon as the linen bag of potatoes had once again been brought to a boil.

After the last laying on of the potato bag, Oma reheated it before pouring out the mushy potatoes. Then she offered them as a treat to the younger children. Even though they must have been hungry, Hubert and the others, still angry at Oma, usually refused to eat them. I always hoped the younger children would refuse the potatoes, because then Oma offered them to Gerda and me. She and I gulped down those soggy potatoes before anyone could change his mind.

In Oma's defense, her recipe always worked. After applying the boiling potatoes every eight hours for two to four days, the glands were no longer swollen.

* * *

From the Palmnicken natives, we learned a little of the history of the amber factory. Up until fifty years before the war, amber had been mined underground in the Anna Pit. After that, it was collected by open strip mining. In 1944, shortages in electricity forced the strip mining operation to shut down. Water flooded the giant open pit. All that was left at the factory was a large stock of raw amber, collected before the end of the war. Skilled workers sorted these pieces by size and quality. Craftsmen turned the assorted raw amber into jewelry, pendants, necklaces, cigarette holders, and buttons.

As day watchman in the amber factory, Opa was sometimes given a few discarded buttons, pendants, and cigarette holders to bring home for my cousins and me to use as toys. The amber was the color of dark, clear apple cider. Even though the pieces all had little chips or rough edges, I was amazed that such beautiful things could be made from the same material I had picked up along the beach the previous summer.

One day Opa gave me a cigarette holder that I liked better than all of the other pieces of amber he had given to me. It had an unusual color, like cream in bright yellow honey. I examined it carefully, but could not find a single flaw. When I sucked on it, I pretended I was all grown up.

Sometimes Ilse would bring home a few potatoes or a piece of bread which she had bartered for a table cloth or a vase left behind by the former owners of our house. When Ilse went out bartering, she always brought her younger sister Gerda along for protection.

I decided to try bartering some of my amber pieces the same way. Nervously approaching the houses of Russian soldiers, I knocked on the door. When someone answered, I held up a flawed amber cigarette holder and said, "Chleb pashalusta" (bread please). Many times I was rewarded with a chunk of bread to bring home. No matter how cold the weather was, nor how hungry I felt, I refused to part with my favorite amber cigarette holder. I treasured it for many weeks and expected a lot of bread for it one day.

* * *

One bitter cold day in the middle of December I set out again to beg for food. For days the only thing I had eaten was thin soup made from turnips or potatoes. The wind howled as I knocked on the doors of three or four houses where Russian officers lived.

Some were not at home or else they did not open the door. A few officers came to the door, shook their heads and said, "Njet" (no). Still others slammed the door in my face or shooed me away like a stray dog. None of them gave me any bread.

The sun was going down when I made up my mind that the moment for my very best amber cigarette holder had come. I chose a large fancy house with a front yard. Frozen snow crunched under my feet as I walked along the path and up the wide stone steps to reach the front door. As I rapped the solid brass door knocker, I wondered what had become of the German family who had lived there before the end of the war.

My thoughts were interrupted by the sound of heavy military boots inside the house. The door flew open and before me stood a huge man with closely cropped blond hair, wearing nothing but military breeches and shiny boots. Below his hairy chest, his big belly hung down over his belt. His chubby face was beet red and he had a glazed look in his bulging blue eyes. The lower part of his face was lathered with shaving soap and in his hand he held a gleaming shaving knife.

From somewhere behind him I got a whiff of fish frying in the kitchen and my mouth got all watery. Even though I was terrified, I showed him my last treasure. I looked up at him with pleading eyes and stammered, "Chleb pashalusta."

Still holding the shiny silver razor, he gestured to me to come inside through the long tiled vestibule. He flashed a nasty grin revealing misshapen metal teeth and blackened gums. His eyes were bloodshot and he reeked of schnapps. With some hesitation, I followed him into a large gloomy carpeted living room. Putting down his razor, he took my cigarette holder and disappeared into the kitchen. When he came back, he offered me a slice of bread so thin it was nearly transparent.

I could not believe how little bread he was giving me. For my other less perfect amber cigarette holders, Russian officers had given me at least half a loaf of bread. A pretty female officer with long black hair once gave me a whole loaf for a small, badly flawed amber pendant.

Although hunger was gnawing at my stomach and I was close to tears, I looked at him and said softly, "Njet" as I reached up to take back my treasure. Above the white shaving lather his red face turned deep purple. Thrusting his jaw forward, he shrieked at me in Russian. With force he threw my precious amber cigarette holder to the tiled floor where it cracked into a thousand pieces.

I slowly backed away from him into the vestibule, my shoes crunching on the amber fragments. As he came after me, I sprang towards the open door, but I was too late. Using his heavy army boot, he kicked me so hard in the seat of my pants that I flew out over the stone steps onto the front walk. The door closed behind me with a loud bang.

Unable to get up, I dragged myself through the snow to a bush to hide. "Dear God," I prayed, "don't let him put on a shirt and follow me."

Not a single person was on the street, not a soul to help me. I had heard about people who died when they fell asleep in the snow. The fear of dying made me struggle to my feet. With tears running down my cheeks, I slowly limped back home.

When Oma let me in, I was sobbing so hard my story came out in little bits and pieces. "He kicked me!" I gasped. "My amber's smashed! My best amber cigarette holder!"

"Lower your pants," Oma ordered. "Let me check you over."

As Oma examined me, I twisted around, trying unsuccessfully to see my bottom.

"Since you managed to get home on your own, I don't think anything's broken," she finally said. "But you're going to be black and blue for a long, long time."

Hitching my pants back up, I washed my hands in a bowl of water next to the sink and limped over to the kitchen table. Oma set a bowl of turnip soup in front of me, saying, "Warm yourself up, but then I want you to go to bed."

Mutti and Opa heard my story an hour later on their return from work. Mutti gave me a big hug and gently stroked my face.

Later as Mutti leaned down to wish me a good night, I could see that she had been crying. "Maybe one day we'll get out of here," she whispered as she smoothed out my covers.

"How?"

"Well, there are rumors that the Russians will send all of us back to Germany."

"Do you think it'll really happen?"

"We just have to be patient a while longer. Good night!"

"Good night!"

* * *

As winter wore on, Mutti no longer received as much food for her work. Our potato supply dwindled away. Oma cooked watery soup made from six or seven potatoes for the eleven of us.

"We should count our blessings," Opa said. "Some Germans in Palmnicken have died from hunger and cold. I've heard that in some villages entire families have starved to death. We are fortunate we still have food on our table."

Before Christmas Opa was given notice at the amber factory. Without his daily ration of bread, we would have even less to eat and no amber to barter. However, there was a silver lining. When Gerda had other chores to do, Opa had time to go with me to collect wood for our furnace. If it wasn't too windy, he and I would go to a pine and fir forest near the Baltic Sea, between Palmnicken and Sorgenau. Collecting suitable wood was slow work. We picked up only the dried branches, twigs, and pinecones from the ground, since green branches cut from the trees did not burn.

If the icy wind coming off the water stung our faces, we avoided the forest, trying our luck instead in the abandoned buildings of Palmnicken and Kraxtepellen. Wood buried under bricks and plaster was hard to dig out and others, Germans as well as some Russians, had already scrounged for fuel ahead of us. Still, Opa and I were often able to find charred beams, a few wooden boards, and old pieces of furniture. Opa no longer had the strength to do all of this work by himself.

"Remember how I said you'd have to be ten before I'd let you chop wood?" he asked me one day.

"I've still got two years to go."

"Well, I've been thinking maybe I was wrong about that. Maybe the time to teach you is now."

Behind our house Opa had put up a chopping block and a sawhorse. One cold day he gave me my first lesson in sawing. We placed a log on the sawhorse. Opa pulled the two-man saw to one side and showed me how to pull it back the other way. Before long, the saw got stuck because I had pushed rather than pulled. Opa patiently reminded me, "Pull. Don't push. Pull. Don't push. Easy does it."

Quickly I got the hang of it. The saw glided back and forth until it began to disappear inside the wood. Finally a wooden block fell down with a big satisfying thump. Once we had sawed a number of wooden blocks, Opa started to chop one of them. As he worked, he explained to me what he was doing:

"To start with, it's important to stand the wood absolutely straight on the chopping block. Then, holding tight to the axe, place yourself directly in front of the wood with your feet spread apart a little, like this." Raising the axe over his head, Opa quickly brought it back down, cleanly splitting the wood. "Now you try it."

Opa set aside a quarter block for me to practice on. I stood it on end, just as Opa had done with the full block, and quickly whacked it apart. Once I had practiced on five smaller pieces, Opa let me chop a half-size block. Swinging the axe with enthusiasm, I was enjoying myself.

"Easy, my boy," Opa said. "It's not a race."

"Let me try a whole block, Opa. Please." Opa set the heavy block on end, but my axe barely made a dent in it.

"With practice, you'll build up those muscles of yours," Opa assured me.

* * *

As Christmas approached, I tried my best not to think about the rich feast we had enjoyed the previous year, but I couldn't help thinking about food. The other children and I did not dare to dream of presents. We all just hoped one day to have enough soup and bread to fill our stomachs. I remembered all the sandwiches with butter, ham, liver sausage, and cheese Mutti had packed into my school lunches in Langendorf. Regretting having thrown them into the hazelnut and elderberry bushes, I imagined what a hero I would be if I could magically retrieve them to serve at our Christmas dinner.

Christmas Eve 1945 arrived. While Opa read us the Nativity story from the Bible, Dieter, who had just had his second birthday, was given the place of honor on Opa's lap. As we sang Christmas carols, Dieter squirmed away from Opa and ran back to Aunt Liesbeth. I couldn't imagine why any child would turn down a chance to sit with Opa. If

I hadn't just turned eight, I would have been tempted to take his place, but I had my pride.

Mutti and Oma had been working hard to prepare a special Christmas dinner. For nearly two weeks we had not had any salt. Shortly before Christmas Mutti had been able to "organize" a bag of salt from one of the Russian houses where she worked. (We all said "organize" instead of "steal.") At supper we savored the taste of the salt in our thin turnip soup. Oma used salty water to "fry" a large frozen clump of potato peels rescued from the waste container of a Russian-occupied house, but she had an even better treat in store for us. Two or three times during the past two weeks, Gerda and I had gotten a whiff of toasted bread when we had come home. "I gave it all to the younger children," Oma had told us. "There's none left for you."

Now Oma proudly poked in the back of a cupboard and pulled out nearly two dozen slices of stone hard bread for us. If a magician had pulled a rabbit from a hat, I wouldn't have been any more surprised.

"I've been stashing away a few pieces now and then," she confessed, "and roasting them on the stove so they'd keep 'til Christmas Eve."

After dinner, we drank a strangely delicious "coffee" made from toasted acorns into which we dunked our hard bread. Dorchen recited a Christmas poem and we all sang "Silent Night." Oma slipped out of the room and reappeared with a grayish pillowcase filled with something soft. Unraveling the yarn from a number of moth-eaten sweaters, she had knitted mittens for all seven of her grandchildren. The smallest children also received knitted caps. With patches of fabric taken from old clothes, she had also sewn caps for the older children. As we paraded around in our new caps and mittens, Oma beamed.

"It's a wonderful Christmas," Mutti said. Tears welled up in her eyes. "There's only one thing that would make it better."

"I know just what you're going to say," Aunt Liesbeth interrupted. "I've never missed my Alfred as much as right now. Do you suppose he and Willi are still alive? If we at least knew ..."

"Willi and Alfred? I'm sure they are." Oma said in her no-nonsense tone of voice.

I put my hand to my cheek, remembering the smack Vati had given me on the railroad platform in Königsberg the last time I had seen him. Life in Palmnicken was hard enough without him, I thought, hoping Mutti could not read my mind.

"Do you really think so?" Aunt Liesbeth asked Oma.

"I feel it in my bones. The real question is whether the two of them have any idea what happened to us."

"Let us pray," Opa said suddenly. As we knelt down on the wooden floor, I noticed how unsteady he had become. "Thank you, God, for bringing the eleven of us together to celebrate the birth of your son Jesus. Please give us strength in the coming year and reunite us one day with Willi and Alfred. Amen."

Dressed in our new Christmas finery, we sang "Silent Night" one more time before going to bed.

CHAPTER 9

More and more often, Opa refused to eat.

"Please, Father, just have a little taste," Mutti would coax.

Opa was stubborn. "I really have no appetite. Let the children share my portion. Can't you see the hunger in their eyes?"

Opa was right. Oma's watery soup left me hungry and I worried how much longer I would get even that. My bottom was still painfully black and blue. The memory of that heavy army boot in the seat of my pants had prevented me from begging for food. Yet, seeing how desperate our situation had become, I decided to try my luck one more time.

On a cold gray day at the end of January 1946, the threat of snow was again in the air as I headed for a row of fancy houses along the bluff overlooking the Baltic Sea. This time I had no amber; this time I could make no deals.

As I approached each house, I carefully checked my escape route in case I had to run away. To my relief, none of the Russian officers who came to the door looked threatening. Three of them even gave me bread. After a while, I began to let down my guard. Stuffing a piece of bread into my pocket to save for the other children and Oma, I went in search of one last house.

I knocked at the door of an old villa surrounded by big trees. A tall Russian officer in a greenish brown uniform opened the door. He was a bear of a man with curly dark hair, big white teeth, and dimples in his cheeks. He smiled at me and used gestures to invite me in, not giving me the time to stammer, "Chleb pashalusta." He knew what I wanted.

Leading me into the huge kitchen, he motioned me to sit down. An iron skillet was on the stove, the burner underneath, glowing warm. The aroma of leftover home fries with bacon and onions filled the room. A glass full of schnapps and a half empty Vodka bottle stood on the large kitchen table. As the officer moved from cupboard to cupboard in the pantry, I could hear him singing a cheerful Russian song in a deep voice. Even though he was tipsy, I felt safe.

It was warm and cozy in the kitchen. The slush from my shoes began to melt, creating little puddles on the clean floor. When the officer came back to the table where I was sitting, he saw my look of concern about the mess I was making. He waved his hand as if to say, "Don't worry about it."

To my amazement he plopped down a spoon and a white enamel chamber pot filled with thick bean soup, home fries, goulash, piroshki, kasha, and boiled cabbage on the table in front of me. For a split second I had a nauseating feeling in my throat when I thought about how the chamber pot would normally have been used. I was too hungry to worry so I just dug in, barely taking the time to chew.

The officer took the skillet from the stove, sat down opposite me, and began eating from the pan. He smiled at me and indicated with his hands that there was no need to hurry. While I stuffed myself, the officer chatted away in Russian. He sounded very friendly, but I didn't understand a word.

As the level of food went down, I discovered a yellow ring around the middle of the chamber pot. It's probably fat, I decided and I kept on eating. The officer added cold scrambled eggs, bacon, and boiled potatoes to fill up the pot.

After a while I could not eat any more. I thought I was going to burst. I grinned at the officer, held my stomach and said, "Kharosho" (good). He took the pot and filled it again to the brim with more kasha and chunks of sausage. Afraid I would have to leave behind the rest of the food, I pointed to the pot and then to the door.

The officer said "Njet," and gestured to let me know that I should wait. He disappeared for some time and for a moment I toyed with the idea of grabbing the pot and running home with it. When the officer returned he was carrying two thick, brand-new bath towels neatly folded. He placed a double layer of towels on the kitchen table and dumped the contents of the chamber pot on top, hitting the bottom three or four times with his fist to make sure all the food fell out. By knotting the towels in two places, he made a neat bundle and then handed the package to me.

Smiling, he also gave me a whole loaf of box type Russian army bread. I bowed as we reached the door and said, "Spassiba" (thank you). He patted me on the head, opened the door for me, waved and replied, "Da svidanye!" (good bye). As soon as I was outside, I heard him start to sing again.

My belly filled, I cried with joy as I walked home in the dark. Feeling warm in spite of the frosty evening wind, I noticed all of the stars in the sky. I could see my breath in the moonlight. When I got back to our house, I had just begun to tell my story when Mutti, Aunt Liesbeth, and Opa walked in and I had to start all over again. Everyone chuckled when they heard about the chamber pot.

"Do you suppose he used the pot for anything else?" I asked when the laughter had died down.

"I wouldn't worry about it," Mutti said reassuringly. "He probably has a second chamber pot for that. What I really worry about is how your stomach will be after all that rich food."

"I've never felt better!" I replied with a grin.

As everyone gathered around to watch, Oma unwrapped the parcel, her eyes darting over the contents, measuring how best to use them. That night Oma used one-third of the leftovers to make a delicious soup for everyone but me.

"You've had more than enough already," she said. For once I agreed with her. There was no way I could have eaten another bite that day.

When we were seated around the table, Opa clasped his hands and bowed his head. With his eyes closed, he was silent for a moment before speaking.

"May the Lord protect our Russian benefactor," he prayed. "I wish him a long life and God's blessings."

My chest swelled with pride as everyone else started to eat.

Dorchen tried a spoon full. "This is the best soup since we've left home," she announced.

Tears of joy trickled down Aunt Liesbeth's cheeks and landed in her soup.

That night I slept better than I had in a long time.

Oma stored the rest of the food in a big bowl on the windowsill of her bedroom. During the week she cooked two more big pots full of wonderful soup from the leftovers.

Two weeks later, full of hope, I went back to the same house, but the generous officer had moved away. The new tenants, several young officers, were also kind and gave me a chunk of bread. After that, whenever I went begging for food, I daydreamed about having another big delicious meal in a chamber pot, but I never again met anyone like that friendly Russian officer in Palmnicken.

* * *

Somehow, as if by a miracle, "and with God's help" as Opa put it, we all survived the winter. Late in March of 1946, notices were posted on the bulletin boards near the Kommandantura and at the former Schloss-Hotel. All Germans who were not natives of Palmnicken were ordered to report to the Kommandantura on April first. The notice stated that Germans were needed to work at a large Kolkhoz (a state-run farm) in the village of Goldbach.

"We can take along whatever we can carry," Opa informed us. Oma became distraught.

"Shame on the Russians!" she complained bitterly. "In Goldbach we'll have to start all over again. They do with us whatever they please."

Oma was right, but there was nothing we could do about it. That was just the way it was.

Only two days later, early in the morning, we left the house which had been our home since the previous summer and headed for the Kommandantura to wait for the trucks to arrive. With the exception of two-year-old Dieter, who was Ilse's "carry on luggage," all of us had at least one cardboard box or a bundle. I lugged three cooking pots and a frying pan tied together with thin rope. The sun was shining and it was warm for that time of the year. Before long we all started to sweat heavily because we were wearing pretty much everything we owned, in three or four layers. To my surprise, Opa complained of being cold. Just two months from his sixty-eighth birthday, he was no longer the man I remembered from Langendorf. His brisk step was replaced by a slow shuffle, his muscular frame by mere skin and bones. He had shriveled up like a stalk after harvest. When we arrived at the departure point, he sat down on an empty oil drum to rest.

"Look over here, Opa," I said, trying to cheer him up. "The walls are full of bullet holes and most of the lettering's gone from the sign. Can you make out what kind of business it used to be?" But he was gazing into the distance and did not reply.

Around noon, five open Red Army trucks arrived. We were told to share a truck with two other German families. The older children hopped on first, full of excitement about the upcoming trip. For the old folks, climbing on board was next to impossible.

Leaving their submachine guns in the truck cabin, two strapping Russian soldiers in their early twenties hurried to our assistance. Effortlessly lifting up Oma, Opa, and the other old folks onto the high truck, they then went back to hand up the little children to Mutti and Aunt Liesbeth, all the while laughing and chattering away in Russian. Finally everyone was on board. The older folks sat on their bundles and boxes. Not wanting to miss anything, Gerda and I decided to stand, but the trucks did not leave.

The younger soldier proudly wore his military cap with the red star tipped down over his left eye. He sat on the running board of the truck smoking a papirossa. Seeing how relaxed he was, I figured I had time to go to pee. I jumped down from the truck and went around behind the big building.

"Günter!" Mutti frantically called. "Hurry up! They'll leave without you!"

Before I climbed back on board, I lingered long enough to read the word "Ford" on the truck. It was written in our regular alphabet, not in the strange one the Russians used.

"Germanski?" I asked the Russian soldier.

"Amerikanski!" he replied with a broad grin.

Suddenly an officer in the lead truck shouted orders and our driver yelled, "Davai! Davai!" The tailgate was already closed, but the soldiers helped me up onto the truck and off we went. We left Palmnicken, quickly gaining speed. We were on the same road Mutti, Mrs. Koch, and I had taken all those weeks back and forth to the cemetery. We raced through Sorgenau. As the open truck sped forward, our many layers of clothes were no longer too warm. The burned out, rusty trucks were still on the left side of the road. All along the road we saw elderly women and small children using little handcarts to collect wood. I had a last fleeting glimpse of the Jewish cemetery in Germau.

We whizzed past villages whose names I had never heard before, Sacherau, Gaffken, Fischhausen, and Heydekrug. Many small villages were completely deserted. Sometimes charred chimney stumps were the only sign that a village had even existed. Fire-gutted tanks, rims without tires, tank treads, and artillery shells were strewn about. Nearby farms lay fallow. Artillery fire had shot the tops off many of the large trees.

After we had been traveling for about an hour, Mutti yelled something, but her voice was swallowed up by the noise of the diesel motor. Gerda pulled on my sleeve. "Königsberg! She's pointing in the direction of Königsberg!" she shouted.

Mutti came closer to us. "We just passed Juditten, otherwise I wouldn't have recognized the road. This must be the Lawsker Allee going directly into the city."

Except for Opa and Oma, nearly everyone was standing by now, clinging to the sideboards of the truck and to each other, their eyes filled with tears.

Although many of the fine houses set back from the wide, tree-lined boulevards were undamaged, the center of the city near the Nordbahnhof lay in ruins. As Mutti called out the names of the different streets, others vainly tried to identify the piles of rubble, all that was left of the once beautiful buildings. Shortly after passing the big pond where Vati had once rented a rowboat when he and Mutti were courting, we took one last look to our right where the old part of town had once been. The beautiful capital of East Prussia was no more.

Our truck rattled on, past Devau, once the site of the Königsberg airport, and then to Lapsau, where we made a brief rest stop. Everyone hopped down and rushed into the bushes. There was no privacy, but no one seemed to care.

Buds had formed on the willow trees at the edge of a small pond. Birds were chirping loudly. An old woman was leaning against our truck, talking to Mutti. "So, as I was saying, there was a trade. The commanding officer in Goldbach needs us to work on the Kolkhoz and the commanding officer in Palmnicken desperately needs vodka for his troops."

"We're being bartered for a few barrels of moonshine?"

"That's pretty much the size of it," the woman said and she shrugged her shoulders.

Oma shook her head. "I wouldn't put it past them. Imagine that!"

With shouts of "Davai! Davai!" the soldiers called us back on board and soon we were underway.

We passed through Tapiau, a small town with tree-lined streets bustling with Russian troops and military vehicles.

"Goldbach can't be more then ten kilometers from here, if I remember my geography," Mutti said.

Suddenly sunk in gloom, Aunt Liesbeth asked, "I wonder what's in store for us there?"

"Cheer up!" Mutti said. "Goldbach can't be any worse than Palmnicken. Why don't we cross that bridge when we come to it?"

CHAPTER 10

*U*nlike Palmnicken, where neglected villas were reminders of the prosperity the amber mine had once brought, Goldbach was a simple farm village along the road between Tapiau and Labiau. When the main road reached Goldbach, it bulged out and curved around, encircling the village like an egg. In the center of the egg a sloping meadow divided the village in half. We were no longer near the Baltic Sea; a brook in the meadow was the only visible body of water. A church standing on a small hill to our left, with its square stone tower, reminded me of a castle. I made up my mind to explore it as soon as I had the chance.

The trucks stopped in the middle of the village and the Russian soldiers jumped out.

"Davai! Davai!" a soldier yelled up at us. Everyone on our truck and on the truck behind ours was ordered to get off.

Roused from a sound sleep, Opa was sweating profusely. A stocky German woman came over to help him down from the truck.

"Thank you," Mutti said. "We're much obliged to you."

"Welcome to Goldbach," the woman replied. "I expect you'll be working with me at the Kolkhoz before long."

"What's it like?"

132

"You'll know soon enough." She began to count heads. "All these people belong to your group?"

"We're eleven all told."

"In that case," she said, consulting a sheaf of papers, "you'll need to walk back in the direction of Tapiau. At the edge of the village, you can have the second to last house on the right. It's a bit run down, but big enough. Good luck. I'll see you at the Kolkhoz."

The two empty trucks zoomed back towards Palmnicken. As we struggled along under the weight of our belongings, I watched them roar right past our new house. Still crammed with refugees, the other three trucks sped off in the opposite direction. Opa leaned against Mutti for support.

"They could've dropped us off at our house," Oma griped. "Anyone can see we could use some help."

"I'll be all right," Opa said with a weak wave of his hand. "It's not far."

* * *

The door to the house was ajar. Dirty footprints crisscrossed the rooms. Even so, at first glance the place didn't look too bad. Sun streamed in through broken windows. Crocuses had already forced their buds upward in the small garden. While Opa leaned against a wall for support, Aunt Liesbeth and Mutti rushed to make him a bed on an old dusty couch in a back bedroom.

"Let's try to keep the noise down," Mutti said when she returned to the living room. "He needs his rest."

"People have picked this place clean," Oma said, "and whatever they didn't take is broken."

"Look on the bright side," Mutti replied. "We actually have more space than we need and the rooms look even bigger without much furniture."

"When will Opa be well enough to repair this stuff?" I asked Mutti.

"Don't worry," she replied, carefully avoiding my question. "Ilse and I are going to fix the place up. You and Gerda can help."

We set right to work. Ilse wheedled a German woman into parting with six worm-eaten wooden boards. Nailed over the broken windows, they blocked out the cold and discouraged intruders. Mutti, Aunt Liesbeth, and Ilse trudged from house to house begging for the things we needed - a piece of furniture, a chair leg, an old blanket. Late into that night and for several nights thereafter, we worked by the light of our two kerosene lamps. Except for Opa, we slept on the floor as the clean up continued.

* * *

Gradually our house became livable. Our main concern, however, was not our house; our concern was Opa. Racked by a deep cough, he lay exhausted, gasping for air. The Kolkhoz office advanced Mutti a loaf of bread and a small sack of potatoes, but Opa refused all nourishment.

Late on April 5, 1946, the fourth day in our new house, Opa began babbling to himself in his room. Worried and upset, I needed a long time to fall asleep. Towards morning, I woke with a start to see Mutti's silhouette in the dimly lit room. She was sobbing. At that instant, I knew that Opa had died during the night.

Mutti led me into the room where Opa lay. Oma, Aunt Liesbeth, and Ilse stood in front of the couch, heads slumped down, hands folded over their aprons.

Opa was wearing one of his beige night shirts. His hands were clasped on his chest, his eyes were closed, his sunken cheeks the color of yellow wax. Rays of sun struck his head from the back window creating a halo like the ones I had seen many times in pictures of the Last Supper.

I touched Opa's hands, but they were cold. Shocked, I pulled away. Opa had never turned away from me when I had needed him, how shameful to be afraid to touch his body now. I began to cry and Opa soon became a blur.

Mutti and I went into the living room. With the exception of Helga, Hubert, and Dieter, the entire family had already gathered there. Everyone was crying. Oma covered her eyes with her hands to try to hide her tears. Until that moment, Oma had never been especially important to me. She was a hard person to get close to, just the opposite of Opa. Most of the time she was serious, rarely smiling, but now even Oma had lost control of her feelings. It was all too much for me. My world had broken apart. My beloved Opa was no more. He had been more of a father to me than my Vati. Who would answer my questions now? Who would do the heavy work, the lifting of furniture, the repairing of broken doors and windows, the sawing and chopping of wood? Opa had held our two families together since we left Langendorf. He had protected us from danger, solved almost every problem.

I would never sit down next to him and hear his pleasant voice tell me Bible stories. I would never see his smile again, until we met in heaven.

* * *

After a while, Mutti and Ilse left the house, returning hours later with an old German man whom Mutti introduced as Mr. Ademeit. He had wheeled a makeshift wooden coffin to our house in his handcart. After placing the coffin on four chairs in the bedroom, Mr. Ademeit gently lifted Opa from the couch.

"He's as light as a feather," he remarked as he laid him in the box. The bedroom door was only left open a crack.

The tone was hushed in our house all day long. Even Helga, Hubert, and Dieter piped down their usual noise level. For supper Oma had made a potato soup for us and mashed potatoes for the younger children.

After we finished eating, Oma, Mutti, and Aunt Liesbeth went into the kitchen.

Suddenly I heard a high-pitched voice in Opa's room. Thinking it must be a ghost, I froze with fright. The door was open a little bit wider than before. I crept over and peeped inside. Hubert stood next to Opa's coffin. He held his little spoon filled with mashed potatoes next to Opa's mouth and kept saying, "Opa eat. It's mashed potatoes. Opa eat."

Silly boy, I thought, choking back my tears. I pulled Hubert away and brought him to Mutti.

"Can you imagine? He was trying to feed Opa mashed potatoes! Can you explain to him please, that Opa will never eat anything again?"

"Come, my darling," Mutti said to Hubert, lifting him onto her lap. "Your Opa can eat all the mashed potatoes he wants up in heaven."

Afterwards Mutti kept the door to Opa's bedroom tightly shut.

That night I had nightmares. Opa had awakened and was walking through the house, searching in vain for mashed potatoes. I lay in a cold sweat, haunted by the smell of rotting corpses in ditches along the road, imagining that Opa would soon end up like that. I remembered how sad Opa had been ever since he dug out the corpses of the slaughtered Jews along the beach at Palmnicken. I thought about the lonely cemetery at Germau where those poor souls had been buried, only to be forgotten again. Now Opa was also going to be laid to rest in a strange place, far from the farm he loved.

In the morning I awoke in dread of the upcoming funeral. The door to Opa's room was wide open. Mutti and Aunt Liesbeth kept rushing in and out. I went in to see him one more time. Was it only my imagination or had his mouth opened a little during the night? A shiver ran down my spine as I studied the lifeless shell Opa had become.

Around noon, Mr. Ademeit returned with another man. Together they carried the coffin out to the front of the house and loaded it onto Mr. Ademeit's handcart. Gerda and I rushed outside to pick a few crocuses. Following the others, we walked up the hill to the abandoned Lutheran church. A grave had already been dug and the closed coffin was quickly lowered into it on ropes. Dark brown earth hit the coffin with a hollow pounding sound, almost as though Opa had already left the coffin and gone to heaven. I tossed in the crocuses clutched in my sweaty hand and whispered, "Auf Wiedersehen."

Tears rolled down my cheeks and onto my neck. A throbbing began in my ears and spread into my chest. I bit my bottom lip to stop the trembling, and listened to Mutti and Aunt Liesbeth speak briefly about Opa's life. We recited the Lord's Prayer: "...Give us this day our daily bread; and forgive us our trespasses, as we forgive those who trespass against us..." and the service was over.

Aunt Liesbeth, Oma, and Mutti thanked the two men, who stayed behind to fill the grave as we left for home. Later Mr. Ademeit and the other man stopped by at our house. Mutti neatly folded Opa's two pairs of worn trousers and gave each man one pair.

"What are we going to do without him?" Aunt Liesbeth asked Mutti once the men had left.

"We'll just have to manage somehow. It's funny though, sick as he was, I was sure he'd pull through. This time last year, he seemed healthier than the rest of us put together."

"That was before Pentecost," Oma said quietly. "He was never the same after that."

"You're right," Mutti agreed. "When he began to disinter those bodies, he seemed to break apart."

"He asked me every night, 'How could God permit this?'" Oma said, "and I never had an answer for him."

* * *

A day or two after the funeral, Mutti and Aunt Liesbeth were ordered to do heavy farm work on the Kolkhoz from dawn to dusk, every day except Sunday. During the harvest season the work would be seven days a week. Ilse, who was thirteen, was assigned to a work brigade with nine other German girls, all aged twelve to eighteen.

At the end of the work day, Mutti, Aunt Liesbeth, and Ilse were each allotted 300 grams of bread. Three pieces together made up one loaf. We would not have any bit more food in Goldbach than we had in Palmnicken.

Since no German in Goldbach had a watch or a clock, an old German man had been given an alarm clock by the Kolkhoz administration. Every morning around four o'clock he walked the few streets of Goldbach ringing a bell to wake up the workers who took care of the farm animals.

A plow share dangled from a rope tied to a tree. At five o'clock the old man struck the plowshare with a hammer warning the other Kolkhoz workers that they had thirty minutes to get dressed, eat breakfast and report for work. Half awake, I would listen as the metal reverberated like an off-key church bell, feeling guilty that Mutti had to get up and go to work while I could snuggle under my covers a bit longer.

Most days, if I slept through the clang of the plowshare, I never saw Mutti in the morning. She left long before I woke up. Many nights I was asleep by the time she came home. I was lonely without Mutti, but although I was only eight years old, I was now the oldest man in the family. I quickly learned not to cry.

* * *

Oma dressed almost entirely in black. In warm weather, she wrapped her long black shawl over her head and her ears and tied it under her chin, like someone with a toothache. In the winter, she folded her square woolen scarf into a triangle and tied it together in such a way that every wisp of her hair was hidden. Even Oma's aprons were black, although a few had tiny designs of gray and white. She combed her long white hair to the back of her head and knotted it in a severe bun.

Although Oma wore glasses, I sometimes wondered whether she really needed them, because she usually bent her head forward a little and looked right over the top of the rims. Still, when she threaded a needle she always asked Dorchen or Gerda to help her. Sometimes late in the evening when she was tired, she took off her glasses. With her sunken eyes she reminded me of a sad owl. During the middle of the day, Oma often escaped to her bedroom and shut the door for a few hours.

"Not a peep out of you!" she ordered. "I'm sixty-four years old and these old bones need to rest once in a while."

Yet we all knew she wasn't sleeping; she was knitting. She was always doing something. Oma had her hands full with six hungry children at home. From daybreak to sundown, she did not brook any nonsense.

Gerda and I were assigned the difficult task of finding and collecting wood for our stove in a village already picked clean. Dorchen was responsible for looking after Helga, Dieter, and Hubert. Of Aunt Liesbeth's five children, Dorchen was everyone's favorite. Gentle and good-natured, she had a turned up nose, brown eyes, dark eyebrows, and long brown eye lashes. She wore her blond hair in thick braids. In the summertime she always had the best suntan of all of us. When she flashed one of her winning smiles, the dimples in her cheeks made her look even prettier.

Barely a month after Opa's death Dorchen turned twelve and should have gone to work at the Kolkhoz, but she was small for her age and Aunt Liesbeth lied to the Kommandantura, claiming she was only ten. When responsibility overwhelmed Oma, she often yelled at Gerda and me, but Dorchen was Oma's darling. Oma never raised her voice to her. Dorchen had been in fifth grade when we left Langendorf. My education stopped at the beginning of second grade. I struggled to read even the simplest text.

Under a pile of old rags in the corner of the living room, we found an illustrated volume of *Grimm's Fairy Tales*, left behind by the previous occupants of the house. Many of the pages were torn; some were missing entirely. Childish scribbles defaced still others. Damaged though it was, we were glad to have it. The Bible and the fairy tale book made up our entire household library. Although I loved Dorchen, I felt jealous when she read fairy tales to the younger children.

"Come sit with me," she offered one day, "and I'll teach you how to read."

But I chose to decline her offer. I could not bear to be taught by a girl who was shorter than I was.

* * *

One day, Oma, Gerda, and I knocked on doors along our street, asking for burlap sacks. The Russians glared at us and sent us away empty-handed, but some German families were willing to spare us a few sacks so we wouldn't have to sleep on the floor. Oma sewed the burlap together to make straw mattresses.

Whenever Mutti and Ilse brought home a bale of straw from the Kolkhoz to use as mattress stuffing, Oma worried that mice might be hidden inside. Sure enough, one day after lunch Dorchen spotted the first intruders.

"You actually saw them? Or did you only hear them?" Gerda asked.

"I saw them all right," Dorchen replied. "Little gray ones with long tails."

That night I lay awake on my straw mattress listening for mice. It must have been around midnight when I heard a woman's screams followed by a deep man's voice yelling outside. The noise finally stopped and I drifted off to sleep.

* * *

When the plowshare clanged early the next morning I got up and grabbed Mutti's arm. "Did you hear it, too? The screams?"

"Don't worry," she whispered. "It goes on nearly every night. It's the one-legged Russian man and his wife who live next door."

"What's he doing to her?"

"He drinks a lot of vodka and then he beats her," she explained. Mutti tiptoed into the kitchen to get dressed, eat a quick breakfast of cold grain soup, and go to work.

During the next few weeks, when Gerda and I pulled the handcart that Mr. Ademeit had given to us to collect wood, we often saw our one-legged Russian neighbor on the street. He was no more than forty years old, with a hangdog expression. Sometimes he walked alone, talking to himself. Other times his wife and his two teenage daughters followed behind him, as though attached to an invisible leash, their eyes anxiously darting about.

Because he was missing a leg, he hobbled along with the aid of two wooden crutches. His shabby civilian clothes were so ragged and worn, he could have been mistaken for a German, had it not been for the array of Russian war medals decorating his chest. He wore an old boot and his medals made a jingling noise with every step he took.

One day I saw him lying in the muddy street, like a pig wallowing in the pigsty back home in Langendorf. He was snoring, an empty vodka bottle at his side. I made a wide circle around him.

* * *

One sunny morning at the end of May, Oma brought Gerda and me to a big meadow outside of Goldbach. Bright red poppies, yellow dandelions, blue forget-me-nots, and purple violets had burst into bloom. The last time we were there, we had looked for yellow and white chamomile blossoms, but Oma had other plans. She held up several small dark green leaves.

"Remember sorrel? Here's a cloth bag. I don't want you to come home until it's full of sorrel. Is that understood?"

"Yes, Oma," we said in unison. After Oma rushed back home to help Dorchen with the little ones, we set to work. We carefully removed the little snails which clung to the underside of the small leaves. The bag filled up slowly. We dragged our feet as we walked home. The later we got back, the less chance Oma would send us back out for wood. Oma was waiting at the top of the stairs.

"Gerda, you stay put. I've got chores for you to do around here." She turned to me. "I want you to take the handcart and your hatchet and get us some wood. None of that wet stuff, mind you."

Full of resentment, I headed for a dilapidated barn Gerda and I had discovered a few days before. I dawdled along the way there and again as I returned home with a load of wood, wondering what other chore Oma would have in store for me. When I finally got back, I was surprised to find both Mutti and Aunt Liesbeth home so early. They were standing next to Oma's bed. Oma had been crying.

"Calm down, Mother. Everything'll be just fine," Mutti was saying.

"If he sees me, he'll do it again," she sobbed.

"He's probably forgotten all about it by now," Mutti reassured her.

"What happened?" I asked.

"Oma and the children went to the Magazin (small food store) to buy matches. On the way back, Oma knelt down beside the small vegetable garden in front of our Russian neighbor's house."

"I just wanted to touch the leaves on the tiny carrot plants. They reminded me of our farm in Langendorf," Oma sniffled.

"That crazy man came storming out of his house and..."

"Why was he angry?"

"I guess he thought Oma wanted to steal his vegetables. Anyway, he whacked Oma across her back with one of his wooden crutches. Can you imagine? The children were terrified. When Oma slumped to the ground, the man's wife hurried outside to try to pull her husband away. It eventually took three Russian men to hold him back."

"But how come you and Aunt Liesbeth are here?"

"Gerda raced over to the Kolkhoz to get us."

"Tell him about the Kommandantura," Aunt Liesbeth said.

"I had to stop by there to tell them what happened before they would let us go home. The officer told me not to worry, that it would be taken care of, but getting Oma not to worry is quite another matter."

"How can we go on with a neighbor like that?" Aunt Liesbeth asked.

* * *

Mutti and Aunt Liesbeth stayed home the rest of the day to tend to Oma.

"How's she doing?" I asked at supper time.

"Her back is black and blue, but she'll be all right after a while."

"Just like my bottom in Palmnicken," I said. "That took weeks and weeks to heal."

The next morning, Mutti, Aunt Liesbeth, and Ilse left for work at their usual early hour. Oma stayed in bed, complaining about her pain. Hours later a Russian Army Jeep stopped in front of our house. Two Russian officers, a man and a woman, got out and knocked at our door.

"Oma, come quick! The Russians are here!" we shouted.

She rose from her bed with difficulty and came to the door.

The male officer consulted a paper in his hand. "Excuse me, are you Berta Recklies?" he asked in fluent German.

"Yes, may I help you?"

"We're here about yesterday's unfortunate incident."

"Yes, of course," Oma said, inviting them in.

As she told the officer her story, he listened carefully, noting down details on his pad. When she had finished, he turned to Dorchen and Gerda.

"Do either of you have anything to add? Was that exactly how it happened?"

Both girls nodded their agreement. "Send the children out, please, Mrs. Recklies. My colleague here is an army nurse. She's going to examine your back."

We waited with the Russian officer until the nurse called us back inside. The two Russians conferred in a corner of the room.

"Babushka, you were lucky," the man finally said. "Nothing's broken. After a few weeks, you'll be good as new."

Bewildered by his unexpected friendliness, Oma bowed her head respectfully. "Thank you, Officer," she said with uncharacteristic humility.

When the Russians left, we peeked out through the windows to watch. Instead of getting back into their Jeep, they went into our neighbor's house, staying there for quite a while. Afterwards they also went to the houses of the Russians who had helped our neighbor's wife rescue Oma. Later that same day they questioned Mutti and Aunt Liesbeth at the Kolkhoz. We did not know what to make of it all.

* * *

Oma was getting better. We had already stopped talking about the incident when, to our surprise, a Russian Army truck pulled up in front of our neighbor's house and two armed soldiers rushed inside. Over the wild protests of his weeping wife, the one legged veteran was led away.

"Imagine that!" Aunt Liesbeth said, "A war veteran with all those medals. You'd think they'd sweep the whole thing under the rug."

Rumors flew. He had been sentenced to ten years in Siberia. Or was it five years? Or even twenty? However long it was, we never saw the one legged Russian man again. Before long, our neighbor's wife and daughters had become as poor as we were. Out of pity for his family, Mutti asked one of the Russian supervisors at the Kolkhoz whether the punishment was perhaps a little harsh.

"We treat all criminals the same," he replied with a shrug. "Why should his war record matter? The war's been over for more than a year."

CHAPTER 11

By the middle of June 1946, when we finally began to feel settled in our new home, Mutti and Aunt Liesbeth were told at the Kommandantura that our house was needed by a Russian family. We would have to move to an upstairs apartment in the middle of the village.

"Remember how you always griped about the outhouse?" Mutti said to me. "Well, I think it's one of the reasons the Russians want the house. Most places in the village aren't this close to one."

We moved the next day, a Sunday. All of us took turns shuttling back and forth between the old house and the new one with our few belongings on the little handcart. A few days later, Gerda and I sullenly watched a Russian family move into the bright, large house we had just vacated.

Our new apartment was in a two-story building on the village street. Because of its location next to a steep driveway, the house had an extra story in the back, which was where the entrance to our apartment was. Storage rooms, locks rusty with disuse, were on the ground level. A family of four lived on the second floor. To get to the next staircase, we had to walk through their sparsely furnished kitchen. They had a stove, a small table pushed against the wall, and three wooden chairs.

Judging from the light-colored patches on the wooden floor, there must have once been more furniture in the room.

The steep staircase to the third floor was more like a ladder, with narrow steps leading to a tiny platform with two doors side by side. The door on the right opened into a kitchen, with two small windows facing the courtyard and the steep driveway. The kitchen sink had a basin with a drain, but no faucet for running water. From the kitchen window we could glimpse a water pump in the courtyard.

The kitchen had another two doors, one leading to a small bedroom, which became Oma's, Mutti's, Hubert's, and mine. The other door led to a large, bright living room, overlooking the village street. Another room beyond the living room became the Reimanns' bedroom.

Outside the kitchen, the door to the left of the landing led to a tiny room, no bigger than a closet. It had a steeply slanted ceiling so low that Mutti had to bend down to avoid hitting her head. The only source of light came from a skylight the size of one roof tile. In the middle of the room stood a large metal pail left behind by the previous occupants. Judging from the dreadful smell, we understood at once what the little room was for. I decided to use the bushes, unless it was dark.

"We can't live here!" Mutti protested, but we knew we had nowhere else to go.

* * *

I got up early the following morning. Mutti, Aunt Liesbeth, and Ilse had already left for work. I wanted to sneak outside, but Oma caught me before I reached the door.

"Hold it right there! I want you to carry the pail downstairs and empty it somewhere. Be careful going down so nothing spills. I'll be watching from the landing."

Grudgingly, I lifted the handle and picked up the pail. Although it was only half full, it was heavy. Holding the handle with my right hand,

I tiptoed carefully down the steep narrow staircase, the contents of the pail swopping dangerously from side to side.

As I moved slowly down, I never let go of the railing with my left hand. Hardly daring to breathe because of the dreadful odor, I let my hand glide down the rail and held on for dear life as I went from step to step. The thought that I might fall and drop the bucket terrified me.

At the second floor landing, an old lady and two girls were eating soup for breakfast in their kitchen. My "good morning" went unanswered, but I could hardly blame them, considering my smelly burden. When I reached the ground level, I went in search of a place to dump out the messy contents of my pail. Crossing the courtyard, I walked around a building with a Russian army truck parked in front, noting that, tucked away behind another structure, stood a chopping block and a sawhorse. Guided by the stench, I turned left towards a small orchard. There, among the trees, I found a shallow round hole reeking of human waste and dumped in the contents of my pail. I suddenly missed the privacy afforded by the outhouse at the other end of the village.

As I headed back, workers were loading the Russian Army truck with wooden boxes full of fresh bread. A bakery! In spite of the smelly pail in my hand, I was instantly hungry. We did not have a single slice of bread in our apartment.

Except for a tiny mouse scurrying across the floor, our neighbors' kitchen was empty on my way back upstairs. When I reached the top of the stairs, Oma was waiting for me.

"Oma, I just saw a..."

She cut me off in mid sentence.

"You did a much better job than I'd expected," Oma said grudgingly. "So emptying the pail every morning and every evening will be your responsibility from now on."

Oma wasn't strong enough to carry the heavy pail herself. Gerda and Dorchen were busy cleaning up the younger children whenever they had diarrhea, which had been nearly all winter and all spring long. Hubert's colon slipped out every time he had a bowel movement, requiring Gerda to squeeze it back inside by pressing the cheeks of his bottom together. All things considered, I decided to accept my daily chore quietly.

* * *

After a breakfast of soup made from small cabbage heads Ilse had stolen from a field on her way home from work, Oma announced that Dorchen would stay with the little ones. "Günter and Gerda will go with me. We're going to look for garbage outside of Russian houses."

"But Oma," Gerda protested, "eating the food we took from the garbage in Palmnicken sometimes made us sick."

"We're not looking for something to eat," Oma explained. "We're going to search for tin cans. We're a family of ten, but we have only four cups among us."

Passing through our neighbors' kitchen on our way downstairs, I saw that the old lady and the two girls had returned. With a little bow, the lady introduced herself to Oma.

"Good morning. I am Mrs. Schmidt."

"I'm Mrs. Recklies," Oma replied as the two of them shook hands. "These are two of my grandchildren, Gerda and Günter."

"Amanda and Martha are my granddaughters," said Mrs. Schmidt. "My daughter-in-law works at the Kolkhoz. We're from Königsberg."

Oma smiled, but kept silent. When Mrs. Schmidt realized that Oma was not about to tell her anything about herself, she switched to a different topic entirely.

"This is hard for me to say, but I need to talk to you about the pail your grandson brought down this morning. He came through our kitchen while we were eating breakfast. That is, if you can call a thin potato soup breakfast." Words poured from Mrs. Schmidt, who was getting more flustered by the minute.

"What I'm trying to say," she continued breathlessly, "is, would it be at all possible for your grandson to bring out the pail earlier in the morning, before our breakfast, and early in the evening, before we sit down to supper?"

"Of course, Mrs. Schmidt, I'll try my best, but it's hard for me because none of us has any way to tell the time."

"I can understand that, Mrs. Recklies. The Russians took all of our watches and clocks, too, but somehow we've learned how to tell time without them, isn't that so? Anyway, I'd appreciate anything you can do."

"You know," Mrs. Schmidt went on, "a family of nine lived in the apartment upstairs before you came. They came and went as they pleased, without any consideration for us. We'd never have brought our pail through their apartment at mealtimes if the situation had been reversed, I can assure you."

"I'll do my best," repeated Oma, who never considered using two words when only one would do. "Good-bye, Mrs. Schmidt."

"Good-bye, Mrs. Recklies. It was a pleasure meeting you."

Throughout the conversation, I had studied Mrs. Schmidt. She had pale blue eyes, evenly spaced, and an upturned nose. Her mouth, however, was turned down in a permanent frown. Her fine featured face was tinged with sadness, her frail body mere skin and bones. Clothes hung loosely on her small frame. I was sure if she knelt down she would not get back up. I had always thought of Oma as old, but suddenly she looked strong and youthful by comparison.

Once we were down in the street and out of earshot, Oma turned to Gerda and me.

"Judging from the way she spoke, Mrs. Schmidt must be a very educated woman who's always had the best of everything. Life in Goldbach must be especially hard on people like her. She's the type who loves to dwell on her own misery without doing anything about it, but, let's try our best to accommodate her."

150

"Yes, Oma," we replied as one.

The three of us trudged up the steep driveway leading to the village street. We passed three or four houses without finding any cans. It was only after we had dug through the garbage behind the Magazin that we found four empty, jagged edged tins. Three smelled of meat; the fourth smelled of fruits. Oma was disappointed that they were all empty.

Back at home Oma placed the cans on our sturdy kitchen table. Using Opa's small hammer and his round heavy steel file, she hammered the sharp top edge of the first can flat. Turning to me, Oma said, "Did you see the way I did it? I hope you were paying close attention, because I want you to fix the other three cans the same way."

"Yes, Oma."

I went to work and a short time later added three more cups to our small collection. Oma washed the cans carefully and boiled them three times before she would let us use them. As the labels peeled away in the hot water, Oma set them aside. On Sunday, when Ilse was off from work, she was called upon to translate the labels.

"They're from America," she explained. "These three were once filled with sausage and that one contained fruit salad."

"Keep your eyes open for empty tins," Oma instructed us. "We're still two cups short."

* * *

One morning Oma supplied Gerda and me with mittens she had sewn from coarse material. She had also used the same material to make a pair of mittens and a huge cloth bag for herself. The three of us went over to a clump of bushes down by the brook.

Oma explained. "We're going to pick stinging nettle and later I will cook the leaves like spinach. It's very tasty that way."

Gerda and I had always known to avoid the nettle plant. The leaves were covered with soft fuzz. Even the slightest contact with the skin caused painfully itchy blisters which burned for hours.

151

"We'll get stung," Gerda complained.

Oma was adamant. "No, you won't. The mittens will protect your hands."

We set to work, trying our best to avoid touching the leaves, which was not easy since we were barefoot. Protected by shoes and a long black dress down to her ankles, Oma plucked the nettle much faster than we did.

"Only pick the top of the stem and the leaves. The thick stems near the roots are too stringy for eating," she reminded us.

"Yes, Oma."

On the way back we also picked chamomile flowers and linden blossoms which Oma used to make tea.

Cooked with a small amount of water in a covered pot, surprisingly little of the nettle plant remained. Oma was right. With a tiny dash of salt, the nettle tasted like spinach.

* * *

Near a stand of trees on the village meadow behind our house, Gerda discovered wild strawberries. Stringing dozens of the tiny berries onto a long stalk of grass, she brought them home for Helga, Hubert, and Dieter. Two days later, all six of us went back with her to the same spot. More strawberries had ripened. Dieter, Hubert, and Helga popped the juicy red fruit into their mouths.

When we had eaten our fill, Dorchen threaded berries onto a grass stalk to bring home to Oma. As we walked behind the bakery, near the wood chopping place, we caught a glimpse of three fat rats running away from a garbage dump. Snatching up the smaller children, we ran home and rushed upstairs. Oma was distressed.

"We've already got mice, but we have to keep those creatures out at all costs," she declared. She slowly lowered herself to the floor.

"Oh, my poor aching back," Oma groaned as she kneeled down. She carefully checked for cracks under our door through which rats could pass.

"Never leave that door open, not even for a minute," she warned us, "especially when you get up during the night."

"Better still, use a chamber pot," she advised. "Don't open that door to go to the pail unless it's absolutely necessary."

Oma sat down and breathed heavily. Smiling at Dorchen, she added, "And thank you so much for the strawberries, my darling."

"You're welcome!" Dorchen replied cheerfully.

Oma ate only three of the tiny berries and gave the rest to Helga, Hubert, and Dieter.

* * *

I frequently hung around the Magazin, gazing longingly at shelves stocked with bread, salt, matches, salted cucumbers, tomatoes and, on rare occasions, salted fish. I came for one simple reason: to beg for tiny pieces of bread from the customers.

A long line of customers had come and gone without handing me so much as a crumb when, out of the corner of my eye, I noticed a man bending down to pick up cigarette butts next to the road. I recognized Mr. Ademeit's craggy face. Ever since I'd met him at Opa's funeral, I had observed him around Goldbach. He was always carrying something home. His right leg stiff from an old injury, he would limp along with all kinds of odds and ends, a piece of broken glass, a block of wood, a damaged drive belt, or some rusty nails. Cigarette butts did not seem to fit the pattern.

A tall, elegantly dressed Russian officer came out of the store. He was smoking. The Russian turned down the dusty path to the right. To my amazement, Mr. Ademeit followed him. Nosy, I tagged along. After a short distance the officer turned to glare at Mr. Ademeit and, with a look of disgust, he flicked his half-smoked cigarette to the ground, spitting on it before walking away.

Mr. Ademeit, ignoring the glare and the spit, rushed over and bent down to pick up the still smoldering cigarette. As he put it in his mouth and sucked in the smoke, he saw me watching him.

"You're the Nitsch boy, aren't you?" he asked me.

"Yes, sir," I answered, eyeing him quizzically. Mr. Ademeit put his hand behind his ear, to hear me better.

"Do you find it strange, me picking up butts like that? One day, when you take up smoking, you'll understand why." As I listened politely, Mr. Ademeit made me a business proposition.

"I'll tell you what. If you collect tobacco for me, I promise to give you a slice of bread for each thumb-sized match box full you bring me. None of that foul-smelling machorka stuff, though, and no cigarette ashes."

With yellow-stained fingers, he handed me an empty match box. "Bring it to me when it's full," he said.

I became an expert collector. Quickly I found out that the younger soldiers only smoked papirossi, which were two-thirds paper tube and one-third tobacco. Papirossi were thrown away only when nothing but ashes were left, so I concentrated on soldiers and officers who smoked real cigarettes and then tossed away the butts.

* * *

Gerda and I needed hours to saw a two meter length of pine into eight short blocks. Our arms were tired after making the seven cuts, so we rested a while before starting to chop the blocks into pieces small enough to fit into our stove.

"Let's chop wood!" I said, confidently swinging the axe at the first of the blocks and quickly cutting it apart, but the second block, gnarled and full of knots, challenged me. A forceful blow of the axe pushed the blade a scant two centimeters inside. With the blade still imbedded, I swung the axe and the wood over my head and whammed the blunt end of the axe down three times on the wood chopping block, but the blade barely moved any deeper. Ingrown branches held the wood together like steel clamps.

"You need a wedge," a gravelly voice said behind me. Setting down the block with the axe still inside, I turned around and saw Mr. Ademeit.

"I know that, Mr. Ademeit," I replied, unable to hide my irritation. "But unfortunately we haven't got one."

Without answering me, he lifted up the axe handle and studied the gnarled block from all sides. "I doubt anyone could chop through that thing without a wedge," he concluded.

Anchoring the block between his feet, Mr. Ademeit yanked out the axe. "A wedge would slip right into this slot in the wood," he explained. "But you'd have to tap gently with the blunt end of the axe to get it started or else the wedge would break or crack. Have you ever used one?"

"No sir, but I watched my Opa do it."

"Well then, if you come with me, I'll give you an old one that's still in pretty good shape."

"We'd really appreciate that, Mr. Ademeit," Gerda said.

"If Oma checks up on me, please tell her I'll be back soon!"

"I will," Gerda promised as she headed upstairs with an armful of chopped wood.

The flat end of the wedge Mr. Ademeit found in his work shop had splintery edges. After chopping them smooth, he handed it to me.

"Are you sure you know what to do with it?"

"Yes sir, I do. My Opa used wedges all the time."

"That's my boy. All the same, if you don't succeed, just leave the block and I'll come around in a day or so to split it apart for you."

"Thank you, Mr. Ademeit!"

Gerda was waiting for me at our wood chopping place.

155

"Can you split the block without damaging the wedge?"

"I think so. Cross your fingers, here goes!"

I slid the wedge inside the gnarled block. Closing my eyes for a moment, I visualized Opa outside the barn in Langendorf and knew exactly what to do. I tapped gently, gradually forcing the wedge into the wood. Finally, after taking a deep breath, I gave the embedded wedge a huge whack. With a cracking noise, the top of the block split open, although two interior branches still held the wood together in the middle.

A few quick blows with the sharp edge of the axe severed the branches. The two halves of the block fell to the ground with a resounding thud, one on each side of the wood chopping block.

"Mr. Ademeit's really nice," Gerda said as we carried the saw, the axe, and the precious wedge back home.

"We couldn't have done it without him," I agreed.

* * *

For certain jobs on the Kolkhoz, like carrying heavy bags of grain or wooden logs or shoveling dung, Mutti, Aunt Liesbeth, and Ilse received a few rubles in addition to their daily bread ration. We used this money to buy a little extra bread at the Magazin. Bread was expensive, but we had no choice. Ten people could not survive on one loaf a day. Oma also bought salt and matches at the Magazin; we had no money for anything else.

Matches were inexpensive. In fact they were so cheap that I always carried a box full of matches with me. Soap and detergents were never in stock at the Magazin. Even if they had been available, we would not have been able to afford them. Somehow Oma knew how to wash laundry without any soap or detergent. First, she ordered Gerda and me to lug up water from the pump. Stirring in a handful of ashes from the kitchen stove, Oma waited patiently until the ash settled to the bottom of the pail and the water on top was clear again. Next, she ladled out the

156

water carefully, trying not to stir up any ashes. Oma used this water to wash our laundry. Our laundry got clean, but whatever had been white at one time turned grey. To keep up with ten people's laundry, Oma did the wash two or three times a week.

"I've noticed some women washing their clothes in the brook," Oma announced one morning. "Dorchen and I are going to give that method a try."

Oma and Dorchen joined a group of German and Russian women using partially submerged tree trunks as scrubbing boards. Oma was pleased with the results, until the day a dead cat floated by. From then on Oma did the laundry in our kitchen and Gerda and I had to carry up the water from the pump again.

* * *

During the warmer weather, Saturday afternoon was bath time for the children. Mutti, Aunt Liesbeth, and Ilse, who had to work until very late at the Kolkhoz, and Oma who waited to bathe with the adults, bathed on Sunday mornings.

In one corner of the kitchen we had a heavy round wooden vat. I fit inside only by pulling my knees close to my chest. Since the kitchen stove had only two burners, Oma had to heat up quite a few pots to fill the vat with hot water. While the tub was being filled, Oma and Dorchen sat side by side on wooden chairs with their backs to the big window in the living room checking us for head lice. Oma needed all the sunlight she could get to spot the tiny intruders since her eyeglasses were no longer strong enough. I never knew whether it was an insult or a compliment when she turned to me with the words, "You, scoundrel, are first."

Oma scraped my scalp with a fine-toothed louse comb. Holding up the comb, she showed me the yellowish lice sitting on the teeth, saying, "Just look what you have hiding in there."

She cracked the lice on the comb with her thumbnail before combing through my hair again. Afterwards she would check my scalp one last time, cracking any remaining lice between both of her thumbnails.

"That's it for now," she said.

"Thank you, Oma," I said, relieved to know I was off the hook for another week.

"Next!" she yelled loudly and Hubert would hop on her lap.

I tried to suppress a giggle.

"What's so funny?" Gerda asked me.

"I imagined Hubert picking lice off of Oma's head, just like the monkeys in the Königsberg Zoo," I whispered back.

"Don't tell Oma!" Gerda replied and she burst out laughing.

The line-up for the bath was always the same. First came the three girls, Dorchen, Gerda, and Helga, while Dieter, Hubert, and I waited behind closed doors in the living room. A big wooden table, a few real chairs and stools, all different from one another, and an assortment of chairs pieced together from wooden crates found in abandoned buildings were the only furniture. Piled in two corners of the room were the wooden boards, sticks, small crates, and large smooth pebbles Helga, Hubert, and Dieter used as toys. The living room wallpaper was streaked gray as high as the dirty hands of the youngest children could reach. Above that, it was a faded shade of beige.

Afterwards it was the boys' turn, first me, then Hubert, and finally Dieter. By the time little Dieter had been bathed, the water was a murky gray. Hubert enjoyed taking a bath more than anybody else. One day I stood behind Oma while she washed him in the tub. Hubert was grinning broadly at me. I gestured to him to hit the water. To my great delight he whacked down with both hands, splashing Oma in the process. Dieter, who was waiting his turn, started to giggle. Unfortunately for me, Oma suddenly looked around and caught me making gestures.

"I saw that, you rascal. You'll pay for this!"

Feeling a mixture of guilt and fear, I retreated into the living room.

"I'm going to get it this time," I whispered to Gerda as I looked desperately for a place to hide.

"Watch out!" she warned me, but it was too late. At that moment I felt Oma's wet wash rag smacking against the back of my head.

"I want you to empty the water from the tub. Gerda, don't you dare help him!" Oma snapped.

I made many trips back and forth with a small pail, scooping the water out of the tub and pouring it down the drain of the kitchen sink. As the water level sank, I replaced the pail with a small tin can.

"Please, Oma, can Gerda help to get out the last of the water? I can't tip the vat and scoop at the same time."

Glaring at me, she waved at Gerda. I tipped the vat slowly and carefully, nearly all the way to one side while Gerda used a rag to wipe out the muddy residue. It didn't pay to get on the wrong side of Oma and I promised myself to be more careful in the future.

* * *

Whether I was walking on the village street, running across the meadows or rambling along the dirt paths outside of the village, I always went barefoot in the summer. I was supposed to save my one pair of shoes for the winter, only wearing them when I went with Gerda into the forest to pick berries or to collect wood.

After a few weeks of running around barefoot, I developed thick, protective calluses on the soles of my feet. One day, however, while running along the dirt path leading from the Kolkhoz through the big meadow to our apartment, I sliced my right foot open on a broken bottle. Bleeding heavily, I managed to limp home. To my relief, Oma and Gerda were at our wood chopping spot. Oma, seeing my limp, greeted me with, "What on earth have you done now, you scamp?"

"I stepped on a broken bottle."

"Why don't you watch where you're going?"

"Sorry, Oma. I saw it too late."

"Excuses, excuses. You're never short of them."

She made me put my injured leg up on the chopping block and examined my wound. Wiping her hands on her stained dark apron, she pressed her index finger above the gash.

"Does this hurt?"

"Ouch. Yes."

"Don't make such a fuss."

"Sorry, but it hurts."

"Wiggle your toes!"

I moved them up and down.

"You'll live," Oma assured me. "For now, stay where you are and don't budge. Gerda! You come with me!"

The two of them headed towards the far edge of the meadow, disappearing behind some distant houses. Feeling abandoned and in pain, I squinted in that direction, waiting anxiously for their return. Just when I had nearly given up hope, they came back and brought me upstairs. Oma cleaned my foot with a wet rag and took a thick, light-green leaf out of her apron pocket.

"This is called a life-and-death plant," she said. "Let me show you what it can do."

Carefully she separated the jagged leaf at the very tip, pulling off the skin on one side to reveal a juicy, dark-green surface. Pressing the moist side of the leaf against the gash like a poultice, she tied an old rag around my foot to hold it in place. The liquid felt soothing.

"I'm going to apply these leaves twice a day for the next few days," Oma informed me. "In the meantime, you're not going anywhere!"

Oma knew what she was doing. My cut healed nicely and, better yet, I never developed an infection. When I was allowed outside again, Gerda took me to an overgrown garden behind an abandoned house. The weeds and thistles growing in the garden were nearly as tall as I

160

was. Nestled among them was the odd-looking life-and- death plant. At the very top was a small cluster of tiny purple flowers. Below them, pointing upwards along a spindly stalk, were jagged leaves just like the ones that had cured my foot.

CHAPTER 12

During the summer I bartered with Mr. Ademeit, a thick slice of bread for each tiny matchbox full of tobacco. Once or twice, when he was out of bread, he told me to come back another time, but he always lived up to his side of the bargain. With a pang of guilt, I ate the bread as soon he gave it to me, never bringing any home to share with my family. How anyone could prefer smoking to food, I would never understand.

Mr. Ademeit lived in a converted stable. One-half of the floor space he had set aside for his sawhorse, two wood chopping blocks, and a storage area for firewood. A large barrel, half-full of rainwater, stood flush against the outside wall, just below the gutter pipe from the roof.

The living quarters consisted of two rooms. His "shop" served as a work area, living room, and kitchen, all in one. Behind it was a small bedroom where he stored his precious millstones, away from prying eyes.

"This place is plenty big enough for me," he explained the first time he showed me around. "I'm all alone in the world, you know. All three of my sons fell in the war. The Tommies shot down my oldest boy over North Africa and the other two ended up as cannon fodder on the Russian front."

"What about your wife?" Mr. Ademeit was quiet for a moment before answering.

"Our youngest was only eighteen. When they told us he was dead, she just gave up. A doctor might call it something else, but I'd say she died of grief."

* * *

One day I knocked on the massive door, and then peeked through the window. Mr. Ademeit was deeply engrossed in his carpentry work. I let myself in.

"Good morning, Mr. Ademeit!"

A sturdy footstool lay on its side on the workbench. Sandpaper in hand, Mr. Ademeit looked up at me expectantly.

"What brings you here, Günter? Got any tobacco for me?"

"Not today, sir, sorry. My mother asked me to bring you her shoes. I know you said the last time that the leather's worn through, but she was hoping you could fix them one more time."

"Give me a week or two and I'll see what I can do. It's not easy to get my hands on a piece of old leather, believe me."

"Thank you, sir!"

Sensing Mr. Ademeit would not mind, I hung around a while longer to watch.

"My Opa loved to work with his tools," I said, "but he didn't have a real workshop like this."

"Why don't you take a look around?" he invited.

Cluttered as it was, his shop had a certain order to it. Faded wooden boards were stacked in one corner. On the shelves along the long wall, corroded metal trays and battered tin cans held rusty nails, screws, and assorted nuts and bolts. Piled alongside were small blocks of wood, broken panes of glass, lengths of rope, chain links, wire, and iron wedges. Short handsaws, planes, and drills of various sizes rested on the bottom shelf next to five hammers, three pairs of pliers, and some chisels. A dozen screwdrivers in size order, hung like organ pipes from nails hammered into the front of the shelves. Mr. Ademeit's large handcart took up the far corner of the room.

"So," Mr. Ademeit said after a while. "You've had a good look around. Any questions?"

"Actually, I do have one. I couldn't help noticing the three rusty horseshoes nailed to the beam over the stove. I know you are a cabinetmaker and a carpenter and you fix shoes. Even my Opa couldn't do all that. But why do you need the horseshoes?"

"They're just for luck. Does that surprise you?"

"For luck? In Goldbach?" I asked.

"Of course, even in Goldbach," he said with a wink.

* * *

In July, the Russians renamed Königsberg.

"Kaliningrad. That's what we have to call it from now on," Mutti told us. "They posted an announcement at the Kolkhoz today."

"Well, among ourselves, I'm going to insist on the old name," Oma said. "You can't throw away seven hundred years of history just like that."

"We have to get used to the idea," Aunt Liesbeth said bitterly. "East Prussia isn't just under Russian occupation. It's been absorbed by the Soviet Union."

"I also found out some good news today," Mutti said with a grin. "About two kilometers from here, over by Uderhöh, people have been finding blueberries in the forest."

The following Sunday we went berry picking. Oma stayed behind to watch Helga, Hubert, and Dieter. Dozens of people were already combing through the blueberry bushes at the edge of the forest. Most of the fruit had been stripped clean. We walked quite deep into the forest before we found any blueberries. Ilse and Mutti carried three small milk cans to which Oma had attached handles made of thick wire. Gerda,

Dorchen, and I were supposed to collect as many blueberries as possible, but during the first hour we ate most of the berries we picked, especially the big ripe sweet ones. It took us more than half a day to fill all three milk cans, about fifteen liters of blueberries in all. Mutti guided us back out of the forest on the long walk home. For dinner Oma cooked us a wonderful blueberry and flour dumpling soup.

* * *

One of Mutti's friends from work, Mrs. Rehm, had a son named Manfred. He and I became good friends. Manfred had a great sense of humor. His trademark was his contagious laugh. Just like me, he was always in search of something to eat.

I found it puzzling that people mistook us for each other. Manfred was my age, but a little shorter. He also had light blond hair and blue eyes, but his nose was sprinkled with freckles. During the summer his skin tanned a nice shade of brown. He also had a better haircut because his mother cut his hair in a somewhat professional manner, whereas Oma cut my hair with her sewing scissors. Despite these differences, on two occasions Manfred was blamed when I had shot overripe elderberries through a hollowed-out elderberry stem at women wearing light-colored blouses. Manfred had a difficult time convincing his mother that I was the one at fault. The news traveled quickly back to Mutti who gave me a sound thrashing.

On a sticky day in July, Manfred and I were heading back home from a small forest outside of Goldbach where we had been collecting wood. As a truck slowly rumbled past us, three cabbage heads tumbled off the back. Two cabbages rolled off to one side, but the third one split open as it landed with a loud splat. We ran after the truck, hoping the two Russian soldiers sitting on top of the produce wouldn't signal the driver to stop. Instead, laughing, they launched two more cabbage heads in our direction.

"Da svidanye, Friitz!" they called out as they waved goodbye. Now we were certain that the truck would not stop.

Manfred and I both yelled back, "Spassiba!" at the top of our lungs, but the soldiers did not hear us over the noise of the engine. By the time the truck had disappeared in the distance we had collected all five cabbage heads from where they lay scattered along the road.

"The first one was the biggest," I noted. "Why don't we start on that one?"

We hid two of the cabbage heads under the wood in Manfred's cart and two under the wood in mine. Pulling our carts to the side of the road, we sat down in the grass and had lunch.

"Why'd that soldier yell 'Friitz' at us?" I asked Manfred.

"It's their way of saying Fritz. They call us Friitz just like we call them Ivan."

"How'd you know that?"

"My mother told me."

Our stomachs swelled as we ate the giant cabbage, but we managed to eat it all, celebrating afterwards by waving and belching at the drivers of passing wagons and trucks.

"My stomach hurts," I grumbled.

Manfred rubbed his bloated belly as we walked home.

"Mine too," he said. "And I'm still hungry, for anything but cabbage."

Manfred went to his house and minutes later I went down the steep driveway behind our apartment to unload the wood at our wood chopping place. Gerda was there with the children. She was busy helping Dieter with his buttons.

"Can you please help Hubert?"

Hubert averted his eyes. "I'll wait for Gerda if you don't mind."

"Come on, don't make such a fuss. Whatever she can do, I can do too."

I picked leaves from a bush to wipe his bottom. Hubert's protruding gut was nearly the length of my little finger. As I tried to squeeze it back inside, Hubert squealed in pain.

"Sorry, little Brother. I'll try to do better next time," I said, imagining how uncomfortable he must feel.

"His problem's getting worse by the day," Gerda confided. "It was about time you saw it for yourself."

After helping Hubert, I began to unload the wood from my handcart. Oma came into the courtyard at that moment.

"Oma! Look what I've got!" I announced proudly. "I've not only brought back wood, but also two big cabbage heads."

"You didn't steal them, did you?"

"A truck from the Kolkhoz lost three on the road and we picked them up. And a Russian soldier threw down two more for us. Wasn't that great? Manfred and I each took two."

"So where's the fifth cabbage head?" Oma asked sternly.

"We ate it for lunch!"

"You should have brought it home," she snapped disapprovingly.

* * *

Oma, Gerda, and I spent many hours in the forest picking blueberries. Due to the oppressive heat, we dragged our feet all the way home. Now and then trucks and horse drawn wagons rumbled past us sending up thick clouds of dust. Oma and Gerda covered their faces with their aprons. I put my hand over my nose and mouth. My teeth felt gritty from the dust. As soon as I got home, I took off my shoes. I hated wearing them in the summertime.

After a supper of nettle spinach and a small piece of bread I felt restless. I went back out to the court yard, lolled against a tree in the sticky night air, and watched flour being unloaded from a big truck. Wondering how much daylight was left, I poked my head inside the door of the Russian bakery. Ever since Oma had discovered the bakery clock, she had sent Dorchen, Gerda, or me over at least once a day to check on the time.

"Dobryj vetsher!" I greeted the bakers. "Good evening!"

Every time I entered the bakery, I compared it to the tidy kitchen behind Uncle Buchmann's shop in Schippenbeil. A dozen sacks of flour lay on the filthy floor along the left-hand wall. Beside them was an open bag overflowing with coarse, gray pebbles of salt, the kind that left wet salty clumps inside the bread. One baker, a woman in a greasy apron, was ladling thick grayish-brown liquid from a giant vat into dented baking tins, each one large enough to make an official kilogram of bread, while the other baker was reaching into the oven with a long flat paddle to retrieve finished loaves in baking tins. My mouth watered at the smell of the freshly baked bread. I envied the circling flies that would surely pick up a few crumbs.

The clock hung on a grimy wall to the right of the entrance. It was a little past six o'clock. I had another three or four hours before dark, enough time to do something.

From past experience I knew that after the flour was unloaded, the delivery truck would creep up the steep hill and come to a full stop, before turning to the left and continuing along the main village road. All I had to do was hitch a ride to the top of the hill and jump off before the turn. I had only a short walk from there to Manfred's house. I clambered onto the right running board of the truck and sat down. The driver said a few words to the baker, climbed into the cabin of the truck, turned on the motor, and drove off.

It felt wonderful to ride up the hill. To my surprise, the truck turned left without stopping, lumbering through Goldbach in the direction of Tapiau. Convinced the driver would make another left turn and stop at the Kolkhoz, I enjoyed the ride, imagining myself sprinting back from the Kolkhoz over the village meadow to Manfred's house, but the truck did not turn towards the Kolkhoz. It kept on going straight ahead. Leaving Goldbach, the truck was gaining speed fast. The houses of

Goldbach disappeared. We zoomed past vast potato fields. I started to shout at the top of my lungs, but the driver did not hear me.

Faced with the possibility of going to Tapiau eleven kilometers away, I panicked and jumped off. Landing hard, I rolled over a few times and lay in a dazed heap on the road. For a moment I was sure I was going to die. Blood gushed from my left foot. Every part of me hurt and I began to scream for help.

The truck stopped fifty meters or so further along and the driver hopped out and ran back to where I lay. He examined my foot, said something in Russian, and carried me to the side of the road. As he walked back to his truck I was certain he would abandon me to my fate, but instead, the driver managed to turn around by backing into a nearby field. He pulled up next to where I was lying. Once again the Russian climbed out of the cab. Shaking his head, he lifted me up, put me into the passenger seat, and slammed the door shut, returning to his seat on the other side. Gesturing to me that I should hold my left foot over my right knee he drove me back to the bakery courtyard.

Gently lifting me down, he pointed at the running board and said to me half serious, half grinning in broken German, "Nix gutt, nix gutt."

At that moment, Oma walked by on her way to join the children at the wood chopping place. Aghast at seeing me all bloody and covered with dust, she was less feisty than usual when she asked me, "What have you done this time?"

Oma gestured to the Russian to carry me to the wood chopping place. She thanked him in German with a "Danke schön."

I thanked him in Russian. "Spassiba, tovarish."

He shrugged his shoulders, got back behind the wheel of his truck and chugged off up the hill.

While Oma went upstairs to get grayish rags to wrap around my foot, I felt ashamed and embarrassed as I told Gerda and Dorchen what I had done. By chance Mutti came home earlier than usual that day. She and Oma trundled me off in our handcart across the meadow to the makeshift hospital recently established by the Russians in what had once been a large farmhouse. A nurse washed the burst skin on the side of my foot with a red violet liquid. She bandaged me and told us to return the next day.

"It could have been a lot worse," Mutti told me on the way home. "And I'm sure you learned a good lesson. You might not be so lucky the next time."

Oma was not so generous. "How could you be so foolish as to take a ride on the running board of a truck? I can't believe anyone could be so dumb, you good-for-nothing."

Worry and pain kept me awake most of that night.

The next morning Mutti went to the Kolkhoz as usual, but she came home around lunchtime. She brought Hubert along with me to the hospital.

The Russian doctor was a tiny woman who spoke German. After examining me, she said I had no broken bones. She washed my foot again with the red violet solution.

"The wound is about five centimeters long. Given time, it will heal by itself."

"What did you put on it?" Mutti asked.

"Potassium permanganate solution."

"And you're sure the solution will do the job? He doesn't need stitches?" Mutti persisted.

"Well, if you must know, even if stitches were required, I wouldn't have the proper instruments and medical supplies. To be on the safe side, I'd like to see Günter again in three days."

"If you don't mind, Doctor, I'd also like you to look at my younger boy as well."

After the doctor examined Hubert, she turned to Mutti. "His condition isn't serious at the moment, but he'll eventually need an operation to correct it."

"Do you think it's safe to wait?"

"Let me put it this way. At the moment there isn't a single hospital in the area equipped to do the procedure. Why don't you check back with me in a year or so? Perhaps we'll have the things we need by then."

I went twice more on the little cart with Oma's and Gerda's help to see the nurse. After that I went to the hospital on my own. Limping over the village meadow and across the brook took forever. How short the distance was when I had been able to run! By the time I passed the weed-covered ruins of an old stone house and climbed the hill to the hospital I was drenched with sweat. Each time, all the nurse could do was to wash my foot in the red violet solution. After a few days my wound became infected. Three weeks went by, but there was no improvement. Oma ran out of patience.

"Something's not right. Maybe they're only using colored water. Who knows? I don't trust that so-called hospital."

"But Oma..."

"I'm going to get more of those fleshy green leaves." She disappeared down the stairs.

She returned with three stems full of leaves which she placed in one of our tin can cups. After Oma applied the green fleshy leaves for a week, my foot finally began to improve. Within another week, all that was left was a long, dark red scar.

For nearly five weeks, I was not able to help Oma get wood or collect berries, chamomile blossoms, sorrel, and stinging nettle. During the entire time, Oma, frustrated by the lack of food and overburdened with work, complained about how dumb I had been. I was anxious to get out of the house, to roam around again with Gerda and with Manfred.

When the day finally came, I felt wonderfully free, but whenever I saw that flour truck in the bakery courtyard, I got a funny feeling in the pit of my stomach. Even so, I always made a point of looking for the Russian driver who had rescued me to thank him one more time, but he never drove that route again.

* * *

Towards the end of August, food was available if one worked for it. We had our choice of blueberries, raspberries, blackberries, strawberries, and acorns in the forest. Oma roasted the acorns in a frying pan and used them to make "coffee" which we drank with practically every meal.

Many of the older German women collected mushrooms. Rumors floated through Goldbach about whole families getting sick or even dying from poisonous mushrooms. If Opa had been alive, he could have taught us which ones were safe to eat, but since Opa was gone, Gerda and I decided to wait until we met somebody who could teach us the basics.

On the way to and from the forest to pick berries we passed by fields of yellow rye and oats, tomatoes, cabbage, and potatoes. With great difficulty we resisted the temptation to run into a field and steal something. The fear of being caught by the Russians was too great. Farm workers and their Russian supervisors were always in the fields or driving by in their trucks and wagons. Punishment for stealing was harsh. Armed Russian soldiers guarded the fields at night and would shoot if necessary.However, Mutti soon found out that the Russians looked the other way if we collected grain from fields that were already harvested. No matter how careful they were, the Kolkhoz workers always left behind some ears of rye, barley, and oats. Once wet, the grains would mold and rot, so we had to hurry to gather them up before they were drenched by rain.

* * *

As we busied ourselves collecting whatever food was available, Oma and Mutti talked to each other about the Schmidt family downstairs, wondering what they were doing to prepare for the coming winter.

"The Schmidts speak such a fine German, they probably come from the upper class," Mutti said one day. "I guess they're not used to working with their hands."

Officially Mrs. Schmidt's daughter-in-law worked at the Kolkhoz, but often she stayed home from work because she felt sick. Although the older Mrs. Schmidt was probably the same age as Oma, she seldom ventured out, spending her time reading poems to her granddaughters or being read to by them. The only thing the Schmidts collected were the scraggly wild flowers drooping in a small vase on their kitchen table.

"I wish I still had my poetry books from school," Gerda said one day, somewhat wistfully.

Oma quickly dismissed the thought. "We don't have time to read poetry or to collect flowers," she snapped. "People can't eat flowers."

"Yes, Oma," Gerda said. We both got the message.

Oma kept us busy picking berries and herbs or collecting wood for our stove. Once or twice, she brought blueberries down to Mrs. Schmidt, explaining to her where they could find more, but Mrs. Schmidt did not show the slightest interest in this information. Although Gerda and I were skinny, the Schmidt grandchildren were even skinnier.

I wondered why Oma concerned herself about the Schmidt family. In my opinion, it was none of our business what they did. One afternoon Oma told us a fable she had learned from her mother.

"Ants worked hard collecting grain for the coming winter. In the late fall a grasshopper came and begged for something to eat. The ants asked the grasshopper what he had been doing all summer long. 'I made cheerful music with my fiddle,' he explained. He had been too busy merrymaking to collect and store away any food. The ants scolded the grasshopper. 'When winter comes,' they told him, 'you can fiddle and we shall eat.' "

"Can you tell us another story, please?" Cousin Helga begged.

"No. That's all for today. I have work to do," Oma said and she disappeared in the kitchen.

Gerda and I were sure Oma had not told us the story just for our entertainment.

CHAPTER 13

One cool evening in September Mutti called us all into the living room.

"Liesbeth," she said, "I think we have to let everybody know. Why don't you tell them?"

Aunt Liesbeth sighed. "Two weeks ago, rumors began flying at the Kolkhoz that we were going to be sent to Germany. Ilse knew about it, of course, and Oma, but we didn't know whether the rest of you did."

We all shook our heads. "Is there any truth to it?" Gerda asked.

"It was a hoax," Aunt Liesbeth said. "A Russian official told me today not to believe a word of it."

"Was he sure?" Dorchen asked.

"He was sure, all right. He felt so bad about it; he tried to make me feel better. 'Believe, day will come when you go to Germany, but now njet.' That's exactly what he told me."

Oma had been unusually quiet, studying the disappointment in our faces. "It's nice to have hope," she said, "but one thing's for sure, while some people daydream about getting out of here, winter's just around the corner. If the Russians ever do decide to send us back to Germany, I want to be sure we're all alive to see it."

* * *

During these autumn days, Gerda and I, often together with Dorchen, would go to the fields two or three times a week to collect the fallen rye and oats. As we worked, we chewed on mouthfuls of grain.

We always filled a bag with ears of rye, oats or wheat to take home. After Oma dried the ears, she put them into a burlap sack. Near our wood chopping place I set the sack on the chopping block, pounded it with a small wooden board, and emptied it into a big, flat bowl. Oma lifted the bowl up and down very fast. As the contents were suspended momentarily in the air, the wind carried away the fluffy chaff, leaving the heavier grain to settle back to the bottom of the bowl.

Grain soup (Oma called it by its East Prussian name Schlunz), was our staple food during the fall. Oma cooked the rough kernels of rye, barley, wheat, or oats, which had been coarsely ground in her coffee mill. When Oma wanted to bake bread and pancakes, she needed a finer grind and ordered Gerda and me to lug a full bag of grain over to Mr. Ademeit.

"I've been wondering where you got the millstones," I asked him one day.

"This old mill? I found it buried under a pile of tools, wooden boards, and dusty junk. The minute I saw it, I knew right away what it was. When I was your age my grandfather had one just like it. I think at one time every household in East Prussia had one, at least out in the country."

Mr. Ademeit's mill consisted of two round stones which ground the grain into grits. The stones were quite heavy. It took a great deal of effort to turn the crank. A second grinding turned the grits into coarse flour. Mr. Ademeit kept some of the grits in payment for his services.

"Are your horseshoes still bringing you good luck, sir? We'll need plenty of it to get through the coming winter."

"That's only a silly superstition."

"I know, sir."

"Tell me Günter, do you ever pray?"

"Yes I do, sir."

"Who taught you how?"

"My Opa."

"The one I buried? He died much too young. I'm sure he was a good man."

"Yes, he was." The words caught in my throat.

"Never depend on luck alone, I always say. For things that really matter, you have to keep on praying."

"I will, Mr. Ademeit."

* * *

In October the weather began to turn colder. Gerda and I went again to search for potatoes on harvested fields, but all we found after a lot of digging with our small hoes were a few potatoes, some already starting to rot.

Oma began to use wood for the stove in the living room. She stepped up the pressure on Gerda and me.

"Winter is right around the corner. I want you to collect as much wood as possible, even if it's not completely dry. It can dry right here in the house."

All of the wooden fences in Goldbach had long since been carried off. Any wood at the edge of the forest had also been picked clean. In order to find more, we had to go deeper into the forest. It was difficult to pull a loaded handcart over the uneven forest floor. Roots jutted up through the narrow dirt path. If we piled the cart too high, the wood on top slipped off and we had to reload it.

Desperate, people started digging out the railroad ties running parallel to the village street. The ties were all that was left of a narrow gauge railway which had operated between Tapiau and Labiau before the end of the war.

After watching for a few days, Gerda and I took our handcart, a shovel, and a pickaxe and attacked a section of railroad ties. It was

backbreaking work because the ties were embedded in gravel. Sweat soon ran down our foreheads. We took frequent breaks. We needed many hours to dig out one tie. With great effort, we lifted the heavy tie onto the cart and hauled it back to our wood chopping place. Once we had the hang of it, we managed to unearth twenty-two railroad ties over the next few days.

Grunting with the effort, the two of us hoisted a heavy tie onto the sawhorse. Sawing the tie proved to be even more difficult. We examined the wood to find the best place to make the cut, but even so, we had only sawed a short way down before hearing the grating noise a saw makes when it hits metal.

We started another cut a short distance farther down, but once again heard that terrible bone-chilling sound. We dared not risk damaging our saw. An unbroken saw was more valuable than a burlap sack full of potatoes. Considering how long it had taken us to dig out all of the ties, we were frustrated and angry. Still, we were finally forced to give up.

Heaving the tie down from the sawhorse, we put it with the others. The following Sunday, Ilse and Mutti helped us to stack the ties into a neat pile.

"Don't feel bad," Mutti told us. "One of these days Ilse and I will try to saw the ties into manageable pieces so they can be chopped apart. From what I've heard, railroad ties make wonderful firewood. They're soaked in a liquid chemical which helps them burn."

"But Oma needs wood now. How soon can you start?" I asked in frustration.

"Just as soon as our work at the Kolkhoz lets up a little bit. Right now I wouldn't have the strength."

"Aunt Gretel's right," Ilse added. "By the time Sunday rolls around, I barely have the energy to stand up."

Goldbach had no gas, no electricity, and no coal. Yet, however desperately everyone needed wood for cooking and heating, it was an unwritten law that wood stored outside would not be stolen. When it came to food, that was another story. In the spring, apples, pears, plums, and cherries disappeared before they had a chance to ripen.

When the cherry trees were bare, as they were in the autumn, I scraped off clumps of transparent resin oozing from the stumps of broken branches. Chewing that sticky stuff took my mind off the emptiness in the pit of my stomach. Tar dripping from the roofs of small sheds and barns served the same purpose, but Gerda shamed me into giving it up. She said the tar left ugly black spots on my teeth.

* * *

One afternoon Manfred and I went up to the cemetery next to the abandoned village church on the hill. Many of the stone markers lay flat on the ground; some graves gaped open, exposing the bones inside. Thick grass and weeds sprouted in the mounds of dirt piled alongside. Bones, bleached by the sun, were strewn about on the ground. Manfred pointed to an especially big bone. "Do you think it's from the upper or lower part of the leg?"

"How do you know it's even human? It could be from an animal."

"It's lying in the cemetery. What else could it be?"

"Maybe you should take it home and ask your mother."

"That's sick."

"Well, you're the one who wants to know."

"Whatever it is, it must be good for something."

Manfred slid his foot under the center of the bone and flung it a short distance away. We competed to see who could fling it farther. The third time we retrieved the bone, we nearly tripped over four skulls lying in the dirt, their vacant eyes staring up at us reproachfully. Our game came to a sudden halt.

We hurried over to the other side of the cemetery, used for more recent burials. To my relief, the small wooden cross with Opa's crudely carved name was still in place.

The doors of the church were missing, the arched window openings empty. All of the glass had long since been shot away. The walls were so thick, both Manfred and I could have sprawled comfortably on the stone sill, had we been able to climb up.

We ventured inside. Our heavy soles echoed loudly in that empty shell of a church. I glared down disapprovingly at my shoes. Already too small, they crushed my feet and pinched my toes. How would I manage if I grew any bigger?

Most of the wooden pews had already been taken away for firewood. Only a few benches towards the front were left. Six, or to be exact, five and one-half carved disciples lay on the dusty floor. The apostles had been carved out of solid wood. Their once bright colors, the blues, the reds, the pinks, and the greens, had become pale under a thick coating of dust. White and black were harder to distinguish because the dust had turned the white to light gray and the black to dark gray over time. Earlier in the summer there had been more disciples, but we had never seen all twelve.

We tried to stand one black bearded disciple on his feet, but the bottom of the statue was too uneven. Perhaps he had once hung from one of the big columns decorating the church or he had been attached somehow to the altar.

"Have you ever been tempted to haul away a bench?" Manfred asked, as he ran his finger over the fine wood.

"I'd have to be really desperate. After all, this is still a church."

In one of the small alcoves of the church were a few remaining fragments of a Bible verse which had once decorated the wall. The colorful lettering reminded me of Opa's Bible in Langendorf. I was glad that Opa could not see the poor state of the church next to which he was buried.

It started to drizzle as we picked up fallen tree branches on our way home. A woman and two girls were also scrounging for wood nearby. As soon as the woman spoke to me in Russian, I recognized her as the wife of the Russian veteran who had been sent to Siberia for beating Oma with his crutch.

"Sdrastvujte," I mumbled. "Good day." It was one of the few Russian expressions I knew, except for some words pertaining to food.

"The three of them were poorly dressed. They're struggling just like us," I reported to Oma later.

"That poor woman," she replied. "She had a hard life with him and now she's even worse off without him."

* * *

Day after day, Gerda and I passed our neat stack of unused railroad ties as we headed for a small forest in search of wood. We had little success, bringing home nothing but thin, wet twigs and soggy pine cones.

"That's all you found, you lazy bones?" Oma would greet us as we dropped our skimpy load next to the stove to dry. "Well, I suppose it's better than nothing."

The roads became muddy and the weather turned decidedly colder. The temperature in the Schmidt's kitchen was no warmer than it was outside.

"Have you seen anyone from the Schmidt family lately?" I asked Oma one afternoon when I got back upstairs.

"Now that you mention it, I haven't. As far as I can tell, they haven't lit their stove for days. It's beyond me how none of them seems to care."

* * *

In November we had the first snow. It was bitter cold outside and raw. In desperation Gerda and I went up to the abandoned village church to search for wood. As we stepped inside, the first thing that struck me was that only two of the disciples were left.

"Three and one-half disciples have disappeared since Manfred and I were here last," I whispered to Gerda, afraid the remaining apostles might hear me. I had secretly decided that the last two statues were Peter and John.

My conscience bothered me as I helped Gerda saw one of the last damaged benches into pieces. We needed four trips to bring all of the wood home in our handcart.

If we didn't take it, someone else would, I rationalized. As Gerda and I headed for home, I wondered how long before the other statues too went for firewood.

* * *

Oma found frozen potato peels in the garbage dump behind the home of a Russian family. She fried them in acorn coffee. It was getting dark early now and after our meager supper of thin potato soup with fried potato peels on the side, we all sat in the living room, huddled together like roosting chickens, the smaller children on the older one's laps for extra warmth.

"Read us about how David killed Goliath with his slingshot!" Hubert begged Oma, but she shook her head.

"We can't waste the fuel for the lamp. How about a story from my childhood instead?"

As our eyes struggled to adjust to the ever darkening room, Oma cleared her throat and, after a dramatic pause, began to speak.

"Many years before I was born," Oma began, "a woman lived in our village with her husband and her two children. One day the husband came home early and caught his wife cheating on him with another man. The husband sold the farm, took their children with him, and moved away. Although the woman tried to meet someone new, she never succeeded. She was shunned by everybody.

"But one day a wealthy man came to the village with a sack full of gold. He bought a vast farm and he asked the woman to marry

182

him. Everyone in the village was invited to the wedding. Radiant, the bride stood with her father in front of the altar, waiting for her rich bridegroom.

"The bridegroom, a tall handsome man dressed in a tuxedo, walked down the aisle. Just then a little girl pointed and shrieked, 'Look, he has a cloven hoof!' Terrified, the whole parish looked down and saw that the little girl was right.

"The bridegroom turned bright red. Suddenly two little horns appeared on his forehead and a long shaggy tail grew out in the back. Before the eyes of the astonished congregation, he rose slowly off the ground and with a loud bang and a burst of fire he crashed right through the thick stone wall. No matter how hard craftsmen worked to fill the hole after that, no one ever succeeded. By then even the infidels knew the bridegroom was the Devil."

Oma put the fear of the Devil into us with this terrifying story. I squeezed Gerda's arm, sure she was also thinking about the bench we had sawed apart in the church.

"I wish we could bring back the wood," I whispered, but of course we both knew it was too late for that.

Oma's story cost me a night's sleep. This wasn't like the tale she had told us in the summer when we asked about the lights flickering among the alder trees in a swamp outside of Goldbach.

"Those will-o'-the wisps are the souls of sinners, waiting to see if God will allow them into heaven," she had declared. Yet after a little detective work on my part, I had soon found out they were actually hovering fireflies. However, Oma's latest story defied explanation. A person of flesh and blood could never have burst through a solid wall like that. Had Satan enticed Gerda and me to steal the bench from the church? Yes, he had! I was sure of it, and God was bound to punish us both. The only question was how and when.

* * *

My cramped toes bled when I walked. Mutti asked around at the Kolkhoz for larger shoes for me. A few days later, an old farmer brought her a pair of leather boots, stiff from years of hard use. The boots were much too big for me and the soles were so thin that my feet felt like blocks of ice the first time I wore them in the snow.

"I've spoken to Mr. Ademeit," Oma told me, "and he says he can solve your problem. Wear your tight shoes when you go over there, and be sure to bring your new boots along."

Wasting no time, I hobbled over to see Mr. Ademeit. He opened the door on the first knock.

"Good afternoon, Mr. Ademeit."

"So what's new? Got any tobacco for me?" he greeted me in a booming voice.

"I'm afraid not," I shouted. "There's not much tobacco right now. I'm here about the boots."

"Yes, I know. I know. Your Oma told me. Take off your shoes, please, and step on this board. I need to see what size you are."

He bent down and drew the outline of my feet on the wood.

"That should do it. You can pick up your boots in three days. And don't forget to give my regards to your Oma and your mother for me!"

"Thank you! I'll do that!"

* * *

Three days later I limped back to Mr. Ademeit's in my tight shoes. A strange-looking pair of boots was waiting for me.

Mr. Ademeit had carefully removed the soles from the boots. He had nailed the boots to hand-carved wooden soles. The back part of the sole covered about two-thirds of the boot. A small platform heel was carved from one piece of wood. The remaining one-third in the front of the boot was made from a separate piece of wood. Both parts were hinged together with a small piece of leather.

My boots looked brand new. Mr. Ademeit had even shined them with grease. Oma always polished our shoes with a wet brush dipped into black soot from the oven. We hadn't had shoe polish or grease for years. I wondered where he'd gotten it.

With a twinkle in his eyes, Mr. Ademeit warned me, "They'll take some getting used to. I left them big, so you can use them for a long time."

They certainly were big. As soon as I got home, I tried them on, wearing two threadbare pairs of socks held together by thick layers of darning yarn, but my feet still swam inside my boots. Oma found me two square rags. She spread one on the ground.

"Place your foot smack in the middle of the rag. Steady now."

She folded the ends skillfully up and around my foot. Holding the rag the way Oma had, I slipped my foot into the boot. Even stuffed with cloth, it was still a little large. I put on the other boot the same way and attempted to walk.

Elevated by the thick wooden platforms, I enjoyed being suddenly taller as I took a few tentative steps. The flexible front third of the sole made walking quite comfortable in our apartment, but the wooden sole was slippery. When I tried to wear the boots in the snow, I had to flex my foot so that the space between the two sections of the sole could grip the ground and give me traction.

Those treacherous platform heels also made it even more difficult to carry out the pail. However cautiously I felt my way down those two cold flights, my feet always threatened to slip out from under me. I was in a sweat by the time I reached ground level.

To remedy my problem, Mr. Ademeit nailed tacks with big metal heads into the soles to prevent me from slipping. "Here you are," he said. "What do you think?"

"Thank you, Mr. Ademeit. I'm sure they'll do just fine," I said, putting the boots back on.

"Feel free to stop by any time if you need a new layer of grease. If you wait 'til it wears off, the water will seep right through the leather."

"Yes, sir. Thank you."

"I should've used those tacks in the first place."

Clicking and clacking as I walked, my spiky footwear reminded me of Vati's hobnailed army boots, tapping out rhythms on Oma's polished vestibule floor in Langendorf. With my feet snug and my toes enjoying the extra wiggle room, I lugged down our pail with renewed confidence, morning and evening.

* * *

Our daily Schlunz became thinner and thinner. I daydreamed often about our dining room table in Langendorf, imagining my cloth napkin in its silver ring and my monogrammed silver spoon dipping into thick cherry soup.

Within a short time Dieter came down with a bad cold; a few days later so did Helga and Hubert. Whenever I ventured outside in my thin woolen cap to beg in front of the Magazin, I dreamt about owning a fur ushanka with earflaps such as the Russian boys and men wore.

Occasionally, one or two Russians gave me a few kopeks which I slipped into my pocket, saving up until I had enough to buy a little piece of bread. One day as I was walking home with a few precious coins jingling in my pocket, I ran into "Horns-head," a Russian boy four or five years older than I was. He was a papirossi-smoking bully, who enjoyed shoving younger children around. I was afraid of him, and he knew it.

Gerda and I had nicknamed him Horns-head because he strutted around in a worn tanker's helmet all summer long. The padded leather protective straps on top of the helmet made him look like a charging ram. Much too young to have been a tank crewman during the war, he wore the helmet only to show off.

186

On this occasion, he was wearing a brand new Russian fur cap with a bright red star on the front flap. Chomping on a raw onion as though it were an apple, he planted himself in front of me and pointed to my pants pockets. I pulled a grayish handkerchief out of my left pocket, but he shook his head. Reluctantly, I took out three kopek coins from the same pocket. He grabbed them out of my hand.

Still, Horns-head was not done with me. Pulling his own pocket completely inside out, he gestured to me to do the same. When I hesitated, he started counting while glaring at me with his dark, deep-set eyes.

"Adin! Dva! Tri!" His meaning unmistakable, I hurried to comply. More coins fell out into the snow. He made me pick them up and hand them to him. Scared he might beat me up, I pulled out my right coat pocket too, although I knew there was nothing in it but a big hole.

"Nichivo, nichivo!" (Never mind, never mind), he said, and he flashed a wicked smile, revealing wide gaps between his teeth. Half of his teeth were yellow, the others only black stumps. His breath smelled of onion and decay.

As Horns-head sauntered off, jingling my coins in his pocket, I was furious. What he had taken from me was not even enough to buy a small piece of bread, but the fact that he had stolen it made me mad; yet I was powerless to fight back. Ashamed, I never told anyone what had happened.

A few days later a well-dressed Russian boy about my age bought a loaf of bread in the Magazin. When he received his change from the clerk, he whipped off his fur cap, tucked the coins inside and quickly put the cap back on his head.

Horns-head must have robbed him, too, I decided.

* * *

"Get up, you lazy boy!" Oma tugged at my comforter. "We're nearly out of wood for the stove."

I hurried into my clothes and put on my coat, cap, and mittens. Grabbing the hatchet, I raced downstairs. Since our woodpile was covered with snow and ice, it took all of my strength to clear off the snow and pry out an armful of wood. By the time I was back upstairs, I was no longer cold.

"Next time, make sure I don't have to ask you first!" Oma scolded as I set the load of wood down in the kitchen.

Gerda, who had been sitting with my cousin Dieter, grinned at me. "What's so funny?" I demanded.

"You probably don't even know what day this is," she teased.

Two days had passed since Mutti's day off. "Sure I do. It's Tuesday," I said.

"Ilse read yesterday's date in the Pravda," Gerda said, "and she said to be sure to tell you the date this morning: December 3, 1946."

"Oh my goodness!" Oma exclaimed. "It's Günter's birthday. With so many grandchildren, I have trouble keeping track. How old are you now?"

"If Ilse's right about the date, I'm nine years old today," I replied proudly.

"You have grown in the past year, haven't you?" Oma looked me up and down as I stretched to my full height. "I was thinking," she continued, weighing each word, "now that you're nine you have even less of an excuse to oversleep. Birthday or no birthday, I want you to run along and fetch another bundle of wood."

* * *

Ilse's work crew was ordered to accompany brigades of German and Russian women into the forest to cut wood. A few days later, Mutti's brigade was ordered to join them. Although the women and girls felled trees and cut them up all day long, our apartment was ice cold. We only had enough wood for the stove in the kitchen.

The Schmidt family still made no effort to help themselves.

"Of course I feel sorry for them," Oma told us, whenever the subject came up, "but what can we do? We don't even have enough for ourselves."

In the middle of December, old Mrs. Schmidt suddenly died. Not long afterwards her daughter-in-law got sick and could no longer go to work. The system was merciless. Unless you were able to work, you did not receive any bread. As the winter deepened, many people froze or starved to death in Goldbach and the surrounding villages.

I remembered Oma's fable about the ants and the grasshopper. When she told us the story in the fall, I smugly considered us to be the ants and the Schmidts to be the grasshoppers. Now I had the eerie feeling that all of us were grasshoppers.

* * *

I woke up in the middle of the night with a terrible pain under both sides of my jaw. My skin was hot to the touch and the whole area was swollen, something I had never experienced before.

I glanced over to my left where Mutti was sleeping, listening to her breathing and resisting the temptation to awaken her. I knew her nights were short and her workdays were long. It was still dark outside when I finally heard her getting up. As she was about to go quietly into the kitchen I whispered to her.

"Mutti, I've been awake for a while. My neck's all swollen up."

She leaned down and felt with her fingers below my ears.

"You've got swollen glands," she concluded. "Stay under the covers and tell Oma when it gets light. She'll know what to do." And with that she left for the Kolkhoz.

I cringed, recalling Oma's brutal treatment of the younger children in Palmnicken. A year had passed, but their screams of pain were still vivid in my mind. While waiting for it to get light, I tried to wish the pain away, but instead it only got worse.

When Oma woke up, I gritted my teeth and told her about my problem. She quickly confirmed Mutti's diagnosis.

"It's your glands," she announced. "I'll heat up the potatoes."

A short while later she was back, clutching a cloth bag of boiling hot potatoes.

"Lie flat on your back!" she commanded. As soon as the bag touched my neck, I moaned with pain.

Oma snapped, "Don't be such a cry baby."

Showing no mercy, she pressed the potato bag down even harder. For the first time I understood how much the little ones had suffered. Angry by now, I grabbed away the bag.

"I'll do it myself!"

"The treatment won't work unless the bag is pressed down firmly," Oma warned. "If it doesn't hurt, it doesn't help."

"I'll really squash it down," I promised.

Soon all of the other children came down with swollen glands. As we all gritted our teeth and submitted to Oma, we had to admit her methods were harsh but effective.

Once, after she had suffered the potato torture along with the rest of us, Gerda took me aside to complain. "Do you sometimes get the feeling she actually enjoys inflicting pain on others?"

"That's crossed my mind more than once."

* * *

Christmas Eve 1946 came. This time there were no surprises for anyone. The little ones and Dorchen continued to suffer with bad colds. Since we did not have enough wood to heat two rooms, we gathered next to the kitchen stove. In the confined area of the kitchen, the foul-smelling kerosene lamp emitted choking clouds of smoke.

As the sooty mark made by the lamp on the ceiling grew wider, Oma, anxious to conserve the precious kerosene, began to sing "Silent Night." Only Mutti, Aunt Liesbeth, and Ilse joined in.

We still had no word about Vati and Uncle Alfred. I barely remembered what Vati looked like. If Mutti didn't mention him from time to time, I would not have given him a second thought. All of my energy was focused on keeping warm, filling my belly, and avoiding Oma's wrath.

"I can't remember a sadder Christmas," Gerda said as Oma hurried to put out the light.

"God has given us the precious gift of life," Oma reminded her. "Let's pray we receive no less next Christmas."

* * *

Throughout Christmas day we huddled around the little stove in the kitchen. We didn't have a single piece of bread left in our house. No one was able to keep a conversation going above the dreadful chorus of coughing and sniffling and blowing of children's noses.

Gerda tried to organize a game of hide and seek in the cold living room to get the little ones moving around a bit, but they showed no interest.

"Look," she said to Helga, pointing to the frozen window facing the village street, "have you ever seen such pretty frost flowers?"

As Hubert and Dieter watched, Helga traced the outline of a frost flower with her fingernail. Suddenly, Oma stormed in.

"Gerda, don't let her do it! The glass might break. That's the last thing in the world we need right now."

In the silence that followed, we waited for Mutti or Aunt Liesbeth to come to Gerda's defense, but they did not dare to contradict Oma. Sullen, Gerda took Helga into the bedroom and closed the door. Christmas was over as far as I was concerned.

CHAPTER 14

*B*y early January 1947 Goldbach was blanketed in snow. Mutti and Ilse felled trees in the forest all day long. After a long day's work, they had to walk from the forest to the food supply office at the Kolkhoz to collect their wages for the day -- still only 300 grams of bread each. Quite often the bread was full of dark doughy clumps, some as big as hazelnuts. They were salt lumps which had not dissolved during the production and baking process. Despite our hunger, biting into one of those salt lumps made us gag. We ate the bread carefully, in small pieces.

"This stuff's a poor excuse for bread," Oma griped. "The only thing that works right in that bakery is the German clock. If I knew some Russian, I'd go over there and give those folks a piece of my mind."

"Well, I'm glad you don't," Mutti replied. "The last thing we need is a fight with the Russians at the bakery."

However bad it tasted, the salty bread was all we had. To keep Hubert from snatching the bread right out of my hand, I always spat on my piece and made sure he saw me do it.

* * *

One evening, as soon as Mutti came home, she went to look for me in the living room.

"Look what I have for you!" she exclaimed as she plopped a Russian ushanka on my head. I was overjoyed.

"Where'd you get it?" I asked with excitement.

"From Mr. Shatin who runs the food supply office at the Kolkhoz. I mentioned to him in passing that you only had a thin woolen cap."

"He must be a nice man."

"Yes, he is. Tell me, does it fit?

"It fits fine, even with the side flaps down."

Aunt Liesbeth looked at me with admiration. "Just look at Günter in his ushanka. He's beaming like a Christmas candle."

"How come there's no red star?" Gerda asked, eyeing me critically.

I pulled off the hat to take a look. The hat was fairly new, but the fur was missing where the star had once been attached.

"Who cares about that? This is the best present I've gotten in years. Please thank Mr. Shatin for me!"

"I'll tell him tomorrow," Mutti said.

Once she had eaten her soup, Ilse told us more about Mr. Shatin.

"When I first met him, he yelled at me for no reason at all, but after a while I noticed he only played the nasty big shot if another Russian official was in the food supply office. When there's no other Russian around, he's very kind."

"It's the crazy system that forces him to act like that," Oma said. (Whenever Oma criticized the "crazy system," she meant Communism).

"Maybe so," Mutti chimed in, "but on the whole, Jewish Russians treat us a lot better than the other Russians do. Take the military commander in Goldbach for example. He's a major in the Red Army, but he's also Jewish. Remember how kind his soldiers were to us after Oma was attacked?"

193

"I think it helps that so many of them speak German," Aunt Liesbeth said. "It's much easier to get along with someone who knows your own language."

"There are also some nice Russians who don't speak any German," Mutti hastened to add. "Natasha in the food supply office sometimes gives me potatoes and turnips. She always claims they're rotten so she'd have to throw them away anyhow, yet we've never discovered anything wrong with them."

* * *

On a bitter cold Sunday, Mutti and Ilse went down with Gerda and me to our snowed-in wood chopping place. Mutti and Ilse sawed the railroad tie Gerda and I had given up on weeks before. When Ilse chopped the first sawed off block with our axe, she discovered that Gerda and I had tried to saw the railroad tie at the very spot where a shell splinter had been lodged inside. Mutti and Ilse sawed six more pieces off the tie and Gerda and I sawed the last cut. Sometimes we had to use a wedge to chop a block apart because an ingrown branch was too tough to tackle. Oma was grateful for the wood.

During the following weeks, Gerda and I sawed and chopped all of the remaining ties. We knew we had to do it in order to survive, but it was hard work and we stopped often to rest. Each time the axe fell silent, Oma's angry voice would echo through the courtyard.

"I don't hear anything, Günter, you lazy boy. Why'd you stop working?"

Oma nearly always singled me out for criticism, seldom mentioning Gerda by name. Between ourselves, Gerda and I called her the "slave driver" or "master sergeant." Opa would never have yelled at me that way. He would have been right there to help us had he still been alive.

* * *

Every week or so new Russian civilians, many of them widows with children, were transferred to Goldbach to work on the Kolkhoz. Just like the German workers, they were supervised by the soldiers posted at the Kommandantura. Mutti and Aunt Liesbeth hoped there would soon be enough Russian workers so that we would be no longer needed and could be sent back to Germany. In the meantime, all of the women, German and Russian alike, worked side by side in the forest.

In addition to the bread they received, the women were promised a few rubles as a bonus if they felled more trees than the quota set by the Kolkhoz. In order to allocate credit to the proper brigade, the exposed cut of each felled tree was stamped by the gruff Russian supervisor, an aging sergeant. The undernourished workers struggled to cut wood in snow piled above their knees. Exceeding the quota was nearly impossible. Russian women who knew how to beat the system taught the others a trick. After a tree had been stamped, they sawed off a partial slice from the same tree, carefully hiding the thin tree trunk disk with the original stamp a safe distance away under deep snow drifts. The new slice had to be thick enough so that the original stamp was cut off, but thin enough so that the splintery remains left by the felled tree were untouched.

Afterwards the tree, which now looked freshly cut, was stamped again by the Russian supervisor, who carefully noted the new count in his book. Had the women been caught, they would have been sent to Siberia, but even the additional rubles earned by this risky maneuver were far from enough to relieve our dire food shortage.

The Russian women sang songs as the brigades walked back to the Kolkhoz. Their voices lifted everyone's spirits, the Germans' as well as the Russians'. One day during one of these walks through the snow, Mutti struck up a conversation with a Russian woman who spoke some German.

"Can I ask you something? The Russian man who lives downstairs always beats his wife. I've heard our supervisor does the same to his wife. Is that true?"

"Oh, yes! Does it surprise you? Many Russian men think it's their right. And of course their wives don't dare object."

"But why do they put up with it?" Mutti asked.

"The men say it's tradition, but I think the real reason is this: who can the wife complain to? If she complains, her husband will run away. With so few men around, she'd never find another one. The war killed them off by the millions."

For a while the Russian woman and Mutti walked in silence. They were joined by the wife of the one-legged Russian veteran who had been sent to Siberia. She spoke in Russian and the other woman translated.

"Life has been hard since my husband was sent to Siberia," she complained. "I'm so poor, if one of my daughters were to die, I couldn't even put a loaf of bread in her coffin."

When Oma heard this story, she shook her head. "His family is paying for what he did. It's never seemed fair to me."

"Something else doesn't make sense," commented Mutti. "We're suffering because we lost the war, but the Russians are suffering even though they won it."

Strangest of all, in my opinion, was the remark about the bread in the coffin. What a waste! I thought to myself. I'd rather eat it, no matter who died.

* * *

One frosty evening Aunt Liesbeth came home from the Kolkhoz in tears. She was carrying a piece of meat. Blood was dripping from inside her sleeve.

"You poor dear, what happened?" Oma asked.

"A dead horse," Aunt Liesbeth said, between sobs. "We heard about a dead horse on the road." Oma pulled back Aunt Liesbeth's sleeve and examined the wound.

"Try to calm down. This couldn't have been done by a dead horse," Oma said. Aunt Liesbeth took a deep breath to compose herself.

"Three women and I raced over to the road to see if we could get some of the meat. By the time we arrived, half the horse had already been cut away. Two Russian officials drove up and dusted what was left of the carcass with chlorine powder."

"Why would they do that to perfectly good meat?" Ilse asked.

"They're always afraid of contagion," Oma explained. "Who knows what the poor horse died from?"

"Anyway," Aunt Liesbeth continued, "as soon as the Russians left, two of the women began tearing at the remaining meat. While I waited for my turn, the third woman frantically shoved past me, with a knife in her hand. I think she was trying to stake her claim to the meat, but instead she cut me right through my coat."

"And you mean to say you still stayed and cut off some meat, after that?"

"No. One of the other women felt sorry for me, so she gave it to me."

After tending to Aunt Liesbeth's wound, Oma scrubbed the horse meat until she felt it would be safe to eat. Over the next few days little pieces of meat and specks of fat turned up in our potato or turnip soup; however, while Aunt Liesbeth recovered from her injuries, she couldn't go to work and we had even less bread than usual.

A few days later, Gerda and I passed by the spot where Aunt Liesbeth had been stabbed. Only the hooves of the horse remained. Dust from the sawed off bones and a few bloody scraps were sprinkled about on the snow.

* * *

Oma was worried. We hadn't heard a sound from the Schmidts' apartment for nearly a week.

"Why don't you go down and find out?" Gerda suggested.

"Later!" Oma snapped.

"Do you want me to ask them what's going on?" I volunteered, curious to see the rooms beyond the kitchen.

"No, absolutely not!" she replied sharply.

Oma disappeared in the kitchen while Gerda and I helped Dorchen keep the little ones busy. Once it got dark outside, Oma rejoined us, wiping her hands on her apron.

"Our kerosene is running low again, so I won't light the lamp until your mothers and Ilse return from the Kolkhoz. How about a hymn?"

Oma led us in singing "In the Midst of Earthly Life," her voice clear and determined as the room sank into darkness. When we finally heard the creaking of the steps, Oma suddenly stood up and rushed into the kitchen to light the lamp.

"Stay put, all of you!" she ordered and, opening the door to our apartment, she called down the staircase, "Gretel? Liesbeth? Ilse? Please don't come up. I'm coming down!" She closed the door and we all sat in the dark again.

"What's going on?" I whispered.

Dorchen spoke up. "I've no idea, but whatever it is, I don't like it."

Although the living room was dark, the moon shone in through the kitchen windows. We sat in silence, staring towards the kitchen door, waiting for the others to come back upstairs.

Finally, we heard Aunt Liesbeth's voice. "I wonder how long they've been like that. It gives me the shivers to think about it."

"They'll just have to wait until morning," Mutti said. "The night shift at the Kolkhoz wouldn't bother with something like this. In any case, we have to tell the children," and, with that, the door opened, and Mutti, Oma, Aunt Liesbeth, and Ilse walked in.

"Tell us what?" I greeted them.

Mutti cautiously set the kerosene lamp down on the little kitchen table, its light flickering crazily from the draft until Ilse closed the door. Aunt Liesbeth looked at Mutti, who nodded quietly.

"We just found young Mrs. Schmidt and her daughters, frozen to death in their beds."

"Oh my God!" Gerda gasped. "All three of them? Are you sure they're all dead?"

"I'm not a doctor, but that much I know. They're gone. There's no doubt in my mind," Mutti said.

"They must not smell when they're frozen," I commented, recalling the pungent odor of decomposing bodies along our escape route from Langendorf, "or we'd certainly have noticed."

"Have some respect for the dead!" Oma chastised me.

"What're we going to do about it?" Dorchen asked.

"We'll report it at the Kolkhoz tomorrow," Mutti said.

Even the little ones were silent as we ate our evening soup. Although no one said a word, we all had the same thought. Who among us would be the first to follow the Schmidts?

* * *

Towards noontime the next day we heard horses and loud commands outside. Rushing to the kitchen window, Oma and I saw two women with a horse drawn box cart.

"There must be some mistake. That looks like the bakery wagon. Gerda and Günter, put on your coats and come down with me!" Oma ordered.

We followed her down the stairs. In the Schmidts' kitchen, I sniffed the air, but could not detect the smell of death. The thought of invisible, odorless bodies lying somewhere nearby gave me the creeps. I hurried down to the street level, glad to inhale the fresh cold air outside.

"Mrs. Recklies?" one of the women was saying to Oma. "I'm Ruth Egger. Your daughter and I were assigned to the same work brigade at the Kolkhoz."

"Yes, of course. Pleased to meet you. I think Gretel mentioned that you're driving the bread wagon now. But what brings you here this morning, if I may ask?"

"Your daughter reported at the Kolkhoz that three people had frozen to death in your building."

"Yes, but..." Oma stammered.

"Oh! Haven't you heard? Our bakery wagon now doubles as a hearse. When we're not carrying bread, we're under orders to use it to transport corpses from Goldbach to the cemetery."

"I've seen a lot in my life, but this is too much," Oma said.

"You'll probably see us a lot more often. Can you imagine? Seventeen deaths in Goldbach just in the past two weeks. The ones upstairs bring the number up to an even twenty."

"I'd no idea so many had died," Oma said.

"We have another stop after this one. So, if you'll excuse me, we have to do our job," Ruth Egger said.

"By all means, go ahead. I'll show you the way," Oma said.

Gerda and I tagged along as Oma led Miss Egger and her assistant up to the Schmidt apartment. We all stepped into the icy kitchen.

"What are you two rascals waiting for?" Oma snapped at us. "Up you go! You shouldn't see this."

"Yes, Oma." We sprinted up to our apartment.

Peeking out our kitchen window, we watched how the two women laid the bodies on the cart.

"They look like oversized dolls," Gerda whispered.

"The ground's frozen solid. How're they going to bury them?" I whispered back.

"I don't think I want to know."

At the sound of Oma's footsteps on the stairs, we hurried to join the others in the living room. For the rest of the day, Oma was unusually tolerant of the noise level of the younger children and she never once hit me with her dishrag.

* * *

"If you don't mind my asking," Oma said to Ruth Egger when she stopped by one evening, "how on earth did you manage to land the extra job transporting bread from the bakery to the Kolkhoz?"

"I've been wondering about that, too," Aunt Liesbeth said.

"I guess Gretel didn't tell you," she began, grinning at Mutti. "Right after the potato crop had been gathered in September, I was called in by the Natshalnik (Chief of the Kolkhoz) himself and told to report to the office of the Kapitan, the Commander of Goldbach."

"You mean the tall officer with the high shiny boots? The one who always rides a beautiful black horse?" Oma interrupted.

"That's him. I was sure he could hear my knees knocking when I walked into his office. 'You wanted to see me, Kapitan?' I asked, and then he said something quite odd. 'I've observed you around the Kolkhoz and have been meaning to ask. Are you Jewish by any chance?' "

"He asked if you were Jewish? How strange."

"That's what I thought, too, and it wasn't clear to me right then on which side of his question my advantage lay."

"So what did you tell him?"

"'Quite frankly,' I said, trying to buy a little time, 'I have no idea, but may I ask you, sir, why you'd like to know?' "

"That was clever," Oma said approvingly. "Try to sound him out first."

"Yes, but he didn't let me change the subject. 'Perhaps one of your grandmothers was Jewish? There's no need to worry. The fascist villains have been defeated.' Now I saw which card to play. ''It's possible, sir,' I conceded. 'Although I don't know for sure.' "

"And what did he say to that?" Aunt Liesbeth asked impatiently.

"Nothing. Nothing at all. He complained that Russian women only know how to knit mittens! 'I've heard from several people that you know how to knit real gloves,' he said. 'My wife will give you enough wool to knit some for her, our two daughters, and several of our friends.' 'But, sir, what about my job at the Kolkhoz?' I asked. 'Don't worry about that,' he told me. 'For the next two weeks I want you to stay home and knit gloves and after that we'll see.' "

Oma leaned forward in her chair. "So what happened then?"

"Well, I did the knitting and the Kapitan's wife rewarded me with leftover kasha, piroshki, goulash, and more bread than I'd ever earned at the Kolkhoz. Not long after that, the Natshalnik promoted me to driving the horse and wagon at the bakery. It sure beats breaking my back in the fields."

"Except now you also have to transport corpses," Mutti said.

"That's true, but I don't think the Kapitan knew that would happen. No one expected the winter to be so brutal."

We sat quietly for at least a minute, digesting Ruth Egger's story. Finally Oma broke the silence.

"You aren't, are you?"

"I'm not what?"

"Jewish. You're not Jewish."

"I never said I was," Ruth Egger replied with a smile.

"There's still one thing I don't understand," Aunt Liesbeth said. "Why on earth did the Kapitan think you were?"

"He's not the first Russian to ask me. You can see for yourself. I have a very crooked nose. When I was nine, I smacked it into an iron pipe and when my poor nose healed, it was all bent out of shape."

"We're living in a crazy world, if people are judged by the shape of their noses," Oma sighed.

"The strangest thing is, the Kapitan is Jewish himself, but his nose is perfectly straight," Mutti added. "Have you heard some of the Russian workers call him and Mr. Shatin 'Itzhak' behind their backs?"

"Just like they call us Friitz and we call them Ivan?" I asked.

"I guess you could say so," said Mutti. "Still, it doesn't make it right."

"May I ask a question?" Dorchen said. "Why did it matter to the Kapitan whether you were Jewish or not?"

"You've got me there," Ruth Egger replied. "I still haven't figured it out."

* * *

"I've been thinking how nice it would be if we could use some of the rooms in the Schmidt apartment," Ilse said a few evenings later. "We're pretty cramped for space while all those rooms are going begging."

"Well, I'm not going to be the one to ask about it at the Kolkhoz," Mutti replied. "I've never understood how they decide who gets what. In my opinion, it's best to leave well enough alone."

Oma shook her head. "It's foolish to dream about having extra space when we can't even heat the rooms we have now."

"The Russians are probably planning to give the apartment to another family, anyway," Aunt Liesbeth said. "It would warm us up a bit to have someone living downstairs." But, to our surprise, the Schmidt apartment remained vacant.

Long after the Schmidts had died, every time I walked through their kitchen I always stopped for a moment to listen. One never knew.

The death of the Schmidt family made quite an impact on me in another way, not because I missed them, but because it made me focus again on what might happen to us. If Mutti and Ilse were to be crushed one day by a falling tree while working in the forest, their bread rations would stop. Would Ruth Egger come to carry us away like the Schmidts?

Rumors continued to circulate in Goldbach about people who had died in the harsh winter. Yet we also heard that in neighboring villages, especially in those without a Kolkhoz, the number of people who had perished was even higher.

* * *

Although it had not snowed for days, the weather was still bitter cold. One morning Gerda and I walked down to get two pails of water in the court yard. The wife of the Russian barber, bundled up in a wadded coat, felt boots, and several head scarves, stood next to the pump, wringing her hands. The pump was frozen shut. Gesturing us to follow her, she led us past our wood chopping place and out onto the village meadow. Breaking through the glaze on the surface with her mittens, the barber's wife pressed handfuls of powdery snow into her pail and we did the same.

Oma took one look at our buckets full of slush and threw up her hands. "It's enough to drive a person to despair!" she cried.

Once the snow had melted in the warmth of our kitchen, only a few centimeters of water were left behind.

Oma called all of the children together. "Listen up, you rascals," she warned, pointing at the pails. "No one is to drink any water made from snow or ice unless I've boiled it first. Is that clear?"

"Yes, Oma."

* * *

February 1947 arrived. Everything was blanketed in snow. For weeks a biting frost made it dangerous to venture outside. Since late fall our food had consisted of thin soup and, on good days, a little bread. The soups really did not deserve their name, consisting as they did mostly of lightly salted water, with little bits of potato or turnip or coarsely ground grain floating inside. I was hungry all the time.

But we were still alive! More and more people were dying of starvation or freezing to death in their sleep, not only Germans, but Russian civilians as well.

"I've never understood why the military gets enough to eat, when we don't," Oma grumbled one evening.

"Not any more," Mutti replied. "According to Ruth Egger, even the soldiers at the big garrison in Tapiau are running out of bread and potatoes."

"God help us," Oma said. "How is this terrible winter going to end?"

* * *

One morning Dorchen and Gerda were taking care of the little ones for a few hours in our cold living room until Oma finished her work in the kitchen.

"Mind if I go to the Magazin, Oma?" I asked.

"No, not at all. Go right ahead." She knew full well I didn't have a kopek to my name and that I really meant to beg for little pieces of bread and spare change.

"All right, see you later," I said, ready to rush off.

"Hold your horses! I want you back around lunchtime. I hope you'll bring something home." I knew she meant bread.

I trudged up the steep driveway in knee-deep snow to reach the village street. Trucks had left deep slippery ruts in the middle of the road. Yellow holes in the snow marked the spots where people had stopped to pee.

Four boys were already waiting outside the Magazin. Bundled in rags, our faces sliced by the sharp wind, we were all in competition for a few bits of bread. None of us was allowed to go into the Magazin because we had no money.

Bread was sold in 250 gram units. Because the sales clerk had to make sure the weight was measured exactly, most people carried one or two loaves with smaller pieces of bread balanced on top. The clerk was forced to use round numbers. Otherwise he could not use his abacus to figure out the amount of rubles for each sale.

Many of the Russians gobbled up their little extra pieces because they were hungry too. Others listened sympathetically when I begged with my eyes and said, "Chleb." I was so hungry, I ate whatever they gave me and ignored Oma's command to bring something home. From past experience I knew that Russians, especially women, got angry when they gave me a piece of bread and saw me pocketing it for later.

A few patrons were drunk and mean. When they cursed at me, I backed off until they were gone. Others, mellowed by vodka, ate their little pieces of bread themselves, but felt sorry for me and handed me a few kopeks. Eventually I collected enough money to buy 250 grams of bread. Now I could go into the warm Magazin.

It felt cozy to be in a heated room. I took a deep breath, enjoying the mixed aromas of fresh bread, salted cucumbers, dried fish, and cigarette smoke. I overlooked the pervasive stench of old human sweat, including my own. All over the wooden floor were little puddles from the melted snow and ice brought in on boots and shoes. Compared to the cold outside, the Magazin was a great place to be. The shelves were crammed with huge loaves of dark rye bread, matches, paparossis, and little packages of machorka, the cheap foul smelling tobacco made of tobacco plant stems and roots. On the creaky floor stood big wooden barrels full of salted tomatoes, cucumbers, sauerkraut, and salted dry fish. Burlap sacks of potatoes leaned against one wall. Stacked next to them were piles of the Russian newspaper "Pravda."

Smelling the food, I daydreamed of coming in with our handcart. I imagined how I would fill it up with ten loaves of bread and a bag full of dried fish, scooting out of the store at top speed! If I stole food, how far would I get? Out of the store? To the steep driveway? Or even into our house? Maybe I would outrun them. Perhaps I would not get caught. The loud clacking of the abacus brought me back to reality.

The abacus stood on the grimy shop counter. Its gray beads had once been white. I was fascinated by the speed with which the clerk pushed those beads back and forth to "ring up" each sale. I was reminded of the large scale and modern cash register in Uncle Buchmann's bakery back in Schippenbeil, but that was a different world.

Eleven Russians, civilians as well as soldiers, were waiting to buy food. Most wore thickly quilted pants and jackets. The jackets did not button; bands the size of wide shoe laces tied them closed. I was jealous of the warm jackets, but I was sure the Russians' felt boots were not as good as my leather boots with wooden soles. Once the snow started to melt, their feet would surely get wet, in contrast to mine!

Lice ran up and down the dark jacket worn by the man in front of me. Each person entering the Magazin immediately took off his ushanka to scratch his head. There was always something to scratch! We all had lice, the Germans, the Russian civilians, even the Russian soldiers. How could it be otherwise when soap and detergent were not available and even the water pumps had frozen shut?

Two Russian women patted me on the head and gave me their extra pieces of bread before leaving the Magazin. I ate that bread too. Since it was cozy and warm in the store and I was not in any rush, I let the "real customers" pass me.

A stocky soldier, his face reddened by frost, took his place in front of me on line. He was smoking a papirossa. When he finished the tobacco part, it started to smell of burned paper. With a wink at me, he took the papirossi out of his mouth. The mouth piece was half dissolved in saliva. He tore the soggy end of the papirossa into two even flaps, creating a miniature propeller at the top of the tube. The soldier put the papirossa between his right index finger and his right middle finger and flicked it upwards. It stuck to the ceiling together with hundreds of other papirossi tubes, some still covered with fresh spit, but most of them old and shriveled up, as if they had always been there. I grinned back at the soldier who was obviously proud of himself.

He asked me, "Kharasho?"

"Kharasho!" I replied with enthusiasm. He was so friendly, I decided not to let any one else in front of me until it was my turn to buy a little bread. I had sized him up right. When the soldier purchased his papirossis, his salted cucumbers, and his bread, he gave me a chunk of bread weighing at least 250 grams.

"Spassiba, tovarish!" I thanked him as he left the shop.

Now I stepped up to the counter and bought a piece of bread with the kopeks people had given me. Satisfied with my success, I hummed one of Oma's hymns all the way home. For once, Oma was actually pleased with what I brought back.

* * *

As I was returning home empty-handed from the Magazin a few days later, a tempting parcel, neatly tied with cord, lay directly in my path on the icy village street. Perhaps it's something to eat, I thought. Looking around to make sure I was alone, I carried the parcel to a deserted courtyard nearby and set it down in the snow.

With the little pocket knife Mr. Ademeit had given me, I carefully cut the strings and peeked at the contents: four fresh horse apples, neatly packed under a snail-shaped mound of frozen human waste. Hornshead! As I kicked away the package in disgust, my tormenter poked his head out from behind a wooden shed, stuck his tongue out at me, and tipped his hat. I had never hated him so much as at that moment. It had been a cruel trap. He knew I was hungry. He knew I'd be unable to resist his surprise package. Angry and humiliated, I ran home as fast as my awkward platform boots would take me.

* * *

Throughout the month of February, new Russians, mostly women and children, arrived in Goldbach. The old-timers chatted among themselves and pointedly snubbed the more recent arrivals. Some of the newcomers had slanted eyes. Others had eyes like mine set into wide faces with high cheek bones. A few had pitch-black hair and such dark skin they looked suntanned in the middle of winter. The newcomers were given jobs at the Kolkhoz within days of their arrival. Mutti heard from her co-workers that many of them did not even speak real Russian. They came from as far away as Siberia. Despite the frigid temperatures, many of them kept the side flaps of their ushankas up. Women and children wore their thickly wadded jackets open. Judging from the bare skin visible between the bottom edges of their jackets and the tops of their felt boots, the women apparently wore no stockings or long pants. The soles of the women's felt boots were worn so thin they practically walked barefoot on the frozen ground.

* * *

In addition to being in charge of the food supply office, Mr. Shatin was responsible for the rooms at the Kolkhoz where German women cooked sugar beet syrup. In early March, after Oma grumbled that our dwindling supply of potatoes was rotting faster than she could cook them, Mutti began to bring home sugar beet slices. I never found out whether she was given them or whether she stole them. No matter how she got them, they were a change from potatoes.

At first they tasted delicious. Oma made soup with them. She also "fried" them in a little water to crisp them up. Sugar beet slices kept us alive throughout the month. The bread earned by Mutti, Ilse, and Aunt Liesbeth at the Kolkhoz was simply not enough.

By the end of March, I began to wish I had never heard of sugar beets. The sight of them made me gag. My survival depended on them, yet many times I could not force down another mouthful.

All of the younger children were suffering from never-ending coughs and colds, lacking the energy to play no matter how hard Dorchen tried to entertain them. When Oma served up the sugar beet slices, they sat listlessly and refused to eat.

* * *

"We had a close call today," Mutti told us over supper. "Mr. Shatin walked into the kitchen just as I was slipping Ilse a metal canteen filled with syrup to take home."

"Then what happened?" I asked. "Are they going to send you to Siberia?"

"Aunt Gretel must have nerves of steel. She dropped the canteen into the bubbling cauldron of syrup!" Ilse said. "But Mr. Shatin grabbed a long iron hook from the stove, fished around for the strap and pulled it right back out."

"He dangled the sticky canteen in my face and asked, 'Is this yours?'" Mutti continued. "I've never heard him sound so angry. 'Yes, it is,' I stammered. 'I use it to bring water to work. It must have slipped right out of my hands.'"

"'That's not the way I saw it. Were you trying to steal syrup?'"

"'No, of course not. I wouldn't dare.'" As Mutti and Ilse retold the story, we sat at the edge of our seats.

"You must have been terrified," Oma said.

"I was scared to death."

Ilse interrupted. "Not just you. What a schlamassel! Aunt Gretel usually knows just what to say, but this time I was sure she wasn't going to talk us out of it."

"So how did you get away with it?" I asked Mutti impatiently.

"At first Mr. Shatin only glared at me. Then he shrugged his shoulders and, without saying another word, he gave me back my canteen and strolled out of the kitchen as if nothing had happened."

* * *

Not long after the syrup episode, Ilse did not come home from work. Mutti and Aunt Liesbeth heard a rumor that Ilse had been caught stealing wheat. I'm sure neither they nor Oma slept a wink all that

210

night. I admired Ilse. Only five years older than I was, she already had adult responsibilities, yet she never seemed bitter. She always had interesting stories to tell about her job when she came home. Ilse also had a remarkable knack for languages. She had managed to pick up even more Russian than Mutti. Sometimes, on especially cold days in the winter, the pail had been emptied before I got up in the morning. Ilse had brought it down for me. Now as I wondered whether she would be sent to Siberia, I wished I had told her how much I appreciated all that she had done. To everyone's relief, Ilse returned home the following evening. We gathered around to listen to her report.

"A German woman and I were walking back from the Kolkhoz together. The minute we left the courtyard, two Russian officials grabbed us and brought us to the administration building."

"What had you taken?" Mutti asked.

We all knew that Ilse, Aunt Liesbeth, and Mutti often smuggled out rye, barley, oats, and potatoes to bring home to Oma. Without these bits of contraband, Oma would have had nothing to put in the next day's soup.

"That's the strange part. Yesterday was one of the few days I hadn't managed to organize anything. So I wasn't worried about the body search. But when they found a small bag of wheat hidden in the other woman's clothing, they locked us both up."

"It's a strange system of justice," Oma remarked. "How did you finally get away?"

"They interrogated me again this afternoon. I guess the Russian officials were finally satisfied I had nothing to do with it, so I was sent back to my brigade."

"That was a close call. You'll have to be even more careful from now on," Mutti warned.

"Aunt Gretel, you're the one to talk," Ilse replied with a sly grin. "No one in Goldbach beats you when it comes to organizing food."

* * *

Towards the end of winter, bringing down the pail became even more unpleasant. As a result of the severe food shortages, nearly everyone had upset stomachs. The stench at the drop-off spot in the little garden beyond the bakery was unbearable. Human waste lay in heaps to all sides and the stuff took a long time to rot away.

Considering the surroundings, it struck me as odd that someone had strung clotheslines between the trees in the garden, although I never saw any laundry drying there, winter or summer. Men, women, and children, Russians as well as Germans, used the "facilities" in the garden. Children came at all hours, unashamed. Kolkhoz workers stopped by when it was still dark in the morning and in the half light before sunset. Only the elderly, seeking a little privacy, were willing to wait until no one else was around.

Finding "bathroom tissue" was my biggest problem. Grass worked well, when it was available, but it was itchy. Large leaves were definitely better than grass, but they were available only at certain times of the year. The most luxurious method was to use a piece of the Pravda. Whenever I found the newspaper lying on the street, I brought it upstairs and put it next to the pail, first stuffing a page in my pants pockets for the garden. Yet sometimes when I was outside in the winter, I had nothing along to use. This was the worst possibility of all.

* * *

"You seem unusually quiet this evening," Oma commented to Mutti, as they cleared the supper table one day in early April.

"According to Ruth Egger, 123 people have died in Goldbach since the beginning of the year and more than thirty in Gross Keylau," Mutti finally said. "Rats have gnawed nearly half the bodies she picks up."

"How dreadful!" Oma's eyes wandered to the crack under the kitchen door, to be sure it was still tightly sealed.

"Ruth's always been so cheerful, but I'm afraid she's beginning to despair. 'Gretel,' she told me, 'I don't feel sorry for the dead. They've been freed from their suffering. I only worry what's in store for us!'"

"Maybe the children should leave the room," Aunt Liesbeth chimed in, but Mutti shook her head.

"No, they should hear this, too. We have to do whatever we can to stay healthy. Our survival depends on it."

"How can we help?" Gerda asked.

"Well, for one thing, I've started to see tiny stinging nettle shoots. By next week they should be big enough to pick. So children," Mutti said, turning to us, "when your Oma sends you out to pick nettle, don't grumble. Spinach soup is chock full of vitamins."

"What about the potato clamps?" Oma asked Mutti. We all knew the harvested potatoes lay wrapped in straw in shallow pits under low mounds of earth.

Mutti shook her head as Ilse rushed to reply. "It's far too risky at this time of year. Guards are stationed near every clamp. The Russians know how desperate people are for potatoes."

Alarmed, I asked, "Have you ever organized potatoes from the clamps?"

Mutti averted her eyes. "No, of course not," she replied after a moment's pause. "Isn't that so, Ilse?"

"And risk being shot?" Ilse replied. "I wouldn't dare."

CHAPTER 15

*A*t the beginning of May, Hubert's gut was slipping out more than ever. Mutti and I took him back to the Russian lady doctor at the hospital. When we came into her examining room, she recognized me instantly.

"Let me see how that foot of yours is doing," she said, motioning me to sit on a chair near her desk.

I hadn't expected to be examined and was embarrassed by my grimy feet. Without any fuss she pressed my foot with her scrubbed pink index finger. She cleaned around the area of the wound with an alcohol-soaked cotton ball, revealing the deep red scar.

"I'm pleased to see that it's healed nicely. I hope you realize how lucky you were. You might have lost your foot. You might even have been killed." I thought again about how stupid I'd been to hitch a ride on the truck and grinned sheepishly.

She turned to Hubert. "What about this little fellow? Has there been any change?"

"I'm worried about him, Doctor. His problem has gotten worse," Mutti replied.

214

As she examined Hubert, the doctor's forehead creased with concern. "I see what you mean. Something has to be done about this boy and soon. I'll try to arrange for him to be operated on in Kaliningrad."

"How quickly can it be scheduled?"

"I really can't say. Perhaps in a week, perhaps in four weeks. I'll do the best I can. You'll have to trust me."

Mutti took Hubert firmly by the hand. "Certainly, Doctor," she said, but she looked worried.

We walked back quietly along the path across the meadow to our apartment. Oma had been anxiously waiting for us.

"So, what did the doctor say?"

"Well, we saw the same doctor as last time. You remember, the one who treated Günter's foot? Hubert needs to be sent to Königsberg for surgery, but when I asked her when, she said 'perhaps in a week, perhaps in a month.' "

"So which is it?" Oma asked impatiently.

"She doesn't know. It was a typical Russian promise. I'm sure she meant well, but I doubt that we'll ever hear from her again."

"If you don't hear anything, bring Hubert to her again in six weeks or so."

"I guess that's what I'll have to do," Mutti said as she left for work. I heard the frustration in her voice.

* * *

Three days later Mutti was astonished when the doctor sought her out at the Kolkhoz.

"This is the form you need. It's already filled out. They're expecting you tomorrow in Kaliningrad. I've written down the address of the hospital for you."

"I can't tell you how grateful I am, Doctor!" Mutti exclaimed.

"One more thing," the doctor said, anticipating Mutti's next question. "The Kolkhoz sends trucks into Kaliningrad three or four times a week. I've also arranged rides for the two of you in both directions."

Mutti and Hubert left the following morning. A day later they were back. Hubert's problem had been fixed by a routine operation. Oma and Gerda no longer had to push his gut back inside.

"How are things in the outside world?" Oma inquired.

"Judging from what I could see out of the back of the truck, not much has been done to fix the place up," Mutti replied. "Many times I didn't even know where we were. The inner city is just a pile of rubble. We swerved constantly to avoid huge potholes. The hospital was one of the few structures still standing."

"Did you see the cathedral?"

"I caught a glimpse of it, but it's just a ruin; only the shell is standing."

"What about..."

"Mother, it's gone. Königsberg is gone. There's no point in asking. I doubt the inner city will ever be rebuilt the way we once knew it."

"I hope you're wrong," Aunt Liesbeth said, shaking her head.

"And before I forget, remember all the red banners with political slogans hanging along Linden Boulevard in Palmnicken?"

"Sure I do," Oma said.

"Well, they're flapping from every post and pole. It's all communist propaganda, I'm sure. Whether they call the city Kaliningrad or Königsberg, I can't imagine what they have to boast about."

* * *

Blueberries were abundant in the summer. Gerda and I went nearly every day to pick them. Dorchen was too weak to join us. She had never bounced back following her siege of winter illness. Painfully thin and pale as a ghost, her body was racked with a constant cough and she tired easily. She no longer had the energy to care for the younger children.

On our excursions, Gerda and I popped the sweet fruit into our mouths until we were satisfied before filling our milk cans with berries to bring home. On their day off, Aunt Liesbeth, Ilse, and Mutti went with us to the forest. Afterwards, instead of going straight home, we walked over to Tapiau, hoping to sell our blueberries at the Russian farmers' market.

Although the truck had whisked us from Tapiau to Goldbach in April of 1946, it was a long way by foot. For once, I had a chance to talk to Mutti for more than a few minutes.

"I've been wondering. How do you last from breakfast until suppertime when you work at the Kolkhoz? Do they give you any lunch?"

"It depends. Up until last fall, we didn't get anything. Then they decided to provide lunch, but only when we were sent far away from the Kolkhoz to do hard labor. And during the winter, when we really needed soup, they stopped feeding us altogether."

"Well, when you do get lunch, what do they give you?"

"If we're lucky, a horse drawn wagon from the Kolkhoz comes with a giant container full of grain soup. It's not as watery as Oma's Schlunz but..."

"I wish I could have a taste of that," I interrupted.

"You didn't let me finish. I haven't told you about the fat maggots floating on top. But I'm usually so hungry I try not to think about them."

"I eat it too," Ilse chimed in. "After you've had maggot soup two or three times, you don't think about it anymore. And besides," Ilse went on, grinning at Mutti, "think of all the protein we're getting!"

"What about the Russian workers?" I asked.

"Many of them pour the soup on the ground, but of course, they get more bread than we do at the end of the work day."

217

"All this talk is making me hungry," Aunt Liesbeth said. "If I remember correctly, the Tapiau bazaar is just around the corner, at the next street crossing."

Moments later we reached the bazaar. Amazing items were on sale, even meat, butter, and sugar. The whiff of freshly baked bread tickled my nose. Baskets full of huge farmer breads covered an entire sales table. Vodka (Mutti called it "moonshine") was by far the fastest selling item.

Most of the sales people were Russians, but we also saw German women offering fine china cups, coffee pots, and cutlery.

"Would you look at that?" Aunt Liesbeth said. "They must have lived around here during the war."

"Our neighbors in Langendorf also buried their silver and their good china," Mutti agreed. "I wonder if any of them got the chance to dig them back out."

With some of the rubles Mutti received for the blueberries, she bought two loaves of peasant bread. Then she steered us back to a table we had passed earlier.

Elderly Russian women were selling little cups of a white substance with a singed brown crust on top. Mutti was curious. Pointing to a cup, she spoke to the saleslady in Russian.

"What's that, please?"

"Kefir," the shriveled old lady replied.

"Kefir?"

"It's made from milk and it's not too expensive," a German woman behind us volunteered. "You should try it."

"Thank you, we will," Mutti said. Turning to the Russian lady, she said, "Pjatj. Five."

Kefir, also called yoghurt, tasted a bit like sour ice cream. I could easily have finished off twelve cups in one sitting.

While we were perched on a low wall eating our kefir, the German woman who had recommended it walked over to us with a cup of her own.

"So? Do you like it? Did I promise you too much?"

"It's delicious," Mutti assured her.

"Where are you people from, if I may ask? I've never seen you in Tapiau before."

"From Goldbach," Mutti said.

"Oh my, that's a long walk. Tell me, do the people in Goldbach also hope to be sent back to the Reich one of these days?"

"Of course we do. We're dreaming of a better life just like everyone else."

"Well, I'm not so sure it's any better in the Reich."

"What makes you say that?" Mutti asked, eyeing her quizzically.

"Because the Russians are there too, from what I've heard. 'To the victors belong the spoils' as the old saying goes."

"I've heard rumors about a Russian occupation, but I've chosen not to believe them," Mutti replied as she jumped down from the wall. "We all need a glimmer of hope. Have a good day, madam."

"Let's go, children," Aunt Liesbeth said. "We have a long walk ahead of us."

As soon as the woman was out of earshot, Ilse exclaimed, "She must be crazy!"

"Talkative, maybe, but not crazy," Mutti replied. "I've the awful feeling there's some truth to what she said."

* * *

Eleven kilometers separated Tapiau from Goldbach. As we trudged home, I daydreamed of eating as many kefirs as I wanted. When we finally arrived at our court yard, we all rushed to the pump for water to satisfy our thirst. I collapsed into bed, too exhausted to do anything else. A few days later, Oma sent me to the Magazin with the remaining rubles to buy two more breads.

I had expected Mutti, Ilse, and Aunt Liesbeth to join us again on their days off, but it was harvest time at the Kolkhoz and they had to work. Since Dorchen was tired most of the time, Oma had to take care of the little ones in addition to doing the cooking and the laundry. Sometimes Oma joined me when I went berry picking, leaving Gerda in charge of Helga, Hubert, and Dieter. I felt sorry for Dorchen. Here we were in the middle of the summer and she still showed no improvement.

* * *

A week or so after our trip to Tapiau, I went to the Magazin to buy matches for Oma. Waiting my turn, I spotted a crumpled ruble bill lying on the floor in front of the counter. I stepped forward slightly, bumping against the Russian woman in front of me on line, and put my bare foot on the bill. Acting innocent, I looked around to see whether anyone reacted.

No one had observed me; however, I was still unsure whether I could safely retrieve the money. Scarcely daring to breathe, I moved my foot back slightly as I pretended to stare nonchalantly at the loaves of bread on the shelves behind the counter. Still focusing on the bread, I clutched the money between my toes, lifted my foot quickly up to my hand, grabbed the bill and stuffed it into my pocket.

By this time I was terrified that everyone could see from my face what I had done. Losing the nerve to buy the matches for Oma, my only desire was to get as far away from the Magazin as possible. As I slowly backed away from the counter, the man behind me on line said something to me in Russian. I felt the hair stand up on the back of my neck.

"He wants to know whether he can take your place on line," a Russian woman explained to me in German.

"Yes, yes," I replied, greatly relieved. The man gave me a grateful smile.

With my heart still pounding, I left the store. The air felt sticky. I had to control myself not to break into a run.

Safely back at our house, I pulled out the crumpled bill and flattened it out. I was stunned by my good luck. It was twenty rubles. Twenty rubles meant two loaves of bread at the Magazin. Mutti, Aunt Liesbeth, and Ilse all worked for two days to earn that much. I sprinted up the stairs two steps at a time and was out of breath when I knocked at our kitchen door.

"It's me, Günter."

Oma flung open the door. "What took you so long? How can I make Schlunz for lunch without matches to start the stove?"

"Sorry, but a number of people were in front of me and..."

"You never run out of excuses, do you?"

"But Oma..."

"Just give me the matches. The little ones are hungry or had you forgotten that?"

"But Oma, I didn't buy any matches! Here are the kopeks you gave me for the matches and twenty rubles besides."

"Twenty rubles! From whom?"

"I found them!"

Surrounded by Gerda and the other children, I explained how it had happened. I saw a hint of a smile on Oma's face as she paid me one of the few compliments I ever got from her.

"Well done. You were smart not to wait around to buy the matches. To be on the safe side, make sure you stay clear of the Magazin for the rest of the day."

Turning to Gerda, Oma continued. "I want you to go for the matches and you may as well buy a loaf of bread, too. Be careful not to lose the change on the way home!"

Gerda was beaming when she returned with her purchases. Although it was not yet lunch time, Oma gave everyone a thin slice of bread.

Neither the bread nor the story of my adventure cheered up Dorchen. Oma fussed over her constantly, bringing her extra covers and coaxing her to eat. I wondered whether Oma knew more than she was letting on about Dorchen's condition.

* * *

I was walking near the Kolkhoz when, by chance, I saw Mutti standing with Ruth Egger.

"Nice to see you again, Günter," she said, shaking my hand. "My, you've grown since I saw you last!"

I went close to Mutti and whispered into her ear.

"He wants to hear about the frogs," Mutti said, turning to Miss Egger.

"What would you like to know?"

"Do you really eat frogs?"

"As a matter of fact, I do, but only the legs. An hour or so before I leave work every day, I grab a few of the little green fellows and pop them into this bag." She showed me a small bag hanging from her apron. "When I get home I pull off the legs, skin them and fry them up. They're delicious. My mother and sister like them, too."

"And they don't make you sick?"

"Not a bit."

I wondered whether Ruth Egger was pulling my leg. Meat rarely found its way onto our table. Two or three times a year we ate horsemeat if a horse died in a farm accident. Occasionally Mr. Ademeit would barter us a rabbit for a small sack of potatoes, but we never ate frog's legs. Oma insisted they were poisonous.

* * *

Dorchen's best friend was eleven-year-old Traute Runau, a tall pretty girl with long blond pigtails. Before the end of the war, Traute's father had owned the huge farm now used by the Russians as the Kolkhoz. In a strange irony, he and his wife had been reduced to feeding themselves and their five children on wages of 600 grams of bread a day, their only compensation for working on what had once been their own property.

Towards the end of August we were all shocked to learn that the Russians had caught Mr. Runau as he tried to leave the Kolkhoz with ten kilograms of barley. In a sense, he had only taken what already belonged to him. The Russians clearly did not see it that way. Mr. Runau was placed under arrest and then sent away to ten years hard labor in Siberia. The Germans were terrified. No one, it seemed, was above the law in Goldbach.

In early September, right after the Runau incident, I woke with a start. Judging by the way the moon shone through our window, it must have been well after midnight. Only a few hours earlier I had watched, half asleep, as Mutti had gotten ready for bed, and now she was gone.

Not daring to awaken Oma, I lay wide-awake through the rest of the night, worrying about Mutti. Towards dawn, I heard heavy steps coming up the stairs. First Mutti's muffled voice and then Ilse's filtered in from the kitchen. I tiptoed into the kitchen. Moonlight shone on two bulky rucksacks and two smaller bags. Wearing dark, long-sleeved shirts, long dark pants, and dark head scarves, Mutti and Ilse looked like silhouettes.

"Where've you two been?" I whispered.

"You're still up? Why aren't you asleep?" Mutti asked.

"Where were you? I was worried about you. Were you working at the Kolkhoz?"

"We were working all right," Ilse said as she slumped into a chair.

Mutti gave Ilse a sharp look. "Don't be silly," she said to me. "Now, get back into bed and don't worry. Ilse and I are going to try to get some sleep. We've got to wake up soon to go to work."

Before I crept back to bed, I brushed my hand against one of the smaller bags and felt the bumpy shapes of potatoes. Mutti dozed off quickly. As I listened to her rhythmic breathing, I worried that what had happened to Mr. Runau might also happen to her.

* * *

The next morning, I pumped Oma for details.

"Oma, I saw Mutti and Ilse coming home late last night. I know they were stealing potatoes. How often do they go? What if they get caught?"

"That's none of your business. And whatever you saw, don't tell anybody about it. Is that clear?"

Undeterred by Oma, I asked Gerda the same questions. She was appalled by my ignorance. "Where do you think we got all of the potatoes for our basement bin last fall?" Gerda asked me.

"Do you mean they do this on a regular basis?"

"Your mother and Ilse began stealing potatoes ages ago. This time of year, they go out three, four, five times a week."

"But isn't it too dangerous?"

"It's safer now than it was in late winter and early spring. That's when they dig up the clamps for potatoes and turnips."

"What about Aunt Liesbeth? Does she go, too?"

"You know how thick her glasses are? Her eyes have gotten so much worse, she can barely see through them in the daytime. At night she's practically blind. The few times she went along, she just got in the way."

"What if they get caught?"

"Russians guarding the potatoes have the right to shoot."

"Then they shouldn't go. The risk is too great."

"Look at it this way. If they go, they may both be killed. If they don't go, our whole family will starve to death this winter."

"Isn't there anything we can do?"

"I say a prayer for them every time they go out."

When Mutti came home just before dark, she refused to talk to me about her organizing trips, but she assured me that she would not leave again that night.

"What about tomorrow?" I asked her.

Smiling, she said, "Let's take one day at a time. Do me a favor and try not to worry."

Two nights later Mutti prepared her dark outfit again. I tried to stay awake until she got home, but after a while I dozed off. The next morning I helped bring heaps of potatoes down from our kitchen to the basement.

My life was easier before I found out about Mutti's dangerous forays. I always had trouble falling asleep after that and the slightest noise during the night woke me up.

* * *

In the early dawn, I got up to use the pail. Mutti was gone. Unable to get back to sleep, I lay on my mattress, wide-awake and frightened. A short time later the old German man rang the bell to rouse the people who did the milking. Still Mutti and Ilse did not come home.

I drifted back to sleep, only to be awakened again by the clanging of the plowshare. The staircase creaked. I rushed barefoot into the kitchen just as Mutti and Ilse stepped into the apartment. Thoroughly drenched, they were not wearing rucksacks nor were they carrying any bags. Puddles of water formed around their feet.

"What happened?" I asked, feeling my heart pounding up to my throat.

"There's no time to talk right now!" Mutti said sharply.

Mutti woke up Oma and brought her into the darkened kitchen. The closed door muffled the sound of their voices. Determined to know what had happened, I strolled through the kitchen, pretending to go to the pail. Mutti and Ilse had already changed into their normal work clothes, ready to rush off to the Kolkhoz. Something had gone terribly wrong during the night.

Later that morning, Gerda and I asked Oma what had happened.

"They left in such a rush; I don't know all the details. As best I can make out, they abandoned the potatoes and spent the night hiding in the brook."

In the evening Mutti and Ilse came home an hour later than usual. To everyone's surprise they were carrying rucksacks filled with potatoes.

"Out with it!" Oma commanded. "I can't have people tracking muddy water in my kitchen without an explanation."

"We're usually the only ones out organizing potatoes, but last night we had a lot of competition," Ilse began, "but, why don't you tell it, Aunt Gretel? You're much better with the details."

"We'd just reached the edge of the potato field with our full bags when we heard Russian voices and warning shots."

"Rifle shots or submachine guns?" I interrupted.

"Rifles, I think. The Russians sometimes send in dogs, so we waded waist-deep into the brook to throw them off the scent."

"Did you hear any barking?" Gerda asked.

"If we'd waited until we could hear the dogs, we probably would've been caught."

"You've no idea how heavy a rucksack gets when it's wet," Ilse added. "Squatting down in that cold water, they were a dead weight."

"We hid the bags and rucksacks in the water and spent the rest of the night in the brook, ducked down behind the bushes. Before it started to get light, we found our way back here, just in time to leave for work."

"You haven't explained about these potatoes," Oma said. "How'd you manage that?"

"Very simple. After work today, we went back where we left them. We needed the rucksacks and, besides, it would have been a shame to waste perfectly good potatoes," Mutti replied with a grin.

"We gambled that the Russians wouldn't be watching the potato field so early in the evening," Ilse added. "And as you can see, we were right."

Mutti and Ilse may have managed to outsmart the Russians, but we still did not have enough potatoes in our basement. The potato season was not over yet and I was worried.

Before I went to sleep, I sat down next to Mutti.

"Gerda says you and Ilse also organize potatoes and turnips from the clamps in late winter and early spring. Is that true?"

"Oh, don't worry about that now. It's a long time 'til then."

"But I do worry about it. Anyway, aren't the clamps frozen at that time of year?"

"The crust's too hard to dig with our hands, if that's what you mean, so Ilse and I slip small weeding rakes into our apron pockets. We chop through near the air holes they leave in the top to keep the straw from rotting."

"What about the armed guards?" I asked anxiously.

"Sometimes they're asleep; sometimes they don't even bother to come," Mutti assured me.

"But what if they're there, wide awake?" I insisted.

"Let's worry about that when the time comes! No more questions for now. Good night!"

"Good night, Mutti."

CHAPTER 16

*O*ma and I often went into the pine forest to collect mushrooms. A year earlier we had only been sure that the golden chanterelles and the yellow Boletus were safe to eat, but recently Oma had met an elderly German woman who taught us how to pick out many other kinds. With a little practice, we learned how to separate the edible mushrooms from the poisonous ones. Yet I found it strange that the prettiest mushroom, the snow white Amanita with its scarlet cap sprinkled with little white dots, was also one of the most deadly.

I preferred to go mushroom collecting with Gerda. Whenever she came along we made sure to look for dried poppy heads in the big meadow. Shaking the poppy heads before breaking them off the stem, we listened for the rattling of the dried seeds inside. Unless they rattled, the poppy heads were not ripe and the seeds were not fully formed.

The gray poppy heads were often discolored from the rain. Many of them had unappetizing brown and black smudges. Yet opening a poppy head was always like opening a little box filled with tiny black candies. The poppy seeds were fatty and sweet and delicious. Sometimes we ate the contents of nearly a dozen poppy heads before heading into the forest.

Gerda and I quickly learned that we would find more mushrooms after a heavy rain. Yet even after it rained we often walked through the forest for quite a while without any success. Then suddenly, we would find a spot in the forest with mushrooms in abundance. Each time it was like finding a treasure.

We filled our baskets with chanterelles, yellow Boletus, and others, and sat down to relax a little and talk. Or we would search for overripe blueberries or blackberries, sometimes getting caught in the rain and slogging home just as soaked as Ilse and Mutti had been after they spent the night in the brook.

If Oma had an onion in the house, she cooked the mushrooms in a little water with onion pieces and salt. Prepared that way, the mushrooms tasted like meat. Oma loved onions. In Langendorf she even served them for breakfast, mixed into the eggs and the potatoes. Of course, in Goldbach Oma only had onions in the kitchen if Mutti or Ilse organized them at the Kolkhoz. On those rare occasions, the smell of onions clung to Oma's clothes for weeks at a time. I suspected she sprinkled onion juice on her apron like perfume.

If Oma did not have onions, she used a little piece of horseradish root to enhance the flavor of the mushrooms. Horseradish grew wild on the meadow near our house. Oma taught Gerda and me to identify the plant above the ground so we could dig out the crooked white roots. She also showed us where to look for caraway seeds to season our potato and cabbage soup.

"These are a sorry excuse for fried mushrooms," Oma complained as the chanterelles sizzled in the pan. "If I only had butter or schmalz (lard), I could fry them up the way I used to do on our farm."

* * *

On a warm, sticky afternoon, Manfred and I dawdled in front of a Russian house on the far side of the village, admiring the huge sunflowers in the front yard. The plants had already lost most of their yellow petals, revealing shiny black seeds clustered in a perfectly symmetrical pattern. I knew they were ripe and the thought made my mouth water.

"I'd love to snatch some," I confessed to Manfred.

"Yeah, me too. But there are too many people around. We wouldn't get very far."

"I know. I was only kidding."

"See the old woman with the dark head scarf? And the little boy? They're biting into onions like Horns-head!"

"Well at least I'm not hungry enough to do that!"

We left the village and walked along a dirt road parallel to a potato field. Wagons filled with sheaves of oats rumbled past us all afternoon long. We stuffed our pockets with the fallen ears. Sitting down on the edge of the ditch, we picked out the sweet-tasting oat grains from the ears and ate them.

The time to go home for supper had long since passed, but for a change, our stomachs felt full, so we decided to have a burping contest. As we belched aloud like two old men, each of us trying to outdo the other, a toothless old woman, her back stooped, approached us on the road. She wore a ragged dark dress, a black apron, and a black head shawl.

"Do you suppose she's German or Russian?" Manfred asked me as the woman came into earshot.

"I can only tell the difference in the winter, when the Russians wear their wadded jackets and felt boots. This time of year, all old ladies look the same to me."

"You two are impossible. Can't you behave yourselves?" the old crone scolded. Her words whistled loudly through her missing teeth. Manfred burst out laughing.

I poked him in the ribs. "Cut it out. She might know my mom."

"Why? Have you seen her before?"

"No, I don't think so, but grown-ups always seem to remember me even though I don't remember them."

"What makes you think you're so special?"

"I don't know what it is. Maybe I look strange to them somehow."

"You don't look strange. You're strange to think that way."

We watched the woman disappear down the road, her shape silhouetted in the glow of the sunset. No more wagons were driving by.

Chewing thoughtfully on my last oats, I asked Manfred, "Have you ever organized potatoes from a Kolkhoz field?"

"Let's do it right now!" he replied without any hesitation.

As we walked alongside the potato field, we unbuttoned the top buttons of our shirts and tightened our belts.

Carefully checking in all directions, we made sure no one else was around. The distant put-put of a tractor gave me cold feet.

"Maybe this isn't such a good idea," I said nervously.

Manfred grinned. "Don't worry. It's not coming this way. Let's not back out now!"

Squatting down, we waddled like ducks, each one in a different furrow. We turned to face the dirt road again, ready to escape if necessary. The tops of the long mounds on either side of us were thick with brownish dry potato plants, ready to be harvested.

Digging my fingers into the soft mounds on either side, I quickly extracted a dozen or so big potatoes. The smell of damp earth reminded me of Opa.

I stuffed two potatoes into each of my pants pockets and the rest inside my shirt.

"Perhaps I took too many," I whispered to Manfred. "My shirt's going to burst open."

"No, you'll be fine. Just fold your hands and hold them underneath."

Daylight was quickly fading away. Clumps of dirt, caked on our knees, fell to the ground as we walked. Pressing the bulging potatoes against our bodies, we crossed the dirt road and soon reached the bushes in the sloping meadow. We ducked down at the sound of a passing truck.

"The coast's clear," I whispered and we continued our way home.

"That was a close call," Manfred replied. "Let's hope no one notices us when we get back into town."

In the meantime, we had safely reached my house.

"See you tomorrow!" I called out to Manfred.

"Let's do this again some time!" he replied cheerfully as he turned toward home.

At that moment, the Russian barber's wife rushed, shrieking, out of her ground floor apartment. Welts on her face and arms evidenced a brutal beating. Her eyes blinded by tears, she did not notice me. Having passed this last obstacle, I arrived at our kitchen door. I could not use my hands to knock or the potatoes would have fallen out of my shirt and rolled down the steep staircase. So I turned around and tapped on the door with my bare heel, calling out, "It's me, Günter."

I heard Oma's footsteps crossing the kitchen floor. The door flew open and there she stood, her wet kitchen rag held high, ready to smack me for coming home so late.

The flickering kerosene light on the table in front of the open window cast a strange glow on my big belly and my bulging pockets. My hair was slick with sweat. Streams of perspiration ran down my face and my neck. Oma lowered her rag in astonishment.

"What on earth?"

"Potatoes!" I announced. With Gerda and the other children looking on in admiration, I leaned over the edge of the sink as far as I could reach. Sucking in my tummy, I quickly untucked the bottom of my shirt from my pants. The potatoes tumbled out into the sink. Even I was surprised by how many there were.

In a final dramatic flourish, I wiped my grimy hands, front and back, over the seat of my pants before pulling the last four potatoes from my pants pockets.

"Did you find them or did you organize them?" Oma demanded.

"I found them in the long mounds of a Kolkhoz potato field."

"You're a wise guy, aren't you?" Oma said. She looked torn between the possibility of punishing me and the delight of suddenly having more potatoes.

As soon as Mutti, Aunt Liesbeth, and Ilse came home, I repeated my story for them.

"Like mother, like son," Ilse said with a chuckle.

"It was a brave thing to do," Mutti said to me, "and I know you meant well, but please don't ever steal potatoes again. The risk is simply too high."

"But, Mutti..."

"If the Russians caught you, it wouldn't matter to them that you're only nine years old. Promise me you'll never do it again."

"I promise," I said solemnly, but I didn't mean it.

* * *

"Who's starting these foolish rumors, I'd like to know?" Mutti demanded when she came home from work the following day. "First word went around that the Russians might send us back to Germany. Now people are saying it's only a matter of days. It's cruel to give us false hope."

Aunt Liesbeth nodded her agreement. "Someone told me the Russians do it just to aggravate us, but I also heard it's a German who wants to stir things up. Either way, it really doesn't matter. It's not going to happen, so let's not drive ourselves crazy."

"Still, I'd like to get my hands on whoever's starting it. The same thing happened last year around this time, remember?"

"It's like the story of The Boy Who Cried Wolf," Dorchen said, her voice scarcely more than a whisper, "but turned upside down. If we disbelieve good news often enough, we may not recognize it when it stares us in the face."

* * *

If Gerda or I complained to Oma that we were too tired to saw and chop wood, Oma would yell at us and call us lazy, but when Dorchen was tired, Oma always gave her a little hug. Dorchen spent part of the day just resting. No matter what topic Gerda tried to discuss with her, she remained listless and sad. Gerda took over the baby sitting. I had to collect, saw, and chop wood by myself.

Oma prepared mashed potatoes for Dorchen and once in a while even made her bouillon with a piece of meat that Mutti had organized, but Dorchen did not get better. One day Aunt Liesbeth and Mutti brought her to the small hospital where they had treated my burst foot and the Russian doctor decided to admit her. Traute Runau, sick with scarlet fever, was also a patient. Worried about her friend, Traute dragged herself from bed to attend to Dorchen. Nurses were never around when you needed them.

Days passed, but Dorchen showed no improvement. Aunt Liesbeth confronted the doctor. "What are you doing for her?" she demanded. "Why isn't she getting better?"

"She has tuberculosis," the doctor said sadly, "and we have no medication to treat it. You might as well take her home."

* * *

On a Saturday in September 1947, our beloved Dorchen died at home in her sleep. It was still dark outside when Aunt Liesbeth called us all into the room. Illuminated by moonbeams, Dorchen looked like an angel, never to wake up again.

Aunt Liesbeth did not join Mutti and Ilse when they left for the Kolkhoz. She and Oma huddled together in the living room and cried all morning. After a while Gerda and I slipped outside.

"It's as if a light has gone out," Gerda said, a tear trickling down her cheek.

"Dieter looks like he's taking things pretty well, don't you think? I suppose he's too young to realize Dorchen's never coming back."

For a few minutes, we sat quietly together on the woodpile, lost in our thoughts.

"I've heard tuberculosis is contagious," Gerda finally said. "I wonder which of us will be next."

Mutti and Ilse stopped by the house at midday. The Natshalnik at the Kolkhoz had let them leave work early. After a quick lunch, they left again to make the necessary arrangements. Later that afternoon, Mr. Ademeit constructed a box out of old, rough boards.

"I wish I had some new wood," he apologized, "but these were the best I could get."

"We appreciate your help," Aunt Liesbeth said between sobs. "Dorchen was never fussy."

I pulled Gerda to one side. "I'm sure he meant to use those boards for firewood," I whispered.

"That's the way it looks to me, too."

After sunset, Mutti sat me down for a chat.

"We're going to need your long beige flannel nightshirt so Dorchen can look pretty when she goes to heaven tomorrow. I hope you don't mind."

I forced myself to smile. "That's fine with me," I said, but secretly I was resentful. My cozy nightshirt had once belonged to Opa. Wearing it made me feel close to him. Besides, without it, I worried about freezing to death in the coming winter.

Lying in bed that night, wide awake, I thought about what "going to heaven" really meant. According to Opa, only the soul goes to heaven. If anyone's soul would go to heaven, it would be Dorchen's, but her tiny body would rot away like all the other bodies I had seen in the spring of 1945, regardless of whether they were German or Russian, civilians or soldiers, men or women, young or old.

I considered asking Mutti if I could take back the shirt before Dorchen's burial, but decided against it. Feeling guilty to have even considered such a thing, I finally fell asleep thinking it was better to be alive without the nightshirt than to be dead with it.

* * *

Dorchen's rough-hewn coffin straddled two wooden chairs in our living room. The lid leaned against the wall, waiting to close her in forever. Cushioned by an old gray sheet, Dorchen lay in my beige flannel nightshirt, her small hands folded on top of her chest. She looked asleep.

We had finished eating our potato soup when we were startled by the arrival of the Russian barber's wife, accompanied by her two teen-age daughters. With tears streaming down their faces, the three of them nodded their respects to Aunt Liesbeth and Oma and approached the coffin. The barber's wife stroked Dorchen's forehead, then bent down to kiss her cheek. She reached into her cloth bag and took out three large ripe tomatoes and a loaf of bread, placing them gently into the coffin. What a strange thing to do, I thought. After all, dead people can't eat. But the barber's wife still was not finished. She carefully lifted Dorchen's folded hands just high enough to tuck a twenty-ruble bill underneath. Finally, the woman went over to Aunt Liesbeth and said a few words in Russian.

"I think she's asking when the burial will take place," Ilse said.

She and Mutti explained as best they could that the funeral would be that evening in the new Russian cemetery. The woman nodded and she and her daughters left as quietly as they had come.

Mutti, Aunt Liesbeth, and Ilse were already debating whether we should take the bread and the tomatoes out of the coffin when more Russian neighbors, all women and children, arrived. Russians continued to stop by all afternoon, bringing long green cucumbers, yellow onions, tomatoes, loaves of bread, and rubles.

Finally, late in the afternoon, when we were certain no more Russians were coming, Ilse and Mutti took all of the bread, vegetables, and money out of the coffin. We children feasted on sandwiches made with bread, tomatoes, cucumbers and sliced onions. A nice change after all that Schlunz! The grown ups in their grief barely ate anything at all.

"Why d'you suppose they left all this stuff?" Gerda asked. "Not that I'm complaining!"

"They must believe Dorchen needs the food on her journey to heaven," Oma said.

"I've counted out the rubles," Ilse said. "We have enough to buy bread for quite a few more meals."

* * *

Mr. Ademeit came up to our apartment to nail the coffin shut. While Mutti and Ilse carried it down the steep staircase and loaded it onto Mr. Ademeit's hand cart, Gerda and I took the children out to the courtyard next to the bakery. Nearly thirty people, Russians as well as Germans, had gathered there to wait for us. Many people carried forget-me-nots and buttercups. Two or three Russian women carried asters and pansies picked from their gardens.

"Where's Traute?" I whispered to Mutti.

"She's at home recovering from scarlet fever. Her mother hasn't told her about Dorchen yet."

"Will she live?"

"I think so. It's in God's hands."

The mourners started to move. Under cloudy skies we walked along the beaten path through the big meadow, crossing over the wide plank bridging the brook. Mr. Ademeit, who was pulling the little handcart with Dorchen's small coffin on top, led our procession to the cemetery. He was followed by our family, the Russian neighbors who had visited us in the afternoon, and by the Germans whom Aunt Liesbeth, Ilse, and Mutti knew from their work at the Kolkhoz.

Among so many women, Mr. Raddatz stood out. A teacher by profession, it was rumored that he had been a Communist during the Nazi times. He claimed the Nazis had thrown him in jail, beating him so badly that he was now quite deaf. He had a hearing aid made of shiny yellow brass, like a small, crooked powder horn. Holding his hearing aid against his left ear, Mr. Raddatz talked to Aunt Liesbeth until we reached the Russian cemetery behind the small hospital on the hill overlooking Goldbach. The Kolkhoz complex lay off to our left.

Fresh dark earth was piled next to the open grave.

"Did Mr. Ademeit dig the grave like he did for Opa?" I asked Ilse.

"No. Aunt Gretel and I did it ourselves. Mr. Ademeit can't do it anymore. His back would kill him."

"But..."

"Shh. Let's talk later," she interrupted.

When I saw the hole in the ground all ready for Dorchen, I thought about how much joy she had brought to all of us. The full impact of her death overwhelmed me and I began to sob. Suddenly the sun burst through the clouds, covering everything with gold. Mr. Raddatz delivered a sermon about Dorchen's short life. "She was an angel," he said. "God is waiting to welcome her in heaven." While he spoke, the coffin was slowly lowered into the ground. The earth shoveled over the top made the same hollow pounding sound I remembered from Opa's funeral. The grave was filled quickly and soon it was topped by a dark brown mound.

Meanwhile, Mr. Raddatz, forgetting his sermon, launched into a stern lecture.

"Whoever refuses to work shall not eat. A person who works enjoys the bread he earns with the sweat of his brow," he admonished us. His voice squeaked with excitement as he concluded his remarks. "If life is good, it is only because of hard work and a lot of sweat!"

Mr. Raddatz stepped back, wiped his forehead, and nodded his respects to Aunt Liesbeth. He looked quite pleased with the attention everyone had given his remarks.

Even though I was not yet ten, far too young to work on the Kolkhoz, I had the uncomfortable feeling he was speaking directly to me. Woodcutting is hard work, too, I thought bitterly. I earn my bread the same as everyone else. I wondered what comforting words Opa would have chosen if he had been with us. I was certain he and Dorchen had already embraced one another in heaven.

When Mr. Raddatz had finally stopped speaking, my family was joined by the other Germans in singing the hymn "Jesus lives! The victory's won!" Since only Oma knew all the words, it was a struggle to get through it to the end. After we had finished, the Russians sang a hymn. In contrast to us, the Russians sang confidently, with strong voices, in unison. Although I did not understand the words, the faith in God inspiring them was clear.

Mr. Raddatz spoke a few words about Dorchen in Russian and the Russian women started to cry. Suddenly the barber's wife threw herself on the grave. She began to scream, trying to reawaken Dorchen. Clawing at the fresh earth, she appeared to have gone mad with grief. As her daughters and her Russian neighbors lifted her up and led her away, her face turned quite blue. Meanwhile, all around us, the other Russians made the sign of the cross.

* * *

When we got back home I took Ilse aside.

"I didn't understand Mr. Raddatz' sermon. Wasn't it strange to say 'Whoever refuses to work is not allowed to eat'? Do you think he meant children like Gerda and me?"

"It sounded like Communist doctrine to me," Ilse replied with a shrug.

"Never mind Communism," Oma corrected her. "It's from Paul's second letter to the Thessalonians."

"Are you sure?" asked Ilse in surprise, "I thought Communists didn't believe in God."

As she spoke, Oma was already on her way out of the room. A moment later she returned with a Bible, already open to the passage in the New Testament.

"See, here it is in Chapter 3, Verse 10: 'For even when we were with you, we gave you this command: Anyone unwilling to work should not eat.'"

We considered the text for a moment. Finally Oma reached a decision.

"All the same, only a Communist would think it was an appropriate thing to say at a funeral."

However strange the customs of our Russian neighbors, we all grew a little closer after Dorchen's funeral. Over the next few weeks, Gerda and I visited Dorchen's grave on our way to the forest to collect mushrooms and wood. Nearly every time, we found fresh tomatoes and cucumbers and flowers left there by the Russian women. Gerda and I always picked wild flowers in the big meadow to pile on top. After making sure that no one was watching, we ate the vegetables. We were too hungry to feel guilty.

* * *

Six-year-old Helga took over Dorchen's bed, no longer having to share with her brother, Dieter, who was nearly four. Oma took in Dorchen's clothes and passed them down to Helga. After Dorchen left us, Hubert became Oma's new favorite. She never hesitated to use her wet dishrag to slap Gerda and me across the face. She had even begun to smack Helga and little Dieter on the bottom if they misbehaved, but she never hit Hubert. Especially after supper, Hubert spent a lot of time snuggled on Oma's lap. Although he was nearly five years old, Oma stroked her hand over his straight, light blond hair as she stared off into space and waited for Mutti, Aunt Liesbeth, and Ilse to come home from the Kolkhoz.

CHAPTER 17

Towards the beginning of October sensational news spread through Goldbach. The Russians were going to open the old schoolhouse near the abandoned church on the hill. We would be taught German, Russian, geography, history, and arithmetic. Even more important, every German child would receive 300 grams of bread for each day he spent in class. This was as much as the Germans got who worked on the Kolkhoz.

"Do you think it's true?" Gerda asked that evening.

"I can't wait!" I added.

Mutti was skeptical. "I'll believe it when I see it."

Against all expectations, school did open a few days later. Gerda and I arrived the first morning full of curiosity and hope.

Only a few weeks before, Manfred and I had knocked out the last fragments of jagged glass in the schoolhouse windows with pebbles from our slingshots. In the meantime the Russians and some German Kolkhoz workers had worked overtime to get the building ready for us. The doors and window frames had been replaced. The classroom was bright and cheerful. New glass sparkled in the windows. The room was furnished with spartan wooden tables and chairs. In the left front corner, on a rectangular piece of thick sheet metal, stood a cylindrical iron stove. An old fashioned blackboard on stilts was in the front of the room. A single piece of chalk rested on the little ledge. Two large portraits adorned the front wall. One I recognized as Stalin; the other pictured a stern bald man with a mustache and a goatee.

Although nobody had instructed us to do so, the boys took seats on the right side and the girls took seats on the left side of the classroom. I was trying to guess the identity of the man in the second portrait when our teacher walked in. To no one's surprise, it was Mr. Raddatz, the former teacher who had spoken at Dorchen's funeral. Since the unheated classroom was cold, a number of us kept on our caps. Mr. Raddatz took one look around the room and bellowed, "Take off your head gear!" I was so surprised by this unusual greeting, I did not take off my ushanka right away.

Glaring down at me, Mr. Raddatz snarled, "Hey, you! That goes for you too!"

"Sorry, sir."

As I ripped off my ushanka, half a dozen kopek coins flew in all directions. The boys reacted with a roar of laughter as the coins clattered onto the floor.

"Do you want to be our class clown?" Mr. Raddatz' voice boomed at me. "Don't you have a pocket in your pants for your coins?" Embarrassed and angry, I worried about the bad start I was making on my very first day.

Even though he showed us some mercy by letting us keep on our heavy coats and jackets, Mr. Raddatz looked stern as he started to talk to us about school. I found myself comparing him to Mr. Tellmann back in Langendorf, who had greeted us kindly on our first day of school. Mr. Raddatz glared at us while he talked, as though he were wasting his time teaching ragamuffins like us. Mr. Raddatz was a tall, skinny man in his forties. From a distance he looked like a scarecrow. His balding head was bullet-shaped. He spoke loudly in a clear High German while gesturing with his right hand. Judging from his nervous behavior, I thought he would have liked to gesture with his left hand as well, had he not needed it to clutch his shiny brass hearing aid to his ear. He was a no nonsense kind of person. Everything he said sounded very official.

"In a few days you will each receive textbooks. I expect you to do homework every day." After devoting considerable time to the taking of attendance, Mr. Raddatz got down to the business at hand. "It's a little cold in here. As of tomorrow, I want each of you to bring a piece of wood to school every day so that our classroom can be heated." As he spoke, I glanced over at the vast empty wooden box next to the iron stove.

"Times are hard," he explained. "The school will not be able to provide you with paper. I want you to bring your own paper to write on. In case you don't have any paper at home, (Who among us does? I thought) buy the Pravda. It's inexpensive and has wide margins to write on. You will also need to use several pages from the Pravda to make protective book covers."

No one in class said a word.

"Are there any questions?"

Silence.

We were given one pencil each.

"Guard them! Don't lose them!" Mr. Raddatz implored us. "They are also scarce. That's all for today. I'll see you tomorrow. Auf Wiedersehen."

Suddenly a hand went up. I looked to the side. It was Gerda.

"Yes, you have a question?"

"Mr. Raddatz, what about the bread? We were told we'd each receive 300 grams of bread each day."

"Yes, what about the bread?" other children echoed.

Mr. Raddatz looked a bit rattled by the question, but quickly regained his composure, "You heard right. That is not an empty promise. Tomorrow you will all get your bread. Auf Wiedersehen!"

In the evening, after a supper of watery cabbage soup, Gerda and I waited until Mutti, Aunt Liesbeth, and Ilse came home from the Kolkhoz to report about our first day of Russian school.

"He promised we'd get bread tomorrow," I said, "but I have my doubts."

"I think they'll just keep stringing us along," Gerda added.

To our astonishment, the Russians kept their word. Bread distribution started the following day. A lanky young Russian from the Kolkhoz food distribution office placed ten loaves of bread on a table. The bread pressed down when it was cut, a sure sign of freshness. Nearly overwhelmed by the delicious aroma, I was tempted to gulp my portion down right away. My eyes met Gerda's.

"Believe me, I'd love to eat mine too," she sighed, "but we have to bring it home to Oma."

"You're right." I reluctantly stuffed my bread into my school bag. Oma had made the bag for me out of the same coarse material she used to make our nettle-picking mittens.

Oma was waiting for us on the landing. She let us each keep a small morsel of bread, saving the rest for the younger children.

"If it weren't for the bread, most of the children would play hooky," Gerda reflected as we tried to make our portions last. "We certainly haven't learned anything so far."

* * *

Over the next few days Mr. Raddatz tested us. We were twenty-nine children, ranging in age from seven to eleven. Among them I recognized fellow beggars from the Magazin. Officially, Mr. Raddatz divided us into first through fifth grade, but in reality we were only two groups. The first and second graders were kept busy drawing or copying letters and words. The other group, to which I belonged, was comprised of everyone else. Although four boys were older than I was, I was the tallest in the class, even without my wooden soled boots.

245

Mr. Raddatz lectured us endlessly about the greatness of the Soviet Union. "Never forget that the glorious Red Army smashed Fascism and liberated Europe, giving us back our freedom. I'm sure you have noticed the two pictures on the wall. Comrade Stalin you probably already recognize. The other man is Comrade Lenin. We will be learning a lot about these great men in the coming days."

We had lessons in German grammar and spelling, arithmetic, and the history and geography of the Soviet Union, but the greatest moment came every afternoon around one o'clock when we each got a chunk of bread at dismissal time.

A week after the start of school, we got our Russian textbook, written entirely in Russian. We also received an arithmetic book, a book about the geography of Russia, and a political history of the Soviet Union, all of which were written in German. The four books had been printed in Moscow. Mr. Raddatz showed us how to fold the Pravda into book covers. The cheap printing ink in these "protective book covers" came off on our fingers. As a result, we smudged every page we touched.

The same day we received the books, we met our Russian teacher. In contrast to the dour Mr. Raddatz, Comrade Semjonov was a tall, jovial man with a warm smile. We were immediately impressed with his gleaming silver wristwatch. As soon as Mr. Raddatz introduced him to us, Comrade Semjonov began his first lecture.

"Menja savut tovarish Boris Michailovich Semjonov (My name is Comrade Boris Michailovich Semjonov)," he said, beaming at us. He spoke entirely in Russian, pointing at different objects in the room.

"Eta chiornaya dacka. (This is a blackboard.)," he would say, or "Eta karandash. (This is a pencil.)" or "Eta stul (That is a chair.)"

My classmates and I were thrilled to discover that the word "stul" was exactly like the German word "Stuhl." The same was true for the Russian word "mebel," which sounded like the German word "Möbel" (furniture). Most of us already knew the Russian words related to food and a few choice Russian curses, but no one in class knew how to form a sentence. Like well-trained parrots, we repeated everything our teacher said. Comrade Semjonov also taught us the Russian alphabet, as well as how to count from one to one hundred.

A few days after we received our textbooks, the bread was no longer cut in our presence. The lanky Kolkhoz worker took the bread, already cut, out of a cloth bag.

"I think the pieces were bigger when he cut them in class," Manfred grumbled. "What d'you think?"

"They look the same to me. Maybe they're a little dried out. You're not going to complain about it are you?"

Gerda overheard us. "Don't look a gift horse in the mouth," she cautioned.

"It's not a gift," Manfred insisted. "We're entitled to it. And I still say we got more bread in the beginning than we're getting now."

I liked Manfred, but sometimes he was a real fusspot.

* * *

Comrade Semjonov knew less German than we knew Russian. Often he was forced to ask Mr. Raddatz for help in explaining words to us. Mr. Raddatz, resentful of being called upon to help, practically spat out the German translation. To make matters worse, since Mr. Raddatz did not own a watch, towards the end of the school day he was obliged to ask Comrade Semjonov for the time. Comrade Semjonov, delighted to show off his fancy timepiece, announced the hour and minutes in Russian, while writing them on the blackboard for our benefit. We always welcomed this pleasant interruption of the lesson, but it annoyed Raddatz to no end. Before long, the two men detested each other.

Even without knowing German, Comrade Semjonov was a wonderful teacher. He made our lessons fun. The girls, especially, were thrilled with him.

"He's so young and good-looking. At least three of the girls have a crush on him," Gerda confided to me.

"Who are they?" I asked eagerly.

"Sorry, my lips are sealed!"

One day, with Mr. Raddatz standing by to help, Comrade Semjonov asked us which Russian words we knew before we came to school. A pudgy child named Müller shot up his hand. He was the only child in our class who looked well fed, undoubtedly due to the fact that his mother worked in the administration office at the Kolkhoz. In rapid succession, Müller rattled off the Russian words for good-bye, please, bread, cabbage, potatoes, and grits. Mr. Raddatz held his crooked trumpet to one ear as Comrade Semjonov printed every word in big Russian letters on the blackboard.

"Come now, class," Raddatz scolded. "Someone other than Müller."

A husky boy named Otto raised his hand.

"Yes, Otto," Mr. Raddatz said expectantly.

Without batting an eye, Otto shouted a vicious Russian curse.

Trying to maintain his pleasant smile, Comrade Semjonov ran his long fingers uneasily through his short-cropped brown hair. He must have known that Russian men, soldiers and civilians alike, used that phrase all the time. Some of the boys even started to snicker.

Mr. Raddatz ran over to Otto and slapped him hard across the face, not only once as he usually did with the rest of us, but three times, leaving bright red hand prints on Otto's cheek.

"That must hurt!" Manfred whispered under his breath. The class became suddenly quiet.

Shaking with rage, his voice trembling, Raddatz said, "Keep your mouth shut! I don't want to hear any more Russian words from you!"

Still steaming, Mr. Raddatz checked for my reaction. He must have been surprised that I looked so serious. Horns-head had yelled the same awful words at me, as had the Russian officer in Palmnicken who smashed my amber cigarette holder. I did not find them funny.

On our way home from school that day, we complimented Otto on his bravery.

"Don't mind Raddatz," one boy said. "He's an idiot."

"You needn't worry about me," Otto replied. "East Prussian blood isn't made of buttermilk," but a moment later he looked angry. "I'll promise you this. If Raddatz ever hits me like that again, I'll hit him right back."

The other boys laughed, but I sensed that Otto wasn't joking. He might actually do it.

* * *

All in all, I was not thrilled to learn Russian. I had not forgotten what the Russian soldiers did to us in the first few months after the war. Mr. Raddatz's seemingly endless praise for the great Soviet Union also sounded hollow to me when I considered that we were living without a toilet, running water, a bathtub, soap, or detergent. We did not even have forks and knives, only spoons. Come to think of it, we never had any solid food where a knife and a fork would have been necessary. We never had enough to eat and I lived in constant fear that Mutti would be caught organizing food and be sent to Siberia.

Sometimes Mr. Raddatz plied us with maddening advice. When he would say, "I want you to do your homework right after lunch," I felt like screaming, "What lunch? I can see the bottom of the bowl, my potato soup is so thin."

Or when he would say, "After you've done your homework, have it checked by your mother," I thought, are you crazy? When my mother comes from the Kolkhoz she's so tired she falls asleep as soon as she sits down.

Mr. Raddatz was obviously doing all right. His wife, also a teacher by profession, did not go to work. She was a housewife, like in "normal times." His attractive daughters were always well dressed. I had never seen them begging for morsels of bread in front of the Magazin; they had rubles and walked inside to buy whatever they liked.

Mr. Raddatz's real passion was neither the German language, nor arithmetic, nor Russian geography. His real passion was music. He checked each of us individually to see how well we sang. Holding his ear trumpet against his left ear, he directed each child in turn to sing directly into the hearing aid. As he yelled "louder" with growing impatience, his victim became so intimidated, he could not utter a note. Frustrated, Raddatz yelled at the same child again, finally giving up and moving on to torture the next student. He had the chronic need to bawl us out all the time. Many days we did nothing but sing folk songs. Other times we practiced singing the Russian National Anthem in German. Sometimes Gerda and I thought we were in a madhouse and not a school.

Mr. Raddatz liked nothing more than teaching us to sing in rounds. He stood in front of the class like the conductor of a thousand-member choir, wielding his arms like a windmill gone mad in a hurricane. Once he had gotten us going, he would hold his hearing aid to his left ear and conduct with his right hand only. We struggled not to laugh in his face.

One day Mr. Raddatz stepped out of the room for a few minutes. The opportunity to have some fun was too tempting. I strode to the front of the class where I began to imitate his wild conducting style using his one meter long wooden ruler. Manfred started to laugh and, as usual, his reaction was contagious. Soon the entire class was howling. Four or five of the children jumped to their feet yelling "More! More!"

All of a sudden, Mr. Raddatz appeared out of thin air. Towering over me, he ripped the long heavy ruler out of my hand and gave me four sharp smacks across my back. "So, you are causing this ruckus?" he yelled. "This is what you get for imitating my conducting. You have nothing but nonsense in your big head."

Remembering the courageous example set by Otto, I bit my lip and refused to cry. My reaction enraged Mr. Raddatz even more. He ranted until he turned quite blue and began to shake.

On the way home I enjoyed playing the hero, but Raddatz's cruel comment about the size of my head hurt me more than the beating. I knew my head was large because the older boys had already teased me about it. Coming from my teacher, it was nearly too much to bear.

Two days later, Mr. Raddatz ran into Mutti and me by chance.

"Good afternoon, Mr. Raddatz," Mutti said. "I hope my son isn't giving you too much trouble."

"Madam," he rasped, glaring at me, "your son is a complete idiot. His only talent is to annoy me constantly."

"That's a rather strong statement," Mutti said. "Can you give some examples?"

"No, I'm afraid not. First of all, I wouldn't know where to begin, and secondly, I'd get too upset. He and some other boys from that school are going to bring me to an early grave. Good day, madam!" and with that he left.

Mutti looked down at me, puzzled. "What on earth have you done to that man?"

"He's strange, isn't he?"

"Now listen to me carefully. I didn't ask your opinion," Mutti admonished. "I'll ask you again. What did you do to him?"

"The only thing I can think of is the time I imitated his conducting in front of the class."

"You did what?"

Flailing my arms, and then grabbing my ear, I showed her my best imitation of Mr. Raddatz. "That!"

"I see! So that was it?" I was sure if Mutti had not bitten her lip, she would have laughed. "Listen, Günter," she continued, "everyone in Goldbach knows Mr. Raddatz has some peculiar habits. Still, he's your teacher and from now on I want you to treat him with respect. Is that understood?"

"Yes, Mutti."

* * *

Besides music, Raddatz's other great passion was the Soviet Union and its people.

"Russian workers have always worked harder than Germans," he claimed. "Russian scientists are smarter than German scientists and have achieved much more in science and industry. The soldiers of the Red Army bore the brunt of the war and have proven that they are superior to the Germans, the Americans, the British, the French, and anybody else in the world. In fact, they are the bravest of all men."

We must have looked skeptical, so he changed his pitch slightly.

"The Soviet Union recognizes that even some Germans have merit. Two such terrific Germans were Karl Marx and Friedrich Engels. I will have the honor of teaching you about their Communist theories and their life histories."

Mr. Raddatz was true to his word. He eventually taught us more about the theories of Marx and Engels than we ever cared to know.

Sometimes, when Mr. Raddatz was on a roll about the blessings of Communism for all of mankind, one of the children failed to pay attention or even dozed off. Mr. Raddatz threw his only piece of chalk at the offender or, if he was in a particularly foul mood, he slapped the child across the face. His favorite targets for chalk pieces and slaps were Manfred and me, or as he used to call us, the Rehm-boy and the Nitsch-boy.

Our physical education class always provided us with a nice diversion. The large empty hall we used as a gym had a creaky wooden floor. As long as we did our exercises while standing in place, everything went well, but as soon as we had to run or to jump, the noise became incredibly loud. After all, I was not the only child in class with wooden soles under my boots.

As we thundered across the floor, like so many elephants, Mr. Raddatz cringed as if the sound hurt his ears. Sometimes he even yelled at us for jumping too high on purpose.

Occasionally, we noticed that Mr. Raddatz heard things that, given his handicap, he should not have been able to hear. If we whispered to one another while he was writing on the blackboard, he whirled around and glared. We wondered whether his deafness was faked and whether his picturesque hearing aid was only part of the show.

Some adults in Goldbach even started to question whether he had been a Communist under the Nazis or whether he had actually been another Nazi who had managed to turn his flag as the wind changed.

One of the few advantages of the school, besides the bread and the "sports hall" were the two clean outhouses, one for the girls and one for the boys. For the first time since the summer of 1946, I enjoyed being able to sit down. Nails had been hammered into both sides of the wooden walls. The heads of the nails had been pinched off. On each nail hung a big batch of neatly cut rectangular pieces of the Pravda to be used as toilet paper. While sitting on the wooden seat, I tried to decipher a few of the words in the newspaper. On two occasions I wiped myself with a picture of Comrade Stalin.

As the weather turned frosty in November, Oma grew resentful about the wood we had to bring to school every day. Mr. Raddatz scolded each child who failed to bring in his allotted share. Our family had collected quite a bit of wood in anticipation of the coming winter, but we were never sure it would be enough. Oma thought of the wood we brought to school more or less as an exchange for two pieces of bread. She complained that the bread was not even 300 grams, although she did not have a scale on which to prove it. Since Gerda and I considered ourselves experts on firewood, we kept careful watch over the classroom supply.

"Have you noticed that there's always wood left at the end of the school day, but the box is empty in the morning?" Gerda asked me.

"No wonder Mr. Raddatz gets so upset if somebody forgets to bring in wood! He's taking it home."

CHAPTER 18

*I*n the middle of November, Goldbach was hit by another incredible sensation. Electricity! One day, out of the blue, the lights came on in our apartment. Not one bulb was missing from the wall fixtures; we had never noticed they were there. In a closet in the kitchen Oma even found spare bulbs. After having lived for one and one-half years with the dim light produced by sooty kerosene lamps (provided we had enough kerosene to spare), we felt as if Christmas had arrived early. Helga, Hubert, and Dieter, who were too young to remember electric lights, shrieked with delight. Oma worried about our lack of privacy.

"It's wonderful to have light in the evenings, but we don't have any shutters or curtains. What are we going to do?"

"Really mother, the things that get you upset," Mutti chided. "That's the least of our problems. No one else has any window coverings, either."

"Whatever you say," Oma replied sullenly.

"We're actually better off than most. Our kitchen is on the third floor, so no one can look inside anyhow," Aunt Liesbeth reassured her.

Over the next few days, we enjoyed the extra light, staying up well past our bedtimes, but all of a sudden we were in the dark again. The Russian officials from the Kolkhoz cut off the electricity to most

German-occupied apartments. They had not counted on the hidden talents of Mr. Ademeit and one of his elderly friends who soon restored our power. The Russians just as promptly shut it back off. The dim light from our kerosene lamp barely illuminated the area around the kitchen table. Beyond that small circle of flickering light, we were once again in darkness.

"Give me a day or two," Mr. Ademeit promised. True to his word, as often as the Russians put us in the dark, Mr. Ademeit lit our homes back up. Eventually, the Russians gave up and our electricity stayed on.

"Congratulations, Mr. Ademeit! Well done!" Mutti said when he stopped by one evening for a chat.

"The way I figured it," he explained, "there are plenty of houses like this one, where both Russians and Germans live. It takes skill to know which wires to cut and which to spare. That meant the Russians had to hire specialists for the job, and specialists are hard to come by."

"You're right. Carpenters, tractor drivers, and mechanics are always paid better than the rest of us at the Kolkhoz," Mutti agreed.

"Well, eventually, the Russians must have concluded it was cheaper to leave the power on."

* * *

Mutti and Ilse brought home a pressed substance the color of my Altenberg Grandmother's shiny black piano. Mutti broke off tiny pieces to give each of us a taste. It was hard to bite into, but I immediately recognized the fatty sweet taste of poppy seeds.

"It's oil cake. The Kolkhoz workers put poppy seeds into a press and squeeze out the oil and this is what's left," Mutti explained.

"How'd you manage to organize it?" I asked.

"The Russians gave it to us in addition to our bread ration!" Ilse said. "Imagine that!"

As soon as Gerda had eaten her little piece, she said, "It's so delicious, I'll call it poppy seed cake."

256

"This stuff's a far cry from real poppy seed cake," Oma said, "but it's probably as close as we'll get, so poppy seed cake it is!"

Oma only permitted us to eat a little bit of oil cake at a time. She claimed too much would cause constipation.

"You're probably right," Mutti said to Oma, "but it would be nice if you gave Günter an extra piece. After all, today's his tenth birthday."

"Really, Gretel, this isn't fair to the other children," Oma grumbled, reluctantly handing me another tiny portion.

The following day, a pot of sauerkraut supplemented the Kolkhoz bread ration. Oma got weepy when she tasted the sauerkraut raw from the pot. Heated up as a side dish, it was a welcome treat for all of us.

"You needn't eat it so slowly, Mother," Aunt Liesbeth chided Oma. "They've promised to give us a portion of sauerkraut at least once a week from now on."

* * *

On December 10, 1947, Aunt Liesbeth was overjoyed to receive an International Red Cross postcard from her husband. Two days later, an official at the Kolkhoz handed Mutti a postcard from Vati. The cards, both from Germany, were the first word we had received from Vati and Uncle Alfred after nearly three years of silence.

"How'd he know where we were?" I asked, staring at the unfamiliar handwriting.

"The Kommandantura gave each of us a blank International Red Cross postcard more than a year ago, so we sent them to relatives who used to live in the Reich on the off chance they'd survived the war. After all this time, we never expected a reply."

"Now that we know they're both alive," Aunt Liesbeth added, "it's even more frustrating."

"Why don't you send them letters?" Gerda asked. "There's so much to catch up on."

"We can't," Mutti said. "No one in Goldbach has any idea how to mail a letter to Germany."

"I'd give anything to know what Alfred's doing right now," Aunt Liesbeth said. "Until I got that postcard, I'd somehow managed not to think about him as much."

"Hopefully, the two of them have found themselves decent jobs," Oma said, "so they can support you when we eventually leave this awful place."

"Speaking of jobs, have you noticed how many Russians have arrived in Goldbach recently?" Mutti asked. "Someone told me they were lured here with promises of milk and honey, but they're suffering nearly as much as we are."

I had already gone to bed when Mutti knelt down next to me. "That postcard from Vati was like an extra-special birthday gift for you," she whispered, trying not to disturb Hubert. "If I had all the money in the world, I couldn't have bought you a better one."

"To tell you the truth, I never thought we'd hear from him again. Do you suppose he'll come to get us out of here?" I asked, knowing full well what Mutti's answer would be.

"Come on, you know he can't," she chided. "We'll just have to wait until the Russians send us back to Germany one day."

"And then he can take care of us," I added.

"That would be nice," Mutti agreed. As she left to rejoin Oma in the kitchen, I wondered bitterly what was so special about Vati's postcard from Germany. At least I collected wood to heat our stove. Vati was no help to us at all.

* * *

In the middle of December, school closed for a one month vacation and our bread rations stopped. Sugar beet slices reappeared on our dinner table and, with them, my gag attacks. Still, our situation was better than it had been the year before. The winter was not as brutal and, thanks to the potatoes Mutti and Ilse had organized during the fall, our basement was fairly well stocked.

At Christmas we actually had a few reasons to celebrate. Although we missed Dorchen, we knew that Vati and Uncle Alfred were still alive. Gerda and I would soon get our school bread rations again. And we had electric light. After a supper of thin potato soup, sugar beet slices, acorn coffee, and poppy seed cake, we sang "A Mighty Fortress is our God," "Holy God We Praise Your Name," and "Now Thank We All Our God," finishing with "Fling Wide the Door" and "Silent Night."

* * *

Rumors kept cropping up, causing elation and disappointment in turn. Most frustrating was the recurring rumor that the Russian authorities would eventually permit us to return to Germany.

"I've heard that one so often, I can't stand it anymore," Aunt Liesbeth griped. "I wish they'd just send us back to our husbands where we belong."

"My thoughts exactly," Mutti concurred. "Every time a new batch of Russians arrives in Goldbach, I hope there'll be enough of them to replace us at the Kolkhoz. Life has to be better in the Reich than it is here."

"That reminds me of another rumor. You know the one I mean? That Germany is divided into Zones with the Russians in charge of one of them," Oma added. "What rubbish!"

"I'm not so sure," Mutti said. "I'm also skeptical about most of the stories that go around, but when I was at the food supply office Mr. Shatin said this one was true and I have no reason to doubt him. As best I can figure it, the rest of Germany is occupied, too. For their sakes, I hope the occupation isn't as harsh in the Reich as it is here in East Prussia."

"Occupied or not, I still wish they'd send us back," Aunt Liesbeth said.

"You can dream about it if you like," said Ilse, "but you're not being realistic. The Russians wouldn't have opened the school for us if they planned to send us away."

Their conversation tired me out, so I excused myself and went to bed. As I lay there trying to get warm, I suddenly felt confident that we would all survive to see the next Christmas. "Dear God," I prayed before drifting off to sleep, "thank you for the many small improvements which have come into our lives. And please protect Mutti from harm. Amen."

* * *

In early January 1948, Mutti, Aunt Liesbeth, and Ilse were each given four frozen, stone-hard potatoes at the Kolkhoz once or twice a week, in addition to their bread rations. After Kolkhoz potatoes thawed in our kitchen, Oma cut away the mushy parts and boiled the rest. They tasted disagreeably sweet.

The only other food we had were the potatoes Mutti and Ilse had stolen in the fall, some of which had already started to rot away in our basement. Oma worried our supply would not last through the winter. Every day she went down to sort out the bad ones to prevent them from spoiling the rest.

"Come down with me!" she barked at me one day. "Bring the kerosene lamp, but be careful not to start a fire!"

"Yes, Oma."

Animals squeaked in a far corner of the basement. My eyes, searching for rats, struggled to adjust to the darkness beyond the small circle of light cast by the lamp. Oma's shadow took on the shape of a giant witch as she set down two small pails and knelt on the ice-cold floor to sort through the potatoes.

"It's a shame so many have turned to mush," Oma muttered. "How will we manage to last until spring?"

At that moment I really didn't care. I only wanted to get out of there, but Oma was in no hurry to leave. She took her time inspecting each potato, cutting away the slimy parts and setting them aside in one of her pails, dropping the good pieces in the other. My fingers and toes were frozen through.

As soon as we reached the top of the basement stairs, I set down the kerosene lamp next to Oma. While Oma waited for me on the drafty ground floor, I ran into the courtyard to toss the mushy rejects onto the huge garbage pile across from the bakery. Somewhere in the dark, rats were waiting to enjoy the unexpected treat. Lured by the smell of freshly baked bread, I stepped into the bakery to warm my hands and check the clock.

"It's 4:46," I reported to Oma when I got back.

"Already?" she replied. "I'd better start cooking our soup."

Oma and I walked up one flight and passed through the empty Schmidt apartment. The rooms had a peculiar musty smell. A year had passed since all of the Schmidts had died, yet I still felt spooked each time I walked across the creaking wooden floor of their kitchen on my way to our staircase.

"Do you also feel strange walking through this place?" I asked Oma. "I can't forget how they all froze to death."

"In a way they had only themselves to blame," she replied. "God helps those who help themselves, you know. Whenever I come through, I wish someone else would move in and heat the place. That would help keep our apartment a little warmer too."

Oma was always so practical.

* * *

Rotting potatoes made our daily soup taste worse than ever. One night, after a meal of thin potato soup, without even a tiny scrap of bread on the side, Oma told us again how Jesus fed five thousand people with some fish and a few loaves of bread. As I listened to the story, my mouth got all watery and I felt hungrier than ever. I wished with all my heart that Jesus would pay us a visit and fill our plates.

My prayers went unanswered until, a few days later, each Kolkhoz worker received a little butter and sugar from the food supply office. It wasn't much, especially not for nine people, but it was something. While it lasted, tiny specks of fat enriched the flavor of our soup and the sugar took the bitterness out of the acorn coffee.

"We must be grateful for what we have," Oma reminded us, "and not expect we'll get any more treats like these."

Despite her stern advice, Oma shared our delight. We heard her sing her favorite hymns as she fussed over the stove in the kitchen.

* * *

The supper dishes had been put away. Aunt Liesbeth and Ilse were home from the Kolkhoz, but not Mutti. Worry lines crinkled Oma's forehead. Long after the little ones were asleep, Mutti finally came up the stairs.

"Thank God you're back!" Oma greeted her.

Mutti had a mischievous grin. She had barely closed the door when she opened her long heavy jacket and pulled out four large chunks wrapped in rags.

"What did you organize this time?" Oma demanded eagerly.

"Believe it or not, it's cheese. The orange color put me off at first, but someone at the Kolkhoz assured me that it's 'processed cheese' from America."

"From America?"

"That's what I heard."

Oma got a knife and cut off a small sample. She sniffed the tiny piece and held it in her mouth, sampling it with her tongue before she swallowed. We waited expectantly for her opinion.

"It's absolutely delicious," she declared. "Helga! Hubert! Dieter! Back in the kitchen right now!"

We heard bare feet patter on the wooden floor as, one by one, they appeared, clad in nightshirts, all three of them with runny noses. Their sleepy eyes lit up when they saw the treat. Oma gave each of them a tiny piece of cheese before giving the rest of us a taste. The cheese had the wonderful flavor of creamed butter. I did not have to chew it; it simply melted in my mouth. No one loved the processed cheese more than Hubert and Dieter. They were crazy about it. Big tears of disappointment rolled down their faces when they did not get any more, but we all knew Oma would not budge. On those rare occasions when especially rich food made it to our house, she claimed that our bodies were so deprived of milk and fat, we would not be able to tolerate larger portions. She set aside the rest of the cheese for the coming days.

* * *

School reopened in the middle of January 1948. Neither Gerda nor I had done the homework Comrade Semjonov and Mr. Raddatz had given us. Our apartment was simply too cold. Except when we were in bed, everyone in the family hung around the kitchen because it was the only room with heat. Finding wood for our stove was more challenging than ever before.

Mr. Raddatz had worked himself into a frenzy over the vacation. Ignoring our lessons entirely, he launched into an angry speech directed at our "older brothers." Gerda and I exchanged puzzled glances since, of course, neither of us had older brothers.

"Some older boys whistled and carried on in front of my house for two evenings following New Year's Eve. I haven't for the life of me figured out whether they wanted to annoy me or whether they wanted to get the attention of my teenage daughters," Mr. Raddatz ranted. Failing to get any reaction from the class, he turned red in the face and bellowed at the top of his lungs.

"Tell the hooligans who disturbed my family's peace, I'll throw a powder charge at their feet if they ever show up at my house again!"

We sat, stunned, not knowing what to make of this tirade. Everyone kept quiet; no one said a word. Afterwards Gerda and I asked around, but we never found any child whose older brother had whistled late at night at the Raddatz house. As we walked home down the hill from school to the village street, a girl about Gerda's age came over to us.

"Did you know that Mr. Raddatz slaps his daughters for no reason at all? And he beats his wife up three or four times a month."

Gerda asked, "How do you know?"

"My mother and the Raddatz's next-door neighbor are friends."

"He sounds like the Russian barber who shares our house with us," I said. "I avoid him whenever I can."

"Well, there's no way we can avoid Raddatz," Gerda said with a sigh. "He stands between us and our daily ration of bread."

* * *

Toward the middle of February, Comrade Semjonov helped us practice for our first Russian dictation. Over the next few days, he had us write certain words and phrases over and over, never giving us the entire text at one time. We felt well prepared for the actual dictation by the time the big day arrived. Afterwards, Gerda and I felt confident that we had done well.

The next morning Comrade Semjonov told us something in Russian. Judging from the expression in his face, we knew it was funny, but the joke escaped us. Seeing our blank expressions, he went in search of Mr. Raddatz.

"You're nothing but blockheads," Mr. Raddatz sneered. "What Comrade Semjonov has been telling you is this: Every single one of you wrote the word 'totshka' at the end of every sentence."

"But that's exactly what he said," I protested.

"You dummies!" Mr. Raddatz said. "It's a wonder we can teach you anything. The word 'totshka' means 'period.'"

Comrade Semjonov chuckled as he wrote three short sentences on the blackboard. After each sentence he pointed at the period and said dramatically, "Totshka!" We had made his day.

On the way home Manfred pulled on my sleeve. "Did you notice how annoyed Raddatz was when Semjonov called him in to translate?"

"Yeah, if looks could kill, Semjonov would be dead. Raddatz is so pompous. He really should be nicer to the guy."

"Both of you are out of touch," Gerda said smugly. "If you promise to keep it secret, I'll tell you the real reason."

"Tell us!" Manfred and I begged.

"I've heard a rumor that Semjonov is chasing after Raddatz' older daughter."

"But she can't be older than sixteen. Semjonov is old enough to be her father," Manfred objected.

"I don't think he's thirty yet, but that's beside the point. The fact is, the whole thing's driving Mr. Raddatz crazy. And he can't do anything about it."

* * *

On a miserable gray day, a Russian soldier drove up to the school in a truck. After a lot of preparation, he set up an odd looking machine in the back of the classroom.

"It's a movie projector," one of the older boys whispered.

We watched in astonishment as the soldier put up a screen in front of the blackboard. By this time, our classroom was humming with excitement. I hadn't seen a movie since Mutti and I had gone to Schippenbeil in 1944. Raddatz strode in and glared at us.

"Quiet! Pipe down! We're going to see a movie about the October Revolution of 1917."

The propaganda movie was narrated entirely in German. When it was over, Mr. Raddatz asked, "So, how did you like it?"

Comments exploded from all sides: "Very good!" "Wonderful!" "Great!" "Excellent!" "First rate!" and "Splendid!"

"Don't talk all at once! One at a time!" Raddatz hollered. He turned to Manfred.

"Rehm! How did you like the movie?"

"It was terrific! When can we see another one?"

Mr. Raddatz nervously scratched his bald head. "I should've known better than to ask you," he sighed. "Müller! How did you like the film?"

"It was absolutely superb, Mr. Raddatz. It clearly demonstrated the triumph of good over evil," was the prompt reply.

A few days after the big movie event Mr. Raddatz asked us, "Who can explain the function of soap?" I thought it was a nasty question since most of us had not seen any soap since 1945.

Several younger children chanted in unison, "It takes away filth."

Mr. Raddatz cringed when he heard their broad East Prussian accents. He turned to Müller. "Do you know a better answer?"

"Yes, Mr. Raddatz."

"Tell the class the function of soap!"

Looking around to be sure he had everyone's attention, Müller spoke in a clear, high German. "Soap, together with water, has the function of dissolving dirt from fabric or from the surface of the skin."

A rare smile brightened his face as Mr. Raddatz praised Müller. "Good boy!" he said, eyes gleaming. "That's precisely what I expected from you."

After school, a few of the older boys punched Müller and threw him down on the icy ground. He got a bloody nose, and I felt sorry for him.

* * *

On an evening in late February, with the younger children already tucked in bed, Oma was reading Bible stories to Gerda and me when

Mutti, Aunt Liesbeth, and Ilse came home from work at the Kolkhoz. All three had a good case of the giggles.

"Hush!" Oma warned. "You'll wake up the little ones!"

Mutti leaned over and whispered in Oma's ear.

"What is it?" I asked. "Can't you let us in on the joke?"

"Gerda can stay put," Oma said, "but I want you out of the kitchen this minute!"

"But Oma..."

"Don't you dare come back until we call you."

"That's not fair!" I protested as Oma gave me a push in the direction of the living room, shutting the door behind me.

I pressed my ear to the door, but all I heard were giggles from the other side. The louder the laughter became, the angrier I was at being excluded. After a while I could not stand it anymore. Flinging open the door, I was met with a startling sight. Mutti had taken off her outer garments. Some of her underclothes were bloody and discolored. Bloody cords encircled her waist. At first I thought Mutti had been wounded or beaten. So, even though Oma yelled at me to shut the door, I stood my ground.

"It's not as bad as it looks!" Mutti said cheerfully, as Aunt Liesbeth and the girls continued to laugh. "I've organized some meat."

Only then did I notice four long slabs of meat, the marks of the cords still visible, on the kitchen table.

"How'd you manage to carry it home?"

"I undressed in an outhouse and tied it round my waist. Then I spent the rest of the day worrying that the blood would seep through my clothes and give me away. I sure didn't want to end up like Mr. Runau."

"Well, that's a relief!"

"Now out you go," Mutti scolded. "And let me have some privacy!"

267

Over the next few days specks of fat and a few tiny pieces of meat floated on the surface of our potato and turnip soup. "We haven't had any meat in our soup since I bartered that rabbit from Mr. Ademeit last fall," Mutti reminded us.

* * *

One evening I went to look for Mutti at the Kolkhoz. I put on my long German military coat, a hand-me-down from an old German man who had died of starvation. To disguise its origins, Oma had carefully unstitched the bright metal buttons, replacing them with a mismatched set of ordinary ones. Oma had also folded the sleeves inside and sewed them down, but they still dangled well below my hands; the hem nearly covered my boots. Pulling the flaps of my ushanka down over my ears, I left the house.

The dark sky was filled with glittering stars. The full moon lit my path over the village meadow, snow crunching under my boots. I asked an elderly woman at the storage room where Mutti was.

"She's probably at the food supply office talking to Mr. Shatin. I'm sure you'll find her there," she replied.

When I finally caught up with Mutti, she was standing next to two enormous Russian women dressed in thickly padded winter coats, talking to a man behind the counter. Mutti introduced me to Mr. Shatin, who had given me the ushanka. He spoke to me in German.

"You look like a real Russian," he told me in a friendly voice.

I was tempted to correct him, because if I had been a "real Russian" I would have worn a heavy wadded coat instead of my old gray cloth coat and I would have had on felt boots instead of my leather boots with wooden soles, but I just smiled back at him as I studied his appearance. I had never seen a Jewish person close up. The word "Jewish" conjured up images of the corpses Opa dug out in Palmnicken and the escaping prisoner Ilse saw in Schippenbeil. I was sure Jewish people would look different from everyone else, but Mr. Shatin certainly did not look different at all.

He was a slim man, about fifty years old, slightly taller than average, with broad shoulders. Most of his hair was hidden under his ushanka, but what I could see of it was entirely white. The laugh lines around his steel-blue eyes and his mischievous grin reminded me of Uncle Ernst. I had expected him to wear a soldier's uniform, but he wore neatly pressed civilian clothes; the cuffs of his trousers were tucked inside his shiny boots.

Mr. Shatin's voice interrupted my thoughts. "Hand me your hat, young man."

He took the cap from me and put something inside. With a sharp glance at the Russian women, he handed the ushanka back to me and said in a low voice, "Draussen (outside)."

Clutching my hat, I bowed as Mutti and I left the room. Once outside, I reached in and, to my pleasant surprise, found a thick slice of bread. Mindful of Mr. Shatin's concern for secrecy, I resisted the temptation to eat it on the spot, instead slipping it into my vast coat pocket for later on. I plopped my now empty ushanka on my head and, no longer bothered by the cold, I walked home with Mutti in the dark. In the frigid night air, the snow on the village meadow reflected cold moonlight. As Mutti and I walked home, we held our hands in front of our mouths to warm the cold air going into our lungs. My breath came in white puffs.

CHAPTER 19

*A*t the beginning of April 1948, crocuses burst into bloom, reminding me that two years had passed since Opa died. One night when Mutti and Ilse came home from work, Mutti spoke to Gerda and me.

"Listen, you two. I have a job for you. Tomorrow I want you to go to the Kolkhoz dairy in Köwe. It's a bit more than two kilometers. Ask for a German woman named Mrs. Schneidereit. She'll give you..."

At that moment Oma called Mutti away.

"How come Mutti knows so many different people at the Kolkhoz?" I asked Ilse.

"That's easy," said Ilse, "She always volunteers when other departments need extra help. With each new job, her circle of contacts grows."

"Is that the way she met this Mrs. Schneidereit?"

"I'd say so. You see, many women are content to hang around with their work brigade, even when there isn't much to do, but not Aunt Gretel. She's always looking for another assignment."

"She even volunteered to make sauerkraut by treading barefoot on chopped cabbage in a giant barrel," Aunt Liesbeth added with a chuckle as Mutti rejoined us.

"What's so funny?" she asked.

"We've been telling them about all of your extra jobs," Ilse explained. "It's a good thing they haven't found out you know how to juggle."

Mutti grinned. "If they need a juggler, then that's what I'll do," she said. "But to get back to what I was telling you, be sure to bring along our three milk cans so that you can carry back some whey."

Opa always gave the whey to our calves in Langendorf to fatten them up. He had offered me a cup, and I hadn't particularly liked it, but now, our circumstances had changed. The thought of whey made my mouth water.

"Should we leave right after school?" Gerda asked.

"Yes, please. And don't forget the milk cans!"

The next afternoon Gerda and I walked along a muddy road to the dairy in Köwe. We had seen the buildings before, but had never been inside. When we asked for Mrs. Schneidereit in the small office, an enormously overweight blond lady with rosy cheeks came out to meet us. She wore a snow white starched coat like a doctor. The buttons in the front bulged as the coat struggled to enclose her wide girth.

Gerda curtsied and made the introductions. In a friendly manner and without much fuss, Mrs. Schneidereit took our cans to another room. When she lugged them back to us, she was short of breath from the exertion.

"Next week, around this time, I want you to come back for more," she gasped, plopping the heavy containers down on the counter.

"Thank you very much," we said in unison while Gerda curtsied and I bowed. Gerda added, "We'll be back next Wednesday. Auf Wiedersehen."

"Until then. Auf Wiedersehen," Mrs. Schneidereit said as she bustled into the back room.

We lugged our milk cans in the direction of home. After ten minutes we stopped to rest. Without exchanging a word, Gerda took a taste of the whey from one of the milk cans and I drank some from another. I gulped down more than a liter before coming up for air.

271

"Hey, don't drink so much," Gerda cautioned.

"Sorry, I couldn't help it."

A quarter of the contents of the second can had disappeared. Undismayed, I poured some of the whey from the third can into the second can to even things up. Clumps of cottage cheese floated on top. We fished them out with our dirty fingers and ate them. As good as the whey had been, the clumps were even better.

"One more dip and I'll stop," I promised, but Gerda shook her head.

"Oma will notice something's missing."

Suddenly we both felt guilty. Fearing Oma's wrath, we carried the milk cans the rest of the way home. Our worries were needless. Oma never suspected a thing.

"Mrs. Schneidereit must have been sent to us from heaven!" she declared, as unaccustomed tears of joy streamed down her cheeks. She filled metal cups for the younger children, and even gave them each a second helping.

* * *

The following week, Gerda and I went back to the dairy. I no longer noticed Mrs. Schneidereit's enormous waistline. To me she looked like an angel in disguise. With a friendly smile she sent us off with a reminder:

"From now on, I want you to come back every Wednesday, and please give my regards to Mrs. Nitsch."

"We will!" I replied with undisguised enthusiasm.

"We really appreciate it," Gerda added, curtseying as best she could while holding the heavy can. I made a solemn bow. The two of us could scarcely believe our good fortune.

Gerda and I always looked forward to Wednesdays. Like two conspirators, whenever we were about half way back from the dairy, we stopped to have a drink and to fish out clumps of cottage cheese.

One time we were so hungry, we were forced to level off all three cans at the pump. We felt guilty, but the stuff was irresistible. To avoid telltale swirls of grime when we dipped in our hands to find the cheese, we always made sure to wash before we left home.

After a couple of weeks, the children's coughing and sneezing stopped.

"It works better than medicine," Oma exclaimed. "Just look at the results!"

"Mrs. Schneidereit must be taking quite a risk," Ilse added. "I can't imagine she's supposed to give things away."

We didn't think Mrs. Schneidereit could be any more helpful, but we were wrong. One Wednesday Oma discovered two pounds of cottage cheese hidden in a cloth bag at the bottom of our largest milk can. It had been invisible under the cloudy green whey.

"Can you believe it?" Oma exclaimed, holding up her astonishing discovery. "If she gets caught, they'll give her a one-way ticket to Siberia. Why does she risk everything for people she doesn't even know?"

"I don't know," Mutti said. "She's been so helpful and she isn't even Lutheran. She's a Catholic!"

"A Catholic, you say? I don't think I've met more than five Catholics in my whole life, but I have to admit, she still seems like a good person."

"Unfortunately, not everyone shares your good opinion of her," Mutti said, shaking her head.

"How could anyone not like her?" Gerda asked.

"Some people criticize her for being so heavy when everyone else is going hungry. And she's living with the Russian man who's in charge of the dairy. The German women think that's how she got the job."

"But you don't think so, do you?" I asked.

"No, of course not. She's fluent in Russian; otherwise she wouldn't be working there. Besides, I don't care who she lives with or how she looks. She's been wonderful to us."

* * *

On a Monday morning at the end of April, Comrade Semjonov, our Russian teacher, did not show up at school. He was never to return. Following an investigation by the Russian authorities, he had been jailed in Tapiau, charged with shorting our daily bread rations and selling the difference.

When Oma heard the story of Comrade Semjonov's downfall, she gloated. "Just as I thought. All I needed was a scale to prove it. Any fool can tell the difference between 200 grams and 300 grams, but why should anyone believe an old woman like me?" she concluded with obvious satisfaction.

In contrast to Oma, I was upset by the news, at first refusing to believe the whole story. If anyone had shorted our bread rations, I would have suspected Mr. Raddatz; it would never have occurred to me that good-natured Comrade Semjonov would have cheated us.

The following Sunday, some of the mothers took their children to visit Comrade Semjonov. He was a broken man. A few days later he was shipped off to a Siberian labor camp.

We waited nearly two weeks for his replacement to arrive. On the appointed day, my heart was pounding and my hands were clammy.

"He's bound to be another Raddatz," I predicted to Gerda on our way to school. "I don't think I can handle another one like him."

Like his predecessor, our new teacher scarcely knew a word of German. Comrade Karpov, a stodgy middle-aged man, was neither friendly like Comrade Semjonov nor nasty like Mr. Raddatz. He was just plain dull. Among the Russians at the Kolkhoz it was rumored that he had been a hog dealer before the war. Comrade Karpov, like

Comrade Semjonov, wore a wristwatch, so Mr. Raddatz knew once again whom to ask for the time.

* * *

On May Day 1948, the Russian barber who lived downstairs got roaring drunk. We could hear the muffled cries of his poor wife from two floors below. When we saw her later on the street, she was covered with dark blue bruises and red welts.

Only Russians patronized the barber shop. The few old German men living in Goldbach could not afford to pay for haircuts. Oma cut my hair, as well as Hubert's and Dieter's, with her precious pair of sewing scissors. Sometimes I caught a glimpse of my distorted reflection in a muddy puddle. I had never seen myself in a mirror since we left Palmnicken, but since Gerda and Ilse always snickered afterwards, I was sure Oma made me look like an idiot.

* * *

On a pleasant day, Mr. Raddatz took all of us outside into the sunshine. Our expectations of a brisk hike were soon dashed. We walked only a short distance until we reached a sandy dirt road.

"This will do," he announced. "I want each of you to find a little stick."

With puzzled faces, we did as we were told. Mr. Raddatz puffed himself up. He was so excited, his face began to twitch.

"Everybody take a spot please! Upper grades, attention! I want you to write these sentences in the sand: 'The Soviet Union has more natural resources than any other country in the world. It has also more time zones than any other country in the world. We love Comrade Stalin because he is a great leader.'"

While dictating, he strutted behind us with his hands clasped behind his back. Satisfied that we were hard at work, he turned to the first and second graders.

275

"And now for the lower grades! Please write: 'The starlings sing a happy song in the spring.'"

We began to giggle and Mr. Raddatz glared at us angrily. As the younger children struggled to write their sentence, the older ones thought the assignment was plain silly. Everyone, that is, except for Müller. He labored to make each word a work of art. No sooner had he stepped back to admire his masterpiece, another boy rushed over and trampled it. Poor Müller was close to tears. Suddenly aware that most of us were only fooling around, Mr. Raddatz rounded us up and led us to the edge of a freshly plowed field. He never even bothered to correct our spelling mistakes.

"I want you to search for little pieces of limestone like this one," he commanded, holding up a small piece to demonstrate what he needed. "The school's supply of chalk is nearly exhausted. From now on, we will use little pieces of limestone for the blackboard."

Manfred and I exchanged worried glances. We were both thinking about all of the pieces of chalk which had shattered when Mr. Raddatz had thrown them at us in class. The idea that we would now be targets for rock-solid pieces of limestone was not appealing. In the interests of self-preservation, Manfred and I did not look very hard, so neither of us found any limestone, but with growing alarm, we noticed that the limestone pieces the eager younger children gave to Mr. Raddatz were even bigger than sticks of chalk and looked downright dangerous.

It wasn't the first time I wondered whether Mr. Raddatz might be insane. Even the adults in Goldbach had heard strange rumors about him. One story in particular, filtered down to us by the grapevine, dealt with Mr. Raddatz's almost pathological hatred of snakes, but as usual, we took all such reports with a healthy grain of salt.

After the limestone hunt, Mr. Raddatz made us all sit down on the grassy edge of a nearby meadow where he gave us a lecture about hibernation. He was unusually low key as he rambled on about the habits of bugs, mice, and rabbits. I had never seen him look so relaxed.

"Any questions?" he finally asked.

With a wink at me, Manfred inquired, "Mr. Raddatz, do snakes also hibernate?"

Mr. Raddatz's reaction was electrifying. With a voice bordering on hysteria, he raged against vipers.

"Yes, those slimy reptiles hibernate and I wish they would never wake up! I hate them! Last summer when I was fishing along the Deime, an enormous viper sank its fangs into my big toe!"

The younger children sat with their mouths agape as he went on.

"As the snake slithered away, I sat down on a log. Fearing that I would die from the venom, I pulled out my pocketknife and cut off part of my toe. Afterwards I limped home in agony and drank half a bottle of vodka. It was a miracle that I survived," Mr. Raddatz concluded proudly.

At a loss as to whether he wanted our admiration or our pity, none of us said a word. Stunned by his strange outburst, we all walked quietly back to the school, collected our rations of bread and went home. From that day on I no longer wondered whether Mr. Raddatz was insane. I was sure of it.

The school year ended in the middle of May. Our vacation would last until the beginning of October. The daily rations of bread would also resume in the fall. We had been urged to study our textbooks over the long summer months, but Gerda and I were too busy minding the children, collecting stinging nettle and sorrel leaves, berries and acorns. Gathering food was much more important to us than reading about the great Soviet Union.

* * *

Next to the Magazin was a high-ceilinged assembly room in which the Russians had been showing movies ever since Goldbach had gotten electricity. Two weeks after the end of school I was hanging out at the entrance of the movie room, daydreaming about somehow getting inside. I didn't have the money to buy a ticket. Even if I had money, I would have used it to buy a piece of bread.

The burly cashier stood like a tower, scrutinizing all the Russians who wanted to get in, to make sure that everybody paid his dues. I edged closer to the door. Standing on my tiptoes, I peeked inside. The room, buzzing with the conversation of eager patrons, filled up quickly. As soon as the performance started, the cashier shut the door, opening it only when another paying customer arrived. Even so, three other raggedly dressed boys my age stubbornly waited close by the entrance.

"Is he going to let you in?" I whispered to the only boy I recognized.

"I dunno. But don't hang with us. Three have a better chance than four."

"All right, all right," I replied, stepping to one side.

A few minutes later, something incredible happened. The burly cashier opened the door and waved the other three boys in. Seizing my chance, I rushed over to the entrance and looked beseechingly up at him. The poor man was so cross-eyed, he might have been looking at me or at somebody else. I glanced over my shoulder, but no one else was there. With a nod in my direction, he let me slip inside.

For a moment I was blinded. The only light came from the movie screen and from the tips of dozens of lighted cigarettes. The room was smaller than expected. It had once been used as a meeting room in a tavern. A portable screen stood against the front wall. All seven rows of wooden benches were occupied. Five to six rows of standees crowded between the benches and the door, leaving open only a narrow aisle. Elevated on blocks of wood to raise it above everyone's heads, the projector rested on a small table in the back. Men stood aside to let me squeeze through.

Finally I managed to join the other boys on the left side of the room, in the front of the first row of standees. My heart pounded with excitement. A newsreel was shown first. Although I could not understand the narrator, I recognized the Kremlin and Red Square in Moscow and the May Day parade. We had similar pictures in our Russian textbook. Since I understood only a few words, I followed the plot of the main feature by concentrating on the soundtrack. The music echoed all of the emotions on the screen - joy, danger, and sorrow.

Men continued to smoke throughout the film. Not wanting to disturb the people around me, I struggled not to cough. When the lights came on at the end of the film, the room looked as though it were enveloped in thick fog. I rushed outside to get a breath of fresh air. It was already dark. Choking on the smoke, I rushed home. Luckily Mutti was home, because otherwise I would have gotten my usual smack with the dishrag. Oma was beside herself. She hurled her favorite East Prussian insult at me.

"You Lorbass (wise guy), where have you been? How dare you stay out after dark? What's your excuse this time?"

"Sorry, Oma, but I was at the movies!"

"The movies? How'd you get in? Don't they charge admission?"

When Mutti heard my explanation, she decided it was time to interfere.

"Your Oma and I were worried sick about you, coming home so late. If you want to go to the movies again, there are two rules. You have to tell Oma before you go and, in case you don't get in, I want you to promise you'll come straight home."

Oma clearly disapproved of these rules, but she grudgingly accepted them. The movies, and especially the newsreels, were eye openers for me. I saw well-dressed people walking on clean paved streets, not muddy roads like those we had in Goldbach. People drove long distances in passenger cars and traveled by train. We had never gone anywhere in more than two years. Passenger cars were unknown in Goldbach. The only transportation was by truck, and even that was reserved for the Russians who worked for the Red Army or for the Kolkhoz.

Until I started watching the newsreels I had somehow forgotten what normal life was like, but now that I knew normal life existed somewhere else, I began to think seriously about my future. It looked rather bleak. The way I saw it, if I managed to survive until the age of twelve, the most I had to look forward to was a life of toil at the Kolkhoz.

After seeing one of these newsreels, I asked Mutti, "Why don't we try to get out of here? Any place else would be better than this."

Mutti smiled sympathetically as she reminded me of all of the reasons. "We have no passports. We have no identification. Officially we don't even exist. We have no money and, even if we had, there's no public transportation. In a way, we're not any better off than prisoners of war. It's as though we're trapped behind a giant, imaginary fence."

"Hasn't anyone ever tried to escape?"

"A few Germans from Goldbach have tried it. All of them were caught by Russian soldiers. The ones with children were sent back to work at our Kolkhoz or another one nearby. The ones without children were shipped off to Siberia."

"So you don't think it's worth a chance then?" I asked with a sigh.

"How far do you think we would get with nine people?" she replied sadly.

"All nine of us? Probably not even to Tapiau," I admitted with a grin.

"That's the spirit. If we keep our sense of humor, things will work themselves out somehow. Perhaps Opa will put in a good word for us. Lately I've felt very strongly that he's pulling strings up in heaven to help us get out."

With Mutti's words still fresh in my mind, I lay down on my straw mattress. Compressed by two years of wear, it was quite flat, providing little cushioning from the hard wooden floor boards underneath. I recalled how Opa had once told me that God punished people who didn't follow the Ten Commandments. What did I do to deserve a life like this? Was it the school sandwiches I threw away in Langendorf?

The church bench Gerda and I had sawed apart? Perhaps I was being punished for that? Feeling guilty and worrying about the future, I stayed up long after midnight.

* * *

The sun was streaming through the window when I woke up. I never heard the old man with the bell. Gerda and I went out to the big village meadow to pick sorrel. We found a spot with an ample supply and collected what we needed. Afterwards, we sat down under a shady tree next to the brook. This was our secret hideout, where we talked about God and the world. Oma was only a few hundred meters away, but in this spot we felt safe from her.

"I've been thinking," I said. "Mr. Raddatz may be an odd duck, but being in class is still better than doing chores for Oma. And I really miss our daily ration of bread. I'm sick and tired of sorrel soup, stinging nettle spinach, and chamomile tea."

"I'm not sure I'll ever go back to school," Gerda replied. "My twelfth birthday's coming up and the Russians at the Kommandantura know it."

"Well, working at the Kolkhoz is probably easier than working for Oma," I consoled her.

"I don't know about that. Perhaps in the summer, but certainly not during the winter. It's a lot of effort for 300 grams of bread."

We sat quietly for a few minutes. Gerda broke the silence.

"I wish, just once, I could have as much bread and milk as I wanted," she said wistfully.

"You can say that again," I agreed wholeheartedly.

The last time either of us had drunk any milk was at the beginning of 1945. I barely recalled how it tasted. We suddenly remembered it was nearly Wednesday when Mrs. Schneidereit would fill our milk cans with whey. With our spirits uplifted, we walked home to Oma and the children.

CHAPTER 20

By the middle of July most of our clothes, but especially our underwear and socks, were falling apart. The crotches of my three pairs of underpants consisted only of Oma's darning, the original material having long since disintegrated. All of our clothes were festooned with colorful patches, none of which matched. New outfits were not sold in the Magazin. If they had been, they would have been unaffordable.

The only way clothing became available was if someone died, but the relatives of the deceased were always the first in line. Occasionally Mutti would bring home an organized burlap sack from the Kolkhoz from which Oma would sew us winter clothing. I got a new pair of burlap pants because I had outgrown my old ones.

In August another batch of Russians, mostly women and children, arrived in Goldbach. Judging by their ragged clothing, they were not much better off than we were. All of them were put to work at the Kolkhoz. We heard that each of them would be given a cow so that they would always have a source of milk.

"Aren't you worried they'll take away your jobs?" Oma asked Mutti one evening.

"No, I don't think so. There's still plenty of work to go around. What concerns me are the people who get the plum jobs. The ones who measure how much we do and the people who dole out the potatoes and bread."

The privileged holders of such jobs had power over everyone else. They could grant or withhold favors, ranging from overestimating the amount of work done to arranging a ride home on one of the Kolkhoz's American made trucks.

"It's not that I'm jealous," Mutti explained, "but those toadies are the first to report anyone they catch organizing."

* * *

At the end of August, Ilse and Aunt Liesbeth came home just as we were starting to eat our oat and blueberry Schlunz.

"You're fifteen years old, but you acted like a two-year-old," Aunt Liesbeth was saying to Ilse as they came into the kitchen.

"Don't start with that again, Mutti. I just couldn't resist."

"Out with it!" Oma commanded. "What's going on?"

"On our way to work this morning, I found a hard candy in front of the Magazin."

"Covered with dirt and saliva," Aunt Liesbeth added, with disgust.

"Did you eat it?" Oma asked. "Back in Langendorf, you were always so picky about food!"

"If I can eat maggot soup, why not second-hand candy?" Ilse replied. "It didn't take me long to suck down to the clean part, and it had a delicious fruit flavor. I could've eaten a whole pound."

"The Russians call it Konfekt. They've been selling it at the Magazin," Aunt Liesbeth added.

"When I hear the word 'Konfekt,' I think of chocolate, not hard fruit candy," Oma said. "What I wouldn't give for a piece of dark chocolate right now!"

"Will you please stop talking about candy?" Gerda said in a loud voice. "I'm trying to eat my Schlunz."

"Don't worry," Ilse assured her. "It won't happen again. I heard that the candies were extremely expensive and besides, the Magazin has already run out of them."

"So much for that," said Oma with a shrug, but we could see the disappointment in her eyes.

* * *

Before I fell asleep that night, Mutti and Ilse put on their black outfits and their huge rucksacks. As they had done the two previous years, they went out three or four nights a week to organize potatoes. The danger was even greater than it had been in 1946 and 1947, because the recently arrived Russian civilians also stole potatoes after dark. Armed Russian soldiers guarded the crops more strictly than ever.

Despite tightened security, the Russians still permitted us to pick over the fallen grain in the harvested fields. Manfred and I had filled our bags with rye one afternoon when we were caught in a sudden downpour. We took shelter under a lone oak tree in the middle of a muddy field. The grain had to be protected from moisture. When the rain finally let up, our feet sank in the muck on the dirt road.

"Looks like perfect conditions to test out loam balls," I commented to Manfred as we stopped to rest.

We cut meter-long sticks from a bush and carved the tips into sharp points. Forming walnut-sized balls of wet loam with our hands, we popped one of the tiny balls onto the tip of each of the sticks.

Using the gnarled oak tree as a target, we held the sticks behind our backs and swung them over our heads with great force. The loam pellets took off like little cannonballs, sometimes flying so far we could barely see where they landed.

"Forget the tree," I finally said. "We'll never hit it. Let's only go for distance."

Engrossed in our friendly competition, we lost all track of time. By the time we resumed our walk, it had started to pour again.

I arrived in our kitchen soaked to the skin. What was worse, the ears of rye were also wet. Still, Oma was not the least bit angry. On the contrary, she was uncharacteristically cheerful. I sensed she must be hiding something from me, but when I asked her about it, she said it was "nothing."

Whenever Oma cooked our supper, she had a look of grim determination on her face, but that evening as she worked she hummed all of her favorite hymns. When she had repeated "A Mighty Fortress is our God" four times, I became suspicious. I went into the next room and whispered to Gerda, who had a better rapport with Oma than I did, "What's going on? Why's she in such a good mood?"

"No idea. I've asked her, but she clams up."

We heard steps coming up the staircase, much faster than usual. Mutti, Aunt Liesbeth, and Ilse burst into the kitchen, laughing and crying at the same time. Mutti was beaming.

"Can you imagine? We heard it from at least half a dozen different people so it must be true. We're all being sent back to Germany!"

"Oh no! Not that old fairy tale again," Gerda protested.

Now that the cat was out of the bag, Oma confessed, "Well, I didn't want to spread any rumors, but I heard the same thing from the old woman with the limp who lives two houses down."

"We've heard it all before, and we're still right here in Goldbach," I grumbled.

Mutti interrupted me. "It's all over the village. This time it must be true."

We stayed up late discussing the possibilities. Mutti and Ilse decided to take the night off. Their black organizing uniforms remained unworn.

The next morning when Mutti, Ilse, and Aunt Liesbeth went back to work at the Kolkhoz, the Russians they spoke to claimed not to know anything about it.

"They insisted the story was started by the Germans, not by them," Mutti reported.

Still, the rumors persisted. The uncertainty nearly drove us crazy. Two days later, when there had been no further developments, we decided we had once again been the victims of a terrible hoax.

* * *

Judging from the position of the sun, it was time to get up. Mutti's bed was empty. She had long since left for the Kolkhoz. Since I had to go outside anyway, I brought along the pail. As I walked towards the back of the courtyard, I was surprised to hear Mutti's voice from the direction of our wood chopping place.

"Up so early?" she called out cheerfully. Mutti, Aunt Liesbeth, and Ilse were returning from work. They were smiling.

"Just throw that pail away; we won't need it anymore," Mutti yelled. She sounded almost giddy. "Let's pack!"

"What? Say that again."

"You heard me right! Let's pack!"

Suddenly I had a lump in my throat. The three of them would not have been sent home early unless it was true. In a state of shock, I waited until they came closer. In the meantime, Mutti had reconsidered.

"Just to be on the safe side, I suppose you'd better bring the pail back upstairs," she said. "We'll be in Goldbach another three hours and, with nine people in the house, you never know who might need it."

"Three hours?" I gasped, scarcely believing my ears.

Ilse and I raced on ahead of Mutti and Aunt Liesbeth. Breathlessly Ilse announced the news to Oma, who kept repeating, "Dear God, this can't be true. Praise the Lord, this can't be true."

Once everyone was back upstairs, the nine of us assembled in the living room. Mutti and Ilse were talking at once. Frustrated about all the rumors, Mutti, Aunt Liesbeth, and Ilse had gone to work at the usual time. No sooner had they reached the Kolkhoz when all of the Germans with young children had been told to wait in a separate group. Several hours later, the Kommandant of Goldbach, magnificent atop his black horse, arrived to make a dramatic announcement.

"You all can go home now and pack whatever you can carry. Around noon be ready with your luggage at the collection point at the edge of town on the village road leading to Tapiau. You will be brought by truck to Kaliningrad and from there you will travel by train to Berlin. The elderly who cannot work will accompany you."

"What about the others?" a mother of four asked.

"Childless young adults are still needed to help with the harvest. They'll follow you in a week or two at the end of September."

He paused and asked, "Are there any other questions?"

Silence. No one dared to speak.

"Da svidanye," he said with a cheerful wave of his hand.

"After he said 'Da svidanye'," Mutti continued, "we all roared 'Da svidanye' like a large choir before he could change his mind. Then we ran home as fast as we could."

Mutti beamed at us and said, "It's been years since I've seen so many happy faces under one roof." She swept Hubert up into her arms and gave him a hug.

"We have no time to celebrate," Aunt Liesbeth reminded her. "It's still warm outside, but we don't know where we'll spend the nights. We need to put on as much clothing as possible and pack our bundles."

"Right you are. Let's get moving," Mutti agreed.

As we had done in Palmnicken two and one-half years before, we packed in a hurry. When Oma started to gather up our pots and pans, Mutti objected.

"I don't think we'll need those again."

Oma was stubborn and packed them anyhow. She handed me the heavy package and said, "Here, these are for you to carry. Watch out you don't lose any. Do you hear?"

"Yes, Oma."

"Ilse, what are you carrying?"

"Just this bundle of blankets. I'm keeping one hand free to hold Dieter."

"Dieter can walk on his own," declared Oma. "He's nearly five. Here, I want you to carry this rucksack and a bag full of potatoes."

"But Oma, they're too heavy. Besides, we won't need them."

"Mark my words, we will. The Russians aren't going to send us to Berlin in a train with a dining car."

"Yes, Oma," Ilse said meekly.

Mutti quietly took over the rucksack full of potatoes. It was the same rucksack she had been using to organize potatoes for nearly three years. Every once in a while Oma or Aunt Liesbeth stopped working long enough to express their doubts we would really leave.

"Cheer up you two. It's going to be all right," Ilse reassured them.

Not expecting visitors, we were surprised to hear footsteps on the staircase. Mutti opened the door and there stood the barber's wife and her daughters. They had not been to our apartment since the day of Dorchen's funeral. The poor woman had tears in her eyes. She shyly pointed at our furniture and the remaining pots and pans. Mutti and Ilse told her in Russian she was welcome to everything she saw. Sobbing quietly, the woman and her daughters took as much as they could carry. They returned at least a dozen more times, leaving only the heaviest pieces of furniture, a few odds and ends, and our bundles.

* * *

Before we left the apartment for the last time, we gathered together in the living room. My feet, barefoot all summer, felt strange in my boots. I had grown over the summer and my toes touched the leather.

On such a warm day, I was uncomfortable in my grimy old coat with the shredded sleeves. Mutti insisted I wear it.

"I'll give you three good reasons," she said when I protested. "First of all, we're still not sure the Russians will let us leave. Secondly, even if we do get out of here, we can't be sure where we'll end up. And finally, you'll need something to sleep on. You heard what Oma said about dining cars. Well, there won't be any sleeping cars either." Her third argument was the one that won me over.

We walked down the steep staircase through the kitchen of the empty Schmidt apartment to the ground level. As we reached the courtyard, I checked the bakery dump for rats and realized I had forgotten my slingshot.

"You'll have to make another one," Mutti advised me. "We've got to hurry or we'll miss the truck."

Dieter began to lag behind. Slowing our pace to his, we lugged our heavy bundles towards the edge of town. The barber's wife and her daughters stood in their doorway, waving and calling out, "Da svidanye."

Newly arrived Russians watched our slow progress, their children gaping at us as if we were part of a traveling circus. The Russian girls wore thin dresses and the boys wore shorts and shirts; they were all barefoot. By contrast, I was wearing knickerbockers made out of burlap sacks, a shirt, a sweater, my old long coat, and leather boots with wooden soles and high platform heels. Sweat ran down my face from under my warm ushanka. At that moment I would have loved to change places with one of the barefoot Russian boys.

Gerda used her elbow to give me a poke. "Look!" she said. "We'll never see that nasty guy again."

Horns-head stood at the side of the dusty road, furiously chewing on sunflower seeds. Like a parrot in the zoo, he skillfully separated the seeds from the husks with his tongue. With a defiant glare, he spat the black and white shells in my direction through the gaps in his teeth.

Gunter Nitsch

Barefoot, he wore his leather tank crew helmet, a tattered dirty shirt, and long, torn pants with patches. I thought about the cruel surprise package he had left for me on that cold winter day and about the bread money he had stolen. When he grinned at me, I took a tighter grip on my bundle of pots and pans and kept on walking.

CHAPTER 21

Our collection point was located close to our first house in Goldbach. Eighty people were already waiting there, among them Mr. Ademeit, whom I had not seen for a while. He looked more stoop-shouldered than before, reminding me of the old farmers back in Langendorf.

"Good day, Mr. Ademeit," I greeted him as we walked by.

"Hello, Günter. I see you're on your way to a better life."

"Aren't you coming with us?"

"I'm coming, all right, but at my age the chance for a new start has probably passed me by."

We were soon joined by Manfred, his mother, and his grandmother. Some adults were becoming impatient. One old woman kept muttering to herself, "The trucks will never come. The trucks will never come."

But Manfred's mother insisted, "The trucks will come, because we're no longer needed here."

"They'll come, I'm sure of it," Mutti agreed. Still, we all felt a mixture of expectation and fear.

Just then a convoy of military trucks arrived. Thick diesel exhaust fumes hung in the stagnant air as we quickly climbed aboard. We heard the all-too-familiar Russian commands, "Davai, davai," and off we went.

I took one last look at the stone church on the hill. Would Opa's wooden cross be left standing after we were gone? Would anyone remember to put flowers on Dorchen's grave? The Kolkhoz flashed by to my left and Goldbach was gone.

No one spoke during the forty-kilometer ride; each of us was lost in private thoughts. I wondered what the future held for us.

To avoid the enormous potholes, we drove slowly through Königsberg. On both sides of the road, houses gaped open, like Sigrid's dollhouse in Langendorf, exposing vacant rooms, bathroom fixtures, and kitchens inside. At a large freight yard on the outskirts of town, the trucks came to a halt.

"Davai! Davai!" yelled the Russian soldiers. We left the trucks and were herded into a giant warehouse. Thousands of people were already waiting there. As the noisy crowd milled about, we soon lost sight of everyone we knew, except for a few families from Goldbach and Mr. Ademeit. With each new group of arrivals, we felt more and more boxed in. No one knew what to expect. I caught snatches of Mutti's conversation with Aunt Liesbeth over the noise of the crowd.

"...be here for days at this rate."

"How will we manage?...didn't bring enough to eat..."

Angry muttering from the front of the crowd drifted back, row by row, to where we stood.

"What're they saying?" Oma asked, cupping her hand to her ear. "Can you make it out?"

"Something about a checkpoint and a body search, as best I can make it out," Mutti replied.

"Body search?" Oma said. "For what? All we've got are the lice infested rags on our backs."

Still, some of the adults near us started pawing through their luggage. Unpacking scissors and needles, they were soon frantically undoing the seams of their coats and jackets.

"What do you make of it?" I asked Mutti.

"I've no idea. Maybe they have Reichsmarks sewn into the linings."

As we moved slowly towards the front, whole families, busy with scissors and needles, stayed back, frantically tearing open their clothing. After a while, we reached a long aisle just wide enough for people to walk four abreast. As a result of this sudden bottleneck, everyone was forced to slow down to a snail's pace. Amidst shoving and pushing, some people jostled to move forward. Yet others seemed just as anxious to move towards the back.

I felt something crunching under my wooden soles. The smooth stone floor was thick with medals. I saw Iron Crosses, Wounded Badges, Infantry Assault Badges, and Close Combat Clasps. Strewn among them lay documents bearing the swastika-and-eagle stamp, savings passbooks, and photographs of soldiers. One awestruck woman grabbed her mother's sleeve and pointed.

"Look! A Ritterkreuz! What a hero of the Fatherland that must have been!"

In a newsreel in Schippenbeil, I had once seen a Luftwaffe officer receive a Ritterkreuz for shooting down enemy airplanes in Russia, but to me it looked like all the rest. Just for the fun of it, I stuck the toe of my boot under the growing pile of trash and kicked some of the medals aside.

"It's absolutely beyond me how people could have held onto this rubbish until now," Mutti said to Aunt Liesbeth.

"I wouldn't have believed it, if I hadn't seen it with my own eyes," Aunt Liesbeth agreed.

Hubert, who was still a few months shy of his sixth birthday, bent down to pick up a golden Nazi party badge.

"Mutti! Look what I found!" he chirped with delight.

Mutti grabbed the badge right out of his hand and dropped it onto the floor.

"Don't touch any of that bad stuff," she pleaded.

As medals and military decorations continued to clink to the floor all around us, I could see the checkpoint up ahead. In front of me, a skinny middle-aged mother with three children waited tearfully, only dropping her husband's war medals when we could make out the features of the Russian soldiers waiting to search us. Just then, Mr. Ademeit somehow worked his way over to us.

"Look for me after we pass the checkpoint," he whispered. "There's something I want to tell you." Then I lost sight of him again in the crowd.

Up ahead, Russian soldiers stood beside six large tables. As the throng crept slowly forward, I observed them as they did body searches and inspected luggage. There were so few of them and so many of us, they were clearly overworked, impatient, and short tempered.

We finally reached the checkpoint. A tall soldier with a chest full of medals looked us up and down. His hair was so blond he didn't appear to have eyebrows or eye lashes. His cornflower blue eyes looked as cold as marbles. In broken German, he angrily pointed at Mutti and Aunt Liesbeth.

"Medals? Photographs with soldiers? You have?"

"We don't have any," Mutti and Aunt Liesbeth declared at the same time.

"Medals! Photographs! You have?" he repeated, even louder than before.

"No, we have nothing," Mutti repeated.

With growing frustration the soldier barked at Mutti, "Documents? Passports? You have documents? Passports?"

Mutti looked desperate. "We don't have any documents or passports. They were taken away from us in 1945."

"On April 15, 1945, to be exact," Aunt Liesbeth added.

The soldier still did not give up.

"You have photographs?"

"We have nothing. No photographs, no documents, no passports," Mutti insisted firmly.

For a tense minute, the soldier glared at Mutti. He gestured to Mutti to take off her coat and lift her arms. Determined to find some contraband, the tall blond soldier and two of his companions next turned their attention to the children. Of course they did not find anything, because we had nothing in the first place.

With the permission of another Russian soldier, the blond man waved us through. He practically spat out the words, "Davai, davai."

Looking back at the aisle along which we had come, I understood why the soldiers working at the checkpoint were angry. We had been wading through discarded medals, documents, and photographs. It must have infuriated the Russians to see how many of the German adults still cherished these mementos from the Hitler times.

We entered another big waiting area. Someone tapped me on my shoulder and I looked up to see the friendly face of Mr. Ademeit. He suddenly reminded me of Opa. We could not have survived the years in Goldbach without his help.

"Here's what I want you to know," Mr. Ademeit said. "All the medals you saw back there, even the ones that look like gold, are just worthless tin badges. None of them was earned for good deeds. They're rewards for killing enemy soldiers and for sending German soldiers to be slaughtered. And, believe me, I know what I'm talking about. I fought for the Kaiser in the last war."

"But the men who got them must have been brave," I protested.

"When you talk about bravery, think about ancient heroes. Knights who fought valiantly and with honor to win the hand of the King's daughter or to receive a big bag of gold." Mr. Ademeit waved his hand in the direction of the room behind us. "But those things! Always remember, a piece of tin, and I don't care if it has a swastika on it or a red star, is just a piece of junk." Having said this, Mr. Ademeit shook my hand, grabbed his luggage bundles, and moved on.

The women around us had just begun to grumble about how many nights we would spend on the floor in the big hall when the mass of people ahead of us began to move again. Slowly, like cattle that have discovered a small hole in the fence, we funneled out of the big warehouse through two narrow gates. Outside, a seemingly endless freight train awaited us. 'Deutsche Reichsbahn' was painted on the sides of most of the boxcars. Ilse counted about one-quarter of the cars and estimated between sixty and seventy of them in all. A dozen or so makeshift food stands were off to one side. Clutching our last rubles, Mutti and Ilse hurried over to shop for provisions.

"If that's our train, the trip to Berlin will take a lot longer than we thought," Aunt Liesbeth predicted.

"I'm afraid you're right," Oma agreed.

Mutti and Ilse rejoined us. "We were among the first customers!" Ilse exclaimed. "We bought eight loaves of bread and a bag of grits!"

"The grits I can cook up into plenty of Schlunz," Oma said. "But what've you got in that pot?"

"Honey! Isn't that amazing? We got a pot full of honey."

I let out a cheer.

"I can scarcely remember how it tastes after all these years," Gerda said, licking her lips. "The little ones are in for a sweet treat. They don't even know what honey is."

"Do you have any rubles left?" Oma asked Mutti.

"Not a one. At this point I think we'd better just take one day at a time."

"Looks as if we got there just in time," Ilse said.

So many people were crowded around, the food stands were no longer visible. Each time a new batch of people left the hall, there was another frenzied rush to buy food. Everyone who had any rubles left wanted to get rid of them, or so it seemed.

* * *

Russian soldiers and German female workers set about assigning groups of approximately three dozen people to each boxcar, taking care not to split up families. The nine of us were joined by several other families, none of whom had been with us in Goldbach. We placed our baggage along the walls of the car, leaving open the space on both sides of the sliding doors. Once everyone was settled on board, the Russians cried out "Davai, davai," and we started to roll. Some of the adults looked jubilant; others were not yet ready to celebrate.

"They might change their minds," one elderly woman warned. "Perhaps they're only going to take us deeper into Russia."

At first I was so startled by the sudden movement of the train, I hardly noticed the scenery outside. Before long I peeked out the door, which stood open just wide enough for two people to stand side by side. In the outskirts of Königsberg, grass and ivy grew over the shells of damaged buildings, partially hiding them from view. Bushes edged in as if to hide what had happened there. The adults standing with me looked glum.

Minutes later, as we reached the East Prussian countryside, an older boy helped Ilse open the sliding door as wide as possible. Children and adults positioned themselves so they could look outside. Three children sat on the edge, dangling their legs. Even the stubble fields, bare of harvested rye and barley, looked beautiful as we zipped past. A feeling of unaccustomed joy came over me. I felt like yelling at the top of my lungs, "We're flying! We're flying!"

A young woman suddenly spoke up. "Why don't we sing 'Nun ade Du, mein lieb' Heimatland' (Now goodbye, my dear homeland)?" she suggested.

Nearly everyone joined in. The song had a catchy melody and it perked me up to sing it, but Oma and some of the other adults started to weep.

Someone called out, "We're passing Preussisch Eylau!"

I thought back to our short stay there in February of 1945. My mouth watered as I remembered the pea soup the German soldier ladled out for me at the field kitchen.

After Preussisch Eylau, we began to sing again. Some of the songs, like "Land of the Dark Forests," were sentimental. Other songs like "Dark Brown is the Hazelnut" were just for fun. The signs along the track were no longer written in Cyrillic letters. We were now in Polish controlled territory.

Aunt Liesbeth called out, "Bartenstein!" She quietly scanned the horizon, and then signaled to us to look outside. "If I'm not mistaken," she shouted over the singing and the clack-clack of the wheels, "if we keep looking, we should be able to catch a glimpse of Schippenbeil."

We gazed out over the flat landscape. Way in the distance, to our left, we saw the town. Towering over the trees, the familiar red brick church of Schippenbeil pointed skyward, its massive steeple built in layers, each one thinner than the one below. The layer on the very top looked like a giant sharpened pencil. Oma, Aunt Liesbeth, Mutti, and Ilse had tears in their eyes. Mutti had been singing, but the words of the song suddenly caught in her throat.

We had not seen that church steeple for nearly four years. As soon as it came into view, memories flooded over me. Fräulein Durbach, my first grade teacher! I knew only too well what the Russians would have done to her had they caught her. I thought of our prisoners, especially Vassily, Armand, and Gustave, and prayed they had all been safely reunited with their families, just as we were soon to be. But most of all, I thought about Opa and the good times we had shared on his farm in Langendorf just beyond Schippenbeil. Still, I felt strangely happy and unsentimental. All of that had happened a very long time ago.

Those times were gone forever. I wanted only to go west, to Germany, where Vati was, where life would be normal again. My only goal at that moment was to get as far away from East Prussia as possible.

The steeple of the Schippenbeil church faded away at the horizon. I was sure we would never see it again. In the meantime, Mutti and Aunt Liesbeth began to wonder why we were traveling southeast, rather than to the west.

"If we continue in this direction, we'll get to Rastenburg," Aunt Liesbeth brooded. "We'll never reach the German border."

At Korschen, after a long wait, our train was shunted over to a switch yard. Late at night we began to move again. Each of us laid claim to a small spot on the floor where we could use our bundles of possessions as pillows. I lay between Mutti and Ilse, my mind filled with new impressions. It took me a while to fall asleep.

We had really left Goldbach! With the exception of our occasional hikes to the market in Tapiau, I had never been anywhere else since I was eight years old. Oma called our time in Palmnicken and in Goldbach a "living hell." Now, after three and a half years of starvation, of lice and fleas, of scrounging and begging for food, of collecting berries and mushrooms in the forest, all under harsh Russian rule, we had managed to get out alive.

Several adults complained about their hard beds on the wooden floor. Others groused that they did not have enough space to stretch their legs. The crowded conditions did not bother me. What upset me was that someone had put a pail into use in a corner. The stench was awful. In spite of everything, once I had taken off my boots and stretched out, I finally drifted off to sleep to the rhythmic clatter of the iron wheels.

* * *

"Where are we?" Aunt Liesbeth asked no one in particular when we woke up early the next morning.

299

"Allenstein," an old woman with a wart on her nose announced.

"That's a relief!" exclaimed Aunt Liesbeth. "At least we're headed in the right direction."

Our train was stopped at a siding. I joined the people who were already in the bushes. Since nothing was moving by lunch time, people began to light little cooking fires next to the track so they could boil potatoes. After some hesitation Mutti decided to join them. Oma looked triumphant, "Aren't you glad I insisted on bringing along some of our pots and two bags full of potatoes?"

"Yes, Mother, you were right as usual," Mutti replied. "I hate to think how badly things would have gone without your help. You've been the glue holding all of us together."

"I'll second that," Aunt Liesbeth chimed in.

"Stop it. That's quite enough," Oma cut them off abruptly. "I had a job to do, and I did it, that's all."

Our potatoes were nearly cooked when the locomotive whistle blew and Russian soldiers began to shout, "Davai, davai!" Groaning with frustration, people started running for the train. A little girl, in the arms of her running mother, kept insisting, "I'm not finished. I wasn't finished."

Mutti hurriedly poured out the boiling water to extinguish the fire. She had barely climbed aboard carrying the hot pot, when the train started to move. The potatoes were raw in the middle, but we ate them anyway.

Our train crept along. I could have walked faster. The changing scene outside was framed in the doorway of the boxcar like a movie. We passed a harvested field with piles of dried potato weeds. A boy and three girls squatted around a column of smoke, holding thin pointed sticks. I knew they were roasting potatoes just like Opa and Vassily had done. Ilse tapped me on the shoulder.

"Have you noticed how many people own one or two cows?"

"And chickens and geese," Mutti added. "From the looks of it, these Poles own their own farms. I haven't seen anything big enough to be a Kolkhoz."

"In that case, they're a lot better off than the Russians," Oma added as she gazed out at the tiny houses, each on its own small plot of land.

* * *

Ours was clearly not an express train. Sometimes we traveled for limited distances before stopping in the middle of nowhere without an explanation from anyone; other times we wound up on a siding in a freight yard before moving on. Each time the train stopped, the scene was always the same. People ran into the bushes to relieve themselves. Mothers and grandmothers, in a hurry to boil potatoes or cook a soup, set up makeshift fireplaces made from two stones or two bricks. Some people walked up to Polish homes to beg for food. Others stole whatever had not been already stripped clean from vegetable gardens and fruit trees.

Food supplies were running out and our situation was becoming desperate. Most frustrating, we were never informed how long the train would wait. It could be a stop of as little as ten minutes or as much as a day and a half. Minutes after the locomotive sounded the whistle, the train would give a jolt and, with a loud screech of the wheels, it would get underway. Each time we saw people running with hot pots in their hands trying to catch their car. Others rushed out of the bushes in a desperate race to reboard.

Once a woman carrying a pot of half-boiled potatoes jumped into our car while the train was moving. She had missed her car which was closer to the locomotive. Her children must have been in agony until they were reunited when the train finally stopped again an hour later.

* * *

In Torun during another long wait I heard two adults from a neighboring car arguing about whether the city had been German or Polish before the war. The woman with the wart butted in. She claimed the town was once called Thorn.

"Of course it was Polish. It was in the Polish Corridor. Remember?" Oma snapped. No one dared to contradict her. One thing was certain, it was Polish now and it did not appear that it would ever be German again.

Just then, I heard a familiar voice. Grinning broadly, Mr. Ademeit came over to us.

"How are you doing, young fellow?" he asked me.

"Not too bad, Mr. Ademeit. It's all very exciting, don't you think?"

"Tell me, is your father still alive?"

"We got a postcard from him through the Red Cross a year ago and..."

"Is he living in Germany?"

"He was the last we heard, but it's been..."

"Wonderful!" he interrupted. "I hope he'll take good care of you, Hubert, and your mother. Good luck! Sorry to rush off, but I have to find something to smoke."

With a twinkle in his eyes, he shook my hand warmly. Then he disappeared in the crowd.

"Auf Wiedersehen Mr. Ademeit," I called after him, but I was not sure he heard me.

* * *

In Poznan, the train pulled onto a siding in a huge freight yard. As we watched the uncoupled locomotive disappear down the track, we knew we'd be stuck there for hours. Since there were no bushes, only boys and a few older men ran to the side to relieve themselves. The women searched desperately for toilets or some hidden corner where they could have some privacy.

I raced along nearly the entire length of the train looking for Manfred. The faces of the hundreds of ragged women and children milling next to the train blurred together; many of them suddenly looked alike, especially from a distance. When I reached the front of the train I gave up my search, turning my attention instead to an abandoned, six-story building in the distance. With the faint hope of finding something to eat, I walked over and ventured inside. An iron doorframe was all that was left of the wide entrance. Right inside, a wide staircase led to the upper floors. On each landing the glass was missing from the windows. The higher I climbed, the better my view of the city of Poznan became, and so I kept on going. From the top floor, our train looked like a long metal snake. Judging from all of the rusty machinery on each level, the building must have been a gristmill at one time; however, to my disappointment, there wasn't a speck of grain to be found. In the corner of the large room on the sixth floor, a huge metal funnel resembling the inside of a snail shell ran down along the outside wall. Apparently sacks filled with flour or grits had once glided down this giant spiral belt to the ground far below. I had the irresistible temptation to use the shiny conveyor belt as a slide.

Pressing down hard on the edge with my hands, I climbed into the silvery open tube. I took a deep breath, let go of the edges, and down I went. Gaining considerable speed, I whizzed round and round as I tried to count the floors. Long before I should have come to the ground level, I was flung through the air, landing hard on a sand heap. Although I was unhurt, I was stunned by the surprising way my fantastic ride had ended. It took me a few moments before I stood up and dusted myself off.

The end of the chute was high off the ground, completely out of my reach. Only then I realized that the sand had saved me from serious injury. What if I had broken my legs? Since no one knew where I was, the train would have left without me. Suddenly aware of how foolish

I had been, my legs got all wobbly. With a pounding heart, I ran back to the train.

Mutti asked me the usual questions. "Where have you been? What were you doing?"

"I walked to the front of the train to look for Manfred, but I didn't find him."

"And that took you all this time?" To my relief, she didn't question me further.

CHAPTER 22

*A*fter sunset, I lay down on my spot on the floor. The constant whispering of the adults was interrupted by the sound of other trains. Some rattled by; others switched from one direction to another. Sometime during the night, our train began to move again. Grateful to be safely on board, content with the world, I drifted back to sleep.

In the morning we made a brief stop at the German - Polish border. The Russian soldiers accompanying us were replaced by German officials. As many of us as possible took a spot at the open door to get a glimpse outside.

"Germany looks like Poland," I noted with astonishment. "When I saw borders on the Russian maps in school, the differences looked sharper."

"It's no wonder," Mutti explained. "The Polish area we just passed through used to be part of the German province of Pomerania."

As we passed slowly through the railroad station of a small town, I saw a waiting passenger train. Men in Russian uniforms, their arms wrapped around the shoulders of bare-breasted female soldiers, leaned out of the windows. Seeing us, they began to giggle and to wave. I grinned and waved back, but Mutti pulled me away.

"That's enough of that. Back you go inside the boxcar."

"Yes, Mutti."

"What's going on?" Aunt Liesbeth asked. She was sitting on the floor towards the front of the car in the shadows and couldn't see outside.

"A train full of Russian soldiers! Mr. Shatin was right. There really are Russian soldiers stationed in Germany. There's no denying it. Our nightmare isn't over," Mutti said.

"So it's true," Oma said. "I didn't believe it in Goldbach. Germany really does have a Russian-Occupied Zone."

Aunt Liesbeth looked shaken. "When we get to Berlin, we should try to get hold of a newspaper."

"I think it'll take a lot more than that to catch up on the last three-and-a-half years," Mutti said.

* * *

"Three passengers have died so far," Mutti reported to Oma. "They leave the bodies next to the tracks, just like dead dogs."

A baby was born on the train. Wart-nose greeted the news with contempt.

"Poor fellow. He must be half Russian. The mother will have a lot of explaining to do when she gets back home." She looked around for our reaction, but everyone ignored her.

We had been traveling for two weeks. For the entire time, just like old Mrs. Schmidt in Goldbach, Wart-nose had never stopped griping.

"Before the War, passenger trains only needed eight to ten hours to travel the 600 kilometers from Königsberg to Berlin," she groused. Then she reminisced about first class service and dining cars and berths with fluffy pillows for longer trips.

Oma could not stand it any longer. "Now you listen up!" she snapped. "If you're so upset, why don't you wait at the next siding for a parlor car? As for me, I'm grateful just to be on board."

* * *

Just when I thought we would never reach our destination, a woman cried out, "Look! The outskirts of Berlin!"

Another shouted, "They must have taken a real pounding during the bombing raids. It looks worse than Königsberg!"

"Anything's better than another night on this train," added old Wartnose.

As people crowded next to the open door, I squeezed to the front to get a glimpse. Up ahead was the largest city I had ever seen. But the excited comments all around me quickly turned to groans when the train ground to a halt at a large siding. I jumped down to stretch my legs. A dozen railway workers were standing nearby.

"Guten Tag! Where're you from?" one of the workers called out to me.

Delighted to find countrymen who could speak my language, I walked over to them. Four of the men wore wristwatches. I had not seen a wristwatch on the arm of any German since April 1945. Life can't be all that bad here, I decided.

"From East Prussia," I explained, hoping to start up a conversation.

One of the men, a stocky man with reddish hair and a handlebar moustache, replied. "So I gathered. Trains packed with refugees have been coming through here for weeks. Welcome home!"

Encouraged by his friendly reply, I gathered up my courage. "Excuse me, sir. Do you by any chance know where I could find Magazin-Strasse 18 in Berlin? That's where my Uncle Ernst lives."

I knew the address of Mutti's brother by heart, just in case we became separated. Before the man could reply, his co-workers burst out laughing. Their reaction embarrassed me and I started to back away. The red-headed man put a reassuring hand on my shoulder.

"Berlin has several million inhabitants," he explained. "Even though I've never heard of Magazin-Strasse, I'm sure your mother will help you find it once you get to the center of the city."

His companions were still doubled over with laughter as I thanked him for his kindness. Ashamed of my ignorance, their mocking laughter was still ringing in my ears as I ran back to the train.

A short while after I had climbed back on board, the train brought us to a freight yard somewhere in Berlin. Instead of Russian soldiers yelling "Davai, davai," this time German railroad officials and policemen yelled "Raus, raus!" (Out! Out!) We grabbed our luggage and obediently left the train.

"Davai, davai" or "Raus, raus." What was the difference? Both expressions were always screamed at us in a threatening tone, just like the barking of a German Shepherd dog. I hadn't expected a band to play music in celebration of our arrival, but this nasty "Raus, raus" made me feel as though we were sheep being herded endlessly from place to place.

German social workers bussed us to a refugee camp in Berlin-Falkensee. High concrete poles strung with barbed wire encircled a series of one and two-story brick buildings.

"This place looks nice and solid," Oma commented to no one in particular. "At least it won't be drafty like that old boxcar."

I pulled on Mutti's sleeve. "Are we going to be locked up in there like Opa's cattle?"

"Let's hope not. Maybe the barbed wire's there for our protection," she replied.

A policeman raised a heavy turnpike to let the buses pass through the wide camp entrance.

"What would anyone want to steal from us?" I asked Mutti, as we drove inside. "Just look at us! I still think they're protecting the outsiders from us."

The bus driver announced, "This is it! Everybody off, please."

As we struggled with our bundles in the narrow aisle of the bus, one camp worker shouted, "Raus, raus," while another yelled, "Hurry up! Hurry up!" I was sick and tired of being ordered around. Suddenly a voice boomed from a loudspeaker. "Achtung, Achtung. This is important. This is very important. Please report to the building on your right for delousing."

"What does that mean?" I asked Oma.

"Wait and see," she replied.

"That's something we really need," Mutti commented delightedly.

"How'll they do it?" Gerda asked.

"They'll probably take our clothes to be chemically treated. I'm looking forward to a hot shower with lots of soap."

Mutti was wrong. Towards the front of the room, grumpy men and women dressed in overalls stationed themselves next to rows of tables. On each table were two pails of white powder. As each person stepped forward, a worker reached over with a look of disgust and used his left index finger to pull the refugee's clothing away from his body. Then he used his right hand to pour in a spoonful of the white powder. After that the refugee had to turn around so that the powder could also be poured down his back. The powder smelled horrible and everyone treated with it began to cough. As soon as the stuff had been dropped inside my clothing, my chest and my back started to itch.

"If this 'delousing' works, I'll eat my hat," Mutti complained.

Oma agreed. "We'll have to deal with the problem ourselves once we get settled."

After our dusting, we were assigned bunk beds in one of the large barracks. We were brought to a huge cafeteria where we each received a delicious meal. Potato soup with a few pieces of franks floating in it, bread with margarine, and skimmed milk. Getting seconds was no problem. I really stuffed myself.

"I hope we get to stay here," I confided to Gerda. "That was the best meal I ever ate."

The biggest treat was yet to come. The loudspeaker boomed. "Achtung, Achtung. You have the opportunity to take a shower. Women and children, please proceed to building No. 5A. Men and boys, aged seven and older, to building No. 5B. Soap and towels will be provided."

"Let's meet up back here," Mutti said as I left our group to head for the men's showers. "I've never looked forward to a shower more!"

Just inside the steamy entrance marked "Männer," I saw two dozen showers in one large room. Boys of school age and a few old men were in the shower room with me. I expected to share a towel, as I had done in Goldbach, but an attendant had a towel just for me. I could not believe such luxury! All soaped up, water streaming over me, I rubbed the skin on my chest, my thighs, and my feet. Dirt came up in rolls, like tiny black sausages. After lathering up three more times and using a lot of hot water, my body appeared to be clean, but I was not at all sure about my feet and my knees. Had the dirt grown in? When I had finished, my skin was itchier than before.

"Too much soap and water," I figured. Still, taking a shower was an exhilarating experience.

Walking towards the exit at the far end of the room, I suddenly saw myself in one of the many large mirrors. In Palmnicken we only had a small, cracked mirror, over the sink in the bathroom. We did not have a mirror in our house in Goldbach. My image caught me by surprise. I studied my skinny reflection and did not like what I saw. My hair stood on end, like the spikes of an unevenly shorn hedgehog. My head looked like a giant egg perched on a bean pole. My upper body was covered with a dreadful rash from the smelly white powder.

That night, in spite of my itchy skin and the noise in the barracks, I fell into a deep sleep. I dreamed we were back in Goldbach. In the morning, I was relieved to find that there was no pail to carry down; I did not even have to run into the bushes. I could use toilet paper and flush the toilet and even wash my hands with soap and water afterwards.

* * *

In the cafeteria, while enjoying a breakfast of rye bread, spread with fruit jam, and malt coffee with milk, the booming loudspeaker voice talked to us again.

"Who's talking?" I asked Mutti.

"Shush, we need to pay attention!"

"Achtung, Achtung," the voice reverberated. "There will be an official welcoming celebration in the cafeteria at 11 A.M."

"What do you suppose that's all about?" Ilse asked.

"We'll just have to wait and see," said Aunt Liesbeth.

Two hours after breakfast, the cafeteria quickly filled up again. A cheerful lady in a nurse's uniform got up on a little podium to greet us officially.

"Welcome one and all! We in the camp administration will try our utmost to make your stay comfortable. We apologize for the crowded conditions. Thousands of refugees from East Prussia have been flooding in for weeks now. All of you will be sent to villages in the greater Berlin area as soon as possible and..."

At this, the audience burst into thunderous applause, drowning out the rest of the remarks.

When the noise finally died down, the nurse smiled at the crowd. "Well, that's actually all I have to say. Once again, a hearty welcome to all of you!"

The next speaker was a well-fed man in his forties, wearing an expensive suit. His fat face was so bloated, it looked distorted. The snow white collar of his shirt was much too tight, his face such a deep shade of crimson, I thought his head would explode.

Before launching into his presentation, he fumbled with the loudspeaker until he had adjusted it to his satisfaction. Then, in a somber tone, he introduced himself with a long-winded title.

"What'd he say?" Oma asked. "What job does he have?"

"No idea," Ilse replied. "I couldn't make heads or tails of it."

Forcing a smile, he roared into the microphone. "A heartfelt welcome to Germany to all of you!" His words sounded hollow and empty, as though he'd said them a thousand times before. Nervously he leaned away from the microphone and snapped at the previous speaker, "A glass of water! I need a glass of water, now!"

The friendly nurse rushed to bring him the water. He took a sip, set down the glass, and began in earnest.

"We are proud to live under the protection of the great Soviet Union. The glorious Red Army has liberated all of Europe and has given us back our freedom."

He sounds just like Mr. Raddatz, I thought with disgust. I glanced over at Mutti, Aunt Liesbeth, and Oma. They sat with stony faces. I couldn't see Ilse's expression. She had buried her face in her hands, trying to block out the words. When the speaker started to rave about the advantages of communism, Mutti shook her head. A number of people, first individually, then eventually in entire family groups, simply got up and left.

The massive speaker finally finished babbling, but there was no applause. The few of us who remained to the bitter end stood up in silence and filed out. Later our family gathered in the corner of the barracks next to our bunk beds.

"Either the man is a complete hypocrite or a complete moron," Aunt Liesbeth said.

"He must know what we have gone through over the past few years," Mutti agreed. "It was as though he gave this speech just to show his contempt for us."

In the afternoon we were all given superficial medical examinations.

"Delousing, ten seconds. Medical exam, thirty seconds," Oma said, shaking her head. "Why bother?"

"So the doctors can claim it was done," Mutti said. "Didn't you notice how they checked each of us off as we went through?"

* * *

Shortly after breakfast the next morning, Uncle Ernst, his wife Aunt Irma, and her sister Aunt Gerda, came to visit us. Mutti had telephoned the day before to notify them of our arrival. All of us were soon teary-eyed with joy. Uncle Ernst hugged Mutti. Then he held her shoulders at arms' length and studied her carefully from head to toe.

"Little Sister, you're so skinny. How did you survive this Russian ordeal?"

"It's not easy to kill weeds like us," Mutti replied.

While Mutti and Uncle Ernst were talking, Aunt Irma moved quietly to Mutti's side. Before Mutti had a chance to protest, Aunt Irma pulled off Mutti's grimy coat and dropped it in a nearby trash can. Then she took off her own nearly new trench coat and put it over Mutti's shoulders. Uncle Ernst slipped some money into the pocket of Mutti's new coat. He also gave some to Aunt Liesbeth. Aunt Gerda took off Aunt Liesbeth's worn old coat and helped Aunt Liesbeth into her own new coat. Mutti and my three aunts dissolved in tears.

Turning his attention to me, Uncle Ernst smiled. "I can't believe how tall you've gotten. Where is that little boy I used to know in Langendorf? You'd better put a little meat on your bones."

"I'll try," I replied.

With a mischievous grin, he asked, "Tell me, which barber has messed up your hair? You look like a badly shorn sheep."

Oma hastened to explain. "All I had were my sewing scissors."

"All the same, it's still a lousy haircut."

With a wink at me, Uncle Ernst pulled out another five marks and handed them to Mutti. "Little Sister, please bring that boy to a barber at the first opportunity! And make sure he uses the right kind of scissors."

"Keep on making fun of me," Oma said. "You haven't changed a bit."

"Do you have any news about the rest of the family?" Mutti asked.

"Herbert's living in Wittenberg, not far from here, in the East. Liesbeth, your husband is living near Würzburg, in the West..."

Mutti interrupted him, "You have to explain this East-West business. I've only a vague idea what it's all about."

"You might as well have been living on the moon," Uncle Ernst said, shaking his head in disbelief. "Didn't they tell you anything?"

"Just when and where to report for work," Ilse said.

"Well, before the history lesson, first let me tell you about Willi. Since June 1945, he's been working as a chef at a British officers' mess in Munsterlager. He's got access to cigarettes, coffee, and chocolate so he's dabbled a bit on the black market. Anyway, Gretel, you're in luck. From what I hear, he's doing well financially."

"I can't wait to see him again!" Mutti beamed. "Can you help us arrange it?"

"It's not quite as easy as all that." Uncle Ernst said.

"Why not?"

"That brings me back to your question. After the war, Germany was split into a Soviet-Occupied Zone as well as into American, British, and French Zones. Living standards under the Americans, British, and French are supposed to be getting better by the day."

"According to our welcoming committee this morning," Mutti said bitterly, "life under the Communist system here in the Soviet Zone is also supposed to be wonderful."

"You should feel blessed to have landed in the greatest paradise on earth for workers and farmers," Uncle Ernst replied in a mocking tone. Then he became serious. Leaning closer to Mutti and Aunt Liesbeth, he whispered, "If I were you, I'd make every possible effort to get out of this shit hole. The sooner, the better."

His face brightened again as he turned to his nieces and nephews. "My apologies," he said. "I hope you all had your ears closed."

Uncle Ernst grasped Mutti's right hand in both of his. "By the way, when you told me on the phone that you were in the camp at Berlin-Falkensee, I thought I hadn't heard you right. This is some place for a welcome ceremony! Did they happen to mention that it was a sub-camp of the Sachsenhausen concentration camp until the end of the war?"

Mutti gasped. "You can't be serious! I hope they're not planning to keep us here."

"I hardly think so," Uncle Ernst said. "Just be sure to let me know where you end up."

A few days later, Oma was sent to live with my Uncle Herbert in Wittenberg. The Reimanns were sent to a village near Potsdam. Mutti, Hubert, and I were assigned to a room in a one family house in the village of Plötzin, not far from Berlin. All three places were, of course, still in the Russian-Occupied Zone.

CHAPTER 23

T he modest one story house stood beyond a small pond, just off the main street of Plötzin. Mutti knocked and the door was opened by our landlady, Mrs. Neumark, who stared at us, thunderstruck, as if we were creatures from another world. Granted, Hubert and I were still dressed in our worn clothes from Goldbach. I had on my knickerbockers made of burlap sacks and my boots with the high wooden soles, but I thought Mrs. Neumark would admire Mutti's elegant trench coat.

Mutti hastened to explain. "Mrs. Neumark? Good morning! We're the refugees from Camp Falkensee."

Mrs. Neumark's face relaxed. With a winning smile and a big wave of her hand, she invited us into her house.

"Please, come in. Forgive me. For a moment, I didn't connect. The social worker told me only this morning that you were coming."

"Of course," Mutti replied.

"I hope you don't mind, but I have only one spare room with a small cooking stove for the three of you. It has its own small bathroom with a toilet and a sink, but no bathtub. You can use my tub every Saturday," Mrs. Neumark explained apologetically.

"Don't worry. We're not spoiled. That sounds just fine!"

I barely heard the last part of her apology. When I learned we would have a bathroom for ourselves, I had to control myself to keep from cheering.

Mrs. Neumark's husband had been missing in action since the end of the war. She had two daughters: Gudrun, nine, and Heidi, five.

"Refugees from Pomerania boarded with us until recently, but the woman's husband lived in the West," she confided. "One day, out of the blue, the mother and her three daughters took off and never came back."

The next morning, Mrs. Neumark knocked at our door and introduced us to Gudrun, a short pretty girl with a vibrant smile and thick black braids. Gudrun was wearing a white dress with narrow red stripes at the waist, short white socks and red shoes.

"The school term has already started," Mrs. Neumark explained. "Gudrun will show you the way to the schoolhouse so you can register your boys."

I broke out in a cold sweat. How would I manage to follow the lessons? All I had learned from Mr. Raddatz was a bit of arithmetic, a few facts about the Soviet Union, and how to take a beating without flinching.

"Thank you," said Mutti. "I've almost forgotten how real schools worked. Perhaps Gudrun can fill us in along the way."

With the self-confidence of an adult, Gudrun walked Mutti, Hubert, and me along the main street to the local elementary school. A cemetery nestled next to a small church in the middle of the village. The beige stones of the church walls were capped with a massive gray slate roof and bell tower, like a mismatched lid on a heavy pot.

Gudrun talked without interruption. "The school's across the street from the cemetery," she said, pointing to a one story building. The tiny school had only five windows on that side. A small playground, shaded by five or six trees, was on the right. "The building's in pretty good shape. The bathrooms aren't so hot, though. Can't complain about our teacher, Mr. Hagemeister. Lucky for us, he is a decent man and..."

"How do people make a living around here?" Mutti asked.

"Oh, that's easy. The local farmers have fruit orchards. They're always looking for workers at this time of the year."

As we approached the wide entrance, six boys tried to squeeze through the schoolhouse door at the same time, causing a temporary pile-up.

"As you can see, we also have some idiots in this school. It's a pity that Mr. Hagemeister..."

"Can't you walk in like civilized people?" said a sharp voice from inside the school. The boys quickly moved to the right side. At the left side of the entrance stood a pleasant-looking man in his fifties.

"More later!" Gudrun said, breathlessly. "Gotta run! Don't wanna be late! See you on the way home!" she called over her shoulder. She was about to dart into the classroom when she stopped abruptly. "Oh, sorry, I nearly forgot. This is Mr. Hagemeister, our teacher," and, to Mr. Hagemeister, "This is Mrs. Nitsch and her sons, new pupils," and with that she left us.

Mr. Hagemeister said to us, "I'll be with you in a minute," and he hurried to the other side of the building.

Once we were alone, Mutti whispered, "Boy, oh boy. Gudrun's never at a loss for words, is she?"

"I've never met anyone who talks so much and so fast," I agreed. "She bubbles over all the time."

"She must be a real handful," Mutti said with a laugh.

Although I didn't say so to Mutti, I had liked Gudrun instantly.

* * *

Mr. Hagemeister didn't seem the least bit surprised at the gaping holes in my education. "We're used to refugee children," he reassured us. "Hubert's easy. He's never attended school before and he won't turn six until November. Nursery school is the place for him. Mrs. Neumark's younger daughter, Heidi, goes there so he won't be lonely."

"As for you," he said, turning to me, "you'll probably move up a grade in a month or two, but for now I think you should start out in fourth grade."

"I'm too big for fourth grade," I protested. "I'm nearly eleven years old! I'll stick out like a sore thumb!"

Mr. Hagemeister answered me with unexpected kindness.

"All of our children sit together in one classroom, so your placement won't be all that obvious. Anyway, you have to face facts. If your education hadn't been interrupted, you'd be in fifth or even sixth grade by now. You were in school in Langendorf for a little more than a year. And judging from what your mother told me about the school in Goldbach, the time you spent there doesn't count for much. You just need a little time to catch up and then we'll move you ahead."

"Yes sir," I answered glumly.

After Mutti left with Hubert, Mr. Hagemeister walked me down the hall and introduced me to the class. Maybe things weren't so bad after all, I thought. For the first time in years, I did not feel like an outsider. I was wearing a pair of shorts given to me at the refugee camp and sporting a proper haircut, my first real haircut since 1944.

During recess, I went to use the boys' bathroom, a makeshift affair, a wide metal gutter haphazardly attached with thick copper wire to a wall inside a concrete shed. From the top edge of the gutter to way above my head, the wall in front of me was covered with a slimy greenish-yellow liquid. The boys evidently held competitions to see who could pee closest to the ceiling.

Suddenly someone gave me a shove. To avoid hitting the wall with my face, I was forced to stop myself with my left hand. Disgusting layers of slime stuck to my skin. Raucous laughter erupted behind me. I swung around and saw four boys who were clearly enjoying my misfortune.

"Who pushed me?" I was dumb enough to ask.

"The boy who did it just ran out," one of them lied.

I glared at them. Trying to look unconcerned, I washed my hands and dried them on my shirt under my armpits. There was no towel.

During class I felt uneasy. The desk was way too small for my long legs. Many of the children were staring at me. I felt suddenly scared and isolated. My only consolation was that Gudrun was also there. Later Gudrun and I walked home together. She had a reassuring smile as she spoke.

"So? What do you think of our school?"

"Uh, it's all right, I guess," I replied, not quite sure what she wanted to hear. I did not want to disappoint her.

"Don't worry. You'll get used to it in a few days," she assured me.

*　*　*

As the week wore on, things only got worse. Even though most of the other children were younger than I was, they knew a lot more than I did. They eagerly answered Mr. Hagemeister's questions, whereas I had trouble grasping what was being taught. They all had fancy Berlin accents. I was ashamed of my broad East Prussian accent. I did not belong there. To make matters worse, Mr. Hagemeister constantly reminded us of the great advantages of Communism and the eternal friendship between the Germans and the people in the Soviet Union. It was the spirit of Raddatz all over again.

Why do they bother us with this? I wondered. With our miserable life in Goldbach still vivid in my mind, I knew it was all a pack of lies.

The worst was yet to come. Some mean boys in my class christened me "Wasserkopf" (Fat Head). Having seen myself in the mirror at Falkensee, I was already self-conscious about my rather large head on my spindly body. My new nickname hurt me deeply.

I looked forward eagerly to the afternoons. Mutti had gotten a job picking apples in the local orchards and I often joined her to help out. When Mutti got paid for the first time we didn't only buy bread, milk, and margarine in the Konsum Food Shop, but also three toothbrushes and a tube of toothpaste.

"Why'd you do that?" I asked Mutti. "Shouldn't we save the money for food?" I had not brushed my teeth since we left Mr. Wittke's farm in Bieskobnicken.

"From now on, we're all going to brush our teeth in the morning when we get up and again in the evening before going to bed. Is that clear?"

"Do I really have to? We've been eating apples ever since we got here. Oma used to say, 'Eating a crunchy apple is just as good as brushing your teeth,' remember?"

"I'm sure Oma never said such nonsense. Anyhow, you can eat all the apples you want, but you still have to brush your teeth twice a day."

"Yes Mutti," I grumbled, "but it seems like a waste of time to me."

In the afternoons Mrs. Neumark was kind enough to babysit for Hubert when he was home from kindergarten. He was a good companion for her daughter Heidi.

Mrs. Neumark and Mutti's co-workers complained constantly about food shortages, annoyed that meat, butter, and eggs were not available in sufficient quantities.

They should spend a week in Goldbach, I thought to myself. Then they might appreciate what they have here. In my opinion, it was silly to be fussy when we always had enough bread, potatoes, margarine, vegetables, and fruits. I never went to bed hungry in Plötzin and that meant a lot to me.

* * *

One day on the way home from school Gudrun announced she wanted to play with me after lunch.

"Be sure to leave your shoes at home," she warned.

After wolfing down a huge serving of potato salad with cucumbers, seasoned with pepper and salt, I raced outside. Gudrun perched barefoot on the top rail of a wooden fence, holding on with her right hand and carrying a small rubber ball in her left. Instead of her starched school dress, she was wearing shorts and a short-sleeved sweater.

"Wanna play ball?" she asked with an inviting smile.

"Sure," I replied while looking down at my toes. I knew I wouldn't be any good at it.

She was skilled in throwing and catching the ball. I could throw the ball as well as she did, but I just couldn't get the hang of how to catch it. It was humiliating being outdone by a girl.

"Actually," I finally admitted, "I haven't played ball since the summer of 1944." She just shrugged.

"Do you like peaches?" Gudrun asked me all of a sudden.

"They're a kind of fruit, right? I've never seen one."

"Well, then you're in for a real treat!" she exclaimed.

A short time later we were skipping along a lonely country road next to a huge orchard. Big reddish-orange fruits hung from the trees. Just as Gudrun was about to run into the field, a farmer rode towards us on a bicycle. She immediately started to do cartwheels.

"Let's have a cartwheel contest!" Gudrun called out breathlessly as she spun around, her long braids touching the grass.

I gaped at her. The only other time I had seen cartwheels had been in a newsreel about gymnasts in Schippenbeil. The man on the bike, as startled as I was by Gudrun's stunt, also turned to stare. As a result, his bicycle spun off into the ditch.

"I've never done a cartwheel in my life," I yelled back as the farmer angrily dusted himself off. My admiration for Gudrun was growing by leaps and bounds.

"C'mon, it's not difficult," she pouted. And by that time the farmer on the bike was gone.

Stopping as suddenly as she had started, Gudrun checked left and right to make sure the coast was clear. As we ran together into the orchard, my conscience began to prick me.

"Listen, Gudrun. I may have stolen potatoes in Goldbach when we were starving, but it's quite another thing to steal peaches just for the fun of it."

"You're kidding, right?" Gudrun teased. She grabbed my hand and pulled me forward.

We had to watch where we walked as there were peaches all over the ground. When we could no longer see the road, we stopped. I bent down to pick up a peach.

"Take them from up here, silly," Gudrun chided. She offered me a peach from an overloaded branch.

I bit into the fruit. The fuzzy skin burst and the sweet juice exploded all over me.

"Bend over when you eat it," Gudrun advised with a giggle.

I had never eaten a tastier fruit. We sat down on the ground and each of us ate four more.

"What do you think about the lectures in school about Communism?" I asked after a while.

"It's just stuff we have to learn."

"I suppose so. We heard about it in Goldbach, too."

We got up and walked slowly back towards the road. Gudrun was munching on another peach. When she had eaten half of it, she pulled out the pit. She held the peach up to my mouth.

"Have a bite," she encouraged. "It's really ripe and delicious!"

Startled, I leaned over to taste the fruit. Gudrun suddenly grabbed the back of my head with her left hand while rubbing the overripe mushy peach all over my face. She flashed a big smile and ran away. I ran after her. Gudrun moved with the speed of a jackrabbit. I was getting

Gunter Nitsch

closer; I could nearly touch her, when she suddenly changed direction. She was very good at tricking me. It took me a while to catch up and grab her and, as I did so, I was suddenly aware of the sweet scent of her hair. Doubled over with laughter, barely able to catch our breaths, we flopped down together on the grassy ground. She embarrassed me by trying to wipe my face with her handkerchief. After eating a few more peaches we giggled all the way back to our house.

During the night I had terrible diarrhea. As I rushed back and forth to our private toilet, I thought how awful the situation would have been in Goldbach.

"I didn't have a very good night, either," Gudrun admitted when we walked to school the next morning, "but it was worth it!"

* * *

I scouted the bushes near the house for a good strong stick, but none of them suited me. A few days later, while exploring an abandoned barn on the outskirts of the village, I found just what I was looking for, a strong flexible branch from a rosebush. It took me quite a while to prune off all the thorns and to cut it to the right length with my pocketknife. Strung with strong cord, it was by far the best bow I had ever made.

Gudrun had never used a bow and arrow before. It made me feel good to give her some pointers for a change. She got the hang of it fast. In fact, she liked shooting it so much, she teased me that she would never give it back.

It was late October. The cardboard Mutti had taped over the broken window in our room no longer kept out the cold. Mr. Grumbach, an old friend of Mrs. Neumark, set aside a piece of glass for us and Mutti sent Gudrun and me to fetch it. On the way we passed the Schadebrot Bakery. To my surprise Gudrun steered me inside. She bought two meringue cookies, one for her and one for me. I would have hugged her if I hadn't been too shy.

324

"Where'd you get the money from?" I asked as the crunchy egg white slowly dissolved in my mouth.

"From my mom, who else?"

"Lucky duck," I said. "I never got pastry money from anyone."

Mr. Grumbach greeted us at the door to his cabinet shop. "You must be here for the glass. Be careful with it! These days a square of glass 30 centimeters by 30 centimeters is nearly as valuable as gold."

"Thank you, Mr. Grumbach," I replied, as he cushioned the bottom edge of the pane with several pieces of newspaper and handed it to me. "You can rely on me."

"Bye, Mr. Grumbach," Gudrun chirped.

As we headed home, I clutched the precious glass under my right arm.

"You can't catch me!" Gudrun teased, sprinting ahead of me. Momentarily forgetting my precious load, I ran after her. The plate slipped out of my hand and shattered on the asphalt road. Stunned, we both walked slowly back to the house. I hardly said a word. Even Gudrun was unusually quiet.

Mutti burst into tears when she heard what had happened. With a stony face, she cut the string off my precious rosewood bow and thrashed me with the stick. As excruciating as the beating was, what came next was worse. Mutti took the stick with her when she left the house and did not bring it back.

* * *

My bad luck continued. Our school was abuzz because parts for the Nativity play were being assigned; Gudrun was overjoyed to get the part of Mary. Everyone wanted to get a speaking part, everyone, that is, except me. I would have given anything to avoid it. Finally, Mr. Hagemeister turned to me.

"Günter, you're a tall boy, so you're going to be Balthasar," he announced.

Someone sitting towards the back of the room called out, "Fat Head? Balthasar?" The boys began to snicker.

"Silence!" barked Mr. Hagemeister, and the laughter quickly subsided.

I felt hurt. I had no idea who had insulted me, but I hated him, whoever he was. At the same time, I was terrified about my part in the play. It was difficult for me to learn anything by heart. After school I went to Mr. Hagemeister and begged him to give my part to someone else.

"You'll do just fine," he assured me and, with that, I was dismissed.

His confidence in me was flattering, but as I rushed out to catch up with Gudrun, I had serious doubts about my ability to play Balthasar. Four boys from my class were waiting for me. One of them, a stocky fellow with red hair mocked me.

"Fat Head's playing Balthasar. Fat Head's playing Balthasar," he repeated over and over. Now I knew who had teased me in class. Sick of the taunts, I turned to slug him. Gudrun stepped between us. She glared at the redheaded boy, who was nearly a head taller than she was.

"First-of-all-your-head-is-not-any-smaller-than-his.

Second-in-contrast-to-his-yours-is-empty.

That-is-the-reason-you-are-so-dumb.

And-if-you-ever-copy-from-me-in-a-test-again-I-will-report-you," she scolded. And with that, she pushed him with both hands so hard, he stumbled backwards.

Gudrun's rapid talking reminded me of a burst from a Russian submachine gun. How could anyone in the world talk so fast? She had barely finished when the other three boys started to laugh at their red-haired friend who stood there, speechless, like a beaten dog.

"Let's go," Gudrun said, turning to me.

As we walked away, Gudrun set a deliberately slow pace, even stopping to window shop at Schadebrot's Bakery, to spite the boys behind us. Neither of us looked back and, as we ambled home, Gudrun chatted up a storm as if nothing had happened. Yet, no matter what we talked about, I could not help thinking about her astonishing performance. How on earth did she dare? I wondered. I had never met anyone like her.

Gudrun's rapid-fire lecture had a long-term effect. It was quite some time before those boys bothered me again.

CHAPTER 24

O ne Saturday morning a few weeks later, Mutti packed an overnight bag. "We're going to visit Uncle Ernst in Berlin," she announced.

"When?"

"Our bus leaves in thirty minutes."

The bus took us to the railroad station in Werder and, from there, we caught the train to Berlin. Once we reached Uncle Ernst's fifth floor walk-up on Magazin-Strasse, he quickly locked the door behind us and led us into the living room. He spoke just above a whisper.

"There was so much I didn't dare tell you when you first arrived in Berlin. You never know who might be listening," Uncle Ernst began. "You must be desperate for news about your Willi."

"That's all I've thought about since we got here."

"The British took him prisoner in May 1945, but as soon as they found out he was a master pastry chef and knew how to cook, they put him right to work."

During all the terrible times we lived through in East Prussia, he probably never missed a meal, I thought, with some resentment.

"Is that what he's doing now? Working for the British?" Mutti asked.

"No, it's even better than that. His unit was transferred to the Middle East."

"The Middle East?" Her face fell.

"Don't worry. He didn't go. They offered him a position, but he decided to stay in Germany. He found a well-paying job as a master pastry chef in the largest pastry shop in Uelzen. I've written down his home address and the address of the shop for you."

"Where is Uelzen exactly?" Mutti asked, as she tucked the slip of paper into her pocket.

"Between Hannover and Hamburg. Your Willi is about two hundred kilometers and one closely guarded border away."

While we were talking, Aunt Gerda and Aunt Irma returned home with our cousins, Hanni and Evi. Aunt Schulz was with them.

"You never told us what happened to you after the war," Mutti said to her sisters-in-law.

"The Russians kept us both busy. We spent three years working in coal mines beyond the Ural Mountains," said Aunt Gerda.

"Since we're only back a short time ourselves, we know just how you must feel," Aunt Irma added with a sigh.

"And how did you get out?" Mutti asked, turning to Aunt Schulz. "And what about Hanni and Evi? How old were they at the time? Five?"

"Ernst and I looked after my granddaughters while Gerda and Irma were gone," Aunt Schulz explained.

Mutti shot a quizzical glance at her brother. "You came back to East Prussia?"

"No, of course not. I brought the girls to Berlin," Aunt Schulz went on.

"You make it sound so easy," Aunt Irma said. "Actually, my mother bribed a Polish railroad official who let her take Hanni and Evi to Berlin in a freight train. They were underway for five days."

"The hard part was keeping the girls quiet," Aunt Schulz added. "I kept plying them with vodka whenever they woke up."

"But they're none the worse for wear," Aunt Gerda hastened to say.

"Is Uncle Schulz coming over, too?" I asked, eager to talk to him again about the African masks and combs he kept in his living room above the Schippenbeil railroad station.

"I'm afraid not," Aunt Schulz said. "The Russians came for him two days after they took Irma and Gerda. When I close my eyes, I can still see him being led away. He turned back just long enough to wave good-bye."

"Try not to dwell on it so much, Mother," Aunt Gerda said. "When my Walter's plane crashed, I forced myself to think about other things."

"He could still turn up," Mutti said. "You shouldn't lose hope."

"I know you mean well, Gretel, but I'm sure I'll never hear from him again. All my letters to the Red Cross and not a word. He probably perished years ago in some Siberian work camp, the poor dear."

During the afternoon, Hubert and I played with our cousins, while the adults talked for hours behind closed doors. Trouble ahead, I thought. Whenever we're shut out of the conversation, things always seem to change.

After a delicious supper of baloney sandwiches and sweet apple cider, my eight-year-old cousin, Hanni, entertained us by singing German folk and pop songs. She had a beautiful voice. Her rendition of "The Capri Fishermen" was so popular we made her sing it three or four times. To my embarrassment, tears rolled down my cheeks each time I heard it. Even years later, whenever I heard that song, I would be reminded of our family reunion in Berlin.

* * *

Shortly after lunch on Sunday we headed back to Plötzin. I proudly carried a big suitcase with a smaller one tucked inside, gifts from Uncle

Ernst. On the train going home, I was burning to know what the adults had discussed in private.

"We'll talk about it in Plötzin," Mutti cautioned, and she put her finger to her lips.

Hubert, exhausted by the trip, was sound asleep soon after we got back home. I was struggling to learn a long poem for school when Mutti sat down next to me.

"In the beginning of December we're going to cross illegally to the West," she whispered. "Don't mention a word of this to anybody, not even Hubert. He's too little to understand."

"Not even Gudrun?" I asked. My heart had already started to beat faster at the news.

"Not a single, solitary soul," Mutti cautioned me. "You're old enough now to be trusted with this secret."

"But I'm supposed to be in the school Nativity play," I protested. "Mr. Hagemeister is relying on me."

"The same rules go for that too. Don't tell him anything. Just act as if everything is normal."

Rehearsals had already started. Gudrun played her role with such feeling that it seemed as if she really were Jesus' mother. The only other student who did nearly as well as Gudrun was the boy who played Joseph. To my great relief, the other children were just as shy as I was and also had trouble remembering their lines, but gradually, we all improved. Although I hated to admit it, I was actually starting to enjoy being in the play.

One night towards the end of November the weather had gotten so cold that I kept waking up with the shivers. The cardboard covering our broken windowpane reminded me about the glass that I had broken, and I felt guilty. For extra warmth, I decided to wear my ushanka with its missing red star to school the following day.

"Great cap," Gudrun complimented me, but the other students weren't as kind.

Some boys called me "Russky," others, "Ivan." Gritting my teeth, I made up my mind to ignore them.

"In Goldbach, the Russians called me Fascist or Friitz. Now the boys call me Russky," I complained to Mutti when I got back home. "I just don't seem to fit in anywhere."

"It took courage to ignore those nasty comments," Mutti comforted me, "but why don't you wear a woolen cap tomorrow instead?"

During the night I had terrible nightmares in which the boys from school called me Fat Head and beat me to a pulp. I woke up soaked in sweat, but full of determination not to let those boys get the best of me. For extra warmth, I wore the beautiful dark blue scarf Mutti had knitted for me. The weather was so cold, she had decided not to wait another week until my birthday. With the stubbornness of an East Prussian, I also proudly wore my ushanka.

If the boys want to call me Russky, so be it, I had decided grimly during the night. I knew it was going to be for only a few more days and, besides, being called Russky didn't get me nearly as angry as Fat Head.

* * *

The first dress rehearsal for the Nativity play was scheduled for Friday, December 3, 1948, which was also my eleventh birthday.

"We're taking off on Friday after school," Mutti confided a few days before.

"But I'll miss the dress rehearsal," I wailed. "And what about Mrs. Neumark? She may decide to take Hubert and Heidi shopping just when we're ready to leave."

"You'll just have to forget the dress rehearsal," Mutti replied, "and I'll let Mrs. Neumark know that I'm taking the day off."

Friday morning Mutti woke me up early to wish me a "Happy Birthday." Hubert was still asleep. "We'll celebrate your next birthday with Vati in the West," she whispered and then she gave me a hug. The world suddenly looked very rosy.

In school, I ignored the boys who called me names. I kicked myself for not having stood up to them sooner, just like Gudrun had done. It was hard to concentrate on the lesson. My mind was far away. Even when the dress rehearsal was being discussed, I could not focus. Now and then I looked wistfully in Gudrun's direction, but all I could see was her back and her long black braids tied up in red bows. She sat diagonally in front of me. What a pity that I could not sit closer to her.

On the way home, Gudrun bubbled with excitement about our costumes for the play, but my side of the conversation was kind of forced. I felt awful that I could not tell her about our planned escape. Most of all I wanted to let her know that she was my best friend and that I would miss her terribly.

"You're so quiet today; is anything wrong?" Gudrun asked with concern. "Did I do something to upset you?"

"Don't worry," I replied, although I had a lump in my throat. "I'm fine."

"Well then, let's meet later and walk to the dress rehearsal together!"

I had to bite my lip before replying. "I'd love to, but if I'm running a little late, I'll catch up with you."

Later, I watched from our window as Gudrun left for school. Feeling a pain I had never known before, I gazed after her until she turned the corner.

* * *

The Plötzin bus stop was on the main street at the edge of the cemetery. To be on the safe side, we arrived well ahead of time. As we waited to catch the bus for the short ride to Werder an der Havel, one of my classmates strolled by us on his way to the rehearsal. I tried to turn away, but it was too late. He gave a me a little wave of recognition. Would he tell his mother he saw me at the bus stop? Would his mother go to the police? Fear gripped my heart as I watched the boy turn the corner behind the church. After all, we must have looked suspicious, standing there with our suitcases.

I barely breathed until our bus pulled in and the driver let us inside. We zoomed along at a good clip on the curvy, tree-lined road towards Werder, retracing the steps we had taken in coming to Plötzin. The trees in the orchards we passed were bare, but I still thought of the juicy peaches Gudrun and I had shared only a few short weeks before. By now, not only Gudrun, but also Mr. Hagemeister and the rest of my classmates must have realized that I was not going to return to school that afternoon for the first dress rehearsal. The boy who saw us in Plötzin would be spreading the word. It seemed to me that everybody was staring at us, on the bus, at the Werder railroad station, even on the train.

Terrified of getting caught, I looked over at Mutti for some reassurance, but judging by the expression on her face, her mind was far away. I was worried about her. A few weeks earlier, while pruning shrubs on a fruit plantation, a rose thorn had lodged deep in her finger. At first she had tried to ignore it, but it had become increasingly painful. Soaking her hand in hot soapy water had been of no help. When pus began to form in the wound, I suggested that she see a doctor, but she had assured me that it would get better by itself. Shortly before we had left Plötzin, I had helped her put a clean white bandage on her right index finger. The bandage was already discolored with ugly yellow pus. What I found most upsetting was that I could not carry the heavy suitcase all the time even though I knew how much Mutti's finger hurt.

"Don't talk about our trip, not even to mention the names of any of the towns we pass through. You never know who may be listening," Mutti had warned me as we left our room in Plötzin, but that rule didn't seem to apply to Hubert, who thought we were going to visit a far-away uncle. As our train poked along, Hubert reported on everything he could see from the window: pine forests, rows of gardens, little villages.

Our train slowed down as it approached the Potsdam station where we had to change trains. By the time we stopped, Mutti and I had our rucksacks on our backs. Mutti grabbed the big suitcase with one hand and held Hubert with the other. I carried our small suitcase and a rolled-up blanket, given to us by a government organization in Plötzin. I had seldom seen so many people in one place. How could anyone know where to go amidst such giant confusion?

A lanky young man with short-cropped dirty blond hair stared intently at Mutti. He didn't look much older than eighteen or nineteen. Remembering Mutti's instructions not to say or do anything that might give us away, I tried not to look in his direction and kept my concerns to myself.

The track number for the train to Magdeburg was announced over the loud speaker. As we rushed to the platform, I could see from Mutti's face that her finger hurt her, even though she had switched the suitcase to her left hand.

Supervised by two officers, thirty Russian soldiers wearing ushankas crowded together on the opposite side of the track. The soldiers were loaded down with luggage and were unarmed. Only the officers carried pistols. Gone were the fish can submachine guns which I remembered from Palmnicken. I studied the Russians more carefully. The soldiers' rumpled uniforms and their greasy garrison caps looked as if they had been slept in. Their coarse leather boots were splattered with mud. The officers wore freshly pressed uniforms, decorated with medals, and tall shiny boots. Both wore the typical Russian peaked officers' caps with wide tops which reminded me of oversized soup bowls. I decided that the Russian officers were better dressed than the East Germans and that many East Germans were better dressed than the Russian soldiers. No one on the platform looked as shabby as Hubert and I did in our long pants made of burlap potato sacks.

After a while, several of the Russian soldiers began to stare back at me, making me uncomfortable. Just at that moment our train pulled in. There were so many people on our side of the platform waiting to board, for a moment I was concerned that we would not be able to get on. Suddenly the same blond young man who had stared at Mutti earlier stepped forward to help with her suitcase. Minutes later we were settled in our seats. Hubert and I even got to sit next to the window. Mutti thanked the young man who settled in with his rucksack and suitcase not far from where we were sitting. He made me feel uneasy and I wondered whether he was spying on us.

As soon as we were on our way, Mutti unpacked some of our provisions from her bag. After a supper of lard and fried onion sandwiches on rye bread, we had sweet crispy apples, a special treat for dessert. Once the sun had set, I tried to look out the window, but all I could see was my own reflection in the glass. My mind was full of questions. I wondered whether we would reach the border near Helmstedt safely. Would we be able to cross to the West? Or would we get caught? My thoughts drifted to the prospect of a reunion with my father. I had not seen him for almost four years and I wondered what he would be like. It seemed strange to think that he would be wearing civilian clothes. I had never seen him in anything but his Luftwaffe corporal's uniform.

I wondered what kind of a place Uelzen was. Would we live with him in a house in a small village nearby or would we live with him in an apartment directly in town? My father's life had been easier than ours after the war. He had not suffered the way Mutti, Hubert, and I had. Now I hoped he would change all of our lives for the better.

I daydreamed about having liver sausage or cheese on a sandwich instead of sugar beet syrup and margarine. I dared to imagine a nice home with all of the windowpanes intact, an apartment with running water, a working toilet, and our own bathtub. I hoped to attend a good school where I would learn how to read and write properly and to study geography, history, biology, English, and French, instead of Communism and German-Soviet friendship.

I had started to drift off to sleep when Mutti tapped my shoulder and whispered, "We'll soon be in Magdeburg. You need to eat something before then. We have a long night ahead of us." It was after 10 o'clock, well past my bedtime, but I was suddenly wide awake and quite hungry. I devoured two more lard and onion sandwiches and ate another apple before we reached the Magdeburg station.

Since the local train to Eilsleben, a village near the border with the British Zone, was not scheduled to leave until the following morning, we walked to the far end of the platform to find the Travelers Aid office. There were two ladies behind the counter.

"We need a place to spend the night," Mutti explained. "Is there someplace where we can be accommodated at the station?"

"I'm sorry," the taller lady replied. "We have no cots. Why don't you check your luggage and sit in the second-class waiting room? It's usually open until after midnight and at least it's warm in there."

The second lady seemed to disapprove of this advice. She gave her co-worker a stern look, but she did not say anything.

"They didn't tell us everything," Mutti said as we went in search of the baggage room. "Did you notice?"

"Maybe it's the way we're dressed," I agreed.

Hubert pulled on Mutti's sleeve. "How far away does this uncle live anyway?" he whined.

"Let me tell you a secret," Mutti said. "It's really Vati we're going to see. Isn't that wonderful?"

"Are we almost there?"

"Just another day or so. But it's a big surprise, so we can't tell anyone about it, all right?"

"I guess so," Hubert said through chattering teeth.

Although it was a cold December night, one of the large windows of the second- class waiting room was open. As we approached, we heard dance music. We peeked through the metal grates covering the window. Inside the huge smoke-filled hall, dozens of couples were dancing. The room was crowded with laughing German girls twirling in the arms of Russian soldiers. Everyone was drunk. The German band was belting out 'The Capri Fishermen,' the song Hanni had sung in Berlin. The music stopped and the band started to play a slow, schmaltzy song.

"Well, of all the nerve!" Mutti exclaimed. "Those women in Travelers Aid knew what was going on. They could have warned us."

"At least it's warm in there."

"Forget it," Mutti snapped. "We'll just have to find someplace else."

After all she'd been through, I guess seeing the German women dancing with the Russian soldiers was just too much for Mutti. Her face twisted with contempt, she yanked me away from the window. By then it was shortly before midnight. We found a wooden bench in the unheated main hall of the railroad station. I bought warm milk from a kiosk and we all huddled together on the bench to wait until morning.

Oma always said, whatever you do on your birthday will most likely continue for the entire year. The thought of sleeping on a cold hard bench for the next twelve months gave me the creeps.

Although I sometimes managed to doze off, most of the time the cold temperature and the blaring music kept me awake. As usual, the only one who slept through it all was Hubert. Around 3 o'clock in the morning, there was a loud commotion as drunken dancers wobbled and swayed across the main hall to the exit leading to the street. When the place quieted down, I leaned against Mutti and finally fell back to sleep.

* * *

The second-class waiting room reopened at six o'clock in the morning. Well ahead of that time, we stood outside the doors, shivering with cold, ready to rush in. The room smelled of old sweat and stale cigarette smoke. Mutti ordered a malt coffee for herself and hot milks for Hubert and me. As soon as the waiter turned his back, we pulled out the stale lard sandwiches left over from the day before, even though it was against the rules to bring our own food inside.

About an hour later, we boarded the Eilsleben local. We had barely settled into our seats in the over-heated train when the blond young man also came aboard. By now I was certain he was following us.

"For goodness sake, what does he want?" I whispered to Mutti, but if she was worried, she did not show it.

We passed strange sounding towns: Magdeburg-Sudenburg, Niederndodeleben, Ochtmersleben and Dreileben-Drackenstedt. At Eilsleben, we left the train and sat down in the waiting room restaurant. Despite our ragged clothing, the waiter treated us with respect.

"Good morning. What can I do for you, please?"

Mutti and I echoed, "Good morning" and Mutti ordered, "Pea soup with bacon pieces for all of us and three lemonades, please."

Bowing his head a bit, the waiter said, "Very well, Madam, three times pea soup with bacon and three lemonades," before disappearing into the kitchen. The last time we had eaten a real meal in a restaurant had been in Königsberg in 1944. Hubert and I pretended we dined like that every day. By the time Mutti ordered a second round of lemonades for us, he and I developed a bad case of the giggles.

In the afternoon we walked from the railroad station to a crowded café nearby. "Uncle Ernst told me we'd have to wait here to get a taxi," Mutti whispered.

Bluish tobacco smoke filled the large room like fog. I could barely see the wall in the back where waiters rushed into the right hand door with empty trays and returned with full trays through the left hand door. The air smelled of cigarette smoke, coffee, pea soup, fried bacon, and onions. Mothers with listless children occupied most of the seats and their parcels were piled up on the extra chairs. Middle-aged men sipped coffee; conversation was in an undertone. We sat down at a small table and Mutti ordered hot milk for us and a malt coffee for herself.

No sooner had the waiter taken our order when the blond young man entered the restaurant. As we gazed in disbelief, he headed straight for our table. Acting as if he had known us all his life, he slipped into the empty seat at our table. He spoke in a low voice.

"From the moment I saw you in Potsdam, I had a hunch you'd end up here. Maybe we can help each other out."

"I have no idea what you're talking about," Mutti said. The color drained from her face.

"No need to worry," he hastened to add. "We're heading the same way. My only problem is, on the trains I can duck into the bathroom to avoid paying the fare. But I can't take a cab without money." He leaned even closer to Mutti. "I'll tell you what. If you take me along in your cab, I'll carry your heavy suitcase. Like I said, we need each other."

Mutti's eyes met mine. "Can we trust him?" they seemed to ask.

Mutti looked down at the oozing bandage on her finger and glanced at her heavy suitcase. She turned back to the young man, her mind made up.

"How do you pick a cab driver? How do you know he'll bring us to the right spot at the border?"

"Just leave that to me." He pointed to the rucksack and the small suitcase he'd set down near our table. "Please watch my things for a minute. They're all I've got."

With a casual glance around the room, he walked over to a group of middle-aged men. One of the men sauntered outside and the young man followed a minute later. We could see them arguing through the shop window.

The price they arranged was more than double the sum Uncle Ernst had led us to expect. Mutti looked worried. The cab would cost us nearly every penny we had left, but at that point we really had no choice. We went outside and squeezed into the cab, which was scarcely big enough to hold all four of us and our luggage. The young man sat in front next to the driver. Hubert, Mutti, and I climbed into the back seat. The stale smell of smoke clung to the tattered upholstery.

We drove out into the country, past an area with a lot of gardens. Suddenly the driver doubled back into the village. A few minutes later, he headed out of town in a totally different direction. Before we knew it, we were driving back through the village streets again. I was certain the driver was taking advantage of us and I glanced at Mutti to see whether she agreed. She shook her head, but did not say a word.

As the cab headed yet again for the outskirts of the village, the young man in the front seat snarled at the cab driver, "Hey pal, do you think we're stupid? We've been going in circles. Where are you taking us?"

"Take it easy, take it easy," replied the driver. "Of course I'm going in circles. I have to take a different route every day. Why do you think I have to charge you so much money? If I went directly there, we'd arrive in fifteen minutes, but I don't want to get caught, and neither do you."

The young man mumbled, "All right, all right. Sorry."

After that, no one dared say a word for the next half hour. We traveled through three or four small villages. The houses stood right against the street without even a sidewalk in between.

Suddenly we turned onto a rutted dirt road. The driver stopped along a curve near the edge of a forest. He took the fare from Mutti, pointed us in the right direction, wished us "Good luck!" and sped away.

As promised, the young man took our big suitcase as we headed towards the tall pine trees. Five or six other families sat on their luggage at the edge of the forest. Hidden by the high dry grass, they were waiting until dark to walk in the direction of the border.

Our helpful young man cursed under his breath. He spoke quietly to Mutti. "I'm awfully sorry, but I have to leave you here. If we get caught with a big group like this, they'll send us all back. Do yourselves a favor. Go alone with your boys." He pointed to the other families. "Don't join them," he warned. Dropping our heavy suitcase, he walked briskly towards the West German border.

Mutti just stared in disbelief as he disappeared into the forest, but I was furious.

"How can he abandon us like that?" I demanded. "With your sore finger and all. If I were bigger, I'd beat him to a pulp."

Mutti shook her head, dismissing my protest. "There's nothing we can do," she said, giving me a little hug. Signaling us to follow her, she began to lug the heavy suitcase in the direction the young man had taken. We steered ourselves in a wide angle, away from the other families.

The sun was setting and the tops of tall pine trees blocked out the fading sunlight so that it looked like twilight. Only when we looked straight up could we see there was still a bit of daylight left. The sweet smell of pine resin tickled my nose. Each time a dry twig or pine cone crackled under my feet, my heart pounded faster in my throat.

Mutti whispered, "We should be in the West by now." As soon as she had spoken, a guttural voice yelled, "Shto takoi? Shtoi! (What's this? Stop!)"

At the edge of a small clearing just ahead, two Red Army soldiers stepped out from behind the trees, their fish can submachine guns pointed directly at us. I was certain they would shoot us. Imagining our stinking corpses abandoned in the forest as food for ants and worms, I broke out in a cold sweat. The soldiers rushed over to us, shouting all the while in Russian. Hubert, Mutti, and I were in tears. Mutti dropped to her knees.

"Please, let us go. My husband is in the West," she sobbed over and over in broken Russian.

The soldiers stood their ground. Hurling a barrage of Russian curses at us, the taller one of the two waved his submachine gun in the direction from which we had come. His meaning was unmistakable. He wanted us to go back to the East.

The louder he demanded our return, the more desperately Mutti pleaded. Finally, the Russians must have decided we weren't worth the trouble. With a look of disgust mixed with pity, the taller soldier pointed towards the West with his submachine gun and grunted, "Davai, davai!"

CHAPTER 25

*M*y heart was pounding as we hurried towards the West. I prayed the Russians would not change their minds. Mutti's face was twisted with pain. Her finger must have hurt her terribly.

"Please let me carry the big suitcase," I pleaded, but she just grabbed it more tightly as we rushed forward. Even Hubert was running on his short little legs.

Minutes later two soldiers wearing unfamiliar uniforms approached us. With a smile, the younger soldier said to Mutti in heavily accented German, "You are in the British Zone." He reached over to help with her suitcase.

Mutti began to laugh and cry at the same time. We followed the soldiers to a small guard station nearby. The soldier who had carried Mutti's suitcase made a phone call to the German police. While we waited for the police to arrive, one of the English soldiers gave us a bar of chocolate. Hubert, who had no memory of chocolate, nibbled cautiously at first, and then stuffed a big piece into his mouth.

"Mmmmmm," he mumbled. "I hope Vati has piles and piles of candy for us in his pastry shop!"

"Do you remember the last time you ate chocolate?" Mutti asked me.

"A solid piece like this, you mean?" I thought about her question. "Oma didn't let me eat the military chocolate I found in Preussisch Eylau. So it must have been when Vati brought some home during the war."

We each took another bite, letting the candy melt slowly in our mouths. "But I'll never forget the last time I drank a cup of hot chocolate," I continued. "It was at school in Langendorf, on Hitler's birthday. Horst threw away his flag on the way home."

"The things you remember! All the way back to April 20, 1944. They really gave you hot chocolate?"

"Yes. I'm sure I told you at the time."

"You probably did, but I guess I forgot. So much has happened in the meantime."

* * *

The German police van arrived. As we were getting in, Mutti tried to thank the British soldiers for their help, but they shrugged as if to say that they were only doing their job.

It was dark and cold when we arrived at the Helmstedt police station. After Mutti filled out some forms, the policeman brought us to the Travelers Aid Society at the railroad station where a nurse changed the bandage on Mutti's finger. The infection had spread to her hand and partway up her arm.

"If you don't get this treated by tomorrow," the nurse warned, "you could be in terrible danger. Blood poisoning should be looked after without delay."

"My husband will bring me to a doctor in Uelzen," Mutti assured her.

Travelers Aid gave each of us a bowl of soup and a slice of bread. After we had eaten, we were assigned to a small room for the night. Hubert and I shared one cot and Mutti slept on the other. I fell asleep right away, but was awakened three times during the night by Mutti's moans of pain.

* * *

The next morning Mutti bought our railroad tickets to Uelzen.

"We only have twenty marks left," she confided in me.

"How'll we manage?" I asked anxiously.

Mutti smiled. "A few hours from now, we'll be reunited with your father and we can put all our worries behind us."

Mutti looked radiant as we boarded the train. Hubert and I were bursting with excitement. Things were certainly looking up. Even the other passengers on the train looked happier than the ones who had traveled with us in the Russian Zone the day before.

"How well do you remember Vati?" Mutti asked me as the train lurched to a start.

"The few times he came home, he was like a distant uncle, just stopping by for a short visit. I was a lot closer to Opa," I admitted.

"I don't remember Vati at all," Hubert said.

"Your father's a gentleman, handsome, an elegant dresser, perfect manners. All the girls adored him."

"How'd you two meet?" Hubert persisted.

"In Bartenstein in the spring of 1934, he asked me for a dance and we danced together half the night. We started dating the following week and before we knew it, we got engaged. In the summer we toured the countryside on our bicycles and in the winter we went skating. He was a real daredevil, racing across the ice and jumping clear over a big water barrel."

"Could you do that too?" Hubert interrupted.

Mutti laughed, "Of course not, silly. I was a good skater, but I couldn't jump that high on the ice. Anyhow, a year later we got married, took out a loan, and opened a café in Königsberg. We both worked very hard; he made the pastries in the baking kitchen and I worked behind the counter in the store. And at the end of 1937, Günter was born."

"Then what happened?" Hubert asked.

"The next two years were wonderful. We were getting ahead in our store, making good money. But then the war started on September 1, 1939. The following month Vati was drafted and we had to close our Café. That's when Günter and I moved in with Oma and Opa in Langendorf."

"I really miss Opa," I blurted out when Mutti had finished her story.

"Me too," Mutti said, "and I feel bad, leaving Oma and Liesbeth and her children behind in the Russian Zone. Maybe Vati will figure out a way to bring them over to join us once we get settled."

In the little town of Lehrte we changed to the train that would bring us to Vati. If it weren't for Mutti's finger, we would not have had a care in the world. We arrived in Uelzen around noon and went to check our luggage. The railroad clerk, an attractive woman with long auburn hair, took out her handkerchief and wiped her hands after picking up our luggage from the counter.

"If you want this stuff back today, you'd better show up before 10 p.m.," she warned.

With trembling hands, Mutti unfolded the paper on which Uncle Ernst had written down the address of Café Mozart where Vati worked and of the apartment house where he lived. We stepped out into the small Bahnhofplatz.

"Excuse me, please," Mutti asked a lady passing by. "Is Café Mozart far from here?"

"No, not at all. The underpass straight ahead will bring you out to Bahnhof-Strasse. Take a left. The Cafe's in a half-timbered building a few blocks down on the left-hand side."

"Thank you," Mutti said. "If you don't mind, I have one more question." Mutti showed the lady Vati's address.

"That's even closer. It's in a small alley right near St. Marien's Church. You'll pass by there on your way to the Café."

"Thank you very much," Mutti said, as she slipped the paper back in her pocket.

"Enjoy your stay in Uelzen!" the friendly lady replied.

Like a magical tunnel in a storybook, the underpass brought us out into a town of half-timbered buildings and narrow twisting side streets. In my wildest dreams, I could not have imagined a prettier place. God was finally answering our prayers.

We passed St. Marien's, a massive brick church with a tall, pointed spire. A short distance further, we saw the Café Mozart sign on a three-story half-timbered house.

Through the shop window, sweets tempted us in their display cases. Towards the back, we glimpsed well-dressed ladies clustered around the tables, eating pastries and sharing midday gossip.

As soon as we stepped inside, the salesclerk glanced at our ragged clothing. She stepped out from behind the counter and put her hands on her hips as if to protect the customers in the room behind her from any unwelcome intrusion. Mutti did not seem to notice the effect we were having.

"I'm Gretel Nitsch," she announced, her eyes sparkling. "Could you please tell my husband I'm here?"

After a long pause, the saleslady replied, "Oh, so you're his wife?" After another pause, she added, "He's not here. He left earlier than usual today. You missed him by about an hour."

"Do you have any idea where he could be? Did he go to his apartment?" Mutti persisted.

The saleslady became more irritated. "I really don't know," she said. "Do you want to leave a message? Perhaps you can come back tomorrow?"

Mutti shook her head and the three of us stepped back outside. "Something doesn't seem right here," she said. Her step had already lost a little of its bounce.

Slowly we walked back towards St. Marien. We asked directions one more time before we finally found Vati's apartment house. A row of metal name plates was attached to the door frame next to the bells. I picked out the name plate which read "Willi Nitsch." He had the apartment on the third floor.

Mutti pressed the buzzer, but there was no response. She tried the doorknob. The door to the building was unlocked. As we walked into the lobby, the wooden soles on my boots thumped against the hard floor. We climbed up the stairs slowly, not knowing whether Vati would be at home. My chest felt as though it were going to explode.

We had nearly reached the second floor landing when we heard the noise of a door being unlocked on the floor above. Someone stepped out into the hallway before closing and locking the door again. And then we saw him. He planted himself above us on the landing between the second and third floors. He looked angry; I could not detect even a hint of a smile.

Mutti made the first move. She stepped up to the landing and said, "Well, here we are. Aren't you amazed to see us?"

Vati continued to block the way upstairs. Staring at Mutti he blurted out, "My God! Your hair has turned completely white."

"That's the first thing you have to tell me after four years apart?" Mutti said and she threw her arms around him. His arms hung limply at his sides.

"Why'd you come here anyway?" Vati asked gruffly.

Mutti took a step down and clutched the railing for support. I was afraid she might faint.

"My apartment's too small for all of us," he continued in a hostile tone. "You have to spend some time in the Bohldamm Refugee Camp in Uelzen to qualify for a place big enough for four people."

"Well, if that's what it takes, then that's what we'll do," Mutti replied, "but at least let us see your apartment as long as we're here."

Vati didn't budge. He stretched out his left arm, pulled back the white starched cuff of his dress shirt and studied his gold watch. "There's no time for that now. I have to bring you to the refugee camp."

Up until that point, Vati had not so much as glanced at Hubert and me, but I had been observing him. He was wearing a stylish, dark blue suit, a white shirt and a fancy tie, an unbuttoned beige trench coat, and a hat. The few times I had seen him before, he had always worn his Luftwaffe uniform. He had gained so much weight since we had last seen him that he reminded me of the overfed Russian officers in Palmnicken.

Mutti was crying as we went back downstairs to the street. We walked in awkward silence to the railroad station. While Mutti and Hubert waited outside, Vati and I went in to claim our luggage.

Ignoring me, the redheaded clerk tipped her head to one side and smiled at Vati, showing off her even white teeth. "And what can I do for you, sir?" she asked, her cheeks suddenly flushed with color.

My father smiled for the first time since our arrival as he handed her the claim check. "I'd like to pick these up, please."

"Of course." She was still blushing when she returned a minute later with our suitcases and my blanket bundle.

My father paid her the sixty pfennig fee. I grabbed the small suitcase and the blanket bundle. My father easily lifted our big suitcase with his left hand, took off his hat with his right hand and flashed another smile at the clerk.

"Good bye, sir, and come back again," she said.

How could he flirt like that with Mutti waiting just outside? Did he think I was stupid?

As we stepped away from the counter, he put the change back in his bulging wallet. It was only then that he took a good look at me.

"You've grown so tall," he commented without enthusiasm. He took my bundle and the small suitcase from me. "I can carry those, too. Tell me, how on earth did you all manage to get here from the Soviet-Occupied Zone?"

Too angry to answer, I stuffed my hands into my pockets and looked down at my boots, hating him for how he had treated Mutti on the staircase, wishing I were big enough to punch him in the mouth.

Although the refugee camp was only a half kilometer from the station, the way there seemed endless. No one talked, not even little Hubert. Set among neat rows of poplar trees, the camp was a large collection of barracks, once whitewashed, but now just drab and miserable. In an administration barrack, Mutti filled out a thick stack of forms. My father watched the whole procedure as if he were an outsider who had nothing at all to do with us. A friendly Red Cross nurse led us to a big hall and showed us to our compartment: two bunk beds, a small square table, and two stools. Our space was separated from the compartments on either side by curtains, but it was open in the front. Our wing of the barrack had twelve such compartments, all of them crowded with refugees. The place reeked of urine and unwashed bodies. Hubert and I lay down exhausted on our bunks, even though it was still afternoon.

"Your father's going to bring me to a doctor about my finger," Mutti said. "We'll come back as soon as possible."

"See you soon," Vati promised as they both headed towards the exit.

* * *

Hours passed and people began to leave for supper. I had no idea what I should do. Finally, Vati came back alone.

"Mutti had to go to the hospital. I'll know more about it in the morning," he explained. He brought us to the camp cafeteria and got us some food, free of charge.

"Well, I'm off for now," he said suddenly. "Something came up. Get to bed early. You can eat all of your meals here."

"So, are you coming back tomorrow?" I asked.

"Of course. I'll see you both tomorrow night; perhaps we can have supper here together," he promised, and then he left us. I felt terribly alone, sitting next to Hubert in that huge cafeteria filled with strangers. Hubert, who had just turned six, began to sob for Mutti.

"Vati promised to be back tomorrow," I repeated, but nothing seemed to calm him down. I tried to be brave for both of us. Since I was still hungry, I helped myself to another bowl of potato soup and a long, thin boiled sausage.

After supper, I escorted Hubert back to our compartment and helped him into bed. He fell asleep right away, but I lay awake for hours, listening to the sounds from the other compartments. People were talking, clearing their throats, whispering, belching, and coughing. An old man kept hollering "Quiet!" at the top of his lungs, only making matters worse.

I thought about how cruel my father's remarks had been that afternoon; how he had smiled at that redheaded woman in the station. During all those hard years when Mutti had risked her life for us under the Russians, it had never bothered me that her hair had changed from light brown to white. Why should it matter to him now? To me, she was still beautiful. As I finally drifted off to sleep, I looked forward to giving Mutti an extra hug when she came back in the morning.

* * *

Awakened by the loud talking and the bustle of the other refugees, I took Hubert to the toilet and afterwards we ventured into a communal men's washroom. I was uncomfortable with Hubert among all those grown men. Some were bent over the rows of sinks, washing themselves. Others lathered their faces and grimaced as they shaved. I hardly saw any boys our age.

Yet I felt dirty from our long trip so I pulled Hubert over to one of the many showers. As soon as we had scrubbed ourselves and gotten dressed, I threw the towels into a corner and hurried with Hubert back to our compartment.

"I want my Mutti," Hubert bawled. "I want her now!"

"She'll be back soon," I replied, trying to sound cheerful.

"Why did Vati leave us alone?" Hubert persisted.

How could I explain to him what I could not explain to myself? I felt sorry for both of us. Why had my father been so mean? What had we ever done to him? After four years apart, this was certainly no way to treat his wife and children. Hubert was looking up at me, waiting for my reply.

"Let's go eat," I said, putting my arm around his shoulder. "We'll talk about it later."

We breakfasted on porridge with raisins, rolls with margarine, and hot milk. After eating our fill, we wandered around for a while, exploring the camp. We looked for a play area, but did not find one. Hubert stamped his foot in the dust. The back of his neck turned a deep shade of red and the veins in his forehead bulged. "I don't want to stay here one more minute," he yelled. "I want to go to Mutti."

I pointed to the guards posted by the big gate. "If we walk out through that turnpike, they might not let us come back inside," I explained. "We haven't any money. Where would we get our meals?"

"When's she coming back?" Hubert whimpered. "When's Mutti coming back?"

"You know what? Why don't we wait for her on our bunk beds? That way she'll be sure to find us as soon as she gets to the camp."

When we went to the cafeteria for lunch, one of the ladies serving the food took us aside. "I've been watching you two. Are you boys here alone? Where's your mother or your grandmother?"

"Our mother's in a hospital here in Uelzen and our grandmother lives in the Soviet-Occupied Zone."

"When's your mother coming back?"

"Vati promised to tell us tonight."

"Oh, so your father is here with you in the camp?"

"No, just us."

"Tell me, what's your compartment number?"

"Nine. Compartment Nine. May we eat now?" I asked impatiently.

"Of course. Help yourselves." She shook her head as she wrote down the number of our compartment.

"Why'd she want to know all that stuff?" Hubert asked me as we sat down to eat.

"Beats me. I'm eleven years old. I can take care of you just fine."

"I guess so," Hubert said, "but I'd rather have Mutti."

It was a long, terribly boring afternoon. When Vati finally returned, he was alone. Even so, I was surprisingly happy to see him.

"Is Mutti all right?" I asked.

"Not really. They took off the first two joints of her right index finger. So she'll have to stay in the hospital for a few weeks."

Hubert and I both began to cry. Vati put one hand on Hubert's head and one hand on mine and said, "Don't cry. Mutti's going to be all right."

"What's going to happen to us?" Hubert wailed.

Vati shifted from one foot to the other and stared up at the ceiling, unable to meet our eyes. Just then a nurse approached us.

"Are you the boys whose mother's in the hospital?"

Before I could answer, Vati rushed to explain, "The doctors had to amputate a portion of my wife's finger. It'll be a while before she's released."

"Your sons can't continue to stay here alone," the nurse said. "Please give your address to the office so they may be officially discharged to your care."

"Totally out of the question! Impossible!" Vati snapped.

"Do you mean to tell me, you're abandoning your children?" The nurse began to write in our folder.

Vati flashed a charming smile. "Of course not. I expect to find a solution by tomorrow. Just give me one more day."

"What's the world coming to?" the nurse muttered to herself as she stormed off.

Vati turned to Hubert and me. "I'll try to bring you a nice surprise in the morning," he said. He wished us "good night" and we were once again alone.

* * *

As we were finishing a late breakfast the next morning, Vati found us in the cafeteria. He was accompanied by a stout lady, a broad smile on her round face. Aunt Käte! My father's sister rushed over to us. She grabbed Hubert and hugged him and kissed him on the cheek. Then she hugged and kissed me, too.

"Goodness, you've grown," she gurgled, tears streaming down her rosy cheeks.

Everything moved quickly after that. Vati filled out another form; we grabbed our luggage and walked back to the railroad station. From behind the luggage check-in counter, the lady with the auburn hair tried to catch Vati's eye, but he was too busy talking to Aunt Käte.

Aunt Käte put her arms around Hubert and me. "No more long faces," she chided. "You boys are welcome to stay with Uncle Hermann and me 'til your mother's able to care for you again."

"I'll let you know how Mutti's doing," Vati promised.

As we boarded the train, I reluctantly shook his hand.

"See you soon!" he called to us through the open compartment window, but I did not know whether I should believe him.

CHAPTER 26

A unt Käte sat on one side of the compartment with Hubert, and I sat facing her. She beamed as she asked me questions about our journey from Plötzin, while plying us with a seemingly endless supply of baloney sandwiches, homemade toffees, and big juicy Russet apples.

"You and your mother have had a terrible experience," Aunt Käte said with concern. "Some of our relatives got off a lot easier. It was all a matter of timing, I suppose. For instance, your Altenberg Grandmother, together with Aunt Hedwig and Aunt Lotte and their five children, reached Pillau by the end of January 1945, a month before you did. A German navy boat took them all to Denmark where they spent nearly two years in a refugee camp before settling in Oldendorf near us."

"I'm glad they got out," I said solemnly. "No one should have had to go through what we did."

"Still," Aunt Käte continued, "you were better off than some. Aunt Hedwig's husband Alfred and Uncle Gerhard were both killed just before the end of the war, Alfred in Budapest and Gerhard in Cottbus, near Berlin."

"What about my Altenberg Grandfather?".

"He stubbornly refused to leave his farm. He stayed behind to feed the animals."

"Wasn't he afraid of the Russians?"

"He was convinced they wouldn't harm a seventy-four year old man. At the end of the First War, they treated him kindly, he kept assuring us." Aunt Käte stopped a moment to compose herself.

"We learned later from several of our former neighbors that two days after the Russians arrived he was seen lying dead in front of his house. His head had been bashed in."

I imagined how a drunken Russian soldier might have swung a rifle butt with enough force to crush his skull. Perhaps Grandfather had merely refused to give up his gold watch and chain. That would have been enough.

In Hanover, we had to change trains. A short time later, we arrived in Osterwald. Mr. Dreesen, the farmer from whom Aunt Käte and Uncle Hermann rented their apartment, met us at the station with a horse carriage to take us the rest of the way to Oldendorf. The well-kept fields at either side of the road reminded me of Opa's farm.

Aunt Käte and Uncle Hermann rented a small apartment on the second floor of the Dreesen's large farmhouse in the middle of the village. We were greeted in the vestibule by Mrs. Dreesen, who looked in amazement at our unusual clothing.

"My nephews, Günter and Hubert, have just spent three-and-a-half years under the Russians in East Prussia," Aunt Käte explained.

We passed through Aunt Käte's spotless little kitchen to get to the living room. The place was so clean and neat, I was hesitant to sit down. Aunt Käte began to unpack our few belongings.

"We don't want to put you to any trouble," I said, glancing around at the small room.

"It's not large, but we'll manage," Aunt Käte said. "You and Hubert are going to share the bedroom with Uncle Hermann. I'll make up a bed for myself right here."

"Thank you, Aunt Käte," I said gratefully.

A thin plywood room divider separated the living room from the kitchen. We could hear Aunt Käte as she bustled about, preparing an afternoon treat for us. When she emerged from the kitchen, she was carrying a tray piled high with slices of dark brown rye bread spread with margarine, and a jar of sugar beet syrup.

"You'll have to gobble the bread down once you pour on the syrup," she warned us. "Otherwise it'll run right down onto the rug." Steaming cups of roasted barley coffee with lots of milk washed down the sandwiches.

"I'll expect you boys are tired of being stared at," Aunt Käte said after some thought, "and I intend to put an end to it once and for all."

"What do you mean?" I asked.

"You'll see!"

Aunt Käte disappeared for a while in the attic. When she came back, she was carrying two old pairs of pants belonging to her son, Siegfried, who sometimes visited on weekends we were told. Aunt Käte sat down at her sewing machine and went to work. By the time Uncle Hermann came home, Hubert was already wearing new long pants made of smooth gray wool.

Uncle Hermann flashed a huge smile as he welcomed us to his home. "I'm glad you boys can stay with us for a few weeks."

"Thank you," I said.

"If I'm not mistaken, the last time I saw you was in Altenberg in the spring of 1943. I can't believe how you've grown from a little boy to a young man in just five years. A few centimeters more, and you'll be as tall as I am."

And to Hubert, "And look at you! You were just a baby when I saw you last."

Uncle Hermann spoke in beautiful High German. "Please don't hesitate to come to me with any questions you may have," he continued.

"You boys have a lot of catching up to do and your aunt and I are here to help you along."

"Your attention please," Aunt Käte interrupted. She held Hubert's burlap knickerbockers at arm's length between her thumb and her forefinger high above the trash can and, with a theatrical flourish, dropped them inside.

"That was my first trick; the second one will make it stick," she announced, with apologies to Wilhelm Busch. The following morning my knickerbockers met the same fate. I was delighted with my first pair of long pants.

* * *

Ever since our arrival in Oldendorf, Aunt Käte had insisted that I wash my hands before every meal, scrub my upper body over the sink in the kitchen morning and evening, and take a bath in the Dreesen's downstairs bathroom every Saturday. Although I had my difficulties with these rules, I accepted them. Aunt Käte even bought me my own comb, the first I did not have to share with Mutti and Hubert, and I was proud to use it.

I drew the line, however, at brushing my teeth. Although I could usually escape notice in the mornings, Aunt Käte kept a close watch over me at bedtime.

"You haven't brushed," she reminded me sternly.

"I didn't have to. We had buttered noodles with sugar and cinnamon for supper."

"What's that got to do with it?"

"My mouth doesn't smell bad. I didn't eat onions or anything like that."

"That's the strangest excuse I've ever heard. How long have you had this habit of not brushing your teeth every night?"

"Mutti made me brush in Plötzin, but in Palmnicken and in Goldbach I never had to do it."

"And why not, may I ask?"

"That's easy. I didn't have a toothbrush or toothpaste. Actually, none of us did!"

"Are you serious?"

"Absolutely."

Aunt Käte sucked in her breath, as if she had uncovered a terrible crime. She wagged her finger at me as she spoke. "Now you listen to me. You have no such excuse in this house. And you will brush, every morning and every night. Is that understood? Because if you don't, your teeth will rot and, one of these days, they'll fall out."

"But if they haven't fallen out in nearly four years, then..."

"I don't want to hear any excuses. If I catch you again going to bed without brushing your teeth, you're in deep trouble. Is that understood?" Aunt Käte's tone of voice was unexpectedly sharp.

"Yes, Aunt Käte," I said.

The next morning Aunt Käte brought Hubert and me to a dentist, who gave us each a thorough examination and took several X-rays. "It's a miracle," he reported to Aunt Käte. "There's absolutely nothing wrong with their teeth."

He turned to me, "You've been lucky, young man, but it's no use tempting fate. You have to brush twice a day from now on!"

* * *

On Sunday, we walked the short distance to the house where my Altenberg Grandmother lived with my Aunt Lotte, my Uncle Bruno, and their two boys. Aunt Hedwig and her three boys lived across the road from them. It was a wonderful reunion. Everyone peppered me with questions about our time under the Russians. As we talked, those terrible years seemed suddenly far away, as though it had all happened to someone else a long time ago.

"How's your Mutti doing?" my Grandmother asked. "Käte tells me she's in the hospital."

"I wish I knew," I said, trying not to cry. "My father," (I could no longer bring myself to call him "Vati") "promised to keep us posted, but so far we haven't heard a word."

Grandmother's eyes flashed with anger, but she did not reply. I was suddenly aware that neither she nor anyone else had mentioned my father all day. It was as if he were no longer a part of the family.

* * *

Hubert and I started school the next day. In honor of the occasion, Aunt Hedwig gave each of us a beautiful pair of high leather shoes, hand-me-downs from my cousins. Rid of the heavy Russian boots, my toes appreciated the wiggle room.

Just as in Plötzin, I was put into the fourth grade. From the front of the classroom, a portrait of Dr. Martin Luther looked down on me. On the wall next to me was a framed print of Albrecht Dürer's engraving "Knight, Death, and Devil." The Devil's horns reminded me of the Devil who had crashed through the wall of the church during the wedding. Oma's story still made me shudder.

Mr. Mückensturm, our classroom teacher, made the introductions. "Welcome to Oldendorf. This is a wonderful school and I'm sure you'll like it here. If you have any questions, come to me."

What a nice teacher, I thought, automatically comparing him to Raddatz in Goldbach.

The children were all well dressed compared to my classmates in Plötzin in the Soviet-Occupied Zone. So I credited my warm reception in large part to my new pants, my leather shoes, and to the mountain cap - passed down from my cousin Jockel to his brother Reinhard to me - which Aunt Hedwig had given me to replace my ushanka.

"Wear this, and let me throw away your Ivan cap," she had said. "We can't have you running around Oldendorf looking like a Russian boy."

* * *

Returning from school a few days later, I ran into old Mrs. Dreesen in the vestibule. Remembering Aunt Käte's instructions to greet everyone I knew by name, I ripped off my cap and bowed slightly.

"Good afternoon, Mrs. Dreesen!" I started to say, but my polite words were drowned out by the clatter of coins landing on the blue and white tiled floor. It was hard to say which of us was more surprised.

"What on earth? Are you carrying money in your cap?" Mrs. Dreesen asked me.

"Sorry, ma'am," I mumbled as I bent down to collect my coins. I felt like a fool and hoped this awkward incident would remain between the two of us. I should have known better. During supper, I found out that the news had already traveled upstairs.

"Mrs. Dreesen was wondering," Aunt Käte began, "why in the world you were carrying your money in your cap?"

"When other boys try to steal it, that's the last place they look," I explained to my startled Aunt and Uncle.

"No one will steal your money in Oldendorf," Uncle Hermann assured me. He pressed an old leather wallet into my hand. "Keep this wallet in your pants pocket. I guarantee it will be safe there." Sensing my hesitation, he added gently, "In time you'll put all of your bad Goldbach habits behind you, but first you'll have to learn how to trust people again."

* * *

The following Saturday, my cousin Siegfried, the twenty-four year old son of Uncle Hermann and Aunt Käte, came for a visit. He was a burly giant of a man. His hands were as big as shovels and when he shook my hand I was afraid he would crush it. During the war he had served as a First Lieutenant along the Russian front. Although he had only recently become a journeyman bricklayer, he was already

362

supervising a big crew at a construction site in Hanover. Siegfried had a strong Berlin accent and he spoke in a booming voice. He was quick to tease me about the way I talked.

"You roll your 'R' like an East Prrrussian," he mimicked. "Why don't you practice speaking like my Old Man?"

"It's just the way I talk," I snapped back. I was angry about his criticism and startled by the disrespectful way he talked about his father.

Still, he was right. My broad accent embarrassed me in school. As long as I sounded so different, I knew I would be too shy to make good friends.

* * *

In order to eke out the skimpy salary he earned at the lumber mill, Uncle Hermann gave private language lessons in the evening after work. His students were boys and girls attending the high school in Hameln. As I sat in the kitchen and listened through the thin partition, he instructed farmers' children in English, French, and Latin. In exchange for the lessons, Uncle Hermann was paid with milk, butter, vegetables, and potatoes. I would have given anything to be as smart as he was. Using the same methods he did, whenever I was alone in the living room I read aloud from my German textbook and tried to sound like my classmates. It was not easy to do and I soon became frustrated.

One day Uncle Hermann overheard me as I was practicing. "Well done, my boy," he said cheerfully. "I'm proud of you!"

"It's hopeless," I confessed, even though I was delighted by the unexpected praise. "I'll never get the hang of it."

"Permit me to make two small suggestions," Uncle Hermann said kindly. "Instead of forming the 'R' in back of your teeth, try to start it further down in your throat. It's almost like gargling. You should also make a habit of listening to the news on the radio. At first, try to repeat a few short phrases that the announcer uses. After a while, you might even try whole sentences."

"Thank you, I'll give it a try," I exclaimed, full of new determination. "May I ask you a question, Uncle Hermann? There's something that's been on my mind."

"Anything, my lad. Don't be shy."

"You obviously have a good education. Why are you working at the mill? Why can't you get a better job than that?"

"That's easy," replied Uncle Hermann. "During the war, I was a Lieutenant Colonel on the staff of the German High Command in Berlin. I was the liaison between Protestant and Catholic army chaplains. Of course I couldn't have held such an important position if I hadn't been a member of the Nazi party. Ever since the end of the war, good jobs have been pretty much closed to former party members."

* * *

Quite the opposite of Uncle Hermann, the music teacher at my school, Mr. Bunk, was nervous and skinny. Rumor had it, he had been buried under the debris of a bombed house in Hanover for several days during the war. The holidays were fast approaching and Mr. Bunk was under a great deal of pressure to get us ready to sing Christmas carols. He divided us into small groups so that we could practice more easily in front of the class. If our singing did not live up to his standards, he wrung his hands and his face began to twitch.

One day during recess I met a round-cheeked boy by the name of Hartmut whose face had "trouble" written all over it. He sat towards the back of the room and seemed to delight in annoying teachers in general, and our music teacher in particular. Hartmut was even dumber than I was. He could not read without moving his lips. Even so, he had a great following among the other boys in our class. Whenever a girl's white or pink or light blue petticoat showed below the hemline of her dress, he called out, "Es blitzt! (Lightning!)" The effect this comment had on my classmates was incredible. The effect Hartmut had on poor Mr. Bunk was even more dramatic. He became hopping mad whenever he heard the word "Blitz!" even if it were only whispered. Wiping his perspiring face with a handkerchief, he trembled from head to toe.

"Stop this outrageous behavior right now!" Mr. Bunk's face twitched more than ever.

Because of his enormous success, Hartmut quickly had several imitators. In the hope that it would make me more popular, I soon became one of them. Once again my bad behavior caught up with me. The day before school closed for Christmas vacation, Mr. Bunk paid a call on Aunt Käte.

"Your nephew has fallen in with a bad group of boys," he informed her. "They've been disrupting my class with outrageous remarks."

"Rest assured, I'll speak to Günter about it," Aunt Käte replied.

"But that's not the worst of it," my teacher continued. "In my opinion, your nephew is one of several boys in that class who are girl-crazy."

When Aunt Käte confronted me with this accusation at supper time, I noticed out of the corner of my eye that Uncle Hermann was having trouble stifling a grin.

"This bizarre behavior has got to stop," she said sternly, with a warning glance at Uncle Hermann. "I've never seen anyone as distressed as your teacher was."

"I'm sorry, Aunt Käte." I felt guilty to have put her to so much trouble. "I promise it won't happen again."

* * *

On the 23rd of December, Mutti came and joined us. Father was not with her. The remaining stump of her finger was still bandaged, but Mutti didn't let it bother her as she hugged Hubert and me.

"I really missed you!" I exclaimed, not wanting to let go.

"Me too!" Hubert added.

365

We sat down to coffee and cake in the afternoon. Aunt Käte had made me self-conscious about my atrocious table manners. Now, in order to impress Mutti, I tried my best to adhere to all of the rules Aunt Käte had been drilling into me: "Don't slurp, don't burp, use your knife and fork properly, don't lick your plate, sit up straight, don't talk with your mouth full of food, and don't leave the table before everyone has finished."

I kept peeking at Mutti out of the corner of my eye, but I wasn't sure whether she noticed what a fine gentleman I had become.

"So much has happened in the three weeks since your birthday," Mutti reminded me later, when we had a few moments alone. "I hope you still aren't sorry about missing your dress rehearsal."

"The only thing I'm sorry about is that you didn't go to see a doctor in Plötzin before we left," I replied, trying not to think about Gudrun.

"Well, I suppose I should have had it looked at," she admitted, "but if I had, we might still be stuck in the East."

"Will my father be coming to celebrate Christmas with us?" I asked, already knowing what her answer would be.

"We'll have to manage without him again," Mutti replied and she became very quiet.

* * *

On Christmas Eve we had an early supper of roast rabbit in sour cream sauce, spiced with marjoram. Mashed potatoes, carrots, and Brussels sprouts smothered in butter filled the side dishes. Red fruit jelly with thick yellow vanilla sauce followed for dessert, each portion served on a small china plate with its own matching cup and saucer. I tried to remember whether, even in Langendorf, we had ever enjoyed such a sumptuous feast.

Mutti held up her coffee cup and ran her finger along the fluted edge. "Käte dear, I haven't seen such beautiful china in a long time."

"Aside from our family pictures, this is all we have left from home. Hermann insisted on storing our good dishes and our silverware with friends in the countryside."

"Over your objections," Uncle Hermann added.

"I never expected our apartment in Berlin to be bombed out. Who would have thought it?" Aunt Käte sighed.

"Whatever we lost can be replaced," Uncle Hermann chimed in. "The most important thing is that we got away with our lives and we're getting by. And, believe me, Gretel, your life will also start to improve soon."

"I really shouldn't complain," Mutti replied. "It's just that this isn't exactly what I had expected when we came west."

* * *

From Aunt Käte's living room window, I could see the huge red brick Ludemann farmhouse where Aunt Lotte rented rooms. As soon as the sun had set, we all walked over in the frosty night air to Aunt Lotte's apartment. Aunt Hedwig and her children had already arrived. Over gingerbread and roasted barley coffee, we tried to catch up on the news about the relatives we hadn't seen in nearly four years. My father's name never came up.

Then came the moment to exchange Christmas presents. Each of the children received a Christmas plate piled high with cookies, candies, and fruits. Hubert, who had never eaten an orange before, took a big bite right through the peel, much to the amusement of the other children.

For the most part, we got outgrown hand-me-down clothes. As I tried each item on, I felt like a rich kid from the movies. Of all the clothes I received, my "new" dark green woolen winter jacket, too small for my cousin Reinhard, was the best. When I slipped my hands into the large pockets, I felt like a grownup young man. Aunt Käte's announcement, "Now we can throw away your horrid Goldbach coat," made my day.

There were two more special gifts. Hubert received a little tin trumpet from our Altenberg Grandmother. He soon fell asleep on the floor, still clutching it in his hand. Seeing him lying there so peaceful and happy, Mutti had a little cry.

Uncle Hermann had told me a number of adventure stories about the Indians, so I was thrilled to find among my many presents a German translation of *The Leather-stocking Tales* by James Fenimore Cooper. I flipped the pages and realized it was too difficult for me to read, but Uncle Hermann promised to help.

"Think of it as a challenge," he advised. "You can read aloud to me from your textbooks, and before long, you'll be able to read everything, even those long compound nouns."

As I glanced over at the gifts which my cousins Jockel, Reinhard, Frank, Christian, and Albrecht had received, I felt guilty. Not even counting what Hubert had gotten, I had more presents on my pile than all five of my cousins put together. Still, it felt good to be spoiled for a change. This had definitely been a wonderful Christmas.

* * *

During the Christmas holidays, Uncle Hermann encouraged me to begin a stamp collection. He brought envelopes with canceled stamps home from his office nearly every day. A number of the newer stamps showed German monuments and buildings, such as the Cologne Cathedral, the Frauen Church in Munich, and the Brandenburg Gate in Berlin, but many stamps showed the profile of Adolf Hitler or a swastika.

"You needn't bother with those," Uncle Hermann said, setting them aside. "They've gone out of style."

Although the German stamps were fun, I was fascinated by the colorful stamps from places such as the United States, France, England, Switzerland, and Sweden. Uncle Hermann gave me a Westermann Atlas and made me locate the various countries on the map. Within a short time my world had grown tremendously. Several times a week, Uncle Hermann came home with a new batch of stamps.

"Two from England, one from Spain, two from France, and one from the United States. There's even one from Brazil! Ever heard of that country?" he announced one evening.

My heart pounded with excitement as I pulled out the atlas and waited for Uncle Hermann in the living room. As soon as he took off his coat, put on his slippers, and washed his hands, we went on a world trip. At such times, supper was an inconvenient interruption.

CHAPTER 27

I returned to school at the beginning of January, full of good intentions. Uncle Hermann had inspired me over the vacation and I was determined to learn as much as I could. When my teachers spoke, I hung on every word.

Shortly after the holidays ended, Mutti took Hubert and me to see a general practitioner in the village for a checkup. "Your son, Günter, is in pretty good shape," he informed Mutti after the examination. "He only needs a little more fat on his ribs and he'll be fine."

"And Hubert?" Mutti asked, when the doctor hesitated.

"I'd like you to take him to see a specialist in Hameln. There's no need to be alarmed. It's just that I don't have the proper equipment here to check him out fully."

Two days later the specialist in Hameln ran a series of tests. "Your son has tuberculosis," he concluded. Mutti was devastated.

I thought about how quickly Dorchen had died after receiving the same diagnosis. I worried that the doctor might not have examined me carefully enough, and that I might have TB too. Seeing how trustingly Hubert looked at Mutti as she explained the situation, my heart filled with pity for him and I felt suddenly selfish and ashamed. I hoped the

German doctors would fix his lungs as well as the Russian doctors fixed his gut in Königsberg.

After returning to Oldendorf just long enough to pick up some clothing, Mutti brought Hubert by train to a sanatorium in Bassum near Bremen.

"He'll need to stay there for at least a year, possibly even longer," Mutti reported to us when she got back and then she broke down in sobs.

I was stunned. A year? My faith in the skills of German doctors suddenly evaporated.

"The poor dear," murmured Aunt Käte, swallowing Mutti up in a big hug.

"Who'll be there to comfort Hubert?" Mutti wailed. "He's only six."

After Hubert left, Uncle Hermann spent more time with me than ever. Sometimes he and I pored over the atlas until well past my bedtime. Uncle Hermann always had wonderful stories to tell about the far away countries I located on the map.

Around 9:30 every evening, the beds were set up for Aunt Käte and Mutti in the living room, and Uncle Hermann and I retreated into the unheated bedroom in the back. One of the large bedroom windows was always open. Two huge wooden beds stood against the long wall and a tall armoire covered nearly half the wall next to Uncle Hermann's bed. Several wooden crates full of big fuzzy-skinned Russet apples stood on empty crates near the windows. It was by far the best smelling bedroom I had ever slept in. When I crawled into the ice-cold bed, I disappeared for a few minutes under the down comforter, head and all. Once I warmed up a little, I stuck out my head and asked Uncle Hermann to tell me another story. He related from memory detailed episodes from *Huckleberry Finn*, *Tom Sawyer*, *The Three Musketeers*, and *The Count of Monte Cristo*. I also heard Karl May's adventure tales about Indians in North and South America, daring exploits in the Balkans, in the Arab countries, and in China.

The inspiration to read came to me in other ways as well. Downstairs, just off the vestibule, was the white-tiled bathroom, the only one in the house. Sunbeams passing through the large milk glass window gleamed off the side of the enameled bathtub. Next to the fancy flush toilet stood handy stacks of rectangular toilet paper cut from old newspapers.

One day, Uncle Hermann began to bring home copies of old correspondence from the lumber mill to use instead of the newspaper. The copies were on white, pale yellow, light pink, light blue and light green onionskin, which was a little too smooth for the purpose. Yet, once they were cut into rectangles, they were gentle enough on my bottom. To the right of the toilet, on a little ledge, Uncle Hermann left a tall stack of uncut copies.

Whenever I was in the bathroom during the daytime, I glanced at the old letters. A clerk confirmed an order for lumber in one; a customer sent a complaint about damaged lumber in another. There were dozens and dozens of letters and every one of them ended with "Heil Hitler!" or "Mit deutschem Gruss!" (with German greetings). Only one year earlier I had been using newspaper pictures of Stalin, and now this!

"Since you're nosy enough to read the letters, you should know that Mit deutschem Gruss! is the same as Heil Hitler!"Aunt Käte explained to me later in answer to my question. "Some day soon I hope we'll be able to afford real toilet paper. Maybe then you'll spend a little less time in the bathroom."

Despite Aunt Käte's teasing, I kept on reading the letters. I struggled to determine which words were nouns, verbs, adjectives, and adverbs according to Uncle Hermann's grammar lessons.

"The 'Heil Hitler!' salutations stopped abruptly in the spring of 1945," I reported to Aunt Käte one afternoon. "After that, the letters always end with 'Yours truly' or 'Sincerely.'"

"That's also the way people wrote before the Nazi times," she replied, "but I doubt if you'll find any letters from way back then."

* * *

One weekend my cousin Siegfried came for another visit. The previous evening Aunt Käte had shown me several photographs of her son in his uniform. The medals which decorated his chest reminded me of the medals we had trampled on in Königsberg before we got onto the boxcar. Since Uncle Hermann's heart condition was giving him trouble, Aunt Käte asked Siegfried to help me with my math homework in the living room.

"Your mother showed me pictures of you in uniform. How did you earn all those medals?" I asked as we settled down on the couch.

"I'll tell you one story, but then we have to do math," Siegfried replied. "My unit was stationed in the southern part of Russia. It was summertime and we were playing cards to while away the time. Since there weren't many trees, we dug several deep wide ditches to shelter us from the sun. We covered the ditches with camouflage netting and that's where we played cards from then on."

"But what about the medals?"

"I'm getting to that part. One morning, three Russian tanks approached our position. We rushed out to man our anti-tank guns, but before we had a chance to use them, one of the tanks tumbled into a ditch and disappeared from view. The other two tanks high tailed it out of there. The startled crew of the tank in the ditch surrendered and we took them prisoner and..."

"Did they fight when they climbed out of the tank?"

"No, of course not. We greeted them with submachine guns pointed right at their heads. They looked more embarrassed than scared, believe me. That very afternoon we repainted the tank with the German Cross and put it into action for our side."

"You got a medal for that?" I asked in astonishment.

"That's just how it happened," Siegfried laughed. "Now let's tackle the multiplication tables."

Unfortunately, Siegfried was precisely the opposite of Uncle Hermann. His explanations were as clear to me as thick pea soup. No matter how hard I tried, my answers just didn't seem to come fast enough to satisfy him. After fifteen frustrating minutes, he slapped me in the face. At that moment Aunt Käte walked into the living room.

"How dare you slap that boy?" Aunt Käte demanded reproachfully. "You, of all people! You were a terrible student and should certainly know better."

Siegfried blushed. "Maybe I'm not cut out to be a math tutor," he admitted with a grin.

"That's for sure. I'm going to send Günter over to see Jockel. He has a good head for math."

It was only a short walk to the farm where Aunt Hedwig was staying with her three children. She assured me I could count on Jockel's help.

A tall, skinny, studious fellow with blond curly hair, Jockel was nineteen years old and in his last year of high school. I had never gotten to know him that well because he tended to keep to himself. He shared a room with his brothers, Reinhard and Frank. As I was about to knock on the door, I could hear Jockel singing hymns. When I knocked, the singing stopped and Jockel said, "Come in."

A bunk bed and a cot were crowded into the tiny bedroom. Books lined the shelves and were piled on the table and on the floor.

"Aunt Käte sent me over to see whether you could help me with my math homework," I explained a bit shyly.

"No problem," Jockel replied in a friendly voice. "It's one of my favorite subjects. I'm working on a math problem right now." He turned his notebook around to show me his work.

"What on earth is that?" I asked, staring at the strange jumble of letters, symbols, and figures.

"It's calculus. One of these days I'm sure you'll be able to do it."

Jockel helped me with my math as patiently and efficiently as Uncle Hermann. He was also the source of other interesting information.

"Why were you singing church music before?" I couldn't help asking.

"I guess no one bothered to tell you," Jockel replied. "Just about everyone else in our family is Lutheran, although they rarely attend church. We're Mennonites, through my father's family."

"What kind of religion is that?" I asked.

"Our church was founded by a Dutchman named Menno Simons. One way we're different from the Lutherans is that we don't believe in the baptism of children. We wait until people are in their teens, when they're old enough to decide for themselves whether they want to accept Jesus into their lives."

"And that's what you did?"

"Oh yes, several years ago," he said with conviction. "I've dedicated my life to the church. As soon as I complete my final exams, I'm going to America to study divinity."

"To America? How can you afford it?"

"Some Mennonites in America got me a scholarship at Goshen College in the State of Indiana. I'm counting the days!"

Why can't something like that happen to me, I asked myself on my way back to Aunt Käte's house. Jockel's really got it made!

* * *

Jockel was right. Neither Aunt Käte nor Uncle Hermann went to church on Sunday mornings. While Aunt Käte cooked Sunday dinner, Uncle Hermann and I went to the little shed behind the farm where he raised rabbits. At any given time, he had several dozen. I enjoyed feeding them treats, like crunchy Brussels sprouts. The rabbits were cute and fun to watch.

Unlike the chickens, geese, and turkeys Oma had slaughtered in Langendorf, the rabbits were cuddly pets. I had even given some of them names. The first time Uncle Hermann slaughtered a rabbit, I vowed not to eat it. I lost my resolve once I smelled the delicious aroma wafting from the kitchen as the little creature roasted to a mouth-watering brown.

Uncle Hermann also set aside some time every Sunday morning to saw wood.

"Let me show you how well I can handle an ax and a saw," I bragged. "I chopped and sawed wood nearly every day in Goldbach."

"It's much too dangerous a job for a boy your age," Uncle Hermann insisted, over my protests.

As he worked, Uncle Hermann talked to me about geography, history, and stamp collecting. When it was time to go upstairs for lunch, I resented having to share Uncle Hermann with Aunt Käte and Mutti. As we ate, I daydreamed about how much better my life would be if he were my father, instead of Vati.

One day, I was so busy tagging along after Uncle Hermann that I completely forgot to write an essay about a poem I read for school. Along with Hartmut and three other boys, I was given detention by Mr. Mückensturm. To my mind, the punishment was far too severe. It wasn't as if I hadn't done the work on purpose. I simply forgot. Besides, Mutti and Aunt Käte were waiting for me for lunch.

As soon as school let out for the day, I packed my notebook and my books into my school bag and, full of trepidation, headed for the door. Hartmut and the others looked at me in awe. I was glad they couldn't hear my heart pounding in my chest. Once outside, I felt more confident. No teacher was around to stop me. With a slight swagger, I headed for the street. Many of the boys, and even some of the girls, cheered me on. "Günter!" one boy called after me. "No one, and I mean no one, in living memory, has ever ignored a detention order in this school before." My heart swelled with pride. I was a hero to the entire school.

Before Uncle Hermann got home that evening, Mr. Mückensturm came to our apartment to tell Mutti and Aunt Käte what I had done. Mutti was upset.

"Where do you keep your carpet beater?" she asked Aunt Käte. "I'm going to give Günter a serious thrashing."

"The carpet beater in this house is only used for carpets," Aunt Käte replied, but my relief was short lived. "There are other methods," she added ominously.

Right after supper, Aunt Käte looked me straight in the eye. "It's bedtime for you, young man. Uncle Hermann has no time tonight for stamp collecting and stories."

Stunned, I went to bed feeling sorry for myself. It took me a long time to fall asleep so I had plenty of time to regret what I had done in school. The next day, to my immense relief, the whole matter appeared to have been forgotten. Still, from then on, Uncle Hermann monitored my homework assignments much more carefully. He made me rewrite my essays even though I thought it was a waste of time.

"When it comes to school work, it doesn't pay to take short cuts. You don't learn for the teacher, you learn for life," Uncle Hermann advised me.

He drilled me on the multiplication tables, helped me memorize poems for school, and worked on improving my grammar. Uncle Hermann and Aunt Käte even talked about my taking a test so I could switch to the middle school. Things had been looking up, but then Aunt Käte, Uncle Hermann, and Mutti began to have serious conversations without me. This was never a good sign. What was worse, I had a hunch they were talking about my father.

One evening, when I was supposed to be asleep, I tiptoed along the long corridor outside the bedroom and slipped into the kitchen to get a glass of milk. It was easy to overhear snatches of hushed conversation through the thin partition.

"We can't ignore the situation any longer," Aunt Käte was saying. "His womanizing is a disgrace. It all started with that strawberry blond in Munsterlager when he began working for the Tommies. After that one, he lived with a brunette postal clerk for a while, and now he has this girl who's nearly young enough to be his daughter. How can Willi continue to live with her in Uelzen when he has a family to look after?"

"I don't see what we can do about it," Mutti responded weakly.

I could feel the color rising in my cheeks. Of course that was the reason! I should have known, the minute my father refused to let us see his apartment. I would have liked to grab him and shake him like a rag doll. How could he do this to us!

Aunt Käte's words interrupted my daydream.

"It's very simple. We're going to make it crystal clear to him that he'll be cut out of our family unless he gives up that floozy and takes you and the boys back."

Having heard more than enough, I sneaked back down the corridor and crawled into bed. I cried myself to sleep that night. How could he cheat on Mutti, especially after all the hardship she's gone through? I thought. It's not fair. It was nearly more than I could bear.

* * *

A few days later, toward the end of March, we heard from my father. He had found a room for Mutti and me in a refugee camp in Bodenteich, a village not far from Uelzen. He promised he would live there with us and commute by train from there to his job at Café Mozart in Uelzen.

At our farewell family dinner in Oldendorf, my aunts gave Mutti copies of several of the photographs we had lost when the Russians stole our luggage, among them my parents' wedding picture from 1935. Joyously surrounded by their forty guests, Mutti wore a long white wedding gown and my father sported a tuxedo. Standing nearby, my beloved Opa looked proud of his new son-in-law.

Aunt Käte also gave Mutti the photo taken of me when I was only three years old, the one where I wore my father's military boots and his air force service cap with the eagle carrying a swastika in its claws. In Langendorf it had always struck me as funny. Now it just made me angry. Having been the oldest man in the family since Opa died when I was eight, I was sick and tired of trying to fill my father's shoes.

* * *

We packed on Sunday morning, April 3, 1949. Aunt Käte and Uncle Hermann rode with us to the station in Mr. Dreesen's carriage to see us off. Mutti stared sadly through the train window as we slowly pulled away from the station. I did not have to ask whether she was thinking about my father and our future. I knew it.

I wasn't ashamed to cry when we called out our "good-byes" through the open window. Aunt Käte and Uncle Hermann had spoiled me and loved me and taught me manners. Although I had sometimes disappointed them, they had always set me back on the right path. I quietly thanked God for every minute of the four months we had spent with them.

CHAPTER 28

Mutti stared glumly out of the window as our train poked along towards Bodenteich. The 140 kilometer trip had already lasted nearly four hours. We had changed trains at Hanover and Lehrte. Just before two in the afternoon, we boarded the last train at the Uelzen station, a short walk from the building where we had confronted my father on the stairway. Dreading the reunion with my father, I tried to draw out Mutti who had spoken barely a word the whole time.

Since I had overheard the story while I was in Oldendorf about my father's girl friend, I wondered how much Mutti would tell me about it. "Did you ever find out why Vati wouldn't let us see his apartment last December?" I asked.

"That subject is off limits!" Mutti snapped. Her sharp tone startled me.

"Sorry," I said. After a long pause, I tried to undo the damage. "I'll really miss Aunt Käte and Uncle Hermann. They're two of the nicest people I've ever met. Why couldn't we just stay with them?"

"You can put that thought right out of your head. I felt terrible enough, imposing on them as long as we did."

"They didn't act like we were any trouble."

"Well, we were. I'm sure we were, all cramped together in that tiny apartment for so long. The two of them aren't getting any younger, you know, and Uncle Hermann has his heart problems. Having a wild young boy like you around probably took two years off his life."

"Was I so bad? I was sure they liked me."

"Let me put it this way. Your behavior didn't help. I was always worried about what you were up to. However, the main thing is, they thought we'd only be there a few weeks. No one ever imagined we'd stay so many months. And the whole time, everyone knew your father was making so much more money than they were."

There didn't seem to be much more to say after that. Our train chugged along, past pockets of barren heath land, thick pine forests, occasional stands of oak, and scruffy bushes. Twice we passed clusters of white birch trees, reminding me of our mushroom hunting grounds back in Goldbach. The musty smell of steam and coal dust from the locomotive gave way to the sweet scent of pine needles whenever the track curved to the right. Over the loud sound of the engine, birds twittered welcoming songs to spring.

Finally, the train pulled slowly into the Bodenteich station, an imposing structure of red brick, with white-trimmed windows. The village of Bodenteich lay behind the station to our left. A lone man, wearing a business suit and a black hat, was waiting on the platform. It took me a moment to recognize my father. With his mouth set in a straight line and his chin tilted back, he nervously jerked his head from side to side, as though his collar were too tight. When we crossed over the track to where he was standing, he did not give Mutti a hug.

Picking up Mutti's suitcase, he asked, "How are you?" He didn't seem to care about an answer.

I expected us to go around the station, towards the center of town. Instead, my father walked back with us along the track until we reached a blacktop road. A right turn would have led to the outskirts of Bodenteich, but we went left, across the tracks in the direction of a tall pine forest. Deeper into the forest, a refugee camp, surrounded by a high barbed wire fence, was tucked away on the right side of the road beneath huge pine trees. I glanced over at my father to find out whether this was where we were going, but he shook his head.

Just past the fenced-in area, a dirt road veered off to the left. My father took the dirt road, and we followed him. Light brown pine needles crunched under our feet. Here and there we were forced to step over dried branches, fallen from the high trees. After a while, four squalid barracks came into view in a clearing. Ignoring Mutti altogether, my father spoke only to me.

"This place is nicknamed the 'Ammo Camp.' It was used as an ammunition factory and an ammunition dump during the war. The buildings were so well camouflaged by the trees, the Allies never knew it was here. The barracks were built before the war as sleeping quarters for the Reich Labor Service and later they were used for the foreign forced laborers who worked here."

"Why are you telling the boy such nonsense?" Mutti asked. "We don't want a guided tour."

"I thought you ought to know."

"What we need to know is where we're going to live!" Mutti exclaimed.

"You'll see soon enough," my father snapped. He turned back to me. "At one time, there were over a hundred buildings on this site. Now, all that's left are these few barracks."

I stared at the shabby structures.

"Are you listening to me?" my father demanded.

"Yes, sir."

"Since the beginning of the year, the barracks have been used as apartments for refugees from East Prussia, Pomerania, and Silesia." His hand swept towards one of the buildings. "This is your new home."

* * *

Our barrack, with the painted number "33," stood in the shade of more than a dozen high pine trees. Using the large doorway on the right side, we entered a corridor which ran the entire length of the building. My father turned right and stopped at the third room on the street side. Reaching into his pocket, he pulled out a huge key, as long as my hand, and opened the door.

"It's four and one-half meters by four meters," he informed us without emotion. Two bunk beds were lined up on the left side of the room. A small table and three wooden chairs stood against the wall between two tiny windows looking out onto the dirt road. My father had left his small suitcase on the floor under the table. Along the wall to the right of the entrance stood a stove with two burners and next to it was a sink with a brass faucet.

"You can use the stove for cooking and heating," explained my father. "It's not fancy, but it's pretty new," he added lamely. "I came down from Uelzen last night to make sure everything was in working order." If he was trying to sound cheerful, he was failing miserably.

"What about a toilet and a shower?" Mutti demanded. It was only the second time she had spoken since we left the railroad station.

"There are separate bathrooms for men and women in the middle of the barrack, each with six toilet stalls."

"You mean to tell me there's no bathtub or shower? Then we're not much better off than we were under the Russians," Mutti snapped.

"What were you expecting? A hotel?" My father sneered.

Turning her back to us, Mutti knelt down on the floor to open our bags. As she started to unpack, my father pulled his small suitcase out from under the table, clicked open the latches and took a magazine out of the small leather briefcase inside. He sat rigidly in a chair, thumbing the pages. I hung in the doorway, uncertain whether to stay or leave. Suddenly, he looked up at me, his tone friendly.

"Günter, why don't you have a look around outside for a little while?"

With a sigh of relief, I turned towards the door. As I was leaving the room, Mutti caught my eye. The color had drained from her face, as though she were about to faint. Hesitating, I turned back to my father.

"Out you go!" he ordered. "It's time your mother and I had a talk, just the two of us."

* * *

In front of our barrack, across the road, six boys my age were playing soccer with a ball made of dark rags. Two banged-up metal military cable reels marked the goal. Just as I stepped outside, one boy scored a point. His teammates shouted "Tor! Tor!" One of their opponents, a boy with greasy blond hair, angrily threw down his cap.

I wandered around to the side of our building. Cement foundations marked the location of four long-vanished barracks. Five little girls with the giggles were playing hopscotch on the grayish cement floor. Chalk hopscotch patterns had been drawn on the other foundations as well, but of most interest to me were the long, yellow-brown marks covering most of the surface of the cement, as though it had been singed. What could they possibly be? I had never seen anything like them before.

Beyond the cement foundations, all I could see was pine forest, nothing but pine forest. I was hoping there would be some blueberries back there in the summertime, when a stocky boy with a shock of dark brown hair came over to where I was standing.

He spoke with a broad East Prussian accent. "I saw you when you arrived. Where're you from?"

"East Prussia."

"Me too."

"I could tell by your accent."

"Your mom looks nice," the boy continued. "Be glad you have her. Mine died in East Prussia of typhus. My dad's around though, and I have three brothers and two sisters."

"I just have one brother, but he's not staying with us right now," I said, not sure how much I should tell him about Hubert.

"Is that man who came with you your mother's boy friend? He looked kind of angry."

"No, he's my father."

"I'm sorry. What's wrong with him?"

"I wish I knew."

"My name's Werner Teschner," the boy said with a smile.

"Mine's Günter Nitsch," I replied, and we shook hands like old friends.

Suddenly I heard my father calling me. I hurried back to our room. Mutti had been crying. My father had his leather briefcase in his hand. He said, "I'll see you on Saturday night." He left his small suitcase behind.

* * *

Across from our barrack, on either side of the small makeshift soccer field, two long, narrow structures stood facing each other, separated by about fifty meters of empty space. Each structure was divided into woodsheds. We were assigned a shed towards the center of the building on the left. Every family with a woodshed also had a chopping block and a sawhorse out front.

To my surprise, my father really did return the following Saturday to spend the day with us. As soon as he arrived, he changed out of his customary business suit and tie, into old baggy pants and a black-and-white checkered shirt, the first time I had seen him in casual clothes.

"Let's tackle the pile of wood you've collected out by the shed," he said to me, with scarcely a glance at Mutti. "I've been cooped up inside all week."

My father and I pulled the double-handled saw back and forth, systematically reducing the pile to kindling size. The only noise, other than the rhythmic grinding of metal on wood, was the constant drone of aircraft overhead.

"Why're there are so many airplanes flying past the Ammo Camp? They've been going non-stop, day and night, since we got here."

"Didn't anyone tell you the Russians have blockaded Berlin?" my father answered impatiently. From the way he looked at me, I was certain he thought I was an idiot for asking. "They're the American Raisin bombers. If it weren't for the food and fuel being dropped from those planes, the people in Berlin would either starve to death or be forced to surrender to the Communists."

"No one mentioned it. How far is Bodenteich from the Soviet Zone anyhow?"

"Five kilometers, more or less. Why?"

I imagined Russian soldiers with fish can submachine guns, slipping across the border to search for people, like us, who had crossed the border illegally.

"Do you think Russian soldiers would ever come as far as Bodenteich?"

"Where'd you get a dumb idea like that?" my father asked.

That was the longest talk he and I had. Somehow, after that, I didn't feel like asking any more questions.

For the rest of the day, I left my parents alone as much as possible. I felt no love for my father, but he had the money to provide for us, to put food on our table. It was my hope that by keeping out of their way, they would have the opportunity to set things right, but they did not set things right. The following weekend, my father came back to pick up his suitcase.

"I've landed a job as a pastry chef in Cologne," he announced. "Until I can get us all an apartment, I'll send you money every month and I'll come to visit as often as I can."

"Don't lead us on like that. You don't believe it yourself," Mutti replied, starting to sob.

"How dare you doubt my word!" he snapped.

Seeing Mutti cry made me feel suddenly brave.

"It's a promise then?" I dared to ask him. Whirling around, he glared at me, as angry as the brutal Russian soldier who had kicked me in Palmnicken. I took a quick step backwards.

"Are you both deaf? Of course it's a promise," he answered, but he didn't meet my eyes.

Moments later, as I watched him take the beaten trail through the pine forest, I clenched my fist and pounded it hard against the table. How I would have liked to slug him at that moment! Mutti didn't make the slightest effort to accompany my father the one-and-a-half kilometers to the railroad station. I was proud of her.

* * *

Fathers were also a problem for the other children in the refugee camp. Many fathers had been killed fighting in the war, most of them in Russia. Others were missing in action or were prisoners of war in Siberia. Only a few fathers lived in the camp. Of those, nearly half were amputees, or limped, or were deaf, or were half blind. Some, like Mr. Boltermann, a short, skinny man who lived with his wife and five children at the end of the hall, had lost their minds. Mr. Boltermann took deep drags on a cigarette as he shuffled from his room to the door in the middle of the barrack leading to the outside. His teeth were tobacco stained and crooked. To hide them, he tried to keep his mouth clamped shut, even when he talked.

"The youngest boy is a Russian's child," it was rumored about the baby Mrs. Boltermann recently brought back with her from East Prussia. She had spent nearly four years under the Russians. Mr. Boltermann had been in the British Zone since the end of the war. Whenever he got drunk, and he got drunk at least every Friday, if not more often, he beat up his wife just like the Russian barber had done to his wife in Goldbach. As his shouts and her screams reverberated through the corridor, our neighbors shook their heads.

"There he goes again," one woman confided to another. "A violent man like that should keep away from the booze."

"It'll come to a bad end one of these days," her friend agreed. "Just mark my words."

Their remarks gave me the shivers. I worried about Mutti's safety, as well as my own.

I felt sorry for Boltermann's children, who often ran around with black and blue marks on their faces, arms, and legs. Mrs. Boltermann always wore long-sleeved dresses with long hemlines; only the welts on her face were visible. She was a walking heap of misery.

* * *

The woodshed compartment next to ours was assigned to an East Prussian named Emil Siemokat, a man with a perpetual smile who shared a room in our barrack with his younger sister and his mother. Although Mr. Siemokat was around thirty years old, his mother and his sister still called him "Emilke" or "Little Emil." He was anything but little. He was a tall, skinny man with a red face and a long, narrow nose.

All of the grown ups in our barrack called him Emil although he never dared to call any of them by their first names. No one seemed to take him seriously except me. I always called him Mr. Siemokat. He sometimes called me Günter, other times simply Landsmann (Countryman).

"Why do you call me that?" I asked him one day.

"Even though we're far from our homeland, we East Prussians have to stick together, don't you agree?"

"We sure do."

Mr. Siemokat was always willing to help me split a tough block of wood, or to repair my hatchet. He even knew how to make and install a new handle. Although he was quite handy, he was unemployed. When I asked him one day, what kind of a trade he had learned, he replied, "Actually none. I helped my dad on the farm 'til I was drafted in 1939. After the war I had some odd jobs, but you know how it is."

"Yes, Mr. Siemokat."

In front of his woodshed Mr. Siemokat had built himself a massive, roughhewn wooden table and a large wooden chair. Sometimes, after his chores, he sat in that plank chair and watched the passing scene. He knew everything about everybody. Often, when he was sitting in his plank chair, I hopped up on his sawhorse to ask him questions. He loved to talk.

Mr. Siemokat spoke with a terrible stammer, especially when several people were around; however, I soon found that, if I did not look him directly in the face, his speech problems disappeared. He had been stationed in Poland and in Russia. I wondered whether he stammered as a result of the war, but I never dared ask him.

* * *

The school was two kilometers away in Bodenteich, although in nice weather we could cut the distance by taking a rough footpath through the woods. Once we crossed the railroad tracks, we passed a cluster of tidy brick houses, and then continued down Main Street. The school building was on the other side of the Market Square.

Wolfgang Berg and Rudolf Weber were two of the boys with whom Werner and I usually walked back and forth to school. Wolfgang had never known his father, who had been missing in action since the first months of the war. Rudolf's father had died along the Russian front.

"How about your dad?" Wolfgang asked as we walked to class one day.

"He's still alive," I was ashamed to admit, "but I don't remember seeing him for more than four weeks altogether my entire life."

"Is he in a Russian camp?"

"He might as well be. He's in Cologne. He promised to send for us, but I don't think he will."

"Why on earth not?"

"I've asked myself the same question. Who knows what makes him tick?"

Yet without admitting it to my friends, in a way I felt responsible for his absence. "I don't like you anymore! Go back to the war!" I had yelled at him just before he smacked me on the railroad platform in Königsberg in January 1945. No wonder he didn't want to have me around.

I had not felt welcome at school from the very first day. The minute I walked into my classroom, many of the local children groaned, as if to say, "Another refugee!"

The teacher, Mr. Zimmermann, assigned me a seat with the other children from the Ammo Camp in the rear of the room. The better-dressed Bodenteich children sat towards the front. I counted heads. Including me, forty-seven children made up the class.

"They stick us in the back because we're all such dummies," Rudolf explained later. He had the annoying habit of brushing his dingy blond hair out of his eyes every few minutes.

"I think it's because we're a year or two older and taller than everyone else," Wolfgang countered. "If we sat in front, no one could see the blackboard."

Most of the children from the camp wore ragged clothes, in contrast to the well-dressed "natives." As soon as the temperature began to get warmer in May, we came barefoot to school. The natives wore clean socks and brown leather sandals. Some of the girls wore short, snow-white socks and bright red sandals. My hand-me-down clothes from Oldendorf were nearly all for cold weather. Mutti worried they would be too small for me by the time the next winter rolled around.

Mr. Zimmermann, who taught religion, was an expert on the Old Testament. He was older than the other teachers in Bodenteich, and very tall. Although he was skinny, he had a round potbelly, as if he had swallowed a medicine ball. He did not trust either his belt or his suspenders to hold up his trousers, using both of them every day. During Nazi times, Mr. Zimmermann had been the principal of the school and a Party member. After the war, the British military government demoted him to teacher, replacing him as principal with a woman named Klemens. From what I heard, Mrs. Klemens belted all her students, even the girls, by whacking the fingers of their outstretched hands with a stick.

Mr. Zimmermann, also a strict disciplinarian, could not tolerate a noisy classroom. If the noise level was too high, he would yell, "What's going on here? You're making a racket like a Jewish school!" None of us had any idea what he meant by that remark, but whenever we heard it, we knew we were in for it, or at least the boys were. Unlike Mrs. Klemens, Mr. Zimmermann never laid a hand on any of the girls.

Mr. Zimmermann required us to know the names of all of the books of the Old Testament. He made us memorize many of his favorite psalms. He waved a copy of Dr. Martin Luther's Catechism at us and called out the number of a Commandment. Woe to the student who could not recite Luther's explanation by heart. If anyone was unprepared, Mr. Zimmermann whacked him with a big wooden ruler across the back, just as Mr. Raddatz had done in Goldbach, bringing even the toughest boys to tears.

"You're old enough now to know the Bible," he would snap. "Otherwise, if any of you slackers suddenly drops dead, you'll be headed straight to hell. Don't say I didn't warn you!"

Terrified, I studied hard in an attempt to please him. It was too much to take on God and Mr. Zimmermann at the same time. However prepared I felt, I prayed I would not be called upon to explain the Commandment, "Thou shalt not commit adultery." Those words had never meant much to me in the past, but now, when I thought about my father, they filled me with anger and shame. I wondered why God was punishing us instead of him. If only Opa were alive, he would know how to explain it.

For the good of our souls, Mr. Zimmermann urged us to attend the St. Petri Church in Bodenteich. Two or three times, he took our class there to explain the liturgy and the altar. The interior was much bigger than the tiny church in Goldbach. Twelve giant columns formed a rectangle in front of the elaborate altar. Just beneath the balcony, at the back of the church, were the words, "Bless the Lord, Oh my soul, and do not forget all His benefits. - Psalm 103.2."

One Sunday morning, I talked Mutti into taking me to church. No one else from the Ammo Camp was there. We stuck out like sore thumbs in our shabby clothing.

During the sermon, my mind wandered. I tried to appreciate the benefits the Lord had given us. Admittedly, we were still poor, but we had survived starvation and hardships, gotten out of Goldbach, and had crossed safely to the West. I prayed that some day we would move away from the Ammo Camp as well.

"What did you think of the church?" I asked Mutti on the way home.

"That's the last time I go there," she said. "At least until we have something proper to wear. Did you notice how everyone was staring at us?"

* * *

Most of the three hundred refugees in the Ammo Camp were unemployed. Mutti was one of the lucky ones. Soon after our arrival in Bodenteich, she found work on a farm a few kilometers away where she helped in the kitchen, cleaned the house, did laundry, and weeded the garden. As a result of her job, I came home every day to an empty room. Guilty about my father's abandonment, angry about my teachers in school, I secretly prayed that Aunt Käte and Uncle Hermann would take us back. Like many of the other refugee children, I wore a key on a piece of cord around my neck, giving me the freedom to come and go as I pleased. So sometimes, when life seemed too much for me to bear, I took my handcart and my hatchet and wandered into the forest to collect wood. No one was around to yell at me if I came back late, so I had time to stop and observe the birds, study the bugs, and watch the clouds in the sky, before getting down to work. I scrounged for branches on the forest floor and chopped them apart on a tree stump so they would fit in my cart. The smell of pine resin on my hands comforted me. In the forest, I felt at home.

Unusual treasures awaited me in the sandy ground under the pine trees. Live ammunition, cartridge cases, flattened gas mask containers, and rusted, spent machine-gun belts were scattered everywhere. In one sandy spot alone I found twenty-two shiny brass rifle cartridges and a few cartridge cases. By pressing my lower lip against a cartridge case and blowing inside, I made whistles. I hid the cartridges and cartridge cases at the bottom of the big bin in our woodshed, deciding to keep my ammunition a secret for a while.

My dream was to find a rifle so that Werner and I could go hunting. Sometimes I scouted the forest for deer and wild boar, imagining what wonderful trophies they would be, but the largest game I ever saw were rabbits.

Later that evening, I ran into Werner. "Tell me, has anyone ever found a rifle in the forest?"

"Why d'you ask?"

"Just curious."

"From what I hear, the only ones lying around are all rusted up. If you have any thought of finding one in good working order, you may as well forget about it."

"Well, I'm going to keep on looking just the same," I said, trying to hide my disappointment. "See you tomorrow morning!"

* * *

393

Not all of our teachers were mean. Mr. Heidecker, a jolly man with an easy smile, taught geography. I never saw him hit any of the students. He looked well nourished and had a slight paunch. A razor-thin part ran through thin hair slicked down with pomade. On entering the room, he greeted us each morning with a cheery, "Good morning children!" Setting down his briefcase, he opened the big window next to his desk, rubbed his hands together gleefully and shouted, "So? What are we going to find out today?"He lectured enthusiastically about rivers, seas, and mountains, and far away places like the North Sea and the Bavarian Alps. Once in a while, after a lesson about a particularly beautiful region, his face would beam as he predicted, "Boys and girls, one of these days, when you're grown up, you'll travel there and see for yourself. I'm sure of it. Then you'll remember your old geography teacher Heidecker."

One day, I brought in my Westermann Atlas to show him. "My Uncle Hermann gave it to me in Oldendorf," I explained. "He also started me on stamp collecting."

"That's a fine atlas you have there!" Mr. Heidecker exclaimed. "But all it has are maps."

"Isn't that what an atlas is supposed to have?"

"See if you can scrape together enough money to get one that has descriptions of the countries as well as maps. That way you can study more on your own."

Mr. Heidecker took a special interest in the children from the Ammo Camp, sometimes keeping Werner and me after school to talk to us about Great Britain, France, Spain, and the United States of America, even though we were not supposed to be studying them yet. No other teacher had ever been so kind to me. The only other times I stayed after school were for detention.

"Mr. Heidecker's lessons always seem too short. I could listen to him all day. Why can't the other teachers be like him?" I asked Werner one day as we straggled home.

"Mrs. Schuster could sure learn a thing or two from Mr. Heidecker," he agreed.

Wide-faced Mrs. Schuster, who taught mathematics, combed her hair straight back, twisting it into a tight bun. Teaching was an unbearable burden for her, her constant smile painted on to cover the misery inside. Rumor had it her husband had lost his life at Stalingrad and she was working only because she needed the money, not for the love of teaching. She also had her good qualities, only rarely hitting children who did not know the answers to her questions. Boys who misbehaved in class always received three sharp strikes on the rear with her bamboo stick.

Both Mrs. Schuster and Mr. Zimmermann drummed into us every day their belief that the refugee children would never amount to anything. If we did poorly on tests, Mrs. Schuster would shriek, "You're so stupid and so lazy, you'll all end up as ditch diggers!"

One afternoon, Mutti and I ran into Mrs. Schuster by chance in Bodenteich.

"Your son is hopeless at math," she told Mutti in front of me. "I'm convinced he'll never be able to figure out how to divide a fraction by a fraction. He doesn't prepare his homework and makes absolutely no contribution in class."

Mutti's face flushed, "Quite frankly, I didn't expect him to be your star pupil, but I hadn't realized it was as bad as all that. Perhaps you didn't know that Günter hasn't spent one whole year in school since December of 1944."

"In that case," Mrs. Schuster said, "he'll just have to make up for lost time. I've always done my duty as a teacher, but with nearly fifty children in my class I cannot give him or anybody else special attention."

"Well, thank you for bringing the matter to my attention. I'll see what I can do about it," Mutti replied.

"That would be well and good," Mrs. Schuster said abruptly and she briskly walked away.

I felt like ten pfennigs, but I was getting used to it. Mutti stood quietly for a moment, watching Mrs. Schuster disappear in the market crowd. Finally, she turned to me.

"Why didn't you tell me you were having so much trouble?"

"It's hopeless. There are so many things I don't understand, I don't even know where to begin."

"Don't be so hard on yourself. You just have to study harder that's all. And with those fractions, that's not difficult at all. I'll show you later."

"That would be nice," I replied, although I secretly had my doubts.

As soon as we returned home, Mutti spread out a newspaper on our table and set the smallest of our three cooking pots on top. Guided by the base of the pot, she drew a number of circles, cutting them into halves, thirds, quarters, sixths and eights. Watching her, I suddenly understood why an eighth was smaller than a third or a fourth.

On my next math test, a few days later, the questions seemed easier. Still, I was sure I had botched things, as usual.

When Mrs. Schuster returned my test, she glared at me. "Nitsch, all your answers were correct, although it's beyond me how you did it. However, all of the children you could have copied from made some mistakes, so I have no choice but to give you an 'A.' "

My cheeks burning with a mixture of pride and anger, I could think of nothing to reply except, "Thank you, Mrs. Schuster."

* * *

Mr. Schlemmer, in his early thirties, taught German, music, and history. He was only about two centimeters taller than I was. His dark brown wavy hair was parted on the right, and he spoke in a clear, booming voice. In a vain attempt to cover the smell of liquor on his breath, he crunched on hard white peppermint drops during class, sometimes chewing up an entire roll of candy during the lesson, as pearls of sweat formed on his forehead. Mr. Schlemmer instilled in us a wide variety of muddled information.

"If only the Americans had joined forces with us in the spring of '45!" he complained one day in history class. "Together we could have preserved our Fatherland and destroyed those Bolsheviks!"

"Are there any questions?" he asked, defiantly glaring down at us. No one dared to reply.

"Did you hear that nonsense?" I asked the other boys on the way home. "Has he lost his marbles?"

"He's totally nuts," Werner said.

"What an idiot!" Wolfgang fumed. "Nearly half his students lost their fathers in the war, and he's still dreaming of a Final Victory."

Even during German class, Mr. Schlemmer would somehow weave in a history lesson. He claimed to have found spearheads from the Stone Age in the Bodenteich area. We had our doubts, but he encouraged us to look around whenever we took a walk in the fields and in the forests. According to Mr. Schlemmer, there had never been any people as fine as the old Teutons. "The Teutons would never have tolerated an occupation force in their day," he announced with absolute certainty. He even taught us a number of runic characters.

"That zigzag letter looks like the one used by the SS," one boy pointed out. Mr. Schlemmer smirked and quickly changed the subject.

Very often, without any warning, Mr. Schlemmer's hot temper erupted, and he raised his voice or hit someone. None of the girls was ever struck; however, if a boy had not done his homework, Schlemmer delivered three sharp blows with a bamboo stick on his out-stretched left hand, taking care never to hit a student's "writing hand." As punishment for copying test answers from someone else, he used the bamboo stick on the boy's rear end. One day Mr. Schlemmer caught

Werner whispering to another boy during a German test. Judgment came instantly.

"Three strokes on your bottom after class!"

After the test, Werner strode up to the front of the room. Without the slightest trace of fear, he grabbed the teacher's desk with both hands and bent over. As the bamboo stick struck, it made a dull thud instead of the usual crisp whack.

Mr. Schlemmer looked puzzled. "What's going on here?" he demanded sharply.

He slid his hand down the seat of Werner's pants. A thin notebook had been slipped inside for cushioning. As soon as the notebook was removed, the stick came down with even more force than usual. From then on, Schlemmer patted the rear end of each boy waiting to be hit, carefully feeling for anything hidden under his pants. I dreaded the day when my turn to be tortured would come.

CHAPTER 29

A small, rickety truck stopped at the Ammo Camp. Since the truck had two wheels in the back and only one under its pointed front end, the driver had to take the curves slowly to avoid tipping over. A short, stocky man climbed out, his jet black hair tucked under a greasy leather cap. Ringing a loud bell, he immediately drew a crowd of children. He also got the attention of the women who spent their days leaning out of the barracks windows, their elbows propped up on pillows.

Taking a deep breath, he shouted, "Scrap iron, scrap metal, and paper! Good prices!" I couldn't place his accent.

He casually took out a cigarette, stuck it in his mouth under his waxed handlebar moustache, struck a match, and drew the smoke deep into his lungs. As he exhaled, he again shouted his verse, "Scrap iron, scrap metal, and paper. Good prices!"

So much hair stuck out from the scrap dealer's fleshy red nose, I wondered whether he had to shave his nostrils. Resting against the dark mat of hair protruding from the open collar of his shirt, the Lord Jesus hung from a small, golden cross.

I had heard about the scrap business in Bodenteich, but had not believed anyone would pay good money for such stuff. Certainly no one had paid me for the iron and paper I had brought to school in Langendorf. Three older boys suddenly appeared with a coil of greenish colored wire.

"What've you got?" the scrap dealer asked the first boy.

"Copper wire!"

Without saying a word, the scrap dealer pulled out a jackknife and scraped at the wire coil in several places. Wherever he scraped, tiny patches of reddish gold sparkled in the sun.

"Looks all right to me."

He placed the copper coil on the hook of his hanging scale. "It's nearly 1-1/2 kilos. Tell you what, I'll give two marks for it."

"It's a deal," the boy agreed, holding out a grimy hand for the two bills.

I was amazed. If a boy could get that much money for some corroded copper wire, perhaps I could get in on the act. We desperately needed the money. Mutti was no longer working on the farm. The farmer's daughter, laid off from her job in Hanover, had returned home to take over Mutti's responsibilities.

"Wait for me. I'll be right back," I called over my shoulder to the busy scrap dealer as I raced at top speed to our woodshed. Pitching the dried wood aside, I retrieved my brass rifle cartridges and cartridge cases, nearly five dozen shiny pieces in all, and dropped them into a small pail. I lugged my collection back to the street. Judging by the weight, I hoped to earn at least two marks, maybe even three.

"What've you got there, boy?" the scrap dealer inquired, his voice full of suspicion.

"Brass," I said, out of breath.

He looked into my pail and sneered.

"Piorun! Brass, my ass! That's live ammunition. Get out of my sight, ty balwan! I don't want that shit, piorun. No cartridges live or used, no ammunition, no weapons. Do you understand that, pal? Jesses,

Maria, Joseph! That stuff's as valuable as kamienie. Piorun! Don't you ever come back to me with crap like this!"

Several boys started to snicker. I felt like a fool. Just then, Werner poked me in the ribs. "Don't feel bad. You're new here. Most of us brought him ammunition the first time around."

"Really?"

"Of course. You should've asked me."

"I guess so. But how can we find copper wire or iron scrap?"

"Forget it. It's all gone. Once in a blue moon we'll find some by chance."

"Where'd those other boys find the wire?"

"I wish I knew. They probably stole it somewhere in Bodenteich. But here in the Ammo Camp, there's nothing left, at least nothing this guy would buy. All we find here is ammunition," Werner concluded with a big grin.

"One more thing. The guy talks funny. What did he mean by 'piorun' and by 'ty balwan'? And what is 'kamienie'?"

"He's from Upper Silesia. The people there speak half German, half Polish. I think 'piorun' means 'damn,' but I don't know about the rest."

"Did you see his cross? I've never seen the Lord Jesus hanging around someone's neck before."

"He must be Catholic. I've heard in Upper Silesia everyone is."

After that, whenever I went to collect wood, I hoped to find a coil of copper wire or a lead cable filled with copper wire, but I never did. Werner was right. All I found was a plentiful supply of ammunition.

Since Mr. Siemokat had been in Poland during the war, I went to him about the strange words used by the scrap dealer.

"Excuse me, Mr. Siemokat, but do you happen to know what 'piorun' means?"

"Piorun? It means 'damn.' I heard it in Poland all the time."

"And what about 'ty balwan' and 'kamienie'?"

"Where'd you hear those words?"

"From the scrap dealer."

"'Ty balwan' means 'you blockhead,' 'you idiot'. It's quite an insult. But 'kamienie' isn't anything bad. How'd he use it?"

"He said something was 'as valuable as kamienie.'"

"It means 'stones.' Something as valuable as stones. Why on earth would he say a thing like that?"

* * *

Mutti landed a new job at a construction site not far from our barrack. She often left with me when I went to school in the morning and did not return until after six or seven o'clock in the evening. A printing plant was supposed to be built at the construction site. All that was left of the building which had once stood there was the cement foundation. Giant trucks rumbled in all day long from far away cities. From the rubble left over from the war, workers hauled in loads of individual bricks caked with mortar, and clumps of bricks still stuck together.

Mutti worked with a group of women, sitting all day on stools, knocking the mortar off the bricks with hammers. It took considerable skill to pound and scrape the stuff off the brick without damaging it. Since Mutti was paid by the number of bricks she cleaned every day, I helped her nearly every afternoon. The work was hard, but it paid better than the job on the farm. We needed the money she earned to buy bread, potatoes, margarine, lard, and sugar beet syrup. Although my father had promised to send us money once a month, we had not yet received any.

By the time I got home, I was usually so tired I collapsed into bed right after a late supper. There was hardly any time for homework and I soon forgot the promises I had made to Uncle Hermann to study every day. Most of the other refugee boys I met agreed that homework was only for girls, for the "natives" from Bodenteich, and for sissies.

* * *

One day an unusual couple moved into a street-side room near the middle of our barrack. The wife was at least 1.90 meters tall, an ugly giantess. Her beady-eyed husband was midget-sized. There was no way they could walk arm in arm; it was physically impossible. They always looked serious. I sensed they could not stand children, perhaps because they had none of their own. The other boys and I nicknamed them "Big Mama" and "Shorty."

A week after they moved in, they did something no one else in the barracks had ever done before. They used four sticks to mark out a plot, close to five meters wide and about ten meters long, in front of their two windows. Shorty stretched a long cord from stick to stick. Then they both got down to work. For two days they walked back and forth between the Ammo Camp and Bodenteich, pulling their handcart. Each time, they returned with another load of rich humus soil. With skill and patience, they piled the humus on top of the hard-packed, sandy ground. Although they tried their best to level it out, the plot tilted down slightly, towards the dirt road. Next they planted seeds. Judging from the little colorful paper packages, it was going to be a vegetable garden and not a flower garden. Time passed and the first green shoots came up. Big Mama and Shorty sprinkled them with water at least twice a day. They stood at their open windows and admired their tiny plants for hours.

The women in our barrack were delighted with the garden. The children hated it. We could no longer cut across to the entrance of the barrack. Now we had to go all the way around.

"Who do they think they are?" Werner complained to me. "They have some nerve taking away part of our playground like that."

One morning, there was great excitement because a child had run across the humus beds during the night. Judging from the tiny foot prints, it could not have been any of my friends. We were all sorry we hadn't been in on it.

* * *

On the way home from school every afternoon, Werner, Rudolf, Wolfgang, and I crossed the railroad tracks around the same time that a train left the Bodenteich station in the direction of Uelzen.

"Do you think the train could crush pebbles the size of a walnut?" I wondered out loud one day.

"There's only one way to find out!" Wolfgang replied. He quickly lined up three small stones in neat rows on each of the rails. The four of us ducked behind some bushes as the train rolled into the station. After a few minutes, the train headed our way. It rolled over the stones, grinding them to bits. All that was left was a tiny bit of sand on the slanted edges of the rails.

Satisfied with our experiment, we walked along the path to the Ammo Camp. Once we had turned off the dirt road onto the footpath, we rested our book bags on a tree stump and began to exchange the latest Wild West books about our heroes, Tom Mix, Billy Jenkins, Buffalo Bill, and Tom Prox. The skinny novels cost thirty pfennigs each in the bookstore in Bodenteich. New ones usually came out on the first Monday of the month.

"Sounds like Indians on the trail!" Werner announced dramatically as we heard a branch snap. To our surprise, Big Mama and Shorty appeared, seemingly out of nowhere, walking past us in the direction of the barracks. Although none of us said a word, as soon as they had passed, Werner gave a loud war cry and then we all burst out laughing.

The next day on the way home, Rudolf felt challenged by the empty rail. He picked out two stones the size of small cabbage heads.

"Let's see what the train does with these!"

"They're much too big," I predicted as we rushed into the bushes to watch what would happen. We heard the train leave the station. It slowly gathered speed as it got closer to us, but suddenly the engineer applied the brakes. Cold sweat broke out on my forehead. Before the train came to a full stop, we all started running at top speed towards the Ammo Camp. Avoiding the dirt path, we raced instead right through the forest. After a few minutes, Werner was brave enough to turn around and look back.

"Stop running! No one's after us!" he yelled.

We tumbled onto the ground, out of breath.

"Do you think anyone spotted us?"

"Maybe the engineer thought the stones rolled on there," Wolfgang said hopefully.

"How many rocks have you seen rolling uphill?" Rudolf countered.

"I don't think we should try any more crushing experiments," Werner said with conviction. We were all quick to agree with him.

Later that night a violent thunderstorm woke me up with blinding bursts of lightning followed by terrifying cracks of thunder, as loud as grenade explosions. Clinging to my bed, I remembered Opa's words from long ago.

"Thunder?" he had told me. "Why, it's only God, scolding people who have disobeyed his Commandments." Had I really behaved so badly? Surely Opa hadn't thought God would bother with childish pranks?

"Are you awake?" Mutti asked.

"Yes."

"Don't worry about the storm. There are two lightning rods on the roof. It'll be over soon. Go back to sleep."

"Thanks, Mutti."

* * *

Aside from the scrap dealer's truck and a few old jalopies driven by farmers selling potatoes and vegetables, cars rarely came to the Ammo camp. So when on a warm evening, a few days after the thunderstorm, a car not only arrived in the camp but also parked on the dusty dirt road right in front of our barrack, I watched from our window with great interest.

"It looks like someone has a wealthy visitor," I commented to Mutti while we ate supper.

There was a knock on our door. I opened it to two well-dressed men wearing hats. They introduced themselves as detectives from the Criminal Investigation Department of the German Railroad in Uelzen.

"Your son and some other boys tried to derail the Uelzen train," one of them told Mutti solemnly.

"Is this true?" she asked me.

I could feel the color drain out of my face. My knees felt like jelly and I would have liked to take off at that moment, never to return. "We were only trying to crush some stones," I stammered.

"If you put stones on the track again, there will be very dire consequences," the older detective warned me. "Is that clear?"

"Yes, sir." My voice was no louder than a whisper.

After the men drove away, Mutti started to cry. Without a word, she left our room. Through the window I saw her walking to our compartment in the wood shed. She returned with a bow that I had made from a hazelnut branch. Using a kitchen knife, she cut the string. Then she gave me my biggest thrashing since I had broken the windowpane in Plötzin.

The next day, on the way to school, I told the other boys what had happened. They had also been visited by the detectives.

"Schlemmer has nothing on my mother when it comes to punishment," I complained.

"Same for mine," Rudolf agreed.

"Me too," Wolfgang added.

"The three of you got off easy. My father did the beating," Werner chimed in. "I'm sure I got the worst of it."

We walked on for a while before Rudolf asked, "It's spooky how they found out. How did they know it was us?" None of us had an answer.

From then on, whenever we walked home, we made sure not to kick anything that might accidentally land on the tracks. After a day or two, Mutti acted as if nothing had happened. That was something I loved about her. She never bore a grudge for long.

* * *

On those afternoons when I wasn't helping Mutti clean bricks at the construction site, my only chore was to collect wood and chop it for our kitchen stove. Werner was a year older than I was. He, his younger brother, Bert, Wolfgang, and I would go together into the forest to find wood. Close to our barracks everything had been picked clean. There was hardly ever a dry branch on the ground. We had to go quite a distance to find thick, dried pine branches. The wood was best if the break off point looked as if it had been dipped in white, gray, or yellow crystallized powder. This meant the branches were full of dried resin and would make good fuel for our stoves. I remembered that from Goldbach.

As we searched for wood, we constantly unearthed cartridges and cartridge cases left over from the war. There were calibers for many kinds of pistols and rifles and even big ones for the machine guns installed in fighter planes. I was convinced all this stuff was harmless, if one knew how to handle it. My only fear was of incendiary bombs. Although everyone warned us about them, we had no idea what one looked like so we kept away from large rusty objects and hoped for the best.

* * *

Remembering the loam balls I had played with in Goldbach, I picked up some cartridge cases and stuck them into my pocket.

Werner looked at my quizzically. "Are you out of your mind? What do you need those for?"

"Watch!"

I found a long thin stick and set a cartridge case on top. Holding the stick behind my back, I swung it with force over my right shoulder. The cartridge case flew off the stick with a loud whistling sound, like a rocket. Werner's eyes opened wide with astonishment. He and the other boys rushed to find sticks. The four of us hurled such a heavy barrage into the forest that, within a short while, we used up our supply.

"How far do you think they went before hitting the ground?" Bert wondered.

"Half way back to Camp, at least," Wolfgang guessed.

"Way farther than that!" I bragged.

"Do you really think so?" Werner said, looking worried. "I hope we didn't hit anyone. Then we'd really get it. If we play this game again, let's make sure the barracks are out of range."

Searching in the sand, we also found unused rifle cartridges. After unloading our wood in the sheds, we stuffed the rifle cartridges into our pockets and headed for the concrete platform in front of a deserted barrack some distance away. Werner, who had experience in such matters, had brought along a pair of pliers. After he pried out the bullet from the rifle cartridge, he poured a snakelike trail of black powder onto the cement floor. The powder fell out in a series of tiny dark gray wafers. He dropped a lighted match at one end of the snake and "Shoosh!" the powder flared and was gone. All that was left was a long yellow-brown mark on the weathered gray concrete floor. Judging from the similar marks on the cement and the piles of spent shell cases, the other boys had been at this game many times before.

"You don't need pliers. I'll show you an easier way," Wolfgang boasted. He stuck the bullet end of a cartridge into a tight crack in the wall and wiggled the shell. The bullet popped out. With a little practice, I was soon as good at it as he was.

"I'm going to keep my rifle bullets for my slingshot," I decided.

Werner advised against it. "Forget it, they're too heavy. Pistol bullets are the best for a slingshot, but it's very difficult to pry them out. The cartridge is too short, so there's no leverage."

"But I need something more effective than pebbles!"

"Just use small pieces of lead cable. They're really awesome. I'll show you how to make them."

"But where can I find some lead around here?"

"When we get back to our wood shed, I'll give you a piece of cable."

Meanwhile, Werner had saved his biggest stunt for last. He poured the contents of six cartridges onto one tiny heap on the cement, making a thin snake of powder one meter long, leading away from the pile. Finally he covered the little heap with a small can. Warning us to step back, he dropped a lighted match on the snake. The flame sped along the powder until the can flew into the air with a loud pop. We all cheered wildly. My admiration for Werner had never been greater.

From a distance a tall, pimply boy had been watching us. He must have been at least fourteen years old, perhaps even fifteen, and he had the sort of cocky face that made me want to put my fist into it.

"Do you know him?" I whispered to Werner.

"His name's Ludwig and he lives in a different barrack. I heard he goes to the Middle School in Uelzen, so I figure he's very smart. I can't stand him because he's so arrogant."

Ludwig sauntered closer to us. "That's really kid stuff. Ever see these beauties?" He held out his right hand and showed us little black pieces shaped like broken bits of hollow noodles.

Werner nodded. "Sure. But I don't know whether they're from a smoke grenade or an artillery shell. I just call them smoke bombs."

"Me too," Ludwig agreed.

"They're very hard to find," Werner pointed out.

Ludwig walked with a self-confident swagger over to the cement platform. He stuffed all but one smoke bomb back into his pocket. With a flourish, he took out a real cigarette lighter. Holding the smoke bomb with the tips of the fingers of his left hand, he flicked on the lighter with his right and held the flame against the end of the tiny black noodle. At first the noodle glowed faintly, giving off only a thin wisp of smoke. As soon as Ludwig blew out the flame, black smoke began to billow into the air. He quickly tossed the smoke bomb into a rusty oil drum. What happened next was astonishing. Thick pitch-black smoke belched out of the barrel. For a few moments, we could not even see the forest behind the building.

"If you want to chase someone out of a hole, there's nothing better to do it with," Ludwig bragged.

"Where can we get hold of some of that stuff?" Werner asked him.

"I'm not going to let you in on my stash, but I'll tell you what. If you dig long enough in the sandpit over there, just beyond that crooked pine tree," Ludwig pointed off to the left, "you're bound to find a few pieces." With that, Ludwig strutted away like a king who regretted having talked to the riffraff.

The four of us rushed over to the other side of the tree and set to work. Sure enough, after digging in the sand with our sticks for a long time we finally found a few decent pieces of black noodle. Each one was half as long as a finger and so brittle, they were easy to break into even smaller pieces. Since they had been buried deep in the sand, most of the pieces were damp. Werner lit one of the few dry ones. The acrid smoke made our eyes tear. After we had all taken a turn, we vowed to come back to find some more.

Afraid of crushing the precious pieces in my pants pocket, I tied my damp smoke bombs up in my handkerchief and tucked it away in my shirt pocket. Giddy with excitement, we headed back to our barrack. My conscience pricked me for a moment. Mutti had absolutely forbidden me to play with ammunition and powder of any kind. Certain she'd never find out, I pondered the delicious possibilities of smoke bombs. What if I threw one down a rabbit hole? When the rabbit came up for air, I would catch it in a burlap sack. A fat rabbit for the big pot on our stove would be a nice surprise for Mutti. Although we always had enough bread and potatoes, I had not had any meat since we ate Uncle Hermann's roasted rabbits in Oldendorf.

* * *

It was already early June and we still had not received a single pfennig from my father. Mutti wrote him long letters with greetings from me added on at the end. All he sent were two different postcards, both showing the Cologne Cathedral. Mutti taped the cards onto the wall between the two windows, just above our table. I had to look at them daily, whether I wanted to or not. We can't buy anything with those! I thought.

Two weeks later, on our way home from school, the other boys and I were waiting to cross the tracks. As the train rushed by, Big Mama and Shorty caught up with us. We tried our best to ignore them. Big Mama bent down to her tiny husband and whispered something in his ear and they both exchanged nasty smirks.

Once it was safe to cross over, Werner urged us to slow down. Big Mama and Shorty were barely out of earshot when he asked excitedly, "Did you see them whispering? Did you see how Shorty grinned at Big Mama?"

"This calls for a meeting!" I agreed. "I think we all know what you're getting at."

We ran to a hidden spot, surrounded by bushes. Leaning our school bags against a pine tree, we sat down on huge tree stumps, legs crossed, Indian style. Werner and Rudolf pulled small pipes from their pockets and stuffed them with dried leaves.

"How can you smoke that stuff?" Wolfgang asked. "When I tried it a few weeks ago, it made me sick."

411

"I vowed never to take it up," I said. "When I was living under the Russians, I knew a man who actually preferred cigarettes to bread. Can you imagine?"

"Besides, the Indians smoked when they made peace. How can you smoke that stuff, when we're going to talk about war?" Wolfgang teased.

"Don't talk nonsense!" Werner said. He sat quietly for a moment, puffing contentedly on his pipe. Then he nodded like a wise old Indian chief. "Yes, we're going to talk about war."

"Right!" Rudolf agreed. "They snitched on us for sure. How could we have been so dumb?"

"Maybe they did and maybe they didn't," Wolfgang said.

"Revenge would be sweet, but we really should be sure," I said uncertainly.

Werner looked disgusted. "You guys are too wishy-washy. Rudolf's right. They did us in. And if they didn't, then I'm Kaiser Wilhelm."

The matter didn't look so clear cut to me. Still, I didn't dare argue the point any further.

"It wouldn't be smart to do anything today or tomorrow. We should let a little time go by first," Werner said, quickly taking charge. "Anyhow, I'm beginning to get an idea, but I need to think about it for a few days."

"What do you have in mind?" we all asked at once.

"I'll let you in on it when I'm sure it will work," he answered with a wicked grin.

* * *

Late in the afternoon, a few days later, I was chopping wood in front of our storage shed, while contentedly chewing the pieces of tar I had retrieved in shiny, pitch-black clusters from empty oil drums and rain gutters. Trying not to gum up my molars, I practiced keeping the tar between my front teeth. Cherry tree resin would have tasted better, but in contrast to Goldbach, all of the fruit trees in Bodenteich grew behind the secure fences of private homes. After a while my teeth began to ache, so I spat the well-chewed piece of tar into the sand. It lay in a dark clump, like a miniature hedgehog with its tiny yellow spikes shaven off.

My work finished, I was bored. Even Mr. Siemokat wasn't around to talk to. I needed something interesting to do. A piece of rail, about as long as my lower arm, had been left behind by the former occupants of our woodshed. I often used its surface to shape wire or nails, or to cut thick wire apart. Now I placed the rail on the chopping-block and went back to the old wooden box in the shed. I picked out three cartridge cases from which I had already pried out the bullets. I had also long since put the powder to other uses. Slipping two of the cartridge cases into my left pocket, I set the third one on the rail with the detonator pointing sideways, away from my body. A cluster of small children edged in close to watch.

I lifted my hatchet, blunt side down, and hit the end of the first cartridge case a crushing blow. The exploding primer blasted like a rifle shot and the end of the pounded cartridge case was transformed into a small brass egg with a long discolored hole in the middle. Applause burst from my small audience, much to my delight. Even more satisfying than the children's reaction, an old woman looked on angrily, while Mr. Boltermann, the old grouch, shot me a dirty look.

Inspired by their disapproval, I whammed the hatchet down on the other two cartridge cases even harder than before and was about to go back for more cartridge cases when Werner suddenly appeared. He towered over the smaller children, who quickly scattered, disappointed that the show was over so soon.

"Having fun?"

"Yeah. I love the smell after the explosion, but the best for me is knowing how much it upsets the adults."

"Same here."

"I've got some more, if you'd like to do some."

"No, not now. I've got an important message for you. Meet me at my woodshed about half an hour before dark. Rudolf and Wolfgang will be there too."

* * *

The other boys were already sitting on a sawed off tree trunk when I joined them just before sunset. As soon as I arrived, Werner laid out his plan.

"In the Wild West, Billy Jenkins would have chased people like Big Mama and Shorty out of town with his Winchester," he began. "Compared to him, our revenge will be more like a prank, but I think we'll get back at them where it really hurts." Then he gave us his instructions.

"Let's do it!" Rudolf exclaimed, after we'd heard Werner out. Wolfgang and I enthusiastically agreed.

At twilight, we all went to the men's bathroom. The doors to all six stalls stood open revealing several wet toilet seats. Two of the bowls were filled to overflowing with solid waste. No one said a word. With a nod from Werner, Rudolf and I followed him to the bathroom window overlooking the dirt road. He had chosen Rudolf and me to work with him because we were the strongest. Meanwhile Wolfgang went back to the hallway carrying three finger-length pieces of black noodle, a match, and a matchbox. His job was to shove three smoke bombs through the gaping crack between the floor and the hallway door leading into Big Mama and Shorty's apartment.

As soon as we heard loud screams from the hall, we jumped out of the bathroom window. The thick black smoke pouring out of the building hid us from view as we took our positions next to the huge rain barrel standing to the left of Big Mama's vegetable garden.

"Eins, zwei, drei!" Werner whispered. We pushed with all our strength against the enormous barrel. It would have been easier to push it straight down, but the plan was to tip it to the right so the water would do the most damage. For a second there was panic because the thing would not budge. Once it started to move, the weight of the rainwater brought it down with a thud. Torrents of water gushed out over the frail humus beds.

Rushing back in through the men's room window, we used three big strides to cross the smoky hallway. We cut through the ladies' bathroom and climbed out of the window on the far side of the building. Wolfgang was already waiting for us in the forest. The four of us raced over to the cement platform where we had first fooled around with the smoke powder. Once safely there, we burst out laughing.

"When I slipped the stuff under the door, there were screams from inside," Wolfgang reported. "I heard the key turning in the lock and then the door flew open."

"Did anyone see you?" Werner wanted to know.

"I couldn't see them, so I figure they couldn't see me either. What about your part of it?"

"It couldn't have gone any better," Werner said smugly.

A short while later, trying to look as innocent as possible, we ambled over to the front of our barrack. A half circle of people, mostly children, had formed around the remnants of the vegetable garden. In the glow of the streetlights, Shorty slumped against the wall. He seemed to be at a loss about what to do. Perhaps he was waiting for instructions from Big Mama who stood by his side, wringing her hands, tears streaming down her cheeks.

An elderly woman complained bitterly about the "bad elements" in our barrack. A one-armed middle-aged man was particularly outraged. "Things like this would never have happened under Hitler!" he asserted angrily.

"Did you hear that? He'd better be quiet, or he'll be next," Werner whispered.

"Careful, I know him. He's crazy," I whispered back, "and bow-legged too."

"He sure is. An East Prussian sow and seven piglets could run between his legs and he wouldn't even notice," Werner said, with a wicked grin.

"Are you planning to rebuild the vegetable garden?" a scraggly woman asked Big Mama.

"I don't know what we're going to do," Big Mama replied, with a shrug of her shoulders.

Werner tapped me on the shoulder. "Look at the children!"

Boys and girls were already trampling through the mud, celebrating the return of their treasured playground.

In the bright sunlight the following morning, we could fully assess the damage the rainwater had done. Uprooted baby radishes and tiny carrots, shriveled parsley sprouts, and small soggy lettuce heads floated in shallow pools surrounded by heaps of black humus. A heavy rain the following day washed away every trace of the soil which had once covered the sandy ground.

Werner and the others never seemed to feel sorry for what we had done, but each time I saw Big Mama and Shorty after that my conscience nagged me. What stung me the most was Mutti's comment to me right after the incident.

"I can't understand how parents can let their children behave like that," she said. "To think someone could have been mean enough to destroy that poor couple's beautiful garden."

* * *

In the middle of July, Schlemmer told us one last story about the proud and noble Teutons, and then he dismissed us for summer vacation. I raced home to put away my book bag for the next six weeks. After slathering some bread with a thick layer of lard, and grabbing an apple, I rushed over to the construction site. Mutti's boss, Mr. Lauritz, had seen me helping her in the afternoons. He had asked Mutti whether I could continue to work during my vacation. Mutti decided I would work every day, but only until lunch time, and I was very happy to help her.

Mr. Lauritz was also an East Prussian. His wooden leg and the scarred left side of his face were reminders of his service as an officer in the army. Most of the wounded veterans at the Ammo Camp were bitter, angry men, but Mr. Lauritz always had a cheerful smile. He even sat down with us sometimes and joined in the work. At least once, sometimes twice a week, he chugged into Bodenteich in his old car to buy fresh rolls for all of the workers.

* * *

In August, when we were beginning to get bored with vacation, Circus Haase set up a big tent in town. None of us could afford to buy tickets. Still, we hung around outside, watching the men work and gaping at the wagons full of wild animals. A tall man in breeches and riding boots seemed to be in charge. We were thrilled with his pitch-black handlebar mustache and his greased black hair slicked back. The next time he passed by, Werner startled us by asking, "Sir, do you need any help?"

The man stopped and looked us over. He called out to a young man with an acne pocked face who was leading a team of horses, "Can you find some work for these boys?"

"I'll see what I can do!"

The man with the horses studied us carefully. "It's hard work, carrying wooden beams from the wagons to the proper places around the tent. Are you sure you fellows are up to it?"

"We can handle it, sir," Werner answered promptly.

"How old are you?"

"I'm fourteen and my friends are nearly thirteen," Werner replied solomnly. I was impressed by how fast Werner had made us all a year older.

"All right, here's the deal. You can work for a few hours now, and all afternoon tomorrow. When you finish, each of you will get two free tickets."

"Agreed!" said Werner, without even consulting us. He knew that's what we wanted.

The job was hard, but by working in teams of two it was manageable. By late the following afternoon, we each received our tickets for performances on the second and the third day.

We went first to the evening show, leaving the Ammo Camp much too early in our excitement. Taking a shortcut along the railroad tracks on the Bodenteich side of the tracks we passed a private house. Apple trees heavy with fruit tempted us from behind the sturdy garden fence.

Werner quickly sized up the situation. "I could climb over it, but I'd rather not meet the owner on the other side," he concluded.

"There's more than one way to skin a cat," Rudolf said. He edged up close to the picket fence and calculated the distance between his head and a big firm apple dangling just above him. Without warning, he took a giant leap and landed with the apple in his hand.

"Not bad! Can you do that again? I bet you..."

"Thieves!" a wild-eyed hulk of a man yelled from the open doorway. He limped toward the garden door, waving a gnarled wooden cane. We backed off, but since the man was limping, none of us was in any particular hurry to leave. He could never outrun us.

"Rotten Ammo Camp refugee scum! You're worse than the gypsies before Hitler's time. Go back where you came from and don't come back!"

"What's his problem?" Rudolf grumbled as we walked towards the circus grounds. "There are plenty more apples where this one came from." He took out his pocketknife, cut the apple into four equal parts, and gave each of us a piece.

"Let's go to the circus!" Wolfgang yelled.

None of us had ever been to a circus before. Arriving well ahead of time, we found our seats in the huge tent and waited impatiently for the place to fill up. Once the performance started, we were thrilled to see jugglers, performing elephants, and trained horses in action. Also impressive was a bicycle rider doing headstands. When a lion tamer made four lions jump through rings of fire, I held my breath, awed that one man could have so much power over wild beasts. My favorites, however, were the trapeze artists. One of them, a young girl with black hair and a charming smile, won my heart. Walking home in the dark, we talked about the circus without interruption until we reached our barrack well past my bedtime. After I described everything I had seen to Mutti, I lay awake a long time, my heart pounding with excitement.

The circus was actually better the second time. The clowns were funnier in the afternoon because so many more children were in the audience.

"I'd go a third time if I had another ticket," Werner told us after the performance.

"I think I'm going to join them," I confided. The prospect of one day being able to swing high above the crowd to catch the beautiful trapeze artist in midair enticed me.

"What about your mother?"

"The way I figure it, with me out of the way, she wouldn't have to work so hard. And my father wouldn't care. He doesn't want me anyhow."

The temptation to run away was great, but a day or so later, when the circus pulled up stakes and left town, I was out chopping wood in the forest behind the Ammo Camp.

CHAPTER 30

*B*y the time school started again in the fall, word had gotten around that my friends and I had been to the circus twice. The "natives" were stunned by this information because they had only gone once. We never told them how we got the tickets. We just kept them guessing.

On the first day back, Mr. Schlemmer made an announcement. "As of August 1, 1949, our beloved Mr. Zimmermann has been reinstated as principal of our school. Mrs. Klemens will be an ordinary teacher again, as she was before. All in all, it looks as if things are getting back to normal. The Nazi witch-hunt after the war was rather unsettling to many of us. Now let's get down to work."

A few of the children shook their heads. Some shrugged. A few yawned. No one really cared which job Mr. Zimmermann had. We all knew that Principal Zimmermann would hit us just as hard and as often as Teacher Zimmermann had done previously.

* * *

Mr. Lauritz interrupted the work at the construction site for two weeks in September because so many of the women wanted to pick potatoes at one of the farms nearby. The farmers offered to pay them with potatoes. Winter was coming and we all needed to store food for the months ahead. All the hired pickers were from East Prussia, Pomerania, and Silesia.

After school, I took a shortcut through the forest to join Mutti at work. The farmer had already plowed up the leafy potato plants, tipping them over to one side so that the potatoes attached to the roots were more accessible. Even so, potato picking was backbreaking work. Each potato had to be clawed out of the dirt by hand, brushed clean with our fingers and then dropped into our individual wire collecting baskets. As soon as our baskets were full, we lugged them further down the row, dumped out the potatoes into waiting burlap sacks, and then started all over again. Most grownups knelt while digging for the potatoes. This put less pressure on their backs, but it also meant they had to keep getting up and down with a groan to dump potatoes into the burlap sacks. We younger pickers bent over at first, giving us easier access to the bags. After a while, all of us joined the adults on our knees. A full sack of potatoes, tied shut with string, stood higher than my waist. I admired the muscles of the farm hands who picked up the full sacks, hoisting them easily onto a horse-drawn wagon.

Highlighting the long afternoons were the mid-afternoon meals of white bread, cheese, and ham. We could not afford such delicacies at home.

"You know, I was just thinking about the afternoon meals Oma brought to us in the fields in Langendorf," I said to Mutti as we sat down to eat. "I once asked Opa how Vassily could eat so much. I guess now I understand why."

"One of these days I hope I'll be able to put ham, or cheese, or sausage on your school sandwiches instead of sugar beet syrup or lard," Mutti said, "but for now we'll just have to make do."

Just as Mutti had finished talking, the farmer's wife called me over to her giant food basket.

"Hey, skinny! There's one sandwich left. I hate to take it home. Help yourself!"

Although I was already as stuffed as a force-fed goose, I grinned at the farmer's wife. "If you put it that way, how can I say no? Thanks!"

Mutti shook her head. "Don't you get sick from overeating. That would be a new one."

"Don't worry about me, Mutti."

On our way home through the forest, I nearly stumbled over a whole array of chanterelles hidden in a soft, mossy spot. Mutti and I picked every last one. Mutti's apron pocket and my pants pockets bulged with mushrooms. Later, Mutti washed the mushrooms, cut off their roots, chopped the mushrooms into small pieces, and fried them with lard and onions. They tasted nearly like meat.

"Too bad we can't eat like this every day," Mutti commented after supper.

"Why aren't there more mushrooms around here? I look for them whenever I'm in the woods."

"The ground's too sandy and dry, I suppose."

"I guess so. They sure are delicious."

"Funny, isn't it?" Mutti added. "In Goldbach, there were plenty of mushrooms but we didn't have any fat and onions to fry them in. Now we have plenty of lard and onions, but hardly any mushrooms."

* * *

On Monday of the second week of the potato harvest, I played hooky so I could work the whole day with Mutti. We left early in the morning. On the way to the farm, we treated ourselves to some wild blueberries.

"How come you didn't go berry picking during the summer?" Mutti asked.

"A whole bunch of us went, but we always ended up horsing around so we never brought anything back."

"What kind of horsing around?"

"Well, the last time we went, all four of us peed onto some ant hills."

I thought Mutti would be taken aback by my story, but her reaction surprised me.

"Just like your Uncle Ernst did when he was a boy!" she giggled.

It was three kilometers to the farm, most of the way through the forest. The forest was edged with pine trees, but farther in there was also leafy wood. It was a cool, overcast day. The crowns of high trees blocked out most of the light. We heard cries, like those made by a baby in distress. Mutti and I went to investigate. A huge bird lay, struggling, in a thicket, one of its giant wings hanging down limply, covered in blood.

"It's a crane," Mutti said, "but I have a feeling it would taste very much like goose."

"We can't take it with us to your job. What would the farmer say?" I protested.

"You're right, but I think I know what to do," Mutti said.

The path was quite a distance away. As soon as we reached it, Mutti took out her handkerchief. She bent down a branch from a tall bush, tied the handkerchief to the branch, and let it snap up again.

"This way we won't miss the spot when we come back in the evening," Mutti assured me.

"You're smart. I wouldn't have thought of that," I complimented her.

Picking potatoes had never seemed to take as long as it did that day. Wondering whether the crane would still be there, I barely tasted the afternoon snack. Since we always worked late, there was hardly enough time to get home in daylight. Sometimes we wound up walking the last kilometer in the dark. If the sun went down, we would never find the bird. Finally, the last wagon full of bags with potatoes went to the farm and we rushed back into the forest.

"Do you think it's still there?" I asked Mutti.

"Relax," Mutti replied. "It couldn't get far with a broken wing. I'm sure it's right where we left it, unless someone else found it first."

As we walked, I carved a sharp point in a thick branch. Mutti's handkerchief was still hanging on the bush. We would have never found the spot without it. However, all we heard were the usual noises of a forest. There wasn't a single sound from the crane.

Gripping my weapon, Mutti and I sneaked toward the bush where we had last seen the injured bird. The pitiful creature lay in the same spot, scarcely breathing. With sudden misgivings, I lowered the stick to my side.

"How're we going to kill it?" I asked meekly.

"Don't think of it as a bird," Mutti said grimly. "Think of it as meat for our pot."

She took the dying bird by the neck, held its head over a tree stump, and hit it half a dozen times with the thick end of my stick. Mutti put the limp creature into an old potato sack which she had taken from the farm and we carried it home in the dark.

After we gulped down our supper sandwiches, Mutti went to work. I was dead tired and soon fell asleep. Mutti must have stayed up half the night. The next morning, the bird had been picked clean. Sealed jars of meat lined the shelf and the leftover meat filled our big frying pan. I sampled a small piece.

"It really does taste like goose!" I exclaimed.

"In a way. But there's a fishy flavor to it," she replied, "and the texture's really oily."

The sandwiches I brought to school that day had meat on them for the first time, instead of sugar beet syrup or lard. Everyone wanted a taste, but I only let Wolfgang try some.

The following day, as one of the boys saw me crossing the school yard, he yelled at the top of his lungs, "Here comes Fat Head with his fancy meat sandwich!"

I hadn't been called that terrible name since Plötzin. "Fat Head" quickly caught on with a group of mean boys and I was once again stuck with it. To my great annoyance, Rudolf also joined in. Three or four times, on our way home from school, we got into a fight about it and we both ended up with bloody noses. After a while I ignored him. We never talked to each other again.

* * *

On a Saturday evening in October, Mutti waved a letter at me when I got home for supper. "The Reimanns are in the West!"

"That's amazing. I wouldn't have thought all five of them could sneak across the border."

"They didn't have to. First they took a train to East Berlin and crossed into West Berlin with the S-Bahn. We could have done that, too, but we would have been stuck in West Berlin. Not the Reimanns. A British military airplane gave them a free ride to Schleswig Holstein in the British Zone and from there they got a free train ride to Bavaria in the American Zone."

"How on earth did Aunt Liesbeth arrange all that?"

"Uncle Alfred got them an official Permit to Move to the West." Mutti's voice choked. "He wanted them with him that much."

"So why didn't..." I started to ask, but the look in Mutti's eyes stopped me and I quickly changed the subject. "How're the Reimanns doing?"

"Just fine. Uncle Alfred's working on a large farm. He doesn't make much money, but they also pay him with produce, fruit, milk, and eggs. Ilse's being trained to be a nurse and all of the other children are in school."

"Sounds a lot better than this dump," I said bitterly.

"Still, the main thing is that all of us except your Oma are in the West," Mutti pointed out. She took a postcard out of her apron pocket. "This came today, too." On one side was a picture of the Cologne

Cathedral. On the other, a barely legible penciled message from my father.

Without another word, Mutti attached the picture postcard to the wall between the other two.

* * *

Three days later, to our surprise, my father sent us one hundred marks. Mutti made up her mind right away what to use it for.

"I haven't seen Hubert since the beginning of January," she reminded me, "and this money should be more than enough to buy me a round trip ticket. Be a good boy and do your homework while I'm gone."

"Yes, Mutti."

The first night alone in our room, I felt uneasy. The radio provided some company for a while. Once I turned it off, I couldn't get to sleep. With Mutti away, I was suddenly aware of how noisy our neighbors were. People yelled to one another just outside the window. Wooden soled shoes thumped along the cement floor in the corridor. Adults scolded, children cried. Louder than all the rest, the slurred, angry voice of Mr. Boltermann cursed at his wife. Earlier that day, Mr. Boltermann had been so drunk he had to support himself against the walls of the barrack.

"Just look at him! Killing himself with schnapps!" Mr. Siemokat had said. "I'll promise you one thing; Boltermann will never become as old as he looks." Mr. Siemokat sure could be funny at times.

Just as I was about to fall asleep, I heard the piercing scream of a woman, no doubt Mrs. Boltermann, begging for help. Next came Mr. Boltermann's raspy voice yelling, "Shut your mouth!" By Mutti's clock, it was nearly one o'clock in the morning. When the alarm woke me up for school at six thirty, I felt half dead with exhaustion.

* * *

Mindful of my promise to Mutti, as soon as I got home from school I ate five slices of bread spread thick with sugar beet syrup, fiddled with the radio dial until I found cowboy music, and settled down to do my homework. Distracted only once, by the sound of an ambulance on the road outside the camp, I plugged away diligently, finishing up shortly before six o'clock. With an unaccustomed sense of accomplishment, I ventured outside.

A young mother was addressing a small crowd near the Teschner's woodshed. "I saw them carrying the boys into the ambulance. Such terrible burns! Bits of skin were missing all over their faces and their arms."

"I pray to God my Jürgen wasn't among them!" another mother exclaimed. "I've been looking for him everywhere!"

"It could've been any of ours," the first mother agreed. "They all play with that stuff. This time it was some new boys. They found a tiny aluminum tube, no longer than my index finger, and poured out bright yellow powder onto a tree stump. Then they added some black powder, lit it and poof!"

"I've seen something like this coming for a long time," Mr. Teschner said. He spun around, grabbed Werner by the shoulders and shook him. "If I ever catch you or your brothers with this stuff, I'll thrash you so hard you won't sit down for a month! Is that clear?"

That evening, Werner and his brother came over, bringing with them some new dime novels.

"Did your father say anything else about the explosion?"

"That's all he talked about, all through supper. I don't think I'll touch any of the junk again."

"Me neither. My mother's been warning me for months, but what happened today really scared me."

* * *

427

The Billy Jenkins stories were covered in glossy paper printed in shades of gray. The gleaming cover pictures hinted at the exciting story inside. Billy Jenkins traveled wherever he was needed to protect good people, especially women and children, from vicious criminals.

I collected Billy Jenkins stories as well as books about his best friend, Tom Prox. Werner and Wolfgang were the only boys I trusted not to get grease spots on the pages and not to dog ear the corners. Werner and Wolfgang preferred the Buffalo Bill and Tom Mix stories. Their books had colorful covers and dealt mainly with Indians. The three of us debated endlessly which of our four heroes was the best shot, the best rider, and so on. The one thing we all agreed on was that, one day, we would go to America to become cowboys.

From the Kaiser's food store carton which I kept under my bunk bed, I took out my precious copy of *The Leatherstocking Tales* and handed it to Werner.

"You can borrow the book if you promise to take good care of it," I told him. "I've already read it three times."

"Your mother must make more money than I thought. There's no way we could afford to buy a book like that."

"It was a Christmas present from my Uncle Hermann," I assured him. "I've never bought a real book in my life."

* * *

I slept better the second night. Mutti came back the next day.

"How's Hubert doing?" I asked.

"Remember how skinny he was? Well, they've really fattened him up."

"It's good he's put on some weight!"

"No, it's a good deal more than that. He's really fat. I was shocked when I saw him."

"But why did they let him get so heavy?"

"The doctor told me to cure tuberculosis the lungs must be swimming in fat. They give the children rich food all day long."

"Did they tell you how much longer he'll have to stay there?"

"At least another year, according to the doctor. Now I'm sorry I didn't wait a few more weeks to go there. I would have liked to be with him on his seventh birthday."

"Hubert will be all right. Anyhow, I'm glad you're back," I said to Mutti.

"Did anything exciting happen around here while I was away?"

"Some strange powder exploded and three boys ended up in the hospital."

"How many times have I warned you...?" Mutti began.

"Don't worry! I've given the stuff up."

"Thank God," Mutti said.

In the evening, while I was doing my math homework, Mutti wrote a long letter to my father, telling him all about her visit with Hubert. I signed the letter too and the next day I mailed it on my way to school. Mutti did not receive a reply.

* * *

November arrived and, with it, colder weather. Autumn leaves, orange and gold, fluttered to the ground, encircling the pond in Bodenteich with color. In puddles left by a steady rain, the leaves turned brown and quickly rotted. Mutti was laid off at the construction site, although Mr. Lauritz promised there would be more work in the spring.

"We have very little money set aside," Mutti confided. "I know it's hard, but please try to eat a little less bread. And another thing. You know the beef bones I've been using to flavor our soup? Well, we can't afford any right now. We'll just have to stretch our budget as best as we can if we're going to make it through the winter."

A few days later, as Mutti and I sat eating a lunch of pea soup and bread, and watching the steady rain fall outside, I saw the mailman walk by our window. A few minutes later he knocked at our door.

"Mrs. Gretel Nitsch?"

"Yes, that's me."

"There's a parcel from America for you at the post office. Please bring this slip with you when you claim it."

"There must be some mistake. I don't know anybody in America."

"All the same, it's addressed to you. The sender's a Mrs. Peachey."

"It's certainly a mystery. Why didn't you bring the parcel with you, if I may ask?"

"Out of the question. I couldn't, even if I wanted to. It's too heavy. When you go to the post office, be sure to bring a handcart."

As soon as the mailman left, ignoring the rain, Mutti and I walked to the post office in Bodenteich with our handcart.

"I can't imagine who this Mrs. Peachey could be, or what she could have sent us," Mutti said.

"Maybe it's got something to do with Jockel. He's studying theology in America," I suggested.

"Don't be silly. Jockel couldn't afford to send us anything. He's only a student with barely enough to live on as it is."

The parcel from America was bulky and extremely heavy. By the time we got back home, the rain had changed into drizzle. We rolled the handcart on wet sandy wheels right into our room and unloaded it on the floor. I raced over to our woodshed and stowed away the cart, bringing back a pair of pliers which I used to snap open the wide metal straps that held the lid closed.

Impatient, we set aside the letter resting on top. Beneath it lay an incredible collection of packages and cans. Judging from the pictures on the labels, they contained rice, ham, raisins, dried plums, fruit salad, coffee, cocoa powder, and chocolate. Two cans contained some kind of meat. One label read "Corned beef" and the other, "Spam."

"Just look at this stuff!" I exclaimed, hopping from one foot to the other.

"It's a miracle!" Mutti said as she reached for the letter. She had gotten all weepy.

"Who sent it?"

"They write in a mixture of old fashioned German and some English," she finally said. "As best as I can make out, Mr. and Mrs. Peachey are Mennonite Christians. Jockel spoke at their church about East Prussian refugees."

"I told you so!" I said triumphantly. "Mr. and Mrs. Peachey must be the best people in all of America." After a moment, I added, "And they must be very rich."

"No, I don't think so. According to what they write, they're farmers in a small village in Pennsylvania and they have four children."

I rushed for my atlas, but was disappointed to discover Pennsylvania in the Eastern part of the United States. I would have preferred it to be one of the "cowboy states" like Texas or Montana, so I could brag about it to my friends.

Mutti used a can opener to open a colorful tin filled with exotic fruit salad. As I savored my first spoonful, I was sure that fruit salad was the kind of food the angels ate in heaven. After we had eaten, Mutti looked again at the letter.

"They refer to five or six passages from the Bible. If we owned one, I'd look them up."

Oma had kept our Bible from Goldbach. So, although we had very little money, Mutti bought a Bible the next day in the bookstore in Bodenteich. As we read the passages, I imagined Opa sitting there beside us, following along in his big leather Langendorf Bible. Two passages, in particular, appealed to me. The first, from the 16th Psalm, read: "Preserve me, Oh God, for in Thee do I put my trust." The other was from John 6:35: " 'I am the bread of life,' Jesus told them. 'Those who come to me will never be hungry; those who believe in me will never be thirsty.'" Mutti sat down to write a long thank you note to the Peachey family. I tapped her on the shoulder. "Shouldn't we go back to church in Bodenteich some time?"

"What makes you ask that now?"

"The package from the Peacheys made me think about Opa. He would've helped complete strangers, too."

"Yes, he certainly would have."

"I think he'd want us to go to church. He never used to miss a Sunday."

Mutti chose her words carefully. "Remember how Opa always wore his finest clothes when he went to church? It still doesn't feel right to me, going in these old patched things, but I promise it's the first place we'll go, if we ever get something decent to wear!"

*   *   *

For four days in a row, I had thin slices of corned beef or Spam on my school sandwich. When Wolfgang asked me what it was, I decided to impress him.

"It's buffalo sausage."

"Buffalo sausage?"

"Yep."

"How'd you get buffalo sausage?"

"We received a parcel from friends in America. They have a huge ranch with lots of cowboys in the Rocky Mountains."

"Wow! Are you going to go there one day?"

"I sure am."

"When?"

"When I'm grown up," I said, suddenly warming to the idea myself. I let him have a bite of my sandwich.

One of the cans in the parcel contained two pounds of coffee. Compared to the stuff made of toasted acorns or barley which Mutti had been drinking since we left Langendorf, a cup of "real coffee" would have been a wonderful treat for her. Still, she did not open the can. Instead she bartered it in the big shoe store in Bodenteich for a brand new pair of high top leather shoes for me, a pair of normal leather shoes for herself, and a pair of fine slippers which she sent to Oma in the Soviet-Occupied Zone. She also bought me black polish so I could buff our new shoes to a fine shine every day.

"I didn't realize coffee was so valuable," I remarked, after seeing how much Mutti had gotten for it.

"Some people claim they can't live without it. They need it just to wake up in the morning."

"Mr. Ademeit told me about addictions like that in Goldbach," I said, remembering how he was willing to trade bread for tobacco.

* * *

Christmas was approaching. It was hard to believe a year had gone by since I skipped out on the Nativity play in Plötzin. At the beginning of December, my father sent me a card for my twelfth birthday. It was the first time I had ever received anything from him since the war. He also sent Mutti a small amount of money. To celebrate, Mutti took me by train to Uelzen to see a Tom Mix movie. The soundtrack inspired me to listen to even more cowboy music on our small radio at home.

On the morning of the last day before our Christmas vacation, a sensational rumor spread through our school: "Every child would receive a hundred gram bar of chocolate and a two hundred gram package of butter cookies."

"That's the biggest lie I've heard in a long time," Werner commented to Wolfgang and me.

"Maybe it's true," Wolfgang replied. Clinging to hope, I waited impatiently for school to end.

433

An hour before classes were over, the treats were distributed, "compliments of the British Military Government."

"Imagine that! This is the second time I've gotten chocolate from the British and both times right around my birthday," I told my friends.

"You weren't here last year, were you?"

"No, I was more or less in no man's land, but I got chocolate all the same."

"You really expect us to believe that?" Werner scoffed.

"It was the day after my birthday, to be exact. That's how the British welcomed us to the West."

The native children devoured their chocolate right away, but my friends and I took ours home to share with our families.

Our good fortune continued. Two days before Christmas, we received another parcel from the Peacheys. Mutti was overwhelmed. She had not expected to hear from them again. This time the package contained two woolen blankets, leather soles for two pairs of shoes, two pieces of soap, a thimble, a meter long piece of elastic, two spools of thread, and a Bible. Weeping, Mutti looked up at me.

"I can't believe this. It's heaven sent."

"Did they send the picture you asked for in your letter?" I asked.

"No," Mutti replied. "Mrs. Peachey writes they don't make photographs of themselves because graven images are forbidden by the Bible."

"Then what pictures did they send?"

"They're aerial shots of the Peachey's farm."

I reached for the photos. They were taken at an angle and covered a wide area. The buildings looked tiny. I could barely pick out the silo and the barn. Looking at them made me homesick for Opa's farm.

The Bible we received from the Peachey family was bigger and finer than the one we bought in Bodenteich. Although it was in German, it had been printed in Philadelphia, Pennsylvania, I noted proudly.

"We'll keep this one at home. Once you start confirmation classes, you can take the other one along," Mutti decided.

"It's a while to go until then," I said.

Mutti and I celebrated Christmas Eve alone. "Our first Christmas without Hubert," Mutti reminded me. "It breaks my heart to think of him in that sanitarium."

"Well, at least he has other children to play with and plenty to eat," I said. The selfish thought had often crossed my mind that, if Hubert were with us in Bodenteich, our food budget would be stretched even thinner.

"You have a strange idea about the place," Mutti said sharply. "It's not a hotel. All of the children may look healthy and many of them are chubby like Hubert, but they all have tuberculosis and I'm sure they miss their families, especially at this time of year. The worst for me is that the doctors are always so evasive about his progress."

I tried to comfort her. "Opa always used to say, 'Never give up hope'."

"I know," Mutti said, "but that's not always easy. Sometimes I think we'll never get him back."

We read and reread the long letter from the Peacheys and the many letters and cards we received from relatives in the American and British Zones and from Oma and Uncle Ernst in the Soviet-Occupied Zone. As expected, my father did not come from Cologne and I wasn't sorry.

CHAPTER 31

In late January 1950, Mutti and I walked into Bodenteich to shop for bread, noodles, sugar beet syrup, and lard at Kaiser's Food Market. As we lugged the groceries back home in our string bags, we passed the big frozen pond in the middle of town. The children from town were ice skating. Watching them glide effortlessly across the ice, I suddenly felt inadequate. Except for the unusual pair Opa had made for me in Bieskobnicken, I had never owned skates. In fact I had never owned any sports equipment other than the leather soccer ball Uncle Ernst had given me in Langendorf. In the summer I had seen the same children riding bicycles. None of the children in the Ammo Camp owned a bicycle, nor did we know how to ride one.

Mutti interrupted my thoughts. "Why so sad?"

"I feel cold," I said, evading the question and pulling the visor of my peaked cap a little further down on my forehead. I knew there was no point in asking Mutti to buy me my own pair of skates.

* * *

In February 1950, a small Edeka food store opened in the Ammo Camp. It was no longer necessary to trek two kilometers into Bodenteich to buy basic food items. Although this was certainly an improvement,

436

it isolated us even more from the people who lived in town. The footpath we used as a shortcut in warm weather turned to mush after the first snow. So since the start of winter, I was forced to go the long way around to school on the dirt road. This took me past the big camp surrounded by barbed wire that I had first seen the day my father brought us to the Ammo Camp.

As I had learned in the meantime, the people in the camp were displaced persons from Lithuania, Estonia, Latvia, Poland, and Hungary. They stayed for a short time, waiting to emigrate to America, Canada, and Australia. The few times I had seen children beyond the fence, I hadn't dared to talk to them.

One morning before I went to school, Mutti asked me to pick something up for her in Bodenteich after classes. The other boys went on ahead. While walking home alone past the big gate of the DP camp, I started to sing a German cowboy song at the top of my lungs. A boy and a girl grinned at me from beyond the fence. Embarrassed, I was about to run away when, to my surprise, the boy talked to me in German.

"So you like cowboy music too?"

"Yes. I sure do."

"Have you ever been to the movies in our camp?"

"No. I didn't even know there were any."

"There's a cowboy movie at five this afternoon. If you'd like to see it, be back at this gate at ten minutes to five and we'll get you in."

"Are you sure? I'm from the Ammo Camp, you know."

"I can see that. Don't worry about it."

"Well, in that case, I'll see you later!"

Shortly before five o'clock, my new friends met me at the gate. The boy's name was Kalju. His sister was Asta. Originally from Estonia, they had learned German while living in a refugee camp in Bavaria.

From outside the barbed wire fence, I could barely see the two-story buildings in the DP camp, which were set well back from the dirt road. Close up, they were clearly of better quality than our barrack, with new window frames and solid wooden doors. Mr. Siemokat had once asked, "How come foreigners from Eastern Europe get to live in solid brick Wehrmacht buildings and we're stuck in barracks where forced laborers used to live?" Now I understood what he meant.

Kalju interrupted my thoughts. "Here we are!"

We walked right into the movie theater. To my relief, no one charged admission. Waiting for the film to start, I heard a number of different languages being spoken, but no German or Russian. The movie was in English. There were no subtitles.

"That was fantastic!" I said to Kalju and Asta after the show. "Is there any chance I could go with you again some time?"

"I'm afraid not," said Asta. "In a day or two we'll be on our way to Bremerhaven to board a ship for America."

"Tell you what," added Kalju, seeing my disappointment, "If you were to come alone, or with just one other child, I'm sure no one would mind."

"Thanks again! And good luck in America. I'll be going there myself one day, no matter what, and when I do, I'll be sure to look you up."

From then on, I went back to the movies at the DP camp most Wednesday and Saturday afternoons. Although Wolfgang or Werner sometimes came along with me, I usually went alone. I saw Western movies, pirate movies, detective movies, and lots of schmaltzy romantic movies, all of them in English. A few funny cartoons always came on before the feature. Mickey Mouse, Woody the Woodpecker, Donald Duck, and Tom and Jerry quickly became part of my vocabulary, as did "Howdy!" and "Good bye."

The lives of the Americans on the screen astonished me. I was awed by what they ate, how they dressed, the kinds of houses they lived in, and the chrome-covered cars they drove. Imagine a car big enough to seat six grown-ups!

I always left the movies humming American music. Before long I fell in love with the America portrayed on the screen. I daydreamed about looking up at towering New York City skyscrapers before heading out to the Wild West.

Once I saw a short film between the cartoon and the main feature. An old bearded immigrant from Russia had recently arrived in America. Although he only spoke a few words of English, he quickly landed a job shoveling snow in a big American city. The old man ordered lunch in a fancy coffee shop. He simply pointed to the food he wanted, using fingers to indicate how many eggs and how many franks. His lunch consisted of a bowl of thick beef stew, two franks on the side, buttered toast, and three fried eggs. He took only one bite of the buttered toast, leaving the rest untouched. Before he left the coffee shop, he even put a tip on the counter. This simple movie left a deep impression on me.

"If a poor man like that can get a job and eat like a king, then someone like me should have a chance there," I informed Mutti when I got home. I was even more determined to go to America myself one day.

Mutti was worried about me. "Those movies are putting foolish ideas into your head," she complained. "You should concentrate more on your school work if you ever want to get out of this miserable place."

"As a matter of fact, I've decided to study English in school," I replied with newfound confidence.

Desperate to speak like an American, I signed up for an English class taught by Mr. Schlemmer Mondays and Wednesdays after school. He did his best to discourage me.

"You don't even know German grammar," he pointed out. "You'll just be wasting my time in here."

* * *

Throughout the winter months, Mutti worked on several odd jobs, barely earning enough to buy our food. Fortunately, her old boss, Mr.

Lauritz, was a man of his word. In March, he hired Mutti to work in the newly built printing plant. She and two other women sorted dime romances and packed them for shipping. It was an easier job than cleaning bricks and the pay was better. My services were no longer needed.

The following month, the postman slipped another postcard from my father under our door. He promised he would pay us a visit. In May, to my immense surprise, my father actually showed up.

He spent most of the time alone with me, collecting wood in the forest. The first day we went out together, I nearly stepped on a viper. It was the first one I had ever seen near the Ammo Camp.

"Look out!" my father yelled. He reacted in a split second. Grabbing a stick, he bashed the snake until its head was crushed and bloodied. Then he lifted the dead viper and flung it into the bushes.

"Next time, watch where you put down your foot," he warned.

"If he had bitten me, would you have had to chop off my toe?" I asked.

My father shook his head. "Where'd you get a silly notion like that?"

I decided not to tell him about Raddatz in Goldbach.

Mutti took me aside at bedtime. "Your father will sleep in your bunk bed so you'll have to sleep in the bunk above mine."

I climbed up to the top bunk and pretended to go to sleep, waiting to hear what my parents would say to each other. Neither one of them said a word. I finally fell asleep to the rustling pages of the newspaper my father was reading.

Two days later, my father and I were in the forest again, loading our handcart with wood. He suddenly pointed up ahead.

"Did you see that fox running away over there?"

In its haste, the fox had left behind a bleeding hare. It was still alive. My father grabbed it by the hind legs and held it high up in the air. He whacked its neck with the side of his right hand. Then we rushed home with it. While my father skillfully skinned the rabbit and removed its guts, Mutti bought sour cream and marjoram at the Edeka food store. An hour later, we sat down to a delicious meal of roast hare, prepared by my father. It was our first real family dinner since the end of the war, although it would have been even nicer if Hubert had been with us.

For weeks I had worried that Mutti would not have the money I'd need to take a school trip. During supper, I gathered up the courage to ask my father for help.

"Our school's making a year-end excursion to Hamburg next month," I finally blurted out. "It's going to cost three marks."

"Three marks?" my father repeated. He didn't look friendly.

"Don't worry about it, Willi," Mutti said hurriedly. "I'll scrape the money together somehow."

"Of course I'll help you, son," my father said, ignoring Mutti. He handed me a five-mark bill. "Go and enjoy yourself."

We ate the rest of our meal in silence. As Mutti was clearing the dishes, my father stretched out his legs in front of him, lit a cigarette, and sucked the smoke deep into his lungs.

"So," he said to me, "maybe you'd like to hear how I avoided being captured by the Russians." Flicking his cigarette ashes onto an empty plate, he waited for my reply.

"Yes, sir, I would."

"It's a bit of a long story. After my leave in Altenberg in January '45 when I saw you last, I took the night train back to Berlin. While I was gone, the military hospital where I worked as a chef had been blown to bits. So, they put a Red Cross armband on me and sent me to Schwedt an der Oder."

"You mean the river Oder?" I asked.

"It was wider than a river, because the meadows on both sides were flooded. The Russians wanted to cross and our boys were supposed to stop them. Casualties on both sides were horrible, a real bloodbath. Our job as medics was to get our wounded soldiers out, but of course, we came under enemy fire. Come to think of it, it was my first dangerous assignment in the whole war. When we were forced back, I was assigned to a FLAK unit."

"To shoot down Russian planes?"

"Not planes, motorboats. The Russians were using them to cross over to our side."

"How'd you feel, shooting at the Russians like that?" I asked.

"Pretty good at first. That is, I enjoyed mowing them down until we came under Russian artillery fire ourselves."

"How many hours did the battle last?"

"It seemed like forever before we received orders to retreat. During the night, a military convoy transported what was left of our outfit to a village north of Berlin. It was just a matter of time before the Ivans would overrun our position and ship us all off to Siberia."

"But you were captured by the British. How'd you manage that?"

"One morning our company took off towards the west. We walked for four straight days and nights. Anyone who sat down to rest couldn't get up and go on. People were pouring blood out of their boots. I don't know how many men we left behind to die. Only twelve of us managed to keep going until we reached a British-controlled area and that's where they took us prisoner."

I glanced over at the stove. Mutti began heating up water to make barley coffee. If she was listening, she did not show it.

"Were you still armed when they caught you?"

"Of course not. We threw everything away, our rifles, steel helmets, rucksacks, the whole bit. Anyhow, when the British captured us, we got exactly what we wanted."

"You were very lucky!"

"Luck had nothing to do with it." His tone was belligerent. "The tough survive; the weak fall behind. I've always kept myself in top condition."

"Mutti told me you could leap over barrels on the ice."

"That's kid stuff. Boxing's the way to build your strength. See these muscles? I started to box in middle school. You ought to take it up."

As Mutti set the coffee cups on the table, her hand was shaking. "Just in case you've forgotten," she said, glaring at my father, "Günter spends his free time collecting and chopping wood. He has no time to waste on boxing."

"I don't want to hear any more of your complaints," he snapped. "I was just giving the boy a piece of advice." He turned to me. "Why don't you go leave us alone for a while," he said, his voice low and ominous. "Your mother and I need to talk."

"Thank you both for supper," I said, forcing myself to smile. Then, needing no further encouragement, I rushed outside for a breath of fresh air.

After a three-day visit, my father took off again for Cologne. Nothing had been said about our joining him. Mutti's face was clouded with bitterness.

* * *

The day of the big excursion to Hamburg, several huge buses pulled up in front of the school. I had seldom been so excited. In honor of the occasion, Wolfgang, Werner, and I wore socks and shoes. Even though we weren't barefoot, our clothes were still ragged compared to those of the children from town. Three of the mothers who were chaperoning glared as they looked us up and down. Schlemmer must have warned them about us.

In Lüneburg, we had a rest stop at a garden café full of soldiers. From their uniforms I recognized right away they were British. Some students from the upper grades dared to walk over to them to practice their English. I was jealous. It would have been nice if I could have told the soldiers about how kind their countrymen had been to us at the border.

Werner came over to where I was standing. "Have you been watching Schlemmer?" he whispered. "He keeps avoiding the British soldiers."

"You're right."

Schlemmer sat alone, tapping the fingers of his left hand nervously on the metal table while gnawing on the fingernails of his right hand.

"What do you make of it?"

"I'd say he couldn't speak English to save his life," Werner replied with a grin.

"Have you seen him bite his nails before?"

"Sure have. He doesn't only bite them; sometimes his teeth cut right through the skin on his fingers. One of these days, he'll have nothing left but bloody stumps."

Before we left the rest stop, I used some of my pocket money to buy myself two frozen ice cream bars. Since I couldn't hold the sticks and unwrap them both at the same time, I stuck one bar in my shirt pocket for a moment. One of the elegantly dressed mothers from Bodenteich was watching me.

"You know, you can't take the ice cream home. It will melt," she told me.

"Really?" I said politely, playing along. I had to control myself not to reply, "Do you think I'm that dumb?"

Wolfgang burst out laughing. He covered his face with his hand and turned his back to us.

We took a breezy harbor cruise in Hamburg. Later we spent hours walking around the Hagenbeck Zoo. Our last stop before driving home was a tour of the tunnel under the Elbe River. It was a popular tourist attraction and we had to wait for our turn on the elevator. My feet hurt. Since it was a hot day, I took off my shoes. Werner and Wolfgang quickly did the same. The mother who had given me the advice about the ice cream rushed over to us. Her tone was strict.

"Now you listen to me! This is Hamburg, not some refugee camp. You can't walk around here barefoot."

"Why not?" countered Wolfgang. "We like it this way. It's just like home."

As the three of us began to laugh, our indignant chaperone tried to storm off in a huff. She didn't get far. The sharp heel of her right shoe stuck fast in soft tar. When she lifted her foot, it came clean out of the shoe. She was suddenly barefoot, just like us. She pried out her shoe. A long thread of tar connected it to the sidewalk. Schlemmer rushed to her aid.

"Permit me, madam," he murmured gallantly, gently supporting her with his hand as she put her shoe back on.

"My dear Mr. Schlemmer, you're so very kind!" she replied sweetly.

Her manner didn't fool us. Just as soon as Schlemmer turned to rejoin our group, the mother shot us a look that was anything but ladylike.

"If she could have managed it, she would have left us in Hamburg," I reported to Mutti on our return.

"Well, I certainly can understand why you got angry about the ice cream. We may be poor, but we're certainly not stupid."

"That's just what I thought, too!"

"All the same," she added, trying not to smile, "next time you find yourself near the Elbe Tunnel, try to keep your shoes on."

* * *

When our school vacation started in July, my Altenberg Grandmother came up from Oldendorf to visit us for a few days. She brought me a new shirt and a half pound of taffy candy.

"If you don't mind," my grandmother said to me after half an hour, "your mother and I need some privacy."

"Sure, Grandma, I don't mind," I said, but as soon as I got outside, I ducked down next to our open window to listen to their conversation.

"You mean to tell me, Willi still isn't sending you money on a regular basis?" I heard Grandma ask.

"I can count on one hand the number of times he's sent us anything. If we'd been relying on him, we'd have starved to death by now. It's funny in a way. If Willi were missing in action, the government would have helped us out. But since I know where he is...," Mutti started to explain.

"How about visiting? How often has he come to see you?"

"He was here a few weeks ago. That was the first time since he went to Cologne."

"Oh, my dear Gretel! I had no idea! He really doesn't treat you nicely at all. The war has destroyed many good marriages, turning good men into bad ones. I never thought it would happen to one of my own sons."

"Please don't blame yourself," Mutti said, trying to calm her mother-in-law.

"No matter whose fault it is, I promise you this. Our family in Oldendorf will put pressure on him again to..."

Werner approached at that moment. I shook my head and put my index finger on my lips. He nodded and kept walking to the entrance of the barrack. I sneaked away from my spot under the window and caught up with him.

"What's the matter with you?" he asked. "You look terrible."

"They're talking about getting my parents back together again. I don't know why they don't just leave well enough alone."

"Well, you'd better look more cheerful than that when you go in for supper, or they'll know you were listening."

Half an hour later, forcing a smile, I walked into our room.

"There you are!" my grandmother greeted me. "Are you hungry? I bought sausage and cheese for our sandwiches so I hope you'll enjoy them."

"I'm sure he will. He eats like a horse," Mutti said.

During supper, we spoke about everything except my father. The major topic was Korea.

"Hermann and Bruno are convinced there'll be another world war," Grandma remarked, "this time between the Russians and the Americans."

"I try not to think about it. As far as I am concerned, the last war isn't over yet, at least not for us," Mutti said.

"I looked up Korea in my atlas," I said. "It's so far away. Is there really any reason to worry?"

"You're right. We're foolish to bother about it. Korea is all the way on the other side of the world," Grandma said, smiling at me. "By the way, Uncle Hermann will be glad to hear you're still using your atlas."

Mutti was not convinced. "All the same, if, God forbid, another war should start, the Russian troops are at the East German border, only five or six kilometers from here."

"Some things are out of our hands," Grandma replied. "Let's concentrate on the problems we can solve ourselves."

At least three times during supper, I considered talking about my father, but I did not want to get Mutti all upset. Two days later, when we brought Grandma to the train station, she gave Mutti a hug and shook my hand.

"Never give up hope!" Grandma exclaimed as she boarded the train. "There's more than one way to skin a cat!"

* * *

In late September, after the potato picking season, the other boys and I had some extra time on our hands. Inspired by our Wild West dime novels, we took turns lassoing tree stumps and roping dry pine branches hanging two to five meters above the ground. Pulling down the captured branch could be dangerous. It was hard to keep it from snapping back at us. We were in training for possible jobs as cowboys in the American West. Our mothers did not share our enthusiasm.

I also used my hatchet as an Indian tomahawk. With a lot of practice, I could throw it so it would stick into a tree trunk. I could do it from a distance of three meters and six meters, and, once in blue moon, even from nine meters. Distances of six meters or more were risky. A few times the hatchet handle split from the force of impact. Mr. Siemokat was always willing to repair the damage for me.

In our search for good firewood, Wolfgang and I set aside an entire Sunday to attempt to dig out a large pine tree stump. The stump stood next to a sandy bomb crater with very little vegetation in it. Werner walked by and saw how hard we were working.

"You're both crazy," he said. "You'll never be able to uproot that tough old thing."

Ignoring his comment, I kept doggedly hacking away at a thick part of the root with my hatchet. Werner watched us for a while. Finally, with a shrug, he picked up my shovel and started to dig on the other side of the stump.

"What's this?" Werner exclaimed. He held the edge of a piece of oilcloth in his hand.

"Maybe it's tracer ammunition," I suggested. The thick aluminum tracer tubes were stuffed with little silk parachutes. I had been trying to collect enough of them so Mutti could sew herself a new blouse, like the beautiful one Werner's oldest sister wore.

"No one in his right mind would go to so much trouble to preserve tracer ammunition," Werner snapped.

"Easy now. Whatever it is, we should put down our tools. There could be live grenades down there," warned Wolfgang.

We got ourselves short wooden sticks and carefully excavated more of the black oilcloth. After we had dug out quite a bit of dirt, Werner gave the cloth a yank. It sprang back, revealing three sheets of thick tar paper which broke apart when we tried to lift them out. Patiently, we removed chunks of the stuff piece by piece. More black oilcloth was hidden beneath it. This time there was something wrapped inside.

"We've struck it rich!" I said, my heart pounding with excitement.

Werner lifted out the long package. Its contents thrilled us even more than gold. We laid out on the ground a dozen beautiful sabers, some still in their sheaths. The sabers were oily, and some of the grips had corroded, but the blades were in excellent condition.

"Before we do any more digging, let's agree to a three-way split," Werner suggested. "Who knows what else we're going to find."

"It's a deal," Wolfgang said, and I readily agreed.

We worked feverishly, completely forgetting about the tree stump. By the time we were through, we had uncovered a cache of forty-two bayonets, twenty more sabers and two dozen daggers.

"I had hoped for a couple of rifles or pistols," I said. "All the same, this is quite a haul."

Wolfgang and I rushed home to get our handcarts. Werner, who was the strongest, stayed behind to guard the treasure. It took us a number of trips back and forth to haul it all to our woodsheds. We camouflaged the weapons under piles of oil rags and wooden sticks. Even so, some other boys got wind of what we had found. They started to dig at the same spot. All they found were a few bayonets. We had done a thorough job.

Wolfgang, Werner, and I divided the weapons into three equal shares. Every spare minute we had over the next few days, we spent holed up in our individual woodshed compartments. In the light that came through the open doors, we used rags and lots of elbow grease to wipe away caked on layers of black grease and sand. Although we could not see one another as we worked, we were all within hearing distance.

"I've got sabers engraved 'Mit Gott für Kaiser und Vaterland,'" Werner called out.

"Most of my daggers have swastikas. This one says 'Alles für Deutschland!' " Wolfgang yelled back. "There's even one with two swastikas, one on the grip and one on the blade."

"You've got to see this one. The end of the handle is shaped like the beak of an eagle!" Werner shouted. We rushed out of our compartments to have a look. "And on its blade are the words, 'Work ennobles.' Have you ever seen such horseshit?"

"Here's one that says 'Blood and honor,'" I said, holding up the dagger I had been working on.

"What's that supposed to mean?" Werner asked.

At that moment Emil Siemokat walked by. He gave us a disapproving glance before heading to his woodshed. Once the other boys had gone back inside, Mr. Siemokat stopped chopping wood and came over to me.

"Tell me, where do you find all this s-s-stuff?" he asked. I knew from his stutter that he was upset.

"Not too far away from here, while trying to dig out a tree stump."

"I reckon, this m-m-must have been the p-p-private collection of some N-N-Nazi big shot. Find any g-g-guns?"

"No, only bayonets, sabers, and daggers."

"Thank G-g-god for that."

Mr. Siemokat picked up the dagger with the words 'Blood and honor.' "D-d-do you know who used these under the Nazis?"

"No idea." I looked down at the dagger, rather than directly at Mr. Siemokat, so he could speak without stuttering.

"Hitler Youth. They were carried by Hitler Youth. I used to have one of these stupid things myself. Just about every Nazi organization had its own specially designed dagger. You couldn't find a man or a boy over the age of fourteen without a dagger."

I had never heard him say so much at one time.

"What were they good for?"

"For nothing, in my opinion. After we attacked Poland and connected East Prussia to the Reich again, everything was in short supply, everything except those worthless daggers."

The dagger gleamed in my hand. It didn't look so bad to me. Mr. Siemokat read my mind.

"The best would be if you and the other boys threw all that junk away. At the very least, promise me you won't fool around with it." I kept on polishing the blade and didn't meet his eyes.

Mr. Siemokat changed the subject. "Tell me, have you ever heard of the catastrophe in Bodenteich shortly before the end of the war?"

"A catastrophe?"

"That's what I said. At the end of March in 1945, three freight cars full of gunpowder and ammunition exploded on the tracks at the railroad station. More than seventy people were blown to bits. No one knows the exact number. A dozen houses were wiped off the map, over one hundred and fifty more were heavily damaged and..."

"How'd it happen?"

"No one ever found out. Some people thought it was sabotage by forced laborers from the ammunition factory, others thought it was caused by sparks from the locomotive."

"There must also have been a lot of wounded."

"Plenty. I don't know how many though. It was chaotic following the explosion. People did all kinds of crazy things. I heard they caught a looter, one of the workers from the Ammo Camp. First they shot him, and then they hung his corpse from a tree on the Bahnhofstrasse. Things quieted down after that."

"Mr. Siemokat, you're not making this up, are you?"

"Certainly not. I'm surprised no one told you this in school. Your teachers should have warned you not to play with the junk lying around here."

"It sounds like a bad movie."

"Never mind a movie. It's all true and, believe me, I've spared you a lot of gory details."

"Yes, sir."

Mr. Siemokat grabbed me hard by my shoulders and spoke in a sharp tone I had never heard from him before. "Listen carefully! Bayonets, sabers, and daggers are real weapons, not toys. If the police catch you with them, your life will be ruined."

I began to shake. Mutti had also begged me not to play with weapons. Perhaps she had told Mr. Siemokat about the detectives from the railroad criminal investigation department?

"Yes, sir. Thank you, sir," I stammered. Rushing into our woodshed compartment, I quickly hid all of my treasures under some kindling wood in a big crate.

All, that is, except for one shiny steel-blue bayonet. I thought it might make a perfect throwing knife, like the ones I had seen in the circus, but it proved to be too heavy.

* * *

October arrived. Except for an occasional postcard, there was still no word from my father. I was convinced he would never want us back. Yet, for the first time in years, the approaching winter didn't scare me. Like clockwork, every five or six weeks, we received a food parcel from the Peacheys in America.

"Our American friends live in Pennsylvania," I confessed to Wolfgang one day because my conscience pricked me. "They're not really cowboys."

"So, if they are not cowboys, what are they?"

"Farmers. They may not have a ranch exactly, but they do have a really big farm."

"Farmers, huh?"

"Yep."

He took the news well, much to my relief. Since he was in on the secret, I let Wolfgang come with me to pick up the parcels from the post office. From then on, Mutti always let him break off a piece of the giant chocolate bar that was in each package.

"Do you suppose you'll meet them one day?" Wolfgang mumbled, his mouth stuffed with chocolate.

"Who d'ya mean?"

"Your friends in Pennsylvania. Do you think you'll ever get to stay on their farm?"

"Don't I wish," I replied with a deep sigh. We sat quietly at the wooden table, munching on chocolate, reflecting on distant possibilities. *Perhaps the Peachey farm is where I'll get my start in America one day,* I thought.

* * *

I was chopping wood in front of our wood compartment while Mr. Siemokat was cleaning up his compartment next door to ours.

"I've decided to raise rabbits," he announced. "Perhaps you can give me a hand with the work."

"Sure, why not? I'd be glad to help, Mr. Siemokat. How're you planning to go about it?"

"I rather thought," he replied with a smirk, "I would buy a male and a female, put them into a cage filled with a little straw, and let them go about it for me."

"How much does a rabbit cost these days, if I may ask?" I went on, trying to change the subject.

Mr. Siemokat was suddenly alert. "What's that noise? Sounds like a hog. D-d-do you hear that? Does Mr. B-b-boltermann have a p-p-pig?"

"What? A pig? No, I don't think so."

"Oh n-n-no! I think he's hanged himself!" He raced around the left side of the woodshed to the compartments in the back. I dropped my hatchet and followed on his heels. The closer we got, the louder the horrible, squealing noises became.

Mr. Boltermann's compartment door was slightly ajar. He hung on a thick rope from the low ceiling. His eyes bulged from their sockets and his tongue hung out. Mr. Siemokat lifted Mr. Boltermann a little to give the thick rope some slack.

"G-g-grab that little stool. He must have kicked it to the s-s-side. C-c-climb up and loosen the rope."

Mr. Siemokat struggled to lift the weight of Mr. Boltermann's body with his scrawny arms. Stepping up on the little footstool, I was soon face to face with Mr. Boltermann. His features were terribly distorted with pain and fear. As he gasped for air, I could smell the schnapps on his breath. My knees nearly buckled out from under me. It was difficult to loosen the noose from around his neck, because the rope was so thick and hard. I finally managed to pull the loop over Mr. Boltermann's head. Mr. Siemokat, close to collapse, eased Mr. Boltermann to the ground.

"You idiots!" Boltermann gasped at us. "Why'd you get me down?"

Dumbstruck, I turned to Mr. Siemokat. He ignored the question.

"Run!" shouted Mr. Siemokat at me. "G-g-get someone from the Boltermanns!"

"Yes, Mr. Siemokat!" I answered, glad to get away from there.

When I got to the Boltermann apartment, his wife opened the door.

"P-p-please, come to your wood compartment immediately. Something terrible has happened!" The shock of it all had made me stammer too. She and I rushed back together.

Mrs. Boltermann stopped when she reached the door. Her eyes darted from the rope hanging from the ceiling to her husband lying limp on the floor. She began to weep.

"He'll be fine. It's all right," Mr. Siemokat reassured her. "As for you, Günter, I would suggest you wait for me back at your woodshed. I'll join you in a little while."

I didn't wait for him to change his mind. Once back at our shed, I chopped wood like a maniac. I knew Mutti wasn't home yet. The thought of returning to our empty room terrified me. Half an hour later, Mr. Siemokat came back, visibly shaken.

"That poor family," he said. "What a moron, this Boltermann, trying to hang himself! But, life's like that sometimes. Things don't always add up. Do me a favor, try to forget the whole thing. There's no point in worrying about it."

Mutti had the same advice for me later that evening, but it was easier said than done. That night I stayed up late. Remembering Boltermann's distorted face and his foul breath made me shudder. I was afraid to go to sleep, terrified that Boltermann would seek revenge because I had loosened the noose and kept him from kicking the bucket.

Whenever I saw Mr. Boltermann after that, I tried not to look him in the eyes.

"Boltermann hates me," I said to Werner. "One of these days, he's going to beat me up or maybe even murder me in my bed."

"Don't worry about him. If he so much as touches you, we'll take care of him."

"That's good to know," I replied with a nervous laugh.

Many times, when I saw Boltermann in the distance I changed my direction just to avoid him. Each time I saw him, he gave me a dirty look, and my heart beat faster. Even weeks later, I dreamed of his distorted face, his bulging eyes, and his swollen tongue. In my dreams Boltermann was always breathing down my neck, trying to hang me with the same thick rope I had pulled over his head.

CHAPTER 32

*A*t the end of October Mutti went by train to Bassum to bring Hubert back. After nearly two years in the tuberculosis sanatorium, the doctors considered him healed.

Their train was due to arrive at 1:51 P.M. At one o'clock, right after school I sprinted over to the Bodenteich railroad station. As the train finally appeared in the distance, I began to worry. When I had last seen Hubert, he was a puny six-year-old. Would I recognize him? Would he still remember me? The train arrived precisely on time. Hubert stood behind Mutti in one of the doorways. I smiled and waved when they stepped down onto the platform. Looking pale and miserable, Hubert gave me a limp handshake and stared down at his shoes.

Hubert had certainly become fat. Although he was still a few weeks short of his eighth birthday, he was heavier than any boy in the Ammo Camp. He looked like a blimp. The minute I saw him, I knew he would be teased.

"How are you?" I asked as we headed back to the Camp.

"Not bad."

"Did you go to school at the sanatorium?"

"Yes."

"How many children were there?"

456

"Dunno."

"What's Bassum like anyway?"

Hubert could not reply. Although we were walking at a snail's pace, the poor little guy was completely out of breath. I worried what my friends would think of him. Even if Hubert were five years older, he would not fit in with Werner, Wolfgang, and me.

Back at the Ammo Camp, Mutti flung open our door. Hubert hung back, his eyes glancing anxiously around the tiny room.

"Come in, my boy!" Mutti encouraged.

A white placard stood on the table between the windows on which Mutti had printed "WELCOME HOME, DEAR HUBERT!" in bold black letters.

A smile creased Hubert's face, the first since his arrival, but his worried look returned when he saw the bunk beds. He knew he could never climb to the top. Without being asked, I moved my pajamas and my two newest Billy Jenkins novels from the bottom bunk to the top.

"You can sleep in this one," I said, patting the mattress.

"Thanks," Hubert replied. His face still flushed with the effort of walking up from the station, he sank into the nearest chair and watched, listless, as Mutti unpacked his few belongings.

Hubert had acquired several strange habits in the Bassum Sanatorium. He had an aversion to fish, which had been one of the main staples of his diet. Just mentioning the words "cod liver oil" made him gag. Every morning before he combed his hair, he would wet his hands, put a tiny bit of sugar in his palm, rub his hands together, and brush them over his hair.

"My hair's too thin and too straight," he explained. "Sugar water holds it in place." Mutti was able to solve this problem. She bought him a small jar of pomade.

Strangest of all, any time Mutti or I would say something to him while he was doing his homework, he would jump up instantly and take a defensive position, closing his small fat fists like a boxer.

"Why's he so jumpy?" I asked Mutti when we were alone.

"He was the shortest patient in the sanatorium. One of the nurses told me he was used as a punching bag by the older children."

During the following weeks, my feelings about Hubert were mixed. I pitied him because his classmates called him "Fatso." I also resented having to look after him again. He followed me around after school like an oversized shadow.

CHAPTER 33

*W*olfgang loaned me his copy of *Tom Sawyer* which I devoured in three sittings. As my thirteenth birthday approached, I hinted to Mutti about how much I would appreciate receiving a copy of *Huckleberry Finn*.

December 3, 1950 fell on a Sunday. Mutti let me sleep until nearly lunchtime.

"Time to get up, lazybones," she said. "Remember, what you do on your birthday is what you'll do all year!"

Hubert stood alongside her, his eyes moving back and forth between my face and the corner of the room where I kept my school bag. There, resting on the bag was a brand-new copy of *Huckleberry Finn*. I let out a joyful Indian war whoop.

"I didn't think you'd be able to manage it," I said, beaming at Mutti.

"If you'd wanted a toy, I might not have tried so hard," she said with a grin, "but a book, that's worth scrimping for."

I gave Mutti a big hug. "Thank you! Thank you! Thank you!"

"Will you tell me the story?" Hubert asked.

"Just as soon as I've read it," I promised.

"Speaking of promises," Mutti said, "how about starting off the year on a new leaf? No reading until after you've finished your homework!"

"I'll get to work right after lunch," I agreed with enthusiasm. Thirteen suddenly felt very grown up.

* * *

The day after my birthday, the postman slipped a letter from my father under the door. He invited us to come live with him in Cologne. Enough money was enclosed to pay for one way train tickets.

"You don't seem very excited," I commented to Mutti.

"Why now? It's all too sudden. How can I trust him?" she replied. "The last time he sent for us, he abandoned us in the Ammo Camp."

"People change. Maybe he has, too."

"We don't have much choice, do we? It's hard enough trying to raise one boy in this place. Now I've got Hubert to worry about. It's only a matter of time before one of you gets blown to bits."

I went outside to find Werner. "I never thought it would happen," I burst out. "My father's taking us back."

"You're leaving this dump? You lucky dog!" Werner said brightly.

"I suppose I am," I replied, "but if even my mother doesn't know why he wants us back, I don't think there's much to celebrate. He's a real deadbeat."

"Maybe he realized how much he really loved all of you," Werner said, sounding doubtful.

"And maybe I'm Kaiser Wilhelm," I replied. "If he really loved us, he had a strange way of showing it."

Werner chewed on his fingernail, deep in thought. "How old is your father now?" he finally asked.

"Going on forty, I think."

"Forty? He's probably too old to find a girl friend. That's why he wants your mother back!"

"I really doubt it!" I replied, although Werner's explanation had a ring of truth to it.

"Whatever the reason," Werner concluded, "I smell a rat and if I were you, I wouldn't trust him for a minute."

Over the next several days we packed our few possessions. It never crossed my mind to bring along my bayonets, sabers, and daggers. Other things were harder to leave behind.

"Why can't I bring my Billy Jenkins and Tom Prox books?" I pleaded. "It took me forever to collect them!"

"I'll repeat the list one more time," Mutti said firmly. "Just *Huckleberry Finn, The Leather Stocking Tales*, the atlas, your stamp collection and the Bibles. We'll have more than enough to carry as it is."

Later that evening, as Mutti did the final packing, I divided my precious Western novels between Wolfgang and Werner. "I know the two of you will take good care of them," I explained as I stacked the books in two neat piles, "but I really wish I could bring them with me."

"Are you sure your mother won't change her mind?" Werner whispered with a glance at Mutti.

I shook my head. "I'm sure. I guess I'll see you both in school tomorrow. It's my last day."

"Lucky you," Wolfgang said. "I wish I could say that!"

* * *

The next day, during recess, Werner and Wolfgang joined me.

"I'll bet you're gonna miss this place, huh?" Werner teased.

"Not likely, but we've had some really great times together. I'll miss that."

461

"I've been thinking," Werner said with a mischievous grin. "You're at least eight centimeters taller than Schlemmer by now. How about punching him one on your way out?"

"That's your most dangerous scheme yet," I chuckled, "but I'll have to pass on it."

After school I sought out Mr. Siemokat in front of his woodshed compartment. He put down his axe when I approached.

"What's new?"

"We are going to move to Cologne to live with my father. I wanted to say good-bye."

"That's good news. What a surprise! When are you leaving?"

"Tomorrow morning. We're taking a train tomorrow morning."

"Tomorrow morning? That's too bad. I would have liked to help you and your mother, but I have an appointment at the Unemployment Office."

"That's all right," I said, "And thanks for everything."

"Don't mention it. Anyway, good luck, Landsmann, and stay out of trouble. You hear me?"

"I'll do my best! Auf Wiedersehen!"

"Auf Wiedersehen," he said, and shook my hand.

* * *

On Tuesday, December 12, 1950, Mutti, Hubert, and I boarded the train at the lonely Bodenteich station. No one came to see us off.

While waiting to change trains in Uelzen, Mutti stopped at the newsstand to buy me the latest Billy Jenkins book. "To soothe my conscience," she explained, with a smile.

From Hanover, an express train took us the rest of the way.

"What's Vati like?" Hubert asked after a while. "I only remember seeing him for a few moments in Uelzen."

"We'll find out when we get there," Mutti said grimly.

As the train tore through the countryside, I read and reread my new Billy Jenkins. It suddenly dawned on me that ever since we left Goldbach, we had been heading slowly west. Now we were taking that direction again, always a little closer to America. If I had any hope of living there one day, I would need a good education. It was too late for me to qualify for high school. That meant leaving school at fourteen to find an apprenticeship or a job. Mr. Schlemmer had beaten it into me every day at school that a stupid boy like me could never get back on track. What chance would I have of ever realizing my dreams? Until that moment, I had been worried about how my father would treat us. Suddenly it struck me that it worked both ways. My father might also be disappointed in me.

Still, looking back at all the obstacles we had overcome since Mutti, Hubert, and I left Langendorf on January 27, 1944, I decided not to give up hope. At a moment like this, Opa would have put his hand on my shoulder and said, "You can do it, young man!" I straightened up in my seat. Maybe we could start again, be a real family. I wasn't sure after all that had happened, but I was willing to try, for Mutti's sake. After all, I was only thirteen and my whole life still lay ahead of me.

* * *

At Düsseldorf, an elderly lady joined us in our compartment. She wore lots of makeup and a heavy perfume. Her gold necklace glittered beneath her fur coat.

"Is this seat free?" she asked. Before Mutti could answer, the lady continued, "This train's so crowded! It's simply terrible." She sat down and breathed loudly and dramatically for quite a while.

A short while later we passed through the suburbs of Cologne. As the train slowed slightly at each station, I saw the word "Cologne" on the railroad station.

"We must be nearly there," I said with impatience.

"The main railroad station will be much bigger than any of these," Mutti assured me.

Just past Cologne-Deutz, our train rolled over a long bridge. The Rhine River lay below us.

"Pardon me, please," I asked the fancy lady, "does this bridge have a name?"

"It's the Hohenzollernbrücke. It was only rebuilt about two years ago."

"Hohen...zollern...brücke?" I repeated, a bit hesitantly. The name made me giggle. The lady looked annoyed.

"Yes, that's what I said. Don't you know who the Hohenzollerns were?"

"Not really," I confessed.

"Dear me. Where on earth have you been going to school? Don't they teach German history anymore?"

Before I could say anything, Mutti tapped me on the shoulder. "It's nearly time for us to get off," she said, glaring at the lady. She turned back to me. I was peering out at the reddish-gold glint of the windows in the few buildings left standing along the riverbank. The glare was blinding.

"You're looking the wrong way. Look out this side," Mutti said. "What do you see?"

"It's the Cologne Cathedral! I remember it from the postcards and from my stamp collection."

With the sun behind it, the Cathedral looked massive and dark, towering over the bombed out ruins around it, taller than any structure I had ever seen. I suddenly felt very small.

* * *

The train pulled slowly into a vast, gloomy railroad station. I poked my head out of the window and scanned the crowd, searching for my father among the hundreds of people waiting on the platform.

As soon as our train screeched to a halt, I saw him. He was wearing a fancy, dark gray suit, an open camel hair overcoat, and a stylish felt hat. In his left hand he held a bouquet of red and white carnations, garnished with asparagus fern.

Grabbing our few possessions, we stepped down onto the platform. He handed Mutti the flowers and kissed her on the cheek.

"Hallo!" he said. "How was your trip?"

Printed in the United States
107385LV00003B/16/A